Her Story, N

Judith Tydor Baumel-Schwartz / Dalia Ofer (eds.)

Her Story, My Story?

Writing About Women and the Holocaust

PETER LANG
Bern · Berlin · Bruxelles · New York · Oxford

Bibliographic Information published by the Deutsche Nationalbibliothek
The Deutsche Nationalbibliothek lists this publication in the Deutsche Nationalbibliografie; detailed bibliographic data is available online at http://dnb.d-nb.de.

Library of Congress Cataloging-in-Publication Data
A CIP catalog record for this book has been applied for at the Library of Congress.

We thank the Fanya Gottesfeld Heller Center for the Study of Women in Judaism at Bar-Ilan University and the Arnold and Leona Finkler Institute of Holocaust Research at Bar-Ilan University for their generous financial and academic support of this project.

ISBN 978-3-0343-3643-7 (Print)
E-ISBN 978-3-0343-3644-4 (E-PDF)
E-ISBN 978-3-0343-3645-1 (EPUB)
E-ISBN 978-3-0343-3646-8 (MOBI)
DOI 10.3726/b16704

This publication has been peer reviewed.

Wabernstrasse 40, CH-3007 Bern, Switzerland
bern@peterlang.com, www.peterlang.com

Printed in Germany

Cover picture – Ida Tennenbaum Theilheimer and Ides (Judith) Tidor, cousins, Germany, 1930s. The first escaped to Palestine and then to the United States, the other returned to Poland where she had been born, and was murdered in 1942

This volume is dedicated to the memory of Fanya Gottesfeld Heller (1924–2017)

Contents

Preface

In Memory of My Mother, Fanya Gottesfeld Heller

My late mother, Fanya Gottesfeld Heller, was born in 1924 and raised in a small Ukrainian village in a stable, traditional Jewish home environment. She benefitted from a secure connection to her parents, especially her adoring and empowering father, who lauded her smarts and bookishness.

With the help of two Christian neighbors, her nuclear family narrowly escaped extermination by the Nazis. Initially they hid behind a farmer's chicken coop, and afterwards, for two years they squatted underground in a small ditch dug beneath a drinking trough. With barely any food and little protection from freezing cold winters and stifling hot summers, it is miraculous, unfathomable actually, that four people survived in that dark, cramped, lice and rat-infested ditch.

After the liberation Fanya married my late father, Joseph Heller, a fellow survivor. For years, homeless and stateless, they migrated through Europe, eventually making it to the US. Even during those nomadic years, my mother read voraciously. I believe that nascent intelligence, an excellent education, and outstanding memory contributed to her resilience and drive, but most important were the secure and nurturing attachments in early life. She studied art history at Columbia University, philosophy and literature at the New School, and family therapy at the Ackerman Institute. Fanya Heller obtained a BA and an MA in psychology from the New School for Social Research, and honorary doctoral degrees from Yeshiva University and Bar-Ilan University.

Forty years after their liberation and shortly after my father's death in 1986, Fanya's years of hard work engaged in self-reflection, recovery and renewal, had impressive results. In 1993 she published a candid autobiography of her wartime story (KTAV) under the title of *Strange and Unexpected Love: A Teenage Girl's Holocaust Memoirs*. In 2005 it was reissued under a new title, *Love in a World of Sorrow* (Devora Publishing) and was adapted into a PBS documentary film narrated by Richard Gere. Shortly before her death in 2017 she wrote *Hidden* (Scholastic 2016), a bestseller for school-age children.

In addition to writing, my mother found her own voice, literally discovering powerful speaking skills and became a sought-after lecturer. She introduced herself as a Holocaust survivor with the emphatically added suffix "who survived Hitler once and Stalin twice". Connected to her riveted listeners, she would describe her terrifying wartime experiences while encouraging disadvantaged students and young adults not to give up. My mother taught her children and all whom she addressed that morbid hatred, unmitigated anger, or soul-killing bitterness need not be the outcome of suffering. Her genuine love of life was infectiously uplifting, and motivated many students to take action to improve their life circumstances. This renewed version of herself became a role model, a superheroine who received thousands of letters from young and old the world over. My mother knew the relevance of creating a cogent personal narrative. Storytelling about self, family, and ancestry are important for personal growth and connection to others. Her life affirming excitement was audible, visible, and palpable. Until the final day of her remarkable 93 year- life, she joyfully seized each moment of every day with love, gratitude, and generosity.

Fanya Heller bravely bore witness and championed Holocaust education and awareness with majesty. My legacy is to honor and echo her messages of love, tolerance, hope, and renewal. My personal journey is informed by my being the child of Holocaust survivors (2g), as a humanitarian, medical doctor, psychiatrist. My aim is to diminish epigenetic inherited trauma by guiding us to our hidden past injuries and traumas. Hurt people can inadvertently hurt and damage others. In order to raise well-loved, securely attached, confident, autonomous, and empathic children, we need to reeducate ourselves. By promoting introspection and self- reflection, we can become psychological sleuths, sifting our past for clues as to why we are who we are. Otherwise, self-deception conceals complex emotions like self-loathing, envy, rage, shame and humiliation, all readily cast off and projected into innocents via bullying and scapegoating. I believe these unassimilated emotions comprise the rudimentary precursors to evil itself. In the best of circumstances, my field can help prevent victims from becoming perpetrators; children from growing into hateful, murderous adults, and ordinary people from turning a blind eye to the victimization of their fellow human beings.

In 1998 my mother established The Fanya Gottesfeld Heller Center for the Study of Women in Judaism at Bar-Ilan University, a unique academic initiative that explores female Jewish identity within the context of Judaism. Fanya was particularly gratified when the Center promoted and supported research about women during the Holocaust, while strengthening humanism with the message that each of us must take an active stand against evil. She deemed the successful implementation of these initiatives a pinnacle of the Center's scholarly activities.

Throughout my adult life, my mother and I shared great exchanges about many books we both read. She would be delighted with this volume, a co-production of the Center she established with the Arnold and Leona Finkler Institute of Holocaust Research. Following an illuminating preface by renowned Holocaust scholar, Marion Kaplan, are 27 self-reflective stories by notable women scholars. These women - historians, sociologists, anthropologists, literary and art critics – who devoted much of their lives to writing about women during the Holocaust, are testimony to the necessity of understanding ourselves, including hidden hurts and buried traumas, before we can go further.

Thank you on behalf of the entire Heller family for dedicating this book to the blessed, beloved memory of our sorely missed matriarch, Fanya Gottesfeld Heller. The compilation is a profound contribution to scholarship today. This is indeed "Her Story, My Story", and all of our stories.

Jacqueline Heller, MD ©. All Rights Reserved. Los Angeles 10.27.2019

Marion Kaplan

Foreword

The contributors to this volume have all written extensively about the Holocaust and have thought deeply about what role gender played in it. Many of us came of age in the 1970s and '80s as Holocaust scholarship entered the academy. Similarly, the women's movement in the United States created a parallel body of history, art, and politics. Inevitably, scholars of this generation – mostly women – brought gendered questions to the study of the Holocaust. Like many women's historians who had addressed women's history as it began to flourish, especially in the U.S. and in Europe, we wondered about Nazi genocide and asked, "might women have experienced this nightmare differently from men? And, if so, how? And, if not, why not?" Fortunately, younger scholars in this volume, educated in the U.S., Europe, and Israel, belong to the generation for whom writing about women's experience had been grudgingly accepted by the, mostly male, historical profession.

Although we all had different trajectories, some coming from curiosity about family histories, other addressing burning issues of gender in extreme situations, and still others searching out unexplored Holocaust accounts, we all shared similar experiences of discovery, of an effort to be heard, and of gradual impact on the field. Frustratingly, many in both generations still experienced push back from advisors and from sceptics fearful that women's historians were raising women's suffering above that of all Jews. Still, we persisted.

This book offers memoirs, sometimes called ego documents, by contemporary women historians, sociologists, literary critics and others, in which they tell their personal stories about coming to research the Holocaust while also thinking about women and gender. Memoirs have helped scholars to investigate the lives of non-elites since at least the 1970s. Memoirs have revealed individual's self-understandings, fears and values, and have provided an entrée into unexplored stories. Yet memoirs offer more than individual lives. The essays in this book are personal, but they also situate the authors within their societies and academia. In this collection, the historians who have shared their memoirs illustrate not only very private journeys, but additionally a sense of the cultural context and the historical moment. These memoirs may surprise us – contradicting, illuminating, and deepening the accepted stories. Just as memoirs give ordinary Jewish women and men historical agency, they also give women scholars the opportunity to weave their life stories into the broader historical and cultural moments of their careers and lives.

Critics of ego documents, especially memoirs, contend that memory "selects, condenses, and interprets experience"[1] and memoirs often contradict themselves or fluctuate between "then" – when the events occurred – and "now" – when the writer sees the past with the benefit of hindsight and the influence of current ideologies. Moreover, the way memoirs and even diaries reconstruct the past "is always more coherent" than when it happened.[2] Further, memory and history are distinct despite their links: the "fissure ... between experiencing an event and remembering it ...is unavoidable."[3] They offer, at best, only a romantic gloss on the past.

I do not agree. Scholars who use memoirs know that such texts give details useful for constructing the past. That they can and do reflect certain collective experiences, social and cultural processes. When juxtaposed with other sources, they fill in important gaps and begin to complete and complicate the puzzle. In this collection of personal essays one can appreciate the strength of memoirs as these scholars contend with their own memories, their own discoveries, and self-discoveries, and their own writings.

The research of scholars represented in this volume has resulted in a vibrant field of Holocaust studies in which they have included a broad variety of Jews – females, males, adults, children, elites and masses – from a wide spectrum of countries, while also approaching these stories from diverse methodologies. These stretch from traditional community histories to microstudies, from data culled from Nazi and postwar court sources to memoirs and fiction written by survivors. Notably, the scholars in this volume have exerted great efforts to amass women's voices otherwise hidden from history.[4] Some of these voices come from polished and published writers like Ruth Kluger, others from the memoirs, letters, or diaries of unknown or unnamed women. Most importantly, gendered research and memoirs of the Nazi era are not just practical correctives or wellsprings of detail. Anna Reading has eloquently argued that when a survivor writes a memoir, it is

---

1 Hamida Bosmajian, *Metaphors of Evil: Contemporary German Literature and the Shadow of Nazism*, Iowa City, 1979, p. 23.

2 David Lowenthal, "Nostalgia Tells it like it Wasn't," in *The Imagined Past: History and Nostalgia*, ed. by Christopher Shaw and Malcolm Chase, Manchester, 1989, p. 30.

3 Andreas Huyssen, *Twilight Memories*, London, 1995, p. 3.

4 Sheila Rowbotham, *Hidden from History*, London, 1983.

> not just a book, it is a life: it symbolically replaces books burnt and cultural and social memories destroyed; it provides a testament in the face of Nazi lies...creating a memorial.... It is also a book of death: within each story of a life survived there is the mute reminder of the ...lives untold and abruptly ended....[5]

Giving voice to women's history and to women's historians and highlighting women's perspectives remains a crucial and an ongoing task.

---

5 Reading, *The Social Inheritance of the Holocaust: Gender, Culture and Memory*, Hampshire and New York, 2002, p. 54.

Judith Tydor Baumel-Schwartz and Dalia Ofer

Introduction

"Why in the world would anyone want to write about women during the Holocaust? After all, does anyone write only about what the Nazis did to men? Weren't Jewish women during the Holocaust just Jews like everyone else? Radical feminists want to separate women from men during the Holocaust. Are you a radical feminist? What do you have to gain by writing about women during the Holocaust but not about men? Didn't the Nazis kill Jewish women just like they killed all the Jews? This is a real career risk. Aren't you afraid that you won't be taken seriously if you limit yourself to writing about women during the Holocaust?"

Seven questions. One for each day of the week. Back in the 1980s when it became known that Judy was coordinating a research project focusing on Jewish women during the Holocaust, there was indeed one week in which she was asked each and every one of these questions by well-known academics, both male and female. Sometimes more than once.

Those were the early days in which research pertaining to women lives and experiences during the Holocaust was slowly becoming a recognized academic discipline. Before that time, it had not been considered a "major Holocaust topic" and was mostly ignored by both humanities scholars and social scientists. But soon things began to change. Although the major research shift towards examining the Holocaust's social and cultural aspects would only take place in the 1980s and 1990s, somewhere between the late 1960s and early 1970s the first of these articles began to appear. Together with the rise of interest in gender studies, they propelled a number of scholars to begin examining Jewish women's lives under the Nazis, which, in turn, would ultimately impact upon studies of the social aspects of the Holocaust.

The first academic studies on women during the Holocaust were published during the following decade, from the late 1970s into the early 1980s. Those were the years when groundbreaking scholars such as Atina Grossmann, Marion Kaplan, the late Sybil Milton and Joan Ringelheim braved the new topic, courageously devoting time and effort to what many still considered a minor or unmerited theme. An important turning point was the conference entitled "Women Surviving the Holocaust", organized in New York in 1983 by Joan Ringelheim and Esther Katz, that placed the topic of Jewish women during the Holocaust on the public agenda.[1]

1 See: Ava F. Kahn, Review of Esther Katz and Joan Miriam Ringelheim, *Women Surviving the Holocaust*, New York: Institute for Research in History, 1983,

During the 1990s the topic appeared to blossom when a number of anthologies, academic studies, and sourcebooks were published, all of which focused on women's lives under Nazi rule. The growing awareness of the subject encouraged scholars to begin teaching courses about women during the Holocaust, first in the United States, then in Israel, and eventually in Europe, which were the impetus for graduate students, mostly women, to choose to specialize in the field.[2] In 1995 Dalia Ofer and Lenore Weitzman convened the first international workshop on Women during the Holocaust in Jerusalem which a number of participants in this volume mentioned as a turning point in their careers. Until that time, they had seen women's Holocaust experiences as an almost clandestine topic. Now they were given proof of its legitimacy, having met leading international scholars who were devoting their careers to researching, teaching and writing about it.

Many Holocaust topics, such as Jewish leadership under the Nazis or the political parties involved in the Jewish resistance movements, aroused powerful emotions and reactions among survivors, scholars and laymen. Yet all were accepted as legitimate topics of study. When it came to the study of women during the Holocaust, not only did the topic arouse powerful emotions and reactions, it was the only Holocaust-related topic whose actual legitimacy as a topic of study was being questioned by scholars and public commentators alike. In 1998 it became the subject of a widespread public debate that began with a scathing article written by *Commentary* editor Gabriel Schoenfeld, against the field, was repeated in the *Wall Street Journal,* and continued to play out for a number of years in public and scholarly journals, sending ricochets throughout the academic community. Even after it subsided, "Women during the Holocaust" was still considered a "hot potato" in more than one academic institution, with the criticism that had been articulated continuing to shape the professional attitude towards those who chose to specialize in that and related themes. In time attitudes changed, but here and there one still found the occasional raised eyebrow with regard to the direction that some of the feminist Holocaust scholarship had taken.

---

in: *The Public Historian* 7:3 (Summer 1985): 104–106; "Focus on Issues: Women Surviving the Holocaust", *JTA* March 29, 1983.

2 The first academic course about Women during the Holocaust appears to have been taught by Konnilyn Feig in 1984 at Foothill College in Los Altos Hills in California. See: R. Ruth Linden, "Troubling Categories I Can't Think Without: Reflections on Women in the Holocaust", *Contemporary Jewry* 17:1 (Jan. 1996): 18–33.

How do we know that a discipline has become mainstream? One test is straightforward and self-explanatory: the existence of bibliographical and historiographical studies about its development, which can only be written when a substantial corpus of research already exists. Several bibliographical essays have listed the growing number of books, articles and reviews devoted to women's lives during the Holocaust and its aftermath that have appeared since the late 1970s.[3] A number of historiographical articles have charted the development of the field and analyzed the timing, contents, and character of the various waves of relevant publications.[4] There is also another, more subtle test: when one begins to examine not only the history of the topic but also the story of its authors. And that is what this book – *Her Story, My Story?* - is all about.

Like many interesting things in life, the idea of creating a book of "ego-documents" (academic memoirs) of women scholars writing about women during the Holocaust, was born out of a moment of total serendipity, the unexpected outcome of a conversation on a completely different topic. One of the goals that Judy set when becoming Director of the Finkler Institute of Holocaust Research in 2018 was to create a series of interconnecting "Forums" – academic communities for researchers and active participants in Holocaust education and commemoration. Having just completed a term as Director of the Heller Center for the Study of Women in Judaism, she was helping the succeeding Director, Prof. Yael Shemesh, settle in when she mentioned that the first of these Forums would be "Women Recall the Holocaust", composed of women scholars who specialized in the lives of Jewish women under Nazi rule. "Did you always want to write about women during the Holocaust?" Shemesh asked. "I always wondered what attracts people to such a topic." Just having completed an ego-document for a book on her second field of expertise, academics specializing in the State

3 Vasvári, Louise O. "Bibliography of Central European Women's Holocaust Life Writing in English." *Library Series, CLCWeb: Comparative Literature and Culture* (2012): https://docs.lib.purdue.edu/clcweblibrary/vasvariceushoahbib; **Reference List for the Study of Ravensbrück and Women and the Holocaust,** Prepared by Dr. Rochelle G. Saidel, Remember the Women Institute for "Teaching the Holocaust to Future Generations: A Special Conference for Educators," Yad Vashem, Jerusalem, August 8 – 11, 2004, https://www.rememberwomen.org/Library/Bibliographies/teaching.html

4 Lisa Pine, "Gender and the Family", in: Dan Stone, ed. *The Historiography of the Holocaust,* London: Palgrave MacMillan, 2004: 364–382; Judith Tydor Baumel, "Gender and Family Studies of the Holocaust: The Development of a Historical Discipline", in Esther Hertzog (ed.), *Life, Death and Sacrifice: Women and Family in the Holocaust,* Jerusalem and New York: Gefen, 2008: 21–40.

of Israel, Judy realized that here was another story deserving to be told. The stage was set. Not only would "Women Recall the Holocaust" become a forum, it would also become a book.

Within days the project had taken on form and substance. Dalia Ofer, a friend and well-respected historian who had moved into the field of women's Holocaust studies in the early 1990s, agreed to serve as co-editor. Letters went out to 30 women scholars, 28 of whom enthusiastically agreed to participate.[5] The final list of participants represented the scope and spectrum of scholars from different disciplines worldwide who have devoted much of their academic career to studying, writing, and teaching about women during the Holocaust. They ranged in age from their 40s to their 80s, originated from eight countries on three continents and were now living in five (USA, Canada, Britain, Germany and Israel). Some were Jewish, others were not, and a third group was of mixed parentage. Some only learned of their Jewish background while in their teens or even later. Three were among the originators of the field, a second group joined from the mid- 1980s until the late 1990s, and a third group only began publishing their research in the 21st century.

As we wrote to them:

> For years, many scholars studying [about women during] the Holocaust faced a lack of understanding and acceptance of their topic among their peers. Some were warned that their choice would marginalize them professionally. Others were told that they were playing into the hands of Holocaust revisionists. Not only was the focus of their research delegitimized; Their professional standing was often challenged or they were warned that such a research choice might affect their possibilities of career advancement.
>
> And yet, most persevered. As time passed, more and more scholars in various disciplines of the Humanities and the Social Sciences began examining different facets of Jewish women's lives during the Holocaust and its aftermath…Some of the scholars advanced in rank; others became pivotal members of Holocaust research institutes and Holocaust memorials, or chose to continue researching and writing on the topic as independent scholars while pursuing a different career.
>
> Almost all these scholars are women. Each came to the topic in her own way; each faced different sets of challenges on that journey; each then chose to focus on a different aspect of women's lives during the Holocaust; each has her own story. We believe that these stories deserve a voice and that together they tell a broader story, one that charts not only how a topic was born but how it developed over almost two generations of scholarship. It is the story of academic challenge and courage. It is the story of perseverance. For some, who were mentored by more senior women scholars who encouraged them on their journey, it is the story of sisterhood. For

5 One refused for personal reasons; another as part of the anti-Israel BDS boycott.

> others, who fought the establishment on their own, it is the story of their personal strength. For all it is the story of an unconventional, courageous, and promising choice in Holocaust research.

Emphasizing that we were not interested in an annotated list of their publications, we asked them to chart their personal journey to and through the topic. Why did they choose to write about women during the Holocaust? In what way did their personal, family and educational background influence their choice of topic? Did they come from Holocaust studies, Gender Studies or a completely different field? What made them choose the particular aspects of women's Holocaust lives upon which they decide to focus? How did their family, friends, and colleagues react to their choice of topic? In what way did it affect their personal and professional lives? Did they remain in the field and if not, why and when did they leave? In hindsight, do they regret their choice? In terms of caveats we mentioned only two: to try and write an essay that would be timeless, and to refrain from focusing solely or primarily on contemporary political events.

During the following year we created a forum email group and held meet-ups in New York, London, and Ramat Gan, Israel. At each gathering it became obvious how deeply invested so many of us were in what we were doing, not only professionally but personally. Over and over we were encouraged by the forum members who emphasized how important this project was for them. "The idea of a project on academic autobiographies of women is brilliant", wrote Insa Eschebach, Director of the Ravensbrück Memorial Museum, "especially if your point of departure is international and/or trans-cultural." "I, for one, would love to read the personal narratives of colleagues whose work I cited, discussed and read over the years", wrote literature scholar Esther Fuchs. "Beyond my own curiosity, this kind of project will be an important contribution to the field."

One of the most unique aspects of this project was the creation of a sense of "community". The meetings we held in New York, London and Ramat Gan were more than social-professional gatherings. They served to strengthen the feeling of sisterhood among forum members in the knowledge that we were creating a community of women scholars who were learning from each other and working together to develop a field. Not only did the face-to-face meetings add a new dimension to our group; the discussions that we held in our internet list helped each of us develop our own personal direction in our essays. Recognizing how significant the gender component is in understanding the Holocaust, we also reminded each other of an important balance. Scholars who have a sense of mission are central to developing a discipline. But that mission must always be tempered by a critical inner voice reminding us that as personally as one may be invested in the field, it is imperative to maintain a certain degree of academic distance from one's subject.

As the deadline approached articles began trickling in, filling us with a sense of wonder at the richness of experiences about which we were reading. When the project began neither of us was sure what to expect, and we were both surprised by the broad interdisciplinary nature of how the field developed, and the wealth of knowledge to which we were being exposed. Who could believe that women scholars who had written only peripherally about women in the Holocaust in their academic work, ended up with it being such a central part of their identity?! "As you know, it's impossible not to work on this subject once you become involved", wrote Myrna Goldenberg, one of the book's participants. How could we, two historians who specialized in Jewish women during the Holocaust, have remained unaware of the various angles from which the topic was being examined in other disciplines? Editing this book has been an extremely gratifying experience for both of us, underscoring once again how much there always is still to learn, even when one is an expert in the field.

When dealing with Holocaust studies, one often assumes that there must be a connection between a scholar's personal biography and the focus of their research. After all, who would want to spend years delving into these horrors if they weren't being propelled to do so by a sense of obligation to their personal past! As soon as we began reading the articles, we saw that in more than a few cases, this assumption held true here as well. Some of our authors were children of refugees from Nazism or Holocaust survivors. Others came from families that were also touched, albeit more distantly, by the Holocaust. A few of those with no Holocaust-related family background came to it via a discovery of or encounter with antisemitism; another group through a growing awareness of feminism. Some were drawn to the topic after hearing about the Holocaust yet in childhood; others after visiting a Holocaust locus, often a Nazi camp. There were authors who wrote how writing this essay was part of a "rediscovery" of their families' Holocaust history. Some had been aware of their family connection to the Holocaust since childhood. Others only learned about it, and their connection to Judaism, as they grew older. A third group had no personal connection to the Holocaust or to Judaism and their gravitation towards writing about women in the Holocaust came through a moment of epiphany, a meeting with children of survivors, or an inexplicable attraction to a certain facet or locus of Holocaust history. Here, too, we realized that there was still so much to learn, not only about women during the Holocaust, but about the women who had chosen to make the study of that topic into their life's work, and perhaps on writing the history of the Holocaust in general.

Although we began the book project with a well delineated picture of what we were looking for, there were times that everything seemed up for discussion. One was the book's original title which did not resound well with some of the participants. Claiming that it could be interpreted as exclusive and not inclusive, they asked us to find a title that would express the common denominator of our journeys. Bearing that in mind we consulted with the publisher and decided on the title now appearing on the cover – *Her Story My Story? Writing about Women During the Holocaust* feeling that it expressed an experience common to most, if not all of the participants, the extent to which writing about women during the Holocaust has become part of our own biography.

Then there was the internal order of the essays. At almost every meet-up someone raised the question of how we planned to arrange the chapters. One participant suggested arranging them alphabetically according to the authors' last names in order to present a picture of sisterhood and equality. Another spoke of using age as a criterion, with the oldest scholars being placed first or last. Ultimately we decided on a generational division, mapping out the book to include three sections corresponding to the three waves of publications in the field. An author's chronological age had little bearing upon their essay's placement. Younger scholars can be found in earlier categories while older ones in the later ones. Within each section the articles appear alphabetically and not according to the years that each participant began her journey within the topic.

The first section, entitled "The Founding Mothers", contains a foreword and two essays by three courageous path-breakers who began writing about women in the Holocaust during the late 1970s and early 1980s: Atina Grossmann, Marion Kaplan, and Joan Ringelheim. Entering uncharted waters, they shaped the early years of women's Holocaust scholarship without the assistance of supportive academic mentors who could help them navigate the field. Two were historians, one came from philosophy and they all began dealing with the subject before the "Women Surviving the Holocaust" conference of 1983, a watershed event in the development of the discipline.

The next section, "The Middle Generation", contains essays by twelve historians, philosophers, political scientists, sociologists, theologians, and literary critics who began writing about women during the Holocaust during the decade and a half between the 1983 conference and the polemic of 1998: Judy Tydor Baumel-Schwartz, Pascale Rachel Bos, Insa Eschebach, Esther Fuchs, Myrna Goldenberg, Sara R. Horowitz, Phyllis Lassner, R. Ruth Linden, Dalia Ofer, Melissa Raphael, Rochelle G. Saidel, and Lenore Weitzman. Some, coming from Holocaust studies, had explored the peripheral aspects of women's Holocaust experiences long before it became the major focus of their scholarship. Others came to the subject through gender related projects. A third group progressed to it in stages on a journey that involved many stops and starts. For a few it was a direct outgrowth of their personal biography. For others it began as an intellectual exercise. For all it became a topic in which they found themselves personally and professionally invested, at times much more than they had originally intended.

The essays in the last section, entitled "The New Scholarship" were written by thirteen historians, literature critics, sociologists, and scholars of art and culture, who began writing about women during the Holocaust during the beginning of the 21st century. Having begun their studies when specializing in the Holocaust was already considered a mainstream academic choice, some of the younger scholars even had degrees in "Holocaust Studies", a discipline that had not existed a generation earlier. Contributors to this section include Natalia Aleksiun, Batya Brutin, F. K. Schoeman, Sarah M. Cushman, Sharon Geva, Dorota Glowacka, Esther Hertzog, Janet L. Jacobs, Bozena Karwowska, Lisa Pine, Naama Shik, Louise O. Vasvári, and Zoë Waxman.

The volume's dedication was a third issue eliciting a lively internet discussion among some of the forum members. As a co-production of the Arnold and Leona Finkler Institute of Holocaust Research and the Fanya Gottesfeld Heller Center for the Study of Women in Judaism, already at the outset we agreed to dedicate it to the memory of the late Fanya Gottesfeld Heller (1924–2019), a Holocaust survivor whose personal story has served as inspiration to many. Nevertheless, some of our participants had suggestions. What about this or that founding mother of the field, they asked? Don't they, too, deserve a dedication?

We therefore agreed that the book would be dedicated to Fanya Gottesfeld Heller, a Jewish woman who experienced the cataclysm of the Holocaust and dedicated her life to teaching others about her experiences. But at the same time, we would like to make special mention here in this introduction of the founding mothers of our field, whose groundbreaking work has been an inspiration to so many. Three of them have contributed to this volume. Marion Kaplan and Atina Grossmann's path-breaking work about Jewish women in Nazi German during the 1970 and early 1980s "started the ball rolling" for many of us. Joan Ringelheim and the late Sybil Milton (1941–2000) who was a pioneer in women's Holocaust studies and senior historian of the USHMM (United States Holocaust Memorial Museum) until her untimely passing, were the first to articulate the topics and questions that we should address when dealing with women in the Holocaust. Marion and Atina have taught about women in the Holocaust for many years at their various institutions of higher learning. Joan and Sybil were instrumental in introducing the topic into their work at the USHMM.

Someone once said that writing about Women during the Holocaust in the late 1980s and early 1990s was similar to riding on a road while simultaneously paving it. But such paving could not have taken hold without the groundwork that these courageous women had laid. This is a meager expression of our thanks and admiration for their having created the framework for the discipline which has become our professional home.

Judy Tydor Baumel-Schwartz Dalia Ofer
Ramat Gan Jerusalem
October 2019

Part I The “Founding Mothers”

Atina Grossmann

Hide and Seek: Becoming a Historian of Gender and the Holocaust

New York, Refugees, and Survivors

Where do I start? First I was a New York kid from a German Jewish refugee family, immersed in the *Yekke* and left-liberal culture of Manhattan's Upper West Side, then came the 1960s and the civil rights movement, the New Left, and finally the women's movement, that heady exhilarating moment of second wave feminism when it seemed possible to integrate, surprisingly seamlessly, the personal, the political, and the academic. Already a feminist, I became a historian, studying modern German history. Only years later, did I begin, via an initial focus on flight from Nazi Germany and the experience of Jewish survivors in postwar Germany, to write – always in the context of women's and gender history – about the Holocaust or even Jews in particular. But, of course, that's only one way of telling the story.

I cannot track a properly linear scholarly or personal progression. My trajectory developed, as it did with so many of us who came to call ourselves "second generation," in the shadow of destroyed families and the murdered grandmothers whose photographs haunted the living room. But it was also framed by the much more appealing fraying Bauhaus chairs, Persian carpets, and tiny ivory elephants, remnant artifacts of an irrevocably lost moment of hopeful cultural and political experimentation in the Weimar Republic, as well as the adventurous decade of my parents' flight and refuge in Iran and India. Crucially, it was dominated by the urgency of the exciting social-political project of the American 1960s and 1970s. This transnational collective volume now moves me to re-chart my childhood memories and revisit – while appreciating in deeper ways – the professional engagement with the Holocaust and gender that has marked my career, long before I consciously defined my scholarly work in those terms.

What memory fragments are most retrospectively vivid? I recall the maternal grandfather who delighted me with games of hide and seek; only now does it occur to me that perhaps his choice of entertainment and expert hiding in our small Manhattan apartment had something to do with his improbable survival underground in Berlin after his wife, my grandmother, had been deported to her death in Auschwitz during the 1943 *Fabrikaktion* in Berlin. Uptown in Washington Heights, the "Fourth Reich" as it was dubbed, lived the less urbane and more religious relatives from Fürth,

Nürnberg, and locales somewhere to the East of Berlin, selling Danish modern furniture and kosher hot dogs; some had those strange bluish numbers on their arms.

Only much later, when I was immersed in literature on gender, sexuality, and sexual violence during the Holocaust with no one left to ask, did I think critically about the whispers that followed my always immaculately dressed and just a bit too over-rouged and lipsticked – and tattooed – childless *Tante* Lee, who, it was murmured, must have "used" her body to survive. She was, it seemed, uniquely damaged in a gendered way; perhaps, I intuited without really knowing what that might mean, some kind of "whore." In my public school on Manhattan's Upper West Side, populated by a mix of children of survivors, refugees, newly arrived migrants from Puerto Rico, and "red diaper" babies, we fifth graders were required to listen to a weekly public radio newscast which promised prizes for essays on current events. Challenged to write about the relevance of FDR's "Four Freedoms", I produced an imagined account of a young boy in the Warsaw Ghetto, dreaming of freedom from want and fear. Did it not occur to me that girls also had a compelling story? Perhaps the historical accounts that I surreptitiously accessed, over the objections of the nonplused librarian who requested (and, incredibly, received) parental permission to provide such texts to a ten year old, were all about boys and men? Surely there are many more such moments in my memory bank, but I never thought of myself as a child of survivors. After all, it was my parents' mothers who were killed, my father's younger brother who had actually survived Auschwitz-Monowitz and the death march to Mauthausen, the grandfather who had survived in hiding; my parents had escaped before the war. They carried no numbers, no tattoos.

For a New York child growing up in an enclave of immigrants and intellectuals, the '50s were shaped more immediately by the trauma of McCarthyism, fears of "the bomb," and the hopeful emergence of a civil rights movement. By fifth grade and several years of Tuesday afternoon "Hebrew School" at the German Jewish congregation Habonim on West 66th street I was consciously thinking about the Warsaw Ghetto, but my entry into kindergarten at PS 87 came a year after the Brown v. Board of Education Supreme Court decision (1954) and the first short essay assignment I ever wrote – in first grade – celebrated this assertion of universal civil rights. At the same time, the anti-communist panic threatened to re-traumatize our community of refugees. My father's other brother had made it out in late 1938, along with a huge seaworthy "lift" containing avant garde art and a library of sexual science literature (including a volume with a personal dedication by Magnus Hirschfeld in whose *Institut für Sexualwissenschaft* he had written his thesis on the "third sex"). He protected his hard-earned reputation as a respected physician in Hartford, Connecticut, by burning his correspondence with Bertolt Brecht and other "subversives" and burying under the label of *Hausfreund* (or roommate) the man with whom he and his wife shared a house on Canterbury Street. Only years later when I unearthed his Dr. Med. dissertation in the basement of the Berlin *Staatsbibliothek*, did I start to wonder about the nature of Onkel Walter's relationship with the ubiquitous Felix. Again, it was too late to ask. The evidence of this possible "queer" history was lost in a different sort of ashes than those to which my grandmothers and so many other relatives had been reduced.

Radicals, Feminists, Jews

As New York City schoolchildren, our war memorials were "duck and cover" exercises and the cautionary exhibit on Hiroshima and Nagasaki that introduced our school tours of the gleaming new United Nations building on the bank of the East River. The modest memorial to the Warsaw Ghetto Uprising in Riverside Drive Park where my parents joined occasional commemorations and which might have inspired my fifth-grade essay, was never completed and never the destination for any school field trip. By high school, references to Fascism, Hitler, and the Gestapo, punctuated the rhetoric of the '60s radicals my friends and I were becoming. But the historical associations were quite different. "Never Again" meant not "never again a Jewish victim" but "Never again a good German," never again a perpetrator, or complicit bystander in an unjust regime of oppression, disenfranchisement, murder, and genocide. Bernhard Cohn, the "American" son-in-law and successor of Rabbi Hugo Hahn who had delivered his sermons in German at Habonim, joined the demonstrations in Selma. He was a less well-known partner to Jewish icons of the Civil Right movement such as Joachim Prinz or Abraham Joshua Heschel, along with Andrew Goodman and Michael Schwerner, martyred with James Chaney in Mississippi in 1964.

"This Land Is Your Land" and "We Shall Overcome," the anthems of Woody Guthrie and "negro spirituals" adapted into "freedom songs" by Pete Seeger, the folk music of the Weavers, Phil Ochs, Peter, Paul and Mary; Harry Belafonte, and Joan Baez, as well as the subversive pleasures of the counter-culture—sex, drugs, and rock 'n' roll – offered inclusion and a profound sense of belonging for those of us outsiders to "white bread" culture in the America we found at once so enticing and so objectionable. My strange parents with their accents, their cosmopolitan allures, their skeptical attitude toward everything too *amerikanisch*, suddenly became appealingly exotic rather than just weird and embarrassing. If some young critical Jews elsewhere—certainly my counterparts in the second generation in

Germany—expressed their "difference" by moving to Israel and working on *Kibbutzim*, the civil rights movement and the New Left were my route to feeling at home in America[1]

So far, the story does not yet clearly reference either women or the Holocaust. After 1968, the larger movement was split by tensions around "anti-imperialist" violence, Zionism, and black-Jewish relations. As some activist Jews turned to specifically Jewish causes, especially Soviet Jewry, the most lasting and significant legacy of the '60s for many politicized young women was feminism. Unlike our disoriented male comrades, we felt lucky to have found a meaningful way of practicing "the personal is political". Like Jews in the movement as a whole, Jewish women seemed disproportionately represented among feminists. Some were rebelling against family pressures to marry and procreate, sometimes couched in the need to repopulate after the Holocaust. Others were following models learned in leftist households with activist mothers or simply a tradition that valued education and Jewish women's customary role as breadwinners. But "consciousness raising" around orgasms, abortion, sexual violence, and childcare, and demands for equal rights in higher education and at the workplace, were not specifically Jewish. Within the women's movement, initially firmly focused on the solidarities of gender, there were even fewer direct allusions to the Holocaust.

Second wave feminists have nevertheless retrospectively unearthed specifically Jewish motifs. Whether one had grown up in almost entirely Jewish worlds in Brooklyn or Shaker Heights, in the Communist Party counter-culture, the suburbs, or smaller communities with few Jews, the '60s had finally made it OK, even alluring, to be different, smart with frizzy hair, to be too "much," in ways which were stereotypically associated with Jewish women. Radical politics attracted those who were perceived (and perceived themselves) as loud, assertive, and resistant to Middle American standards of female beauty, work, and intellect.[2] If feminism and radicalism were already central to my self-understanding as a child of the 1960s – and of refugees – I arrived at the University of Chicago in the fall of 1968 in the aftermath of the chaotic Democratic Party Convention, in a city that headquartered SDS (Students for a Democratic Society), the Black Panther Party, and numerous radical women's initiatives including the "Jane Network" which referred women for safe if illegal abortions. The Holocaust which insistently crept

1 On that socialization, see *Tablet* http://www.tabletmag.com/jewish-news-and-politics/184393/holocaust-sixties.

2 See Joyce Antler, *Jewish Radical Feminism: Voices from the Women's Liberation Movement*, New York: NYU Press, 2018.

into my childhood home and public high school for "gifted girls", even when we tried to drown it out with Dylan and Jefferson Airplane soundtracks, Godard and Antonioni films, and marches on Washington (not to mention SATs and intense intellectual conversation), receded even further into the shadows. Virtually all of us, as we only acknowledged at reunions decades later, were the daughters of World War II in one way or another; our parents were survivors, refugees, or World War II veterans. But for us as teenage girls, preoccupied with our tumultuous present, the Holocaust seemed further in the past than it does now after years of study and commemoration.

When then did these strands come together in the context of becoming a historian? Not yet at City College in New York, the hometown to which I returned rather more quickly than intended in Fall 1969 after having been expelled from Chicago for participating in a sit-in protesting the denial of tenure to a female professor and, more generally the university's adversarial relationship with the South Side African American community within which it was located. CCNY, roiled by demands for open admission for black and Puerto Rican students and the Kent State/Cambodia protests, turned me into a budding historian determined to integrate activism and academia. My professors introduced the new social history "from below" as we read E.P. Thompson on industrial time discipline and Rudé on the sans culottes in the French Revolution. A rather dowdy Professor of Renaissance history – the daughter of an Irish cop – and a rare tenured female member of the History Department, opened up an entirely unknown scholarly world when she dispatched me to the card index in the grand reading room of the 42nd St Public Library to catalogue (in lieu of writing my midterm) the astonishingly rich literature by women scholars on women's role in early modern Europe. This was the beginning, as it turned out, of what would become Joan Kelly-Gadol's path-breaking article, "Did Women Have a Renaissance?"[3]

Berlin, Gender, and History

It was graduate school at Rutgers, a pioneering center of social history, that encouraged students and professors alike to build the new field of women's studies and me to pursue German and women's history. My Ph.D. research on the Weimar Sex Reform movement not only connected to my passionate involvement in the U.S. struggle for reproductive rights, but also brought me back to Germany. This time, not as the daughter of a restitution lawyer who had waged a relentless but short-lived effort to exact revenge, or the

3 "Joan Kelly-Gadol, "Did Women Have a Renaissance?" in *Becoming Visible*, eds. Renate Bridenthal and Claudia Koonz, New York: Houghton Mifflin, 1977: 137–164.

cousin who had "gotten away" while the six children of the uncle deported to Auschwitz were raised Catholic by their "Aryan" mother and still lived in Frankfurt/Main, but as a researcher who would be drawn into a direct confrontation with the Nazi past and my family history. Berlin in the late 1970s and early 1980s marked my path to a more immediate, if not yet scholarly, encounter with the Holocaust.[4]

The city, still punctured by bullet holes and empty lots, divided by a wall that presented an eerie but astonishingly normalized post-memory of war and Cold War, was exciting, erotic, and addictive. Jews were barely present, even as ghosts within a creative counter-culture that was probably only possible in a heavily subsidized island of "democracy" inside the Soviet bloc. There were no *Stolpersteine*, no memory boom debates, and an insular Jewish community that had not yet "come out" as it did after unification and the arrival of the "Russians" who revived the new/old capital's Jewish world. Until – and via – the explosive presentation of the series "Holocaust" on German TV in early 1979, to be Jewish was to be simultaneously invisible and exotic. My dissertation research on Weimar sexual and population policy connected me to a rapidly growing community of feminist historians investigating "Aryan" women's role in National Socialism. My Berlin colleagues and friends were coming to terms, more or less, with *their* past.

Well before I was ready to work on the Holocaust I was drawn into transatlantic feminist research on National Socialism and its aftermath, including my counter-intuitive work in the early 1990s on German women as victims of Red Army rape. As the only American and only (openly) Jewish participant in Annemarie Tröger's oral history project at the Sociology Institute (ZI6) of the Freie Universität, I was fascinated by how young (at the time!) German women historians were confronting their own mothers' youth in the Third Reich. In our seminars, not far from where the liberal Prinzregentenstrasse synagogue had once stood, Jewish women were the looming absence in that work of personal and historical recovery. I needed to learn about murdered grandmothers. My colleagues, primed to uncover women's putatively neglected resistance to misogynistic National Socialism, had to struggle with the shockingly happy memories their mothers revealed, of relative freedom from family and male domination enjoyed in the BdM

4 I draw here on previously published personal reflections including; "Historikerin der 'zweiten Generation': Ein Gespräch über biographische Zugänge zur Geschichtsschreibung," with Louisa Reichstetter and Boris Spernol, in Grossmann, *Wege in der Fremde: Deutsch-jüdische Begegnungsgeschichte zwischen Feldafing, New York und Teheran*, Jena: Wallstein, 2012:105–131.

and other homosocial Nazi organizations. Even the marginalized history of women's anti-Nazi activity drew a blank when it came to Jewish women.

In Fall 1978, our Women's Oral History group toured Ravensbrück Women's Concentration Camp, deep in the GDR, together with a formidable delegation of Communist survivors. These "camp sisters," our interview partners, were still closely connected, able to enjoy *Kaffee und Kuchen* on both sides of the Wall, with their special dispensations as members of the West Berlin VVN (*Vereinigung der Verfolgten des Naziregimes*) or as full-fledged luminaries in the SED (GDR Communist Party). They had constituted a precarious "elite" in the camp, as German communists overseeing barracks for "asocials" or "prostitutes" (who included women incarcerated for the officially non-existent offense of lesbianism, very much an emerging topic for the young West Germans and a taboo for our hosts).

Jewish women were barely present in the moving stories they were so pleased to recount to a younger generation eager to listen. For these survivors, preserving the memory of Ravensbrück had become a life's mission. Jewish victims, however, were a distant transient factor, pitiful barely present creatures on their way to some other planet the "politicals" dimly knew they would not have to endure. They recalled the anti-fascist Olga Benario, separated from her comrades because of her "race", or a winter evening when 5000 "Jewesses", including a violinist playing plaintive tunes, had passed through Ravensbrück on a transport to "the East". The next morning the *Jüdinnen* had disappeared and the comrades had wept. I did not publish my critical memories of that excursion until 1997.[5] By then, the New York–based German Women's History Group, a quite different extension of my German collective, had become the anchor for my research, from Weimar Sex Reform to the "baby boom" among Jewish survivors and finally as a historian of gender and the Holocaust. Looking back, I can see that I was doing that work long before I officially claimed the title.

Approaching Gender and the Holocaust

As part of my ongoing excavation of the family archive in a preservation-unfriendly Long Island basement, I recently discovered my mother's scribbled notes on the program of the now legendary March 1983 New York conference on women and the Holocaust. Organized by "The Institute for Research in History," an explicitly feminist collective but held at Stern College, the women's campus of Yeshiva University, the conference entangled

5 "Zwei Erfahrungen im Kontext des Themas 'Gender und Holocaust'" in Sigrid Jacobeit and Grit Philipp, eds., *Forschungsschwerpunkt Ravensbrück: Beiträge zur Geschichte des Frauen-Konzentrationslagers*, Berlin: Hentrich,1997: 124–146.

women's, Jewish, and Holocaust Studies and thereby precipitated one of the main dramas of the event, the insistent intrusion of contemporary feminist debates. I have only vague recollections of my mother's attendance, and no way of deciphering her shaky handwriting, some in a virtually extinct shorthand, carefully learned as preparation for the female skills required for emigration. Some notes, in a mix of English and German, are in legible caps: "scabies," "lesbians," and the observation that a particular speaker was "very nervous." Re-reading the proceedings today, we hear the lament that drives so much of Anna Hájková's work on excavating queer histories in "Audience #4's question: "I am a Jewish lesbian feminist (applause). I don't know how to ask this question but I feel that I am carrying a responsibility for the many lesbians in this audience today and I hope I can do you all justice. What I want to say is that I cannot believe that there were no lesbians in the camps, ghettos, and so forth....I know that there were lesbians who were there, who fought and died in the camps and ghettoes. I just wanted to make this statement here because I think it is important and should not be ignored. (Applause)."

Another woman countered that she would like to speak "as a Jew...for the unborn Jewish children...for the women who were sterilized and could not have children, and for the women who were deprived of that in one way or another; and I'd like to speak of how this clashes with feminine ideal, the feminist ideal of doing your own thing." Survivors themselves repeatedly insisted that gender or sexuality was not the main factor in a fate determined by their Jewishness. Yet the memories they shared clearly reinforced the conviction that had incited the conference, namely that gender had indeed mattered, very much. As the discussion threatened to derail, Joan Ringelheim intervened, "I don't want to have, right now, at this place, at this conference, a political argument about who anybody is going to be or should be. We are trying to figure out women in the Holocaust. Please let's try to keep it within that context."[6] In so many ways we are still trying to do exactly that.

At approximately the same time, Renate Bridenthal, Marion Kaplan, and I were moved to put together our 1984 volume *When Biology Became Destiny: Women in Weimar and Nazi Germany*. Meredith Tax, an editor at the "New Feminist Library" initiated by the old left publisher, Monthly Review Press, had approached us after we presented a panel at an annual Barnard College "Scholar and the Feminist" conference. The gathering was in no way focused on either Jewish or Holocaust Studies; moreover,

6 *Proceedings of the Conference Women Surviving the Holocaust*, eds. Esther Katz and Joan Ringelheim, New York: Occasional Papers from The Institute for Research in History, director, Marjorie Lightman, 1983: 73–74.

the Holocaust itself wasn't central to our volume. *When Biology Became Destiny* was conceived as a feminist project related to New Right attacks on women's emancipation.[7] But we did understand that, in contrast to the significant feminist historiography on women and National Socialism being produced by our British and German colleagues, we needed to include *something* about the actual Holocaust – not an easy task in the early 1980s. We convinced Sybil Milton, for whom this was not a primary area of scholarly interest, to contribute a remarkably comprehensive article on "Women and the Holocaust: The Case of German and German-Jewish Women" which also raised general questions about gender specific experience in the camps. We added one brief memoir excerpt that Marion found, by a German Jewish camp survivor. It is startling to now re-read that testimony which did not receive much attention when we published the book. "The Story of Ruth" addresses the threat of rape by liberating Soviet troops, the cruelty of women guards, the lucky compassion of camp "sisters" and German soldiers and civilians who slipped food to young women in labor camps. As our bookshelves (and PDF files) swell with new or republished literature it is so easy to forget how long we, in different ways and in different places (and I do think it matters greatly whether one was working in North America, Germany, Israel, or Eastern Europe) have been grappling with these questions.

A 1999 conference in Ravensbrück, which had after the *Wende* in 1990 become a center of research on women's role as perpetrators and victims during the NS regime, on *Gedächtnis und Geschlecht,* was another milestone in my own turn toward these topics. Called to lunch, served in eerily resonant huge pots, in a reconstructed barracks by rather surly remaining employees of the old GDR *Mahn und Gedenkstätte* for Communist resisters, I first met Marianne Hirsch, who was to become an important interlocutor for my thinking about the Holocaust, gender, and memory. Hyper-aware of the ironies, we bonded over our intense discomfort with the locale and mutual outrage at the conference's focus on the gendered aesthetics of camp memorials while the Holocaust itself, and Ravensbrück's role late in the war as an extermination and transit camp for Jewish women on death marches from the East, was ignored. We were joined in our lonely critique by Irith Dublon-Knebel, a researcher from Tel Aviv writing about female guards; together with psychoanalyst Ilany Kogon with whom I was assigned to share a German style double bed with two mattresses, we feebly joked about how this peculiar intimacy must have been due to our supposed shared identity. These moments of

7 Forum, "When Biology Became Destiny: Twentieth Anniversary Retrospective," Renate Bridenthal, Atina Grossmann, Marion Kaplan, *German History* 22:4 (2004): 596–606.

anger leavened by bemused astonishment multiplied as the post-1990 German politics of memory unfolded; they became an integral part of my gradual identification as a historian of gender – I had always been that – and the Holocaust.

Building the Field: A Collective Project

There are so many markers that we should document; other authors in this volume contribute their own. In January 2001, Judy Baumel (Schwartz) of Bar-Ilan University invited me to a conference on "Gender, Place, and Memory in the Modern Jewish Experience." It did not focus on the Holocaust and my panel on "Engendered Memories of the Second World War" was otherwise composed of three non-Jewish researchers (including Insa Eschebach who had continued to work on commemoration in Ravensbrück and is now the memorial site's long-time director). It did, however, allow me to present on "Gendered Interactions between Jews and Germans in Postwar Occupied Germany" and to meet with Judy, herself a pioneer researcher on women in the DP camps. By 2002, supported by one of those rare "paradise" fellowships at the Institute for Advanced Study in Princeton, my beginning research on the DP "baby boom" and the "close encounters" it "engendered" among Jewish survivors, Germans, and Allies, had somehow afforded me the credibility to write a review essay on "Women and the Holocaust" in the premier journal *Holocaust and Genocide Studies.* Gabriel Schonfeld's 1998 attack in *Commentary* on gender analysis of the Holocaust as "an intellectual fad" had fueled feminist historians' determination to finally insist on representation in the ever growing archive of Holocaust scholarship.

Digging through my files (so much easier to find when they were arranged in cabinets rather than stored on generations of computers) I am struck by how indispensable collective thinking and arguments at conferences and seminars have been to my gradual emergence as a historian of gender and the Holocaust; how grateful I am for all those trips and dinners and in the hallway conversations, in the US, Canada, Germany, Israel, and France, even if, as I was frequently admonished, all that running around sometimes delayed publication. One of the challenges and pleasures of thinking about this assignment has been realizing how much had been done even before we declared ourselves a field, even while we still felt beleaguered and unrecognized, and in some instances still do.

The April 2001 conference, *Departures: New Feminist Perspectives on the Holocaust* at the University of Minnesota, marked a kind of "coming out" for my place in the field, even if my Roundtable comments at this intentionally interdisciplinary workshop began with "I come to this panel ....as a relative outsider, professionally, if not personally...a historian of modern Germany and of gender, who obdurately tried to skirt the subject by focusing on the before and after in Germany." That symposium featured memorable, if at times tormented, reflections on disciplinary and generational differences, including Joan Ringelheim's deeply thoughtful critique of her early work on female solidarity in the camps. Literary scholar Sara Horowitz blew my mind with her stunning paper on "Engendering Representations of Atrocity" and younger scholars such as Pascale Bos articulated their own understandings of interdisciplinarity, "postmemory, and personal positionality". It was, certainly for me, a turning point; from then on the titles of conferences and the papers they forced me to write increasingly included the term "Holocaust."

In 2004 the United States Holocaust Memorial Museum placed its first imprimatur on the emerging field, mounting a week-long seminar on Gender and the Holocaust led by a hugely pregnant and astonishingly energetic and committed graduate student named Jennifer Evans. My detailed handwritten notepad documents presentations by, among others, Jane Caplan, Sara Horowitz, Nechama Tec, and, only sometimes participating, Joan Ringelheim.[8] I was especially impressed by Tim Cole, a young British historian of the Holocaust in Hungary who intrigued me precisely because his insights about the gendered nature of deportation had not been driven by any particular interest in women's experience. Hungarian Jewish men had already been drafted into labor camps; those left to be killed were mostly women, children, and the elderly. He had become a historian of gender and the Holocaust because that was the only way he could be a responsible historian of the Holocaust. I was reminded of a similar turn decades earlier when another brilliant British historian, Tim Mason, published his hugely important articles on women in Nazi Germany in the first two issues of the radical social history journal *History Workshop*. His interest had not been piqued by any particular prior interest in gender, but because when trying to understand the negative impact of absenteeism and workers' "opposition" on the Nazi war effort, he needed to dig deep into the regime's ideology about women and its reluctance to mobilize them into the work force.[9]

8 Joan's insistence that I interview Zippi Tichauer instigated a challenging series of conversations about gender in Nazi and DP camps; see "Living On: Remembering Feldafing," in *Approaching an Auschwitz Survivor: Holocaust Testimony and Its Transformations*, ed. Jürgen Matthäus, New York: Oxford University Press, 2009: 73–94. A revelatory counterpoint to Joan's early work was Na'ama Shik's paper on "Weibliche Erfahrung in Auschwitz-Birkenau," which I first heard at a Berlin conference in 2003.

9 Tim Mason, "Women in Germany 1925–1940: Family, Welfare, and Work," *History Workshop* 1 (1976): 74–113, 2: 5–32; For a later example of "mainstream" Holocaust historiography requiring attention to women, see Christopher R. Browning, *Remembering Survival: Inside a Nazi Slave Labor* Camp, New York: Norton, 2010.

Challenges: On the Margins and at the Forefront

For those of us steeped in feminist politics and scholarship it seems that our research is making its way, in fits and starts, with frustrating gaps and omissions, into the center of Holocaust Studies. Key teaching texts such as Doris Bergen's *The Holocaust: A Concise History* or the forthcoming massive new *Encyclopedia of the Holocaust* edited by Mark Roseman have a host of female contributors and articles that both integrate and specifically highlight gender as well as those categorized as "unfit" by the racial state – homosexuals and lesbians, "asocials," Sinti and Roma – long neglected by Holocaust historians. The centrality of gender, I would venture to say, is no longer controversial, even if not necessarily put into practice, as evidenced by too many other tables of contents or conference programs.

My own path towards that centrality both culminated and in other ways only began with an unexpected and fortuitous *Schidduch* engineered by the USHMM. In Spring 2012 at the end of a much too short semester-long fellowship, the "5th Floor" Research Center announced its second Faculty Seminar on Gender and the Holocaust (after 2004) and paired me as co-instructor with a cultural studies scholar and philosopher. I had never heard of Dorota Glowacka and her CV, heavy on representation and theory, was daunting and somewhat alienating. But I was lucky; the interdisciplinary seminar we constructed and the collaboration it inspired continues to shape my practice as a historian of Gender and the Holocaust.

Yet, the "gaps and traps" remain.[10] My long-standing assumption that following the gender trail would always guide my research agenda has been much harder to sustain in my current research on "remapping survival" and globalizing the story of flight and refuge. Ironically, our immense progress in writing about 'gender and' or 'women and' or the 'politics of sexuality in', has empowered us to embark on more broadly conceived studies that dispense with such specific themes—where, to my chagrin, I find myself struggling to reinsert gender as the key category I know it is. This is especially the case with topics where there are no rich layers of prior scholarship to build on, complement and critique, such as those that have preoccupied me: the experience of the majority of survivors who earned that title because they managed to escape Nazi occupation, mostly in the unoccupied Soviet Union or in parts of the non-Western world where flight from violent antisemitism and racism in Europe collided with a peculiar (and gendered) privilege as "Europeans" in colonial and semi-colonial societies.

---

10 See Forum: "Holocaust and the History of Gender and Sexuality," with Doris Bergen, Atina Grossmann, Anna Hájková, Elissa Mailänder, Patrick Farges, *German History* 36:1 (March 2018): 78–100.

Moreover, at the same time as we worry about the future of memory in the absence of live witnesses, my generation of feminist Holocaust researchers who emerged in the context of second wave feminism and the establishment of women's and then gender studies, has been followed by cohorts more inclined to include masculinity(ies) and men's experiences. They stress more fluid notions of gender identity on the one hand, and an emphasis on family rather than gender as determining factors during the Holocaust on the other. Urgent questions about the specific or exceptional status of Holocaust studies in the context of a fading "memory boom" and the rise of comparative genocide studies reinforce our sense of an over-determined transitional moment. Indeed – and my thinking here owes so much to conversations with Dorota – in a complicated reversal, the widely acknowledged significance of sexuality, reproduction, and sexual violence in contemporary instances of genocide, ethnic cleansing, or mass violence, and the ongoing prominence of sexual violence in global conflicts, now frames, undergirds, and legitimizes feminist research on the Holocaust.

The challenge of linking those issues, while also figuring out how to responsibly deploy our time and knowledge at a moment when we find ourselves living in states of general political emergency, can and should be quite dizzying. The "hide and seek" process is ongoing but as this volume shows, we are certainly no longer alone, and the list of references for this essay should be very long.

Joan Ringelheim

The Holocaust in My Life

Introduction

Both of my parents were born in Poland. My mother came to the United States with her mother and a sister when she was eight, joining four brothers who were already there. Her father died when she was six years old.

My father left Poland when he was seventeen years old. He came with his sixteen year old brother. His mother, father and two other siblings remained in Poland. Although my father's father had become an American citizen in 1905, he never wanted to stay in the US. However, my father very much wanted to come to the United States.

While we acknowledged and sort of celebrated some holidays (Passover, Rosh Hashanah and Yom Kippur etc.,) neither parent practiced a religious Judaism regularly. I went to Hebrew school as did my brother who had a Bar Mitzvah, but when I told my parents that I wasn't learning anything there and wanted to leave, they acceded to my wishes. Perhaps this scenario had to do with my being a girl. While this may be true, neither of my parents seemed to be concerned with what it meant to be Jewish in a religious sense, and they also believed me. Sensitivity about antisemitism played a large role in my growing up. A number of incidents will reveal this concern.

In 1949 when I was in the 6th grade, I found it problematic that Christmas was acknowledged and celebrated while Chanukah was ignored. Something didn't seem right to me. This disagreement became so vehement that classroom desks divided into the two view-points. I don't remember what the teacher did beyond letting us divide the classroom's seating arrangement, nor do I have any memory about which side "won". At the time, the holidays of other groups played no role in our protest. I may have been sensitive in some ways to antisemitism but I did not have much sensitivity to other prejudices or oppressive behaviors at that point. Racism seemed to be an exception.

When I became interested in getting a summer job in 1953 or 1954, my mother told me that the bank to which I was applying probably wouldn't hire me because I was Jewish. While I don't remember reacting to what she was saying, I never forgot that she said this.

When I entered high school I learned that the DAR (The Daughters of the American Revolution) had never given their high school citizenship award to a Jewish person. I immediately decided that I would get this award and in my senior year I was awarded it. At the same time I thought that I had received the award only because the high school faculty voted for me rather than the DAR.

I was the speaker at our middle school graduation in 1952. The class was supposed to say some things as a group and I found the use of the term "black" problematic. I thought it was insulting, harsh and clearly negative. I lived in a white world and had no idea how much discussion/argument transpired in the African American community about what terms to use. This was not my sensitivity. I won the argument and we did not use the term "black". I cite this because it does demonstrate some other concerns I had as a young person apart from those concerning Jews. It also shows the level of naiveté that surrounded my ideas at the time. It demonstrates how little the concerns inside the community of African-Americans or Black Americans penetrated the consciousness of ordinary white people like me.

I first met survivors of the Holocaust when I was 11 or 12. They were friends of my dad's sister, Claire. At the time I didn't know very much about the Holocaust, although I remember tension. However, I did not ask any questions. I didn't know what to think or feel. I certainly did not know enough to even figure out what questions to ask. When I was in college, I found out that the Nazis killed my aunt's first husband, so her silences became clearer to me.

My father told me that the Nazis killed his mother, father, and youngest brother, but I have no recollection when he told me, nor what impact this had on me at the time. It was not until after college that I met and talked with survivors and began to reflect on the ways the Holocaust may have affected my aunt and my dad. It took a long time for me to find out what really happened to my grandparents and my father's youngest brother (they were shot at Sambor). I think it took a much longer time for me to reflect on the effect the Holocaust had on me.

At first, survivors frightened me. I felt that they might have done something terrible in order to survive. In retrospect I think that I didn't want to hear how awful it was for them because it was too much for me. I am sure consciously and unconsciously, I wondered whether I could have survived in their circumstances or whether I would even have tried to do so. My response was also complex. When being diagnosed for breast cancer in 1993 I remember thinking that I wanted to have cancer, only later realizing that it might have been a possible response having to do with my guilt or shame of not experiencing a ghetto or a camp.

It was probably because of my family's history and the people I met growing up, that the Holocaust became important to me. My interest was not shared with my Jewish or Christian friends in high school or college nor was it an academic topic in college or graduate school. In spite of not having an environment larger than my own family in which to think about the Holocaust, I seemed "attracted" to the topic. So attracted that when I was in graduate school in Philosophy, I put down a list of topics about which I wanted to teach when I received my Ph.D. and at the top of the list was antisemitism and racism. I wanted to be able to connect the history of the Holocaust to the history of antisemitism and I used antisemitism as a way to understand the historical events of the Holocaust. The topics of racism and antisemitism were not at all what philosophers seemed to talk about, but I was persuaded by my own study that these were crucial topics that had to be covered.

I have the sense that what brought me to the topic in the first place was my family's experience. But I have no clear idea about what kept me there? Attraction to horror? Identification with victimization? Some guilt because I was not there? Did I think that studying and talking about it was doing something? Was it a form of activism? Did the Holocaust as a study serve as a substitute for present day responsibilities? It is easy to wrap oneself in moral garb if you work on the past.

How I Began to Study the Topic

I wish that my desire to start a project on Women and the Holocaust arose from a deep and conscious contemplation of the issues. However, that is not what happened. I had studied history and philosophy, my fields of interest were the Philosophy of History, Social and Political Philosophy, Philosophy of Social Science and Ethics, and I had taught courses on these subjects. What brought me to feminism?

During my first years of teaching (1968), I taught about racism, antisemitism and the Holocaust. I did not come to feminism or feminist theory until around 1973. Consequently, the issue of gender during the Holocaust did not come up for me in studying about racism, antisemitism, or the Holocaust. Once I began to teach feminist theory in 1975 or 1976, I recall asking myself a simple question: where were the women or what about the women during the Holocaust? Until then, I had been seeing only men in the historical literature and I had not been sure whether and/or in what ways the lives and experiences of women replicated or were different from those of men. I began to wonder: "Did gender count in some way? If so, then how?" My view may have been similar to people who became critical of my work in that I must have thought that the Holocaust was some sort of sacred territory not to be treated like other events until I no longer held this position. When I look back, my reading of the feminist literature helped me to ask questions about women during the Holocaust. However, I don't think there was any particular contact with feminist theory that pushed me to pursue these questions.

At the time, the 1970's, the Holocaust was not generally an issue for feminists, whether Jewish or not. The Holocaust was considered a narrow interest at best. For some people the Holocaust was narrowly religiously motivated or nothing more than a distraction from what was essential to feminist thinking. While I knew that my grandmother, grandfather and my father's youngest brother had been killed by the Nazis and that some 80 other relatives had also been killed, I don't know whether this knowledge drove my interest. However, I cannot imagine that this knowledge, no matter how slight, did not have some heavy influence on me.

Following the emergence of that simple question, I attended one of my first conferences on the Holocaust in 1978. I vividly recall walking out of a session with two women I had just met: Helen Fagin and Susan Cernyak-Spatz. They were both survivors and both professors at different universities. I knew nothing else about either of them at the time when I asked what I naively thought was a simple and non-provocative question: "what about women?" Helen Fagin did not hesitate for a moment. She quickly began to walk away, facing me (almost as if she were afraid to show me her back) and said in no uncertain terms: "I don't want the Holocaust to be made secondary to feminism." Although I practically shouted: "I have no idea what the question really means yet", she was gone. From the way in which she so immediately fled, you might have thought I had a disease. Clearly I had to think about whether the Holocaust transcended gender. And this became the central question about what I and others were trying to do.

At this time, I then turned to Susan who stayed to talk but proceeded to tell me that she had been a graduate of Theresienstadt, Auschwitz, and Ravensbruek. I internally gulped at this revelation. She immediately said "sex didn't matter." So I tried to explain that sex was not necessarily the primary issue and we continued to talk throughout the day. She kept trying to find examples to demonstrate that studying women during the Holocaust was pointless because being a woman didn't matter. However, the examples she related suggested that more needed to be studied.

For example, at one point she told me that women guards were more vicious than male guards. If true, why wasn't this something to pursue? Also if she had been only in women's camps with female guards, how did she compare the behavior of male and female guards? And supposing that she was able to see both, did women appear to be more vicious even when doing the same things as men? Did the brutality of the women seem more vicious than that of men even if in practice it was similar or the same? By the end of the day, I was convinced that more needed to be investigated. It took Susan more than a day but she did not run away as did Helen Fagin. I don't think Susan ever changed her mind about female guards. I kept mulling over the issue but did not yet pursue it in a diligent way.

A Turning Point

At a Holocaust Conference in 1979, I found myself in an informal discussion with Yael Danieli, Eva Fleischner, Henry Friedlander, Raul Hilberg, and Sybil Milton. Danieli, a therapist who worked with children of survivors, raised the question of why these children tend to fear that their mothers had been raped. She thought that this fear was widespread and that it might represent some reality.

Without apparent hesitation, those of my colleagues who responded claimed that the children were not describing actual incidents of abuse but rather fantasies induced by the media's sexualization of the Holocaust. No one quoted any research; no one referred to any documentation or studies of interviews of survivors, male or female. No other issues were raised, and no other questions posed. No one discussed the relationships between women and children in the Holocaust. No one spoke about the possible relationship between gender and survival. No one talked about German women as perpetrators or collaborators. No one discussed the structure of women's camps, women in resistance, women political prisoners, or the relationships of men and women, women and women, men and men. No one discussed the possible differences between ghetto life and camp life—in the former, women and men were together and in the latter, for the most part, they were not. There was no pursuit of the issue. There was just an immediate and resounding denigration of the question and the discussion ended. No concepts were readily available to shape such a conversation; there was no historical road map. Feminist theory would have helped, but no one at that time was prepared to apply it to the Holocaust. I well remember that scene, and remember being quiet. I just didn't know what to say, but I never forgot it.

I eventually began to pursue a number of questions: Would the Holocaust be portrayed differently if one reclaimed women's lives and voices? Did women survive better than men? What were women's survival strategies? Did women cope better than men? Did women have different relationships with other women than men had with other men? Was women's resistance different from that of men? What were the relationships between women and men in resistance? Did women have different roles than men in the resistance? What were women's particular vulnerabilities?

When I first began to write about women and the Holocaust, it was clear that battle lines were going to be drawn. Lines between those who believed such an investigation would trivialize the Holocaust and those who thought it could change, even transform, the study of the Holocaust.

At the April 1982 Scholar's Conference on the Church Struggle and the Holocaust sponsored by the National Conference of Christians and Jews (NCCJ) in New York City. I gave my first a paper on the topic. It was entitled "The Unethical and the Unspeakable." It was, I think, in the mode of female nationalism and hence problematic. But I didn't see this at the time nor do I think the commentator was upset by this perspective period. He was upset by my talking about women; it didn't matter how I talked about them.

Michael Wishograd was the commentator and said that the most interesting part of the paper was my middle name "Miriam." Miriam was my grandmother's name. She had been murdered by the Nazis along with my grandfather, Jacob and their youngest son, Josef. I took her name as my middle name for a few years as I began this work.[1] And Michael Wishograd thought the only thing worthwhile about what I said was that my middle name was "Miriam", in honor of my grandmother. He also thought that any work on women and the Holocaust was not respectable. To him, there was no issue about women during the Holocaust, certainly not from a feminist perspective. Wishograd's viewpoint became commonplace. Larry Langer was also on the program. I have no recollection about his comments. However, in subsequent years he was directly hostile to feminist ideas on this subject although he never quoted or delineated the ideas of the feminists he derided.[2]

Papers and Conferences

In this first paper, "The Unethical and the Unspeakable", I believe that I correctly eschewed gender neutrality and suggested that one could not simply assume that all survivors experienced the Holocaust in the same way. It was my position that the lives of women had been obscured or erased from Holocaust history. Women's experiences had been neutralized into a so-called "human perspective" so that issues related specifically to women were excluded from Holocaust history. As I stated: "At the very least, we must acknowledge the special abuse of women in sexual and parental roles, in gender-defined conditions and roles within ghettos, in resistance groups, and in the camps." I continued by discussing the need to define women's values

---

1 Consequently, my name is sometimes written as Joan Miriam Ringelheim and sometimes as Joan Ringelheim. To be honest, and perhaps embarrassedly so, I stopped using her name because I did not like how I wrote the letter "M. The "M" in Miriam just did not work for me.

2 See p. 350 in Dalia Ofer and Lenore Weitzman, eds., *Women in the Holocaust*, New Haven: Yale University Press, 1998, Note #3 about Langer.

to show how they helped shape their experiences. I also spoke about the differences between women's relationships with other women as opposed to those of men with other men. Asking how we can find out why or whether it might be true that women survived better, I proposed that we look at how women constructed survival strategies and made meaningful choices in varying conditions of powerlessness.[3] One can see the grounding of something of a nationalist view of women in this paper which I did not hold forever—indeed I changed my mind in a radical way when I gave a paper at the Berkshire Conference on the History of Women (1984).

The next stage was the Conference titled "Women Surviving: the Holocaust" that took place at Stern College, a college for Orthodox Jewish women in Manhattan, on March 20–21, 1983. The endeavor had been in the planning since 1979 or 1980 and I coordinated it together with Esther Katz. As I was the coordinator engaged in gendered Holocaust research, my perspective at the time seemed to ground the ways in which this conference commenced or was organized. In terms of attendance the Conference was a tremendous success: we had expected between 150 to 200 people a day but over 400 people attended. The auditorium could only hold so many, and we even had to turn a number of people away. We brought together those who didn't usually and probably still don't come together at Holocaust conferences: survivors, scholars, children of survivors, feminists of all kinds, as well as other interested members of the community. Between 20 to 30 men attended as well. The combination of people in the audience was rich, if sometimes uneven.

Unlike academic conferences, here the survivors, and not the scholars, occupied center stage. Survivors were considered to be the experiential experts. The scholars had to listen. There was very little scholarly analysis when compared with the personal stories of the survivors. The lack of scholarly analysis caused some unevenness in the conference and troubled some members of the audience who wanted more from the scholars. Some thought that the lack was the conference's strength. On the other hand, there were those who did not attend because they thought that the conference would be primarily led by scholars. There was no winning on this score.

The conference was built on three principles: (1) the emergence of personal stories even from women who don't necessarily speak or feel that they can speak; (2) some scholarly analysis of the women and Holocaust field such as it was at the time; and (3) most importantly, an effort to get people to be aware that women during the Holocaust had to be studied.

---

3 The 1982 talk was published in 1984 as "The Unethical and the Unspeakable: Women and the Holocaust", in *The Simon Wiesenthal Center Annual 1*, Chappaqua, NY: Rossel Books, 1984: 81.

The conference was very volatile. People wanted to say many things and did. There were fights—different ideologies and perspectives on living produced many conflicts. Perhaps the biggest ones were between those of feminist and lesbian perspectives who found it difficult if not impossible to listen to those whose views were not feminist or lesbian feminist.

I can only describe the conference as being one in which the participation was broad and unquiet. The findings were quite limited. It was clear that survivors had a very difficult time thinking about themselves as women. Actually, many simply didn't want to do so. Yet there was something vital about this conference, something about it was genuinely exciting and unpredictable. It was difficult to stop thinking about it.

A letter that author Cynthia Ozick wrote me in response to an invitation to the conference summarizes the level of hostility that accompanied much of what I was doing on the subject: "I think you are asking the wrong question. Not simply the wrong question in the sense of not having found the right one; I think you are asking a *morally* wrong question, a question that leads us still further down the road of eradicating Jews from history. You are—I hope inadvertently—joining up with the likes of [the Revisionists] who [say] that if it happened to Jews it never happened. You insist that it didn't happen to `just Jews`. It happened to the women, and it is only a detail that the women were Jewish. It is not a detail. It is everything, the whole story. Your project is, in my view, an ambitious falsehood…. The Holocaust happened to victims who were not seen as men, women, or children…but as Jews."

And yet, in terms of purpose, the conference may have been seminal even legendary to some who were there, still it was not definitive. Atina Grossmann, Marion Kaplan, and Renate Bridenthal, scholars of German Jewish women's history wrote a letter to me stating: "It gave voice to women survivors and served notice to scholars that even during the extreme events of the Nazi 'Final Solution'…gender mattered".

However viewed, the Women and the Holocaust Conference was a watershed event in the development of the discipline. And it was also a turning point in my own work.

Following the conference I did a number of interviews and tried to think through my research. I eventually realized that my valorization of women was a mistake. It was in the spirit of this self-critique that I presented my paper in 1984 at the Berkshire Conference on the History of Women and later developed the article that appeared in SIGNS in 1985.[4] Stating that

4 "Women and the Holocaust: A Reconsideration of Research", *SIGNS: Journal of Women in Culture and Society* (1985) 10:4: 741–761.

even if our perspective and questions were wrong, the work was not useless but needed a different political and philosophical context, I posited a list of questions that we should ask the survivors about their gendered experiences. I assumed that oppression did not make people better; rather oppression made people oppressed and consequently our first question had to be "What does oppression do to us?" A large crowd attended this talk and the panel discussion that followed. Some in the audience got angry at what and perhaps how I was giving this paper—I suspect I was so strident. It was as if I was a victim.

I continued to do some writing and even had an agent, Candida Donadido, who tried mightily to sell the book I had written. Despite her efforts I received what seemed like 15 or more rejections. One editor, Elizabeth Sifton at Panthenon, was interested, but the publishing house was disbanded. Sifton was still interested when she moved to Knopf, but the head of Knopf stated that they had too many books on the Holocaust. Needless to say the book was never published.

In 1989 I took a job with the US Holocaust Museum in Washington D.C. (USHMM), beginning another chapter of my life that continued until 2007 when I retired. But I continued to write about women and the Holocaust, such as in an article appearing in 1992 in *The Jewish Quarterly* where I explained how the politics of National Socialism radicalized both antisemitism and sexism.[5] My SIGNS article was reprinted in Carol Rittner and John K. Roth's volume *Different Voices: Women and the Holocaust*, with a new postscript and appendices.[6] During that decade I wrote two additional articles, further developing and reconsidering my research, one appearing in Ronit Lentin's volume *Gender and Catastrophe* in 1997 and the other in Dalia Ofer and Lenore Weitzman's *Women in the Holocaust* in 1998.[7] It should be noted that in these beginnings there was little or no recognition of or research on women who were not Jewish.

After the 1998 piece I no longer wrote anything scholarly about the Holocaust although I still gave talks. Life at USHMM became very intense

5 "The Holocaust: Taking Women into Account", *The Jewish Quarterly* 39:3 (147) (Autumn 1992): 19–23.

6 "Women and the Holocaust: A Reconsideration of Research", Carol Rittner and John K. Roth, eds. *Different Voices: Women and the Holocaust:* New York: Paragon House, 1993: 373–418.

7 "Genocide and Gender: A Split Memory", Ronit Lentin (ed.), *Gender and Catastrophe*, London: Zed Books, 1997: 18–33; "The Split Between Gender and the Holocaust", Dalia Ofer and Lenore Weitzman, *Women in the Holocaust*, New Haven and London: Yale UP, 1998: 340–350.

and my work as Director of Oral History and Director of Education took a lot of time and energy. Most important, I didn't think I had more to say than I had already said on the topic. I was not a historian and I sensed that it was up to the historians and others to continue the work. I felt that I had opened a field but I did not think that I could do more than I had done.

Yet another Turning Point

In June 1998 *Commentary* editor Gabriel Schoenfeld wrote a piece entitled "Auschwitz and the Professors" in which he attacked Holocaust scholarship in general and feminist Holocaust scholarship in particular, mentioning me by name.[8] He also published an editorial in the *Wall Street Journal* which had even more impact among the general public than the piece in *Commentary*.[9] There were of course responses, including my own, by numerous Holocaust scholars and survivors, that spun off into additional articles by Schoenfeld and his critics. However, the entire issue caused a kind of firestorm at the Museum where I was, by then, their Director of Education. In spite of the harsh criticism that was levelled against me for my scholarship it took them 15 months to remove me from that position, but they finally succeeded. Ultimately, I became the Museum's Director of Oral History, a position which I held when I was Director of Education and remained until I retired. But the Schoenfeld polemic was definitely a turning point at the Museum. A few months after I left the position of Director of Education, a good friend of mine saw Schoenfeld at a party and he exclaimed how happy he was that I was no longer Director of Education as the USHMM and took credit for my removal. This experience was difficult for me primarily because life at the Museum became so tense. Once I took over Oral History, life at the Museum was no longer problematic in the same way. I don't think this incident had much to do with my not continuing research on women and the Holocaust. I believe I simply, as I said before, believed that I had said all that I could say.

When approached to write this essay, I was hesitant to agree. Did I really want to reconstruct my connection to the topic of women and the Holocaust? Was it truly necessary for me to relive the entire polemic and process that changed my professional trajectory? With everything going on in my life at the present, did I need to dwell on the past, including painful periods which were possibly better forgotten? At first I demurred, but the editors of this

8 Gabriel Schoenfeld, "Auschwitz and the Professors", *Commentary* 105:6 June 1998: 42–46.

9 Gabriel Schoenfeld, "The Cutting Edge of Holocaust Studies", *The Wall Street Journal*, May 21, 1998: 16.

book refused to take "no" for an answer, at which point I asked for a bit more time to consider the request. Ultimately, as the reader can see here, I agreed. I hope that I have given an accurate accounting of how I began working on the topic of Women and the Holocaust, a coherent explanation of why it happened, and a cogent account of how I became one of the founders of the field.

Part II The “Middle Generation”

Judith Tydor Baumel-Schwartz

"How Will They Ever Take You Seriously if You Write about *Veibers*?!"

Introduction

Many of us have made the choice. For some it was a temporary measure that extricated us from a stagnant situation. For others it was the beginning of a long-standing liaison that continued for years. For a third group it became a "Catholic marriage", an unbreakable bond that was to last a lifetime, even if they were far from being Catholic. For all it was a personal choice that came with strings attached, some which would bind us in ways we couldn't imagine.

The choice to write about women during the Holocaust and its aftermath is not an easy one, as I learned when I began three decades ago. For me it was a combination of the above, a long-standing but not exclusive liaison that extricated me from a stagnant situation. Like some, I got there in a roundabout way, although those reading my professional map might have noted the signs during my graduate studies that would lead to this choice.

The story of how I began to work on "Women and the Holocaust" comes in two versions: the short and the long. As a girl I loved history but never thought of it as a profession. I majored in it for personal enjoyment, and when my father asked what I would do with a history degree if I didn't want to teach, I answered that I would become a secretary like my mother and maybe marry the boss as she did. My tongue-in-cheek answer must have satisfied him as he never asked me about it again. I graduated, worked as a secretary and hated every minute. As I was already married I gave up on marrying the boss. At the summer's end I also gave up an extraordinarily lucrative salary for a twenty-year old, and returned to graduate school to specialize in the Holocaust. For years I taught in adjunct teaching positions throughout the country, researching, and ultimately focusing on women, gender, and memory. Over a decade after completing my doctorate I was offered a full-time teaching position at Bar-Ilan University where I am now a tenured professor and direct their Holocaust Institute. Happy end.

This, however, is the bare bones version that lacks the complexities of "the way it really happened".[1]For that we have to go back to my family

1 Fritz Stern (ed.), *The Varieties of History from Voltaire to the Present*, New York: Vintage, 1956: 57.

history and education, our *aliya* (immigration) to Israel when I was fifteen, a dream that changed my future, and a gamble I took when I returned to graduate school, changing my life and that of my family. The second time around I even married the boss, and that, too, will play a part in my story.

How It All Began (1959–1974)

Actually, it began long before I was born. My family was always into family history, and their stories accompanied me from as far back as I can remember. Growing up, I heard numerous family stories that stimulated my imagination. I also learned how to identify an unusual story, and my family was unusual on any scale. My maternal grandmother, a spinster from a Chassidic family, and grandfather, a communist-atheist widower with four teenage sons, fell in love at first sight, marrying two weeks later. My mother, their only daughter, was brought up with a modicum of Jewish tradition, but followed her father's communist ideology. That is, until she met my father: an Orthodox Holocaust survivor twice her age, a widower with two grown children, and her boss. They differed in background, belief and temperament, but in our family, love is love. The boss married his secretary, and my parents moved to the "wild west" where my father managed uranium mines. Eventually they returned to New York for my birth, also returning to the travel business where they first met. Did I mention something about an unusual story?

My childhood in Woodside, Queens during the 1960s and early 1970s was not your typical American childhood. Other than promoting religious practice, the tiny local Orthodox Jewish community, and the Jewish Day School that I attended, focused upon two pillars of American-Jewish identity: the Holocaust and the State of Israel. With that came a heavy dose of mutual responsibility for Jews worldwide.

The Holocaust was a constant presence in my home, a story of devastation, but also one of survival and victory. My birth was part of that victory, as were my father's wartime and post-war experiences: remaining a believing Jew throughout five-and-a-half years in Auschwitz and Buchenwald; founding "Kibbutz Buchenwald", a post-war Kibbutz in liberated Germany; discovering that his two children had survived the war in America, and starting a new family there in his fifties. The message "with God's help we triumphed over Hitler" was one I embodied in my very being.

Many of my classmates were "2gs", with either one or both parents who had survived the Holocaust. Most of us were named for relatives murdered by the Nazis. The Holocaust was a constant presence in our lives, and we were "memorial candles" for those who perished, compensating our parents for all they had lost.

What could save us from another Holocaust? Prayer (which didn't seem to have helped much the first time around), charity, and a strong State of Israel. My personal connection to Israel developed as I visited almost every summer, usually via Europe, giving me a cosmopolitan outlook and exposing me to languages, as if the eight I heard at home weren't enough.

My facility for languages would later be useful as a historian, but then it was the furthest thing from my mind. I enjoyed history but never dreamed of teaching it. In fact, I had no idea what I wanted to do. In ninth grade I wrote a composition about Elie Wiesel's novel "The Oath" which, unknowing to me, my father sent his old friend from Buchenwald. Wiesel answered immediately: "my dear Chaskel… the composition is excellent and touching, tell your daughter she should study Jewish literature: it is her subject, and the time will come when she will teach it to others with great ability, yours, Eliezer." "You see", my father said, "Elie says you will be a university professor just like he is!" I laughed out loud. "Me? A Professor? At a university? Boy do you have the wrong number!" "Patience, she will eventually come around", Wiesel remarked to my father when he described my reaction. Thank you Elie. While I may be teaching history and not literature, the last laugh was indeed on me.

First Steps in a New Land (1974–1979)

As a former communist ideologue my mother took her values seriously. She had already prepared me for the next Holocaust. Now time to move to Israel. In August 1974, when I was fifteen, my family made *aliya*. The nearby university, Bar-Ilan, offered a program for gifted high school students, and I jumped at the chance of an adventure, enrolling in a college history course that I completed along with my last high school requirements. That course lecturer would change my life. Not only would he teach me how to teach and mentor me throughout my undergraduate years; he would teach me how to be a mentor and an academic *mensch*.

David Aryeh Kolieb began lecturing as he walked into the classroom, never referring to notes and focusing on the piquant to keep us interested. He was a renaissance man who spoke ten languages, a master of satire and consummate actor who had little trouble portraying the personalities mentioned in the lessons. Only later did I learn that the childless former refugee from Vienna had secretly supported underprivileged students throughout their studies, colluding with our department Chair to create bogus "scholarships" for them from his own salary. I admired his ability to keep a class spellbound. Years later, I would copy his teaching techniques and mentor my students with the same energetic concern that he showed me and others throughout our studies and after.

For the next three years I studied history and political science. During my last year in college I married a fellow student, agreeing to support us while he continued for a graduate degree, figuring that my bilingual office skills would serve me well in the job market.

They did. I enjoyed tutoring my fellow students, but was determined to emulate my mother as part of my desire to honor my parents. Within days of graduating I was working as personal assistant for a well-known architect, Moshe Zarchi, earning a salary beyond my wildest dreams. During the first week I was introduced to suppliers, in the second I met leading architects, and by the third I realized that this job was not for me. But I was our family's main breadwinner! What could I do? My husband was away on army reserve duty and my level of despair rose daily.

One night I dreamed that I was standing on the ramp in Auschwitz bathed in fog. A train approached and a group of my relatives who had been killed in the war disembarked. Helplessly I watched them being taken to their death and shouted "wait for me!", but they continued marching into the darkness. Suddenly my grandmother Esther, my father's mother for whom I was named, turned around and said: "My child, remain here. You have a task. To make sure they won't forget us." And then they all disappeared into the fog.

I awoke in a cold sweat, alone in our sweltering apartment. What now? What should I do so to make sure that "they won't forget us"? Like most of my important decisions, my mind went "click" "click" "click" as the puzzle pieces fell into place. I would quit my job, return to school, specialize in the Holocaust, and then write about it and teach it. But what about being the "main breadwinner"? Or my promise to Moshe Zarchi to run his office?

That morning I told Zarchi about the dream and my decision. He listened attentively, leaned back in his chair and said: "Return to school, study Holocaust, and one day you will be a famous historian." Smiling, he continued: "And I will proudly tell everyone that you were once my assistant!" My spirits lifted and with Zarchi's blessing I took the day off, went to Bar-Ilan and registered for graduate studies in Jewish history. Dan Michman, who taught Holocaust studies, agreed to be my thesis advisor, and I applied for a clerical job at the university that paid a tenth of what I was earning at Zarchi's. My husband encouraged my ambitions, and my parents were initially cautious ("how will you survive financially?" "All under control", "What about children?" "All in good time"), but became extremely supportive when they heard what I was specializing in. Holocaust studies aren't "just" history, and weren't we supposed to be "memorial candles" anyhow?

"Into That Darkness" (1979–1988)

In October 1979 I began my graduate studies in Jewish history and encountered my first taste of academic misogyny: a Professor who told the women in his seminar that their place was at home and not in the halls of academe. He was joking, so he reassured us, but looking around the department I wasn't sure. The one woman with a tenure track position had her hours cut each semester. Another joined her, but was fired after her advisor retired. Few women taught Jewish history at Israeli universities, and I would face an "old boys' club" of gatekeepers when trying to get a job.

I also realized that I would not get a tenure track position at Bar-Ilan as the department already had a Holocaust scholar. It was time to rethink my employment strategy. Hoping for a research position, I spent long hours in the Institute for Diaspora Research, pouring over material for my MA thesis on Jewish refugee children in Great Britain. The Institute staff, composed primarily of German Jews in their sixties, was fascinated by a young American-born student interested in the Holocaust. For them my sex was inconsequential; they were excited to find "a child" as they called me, wishing to devote her professional life to Holocaust study. The director soon offered me a part-time research position and I joined the "Institute family", lowering the average age there by decades.

Two years later, when the Institute for Holocaust Research was founded alongside the Diaspora Institute, my thesis advisor became their coordinator, and my boss. As he was still junior faculty, I wrote my doctoral dissertation, focusing on Jewish refugee children in the USA, with a more senior but obscure professor. Encapsulating my sibling's experiences, it was my first taste in writing family history. It was also my first taste of writing about women during the Holocaust, only I didn't realize it at the time. Refugee children meant rescue activists, *Kindertransport* accompaniers, and social workers, most of whom were women. Foster parents were of both sexes, but in hindsight I realized that most source material focused on foster mothers.

From my university experience I knew that writing a doctoral dissertation wasn't enough. Academics are judged by their publications and I decided to throw my hat into that ring as early as possible. By the time I completed my dissertation I had published nine articles in peer-reviewed journals, one of which caused a minor rift with my MA advisor. That incident taught me an important lesson in academic politics: when dealing with advisors or colleagues who are still at the "publish or perish" stage, make sure they won't see you as competition.

My graduate years also taught me another lesson. To survive in academe one needs not only ability and publications, but also connections and friends. I was friendly with my department's younger staff but knew few academics outside my university. To broaden my professional network, I attended conferences, initially as an onlooker and later as a participant. My academic circle grew when I began working at the Open University after my thesis advisor, who also headed their Holocaust course, asked me to join their team. It wasn't an academic position but it paid a living, allowing me to meet a fascinating group of people who became my lifelong friends.

Having thought I would never be asked to teach at Bar-Ilan, I was surprised when asked to teach a summer course on the Holocaust to foreign students in the Basic Jewish Studies program. One course led to others, both at Bar-Ilan and elsewhere, but only as an adjunct and never in a history department.

The final piece of the puzzle was my family. As its main breadwinner with four jobs, I worked all day, wrote all night, and "stole" research time in-between the two. There was no opportunity for recreation, vacation, or thoughts on starting a family. My parents unstintingly assisted us, however, one day my 80-year-old father uttered a sentence that changed everything: "you should just know that my life's desire is not to have a grandchild named after me."

Ten months later my older daughter was born, followed by her sister two years later, just as I received my degree. For four years I came home to my daughters at a normal hour before I realized that my husband had finished studying, but I was still the family's main breadwinner. It was time for a major change in plans.

And Now For the Women (1989–1999)

By late 1988 I was working at the Open University as a course coordinator, conducting research at Bar-Ilan's Holocaust Institute, and teaching as an adjunct throughout the country. As the Institute specialized in religious life during the Holocaust, so did I. At the same time, I was writing another chapter of family history, the story of Kibbutz Buchenwald. Years earlier, as I began researching its history, my father had mentioned a group of young women survivors, teachers and students at the Beth Jacob Orthodox girls' school network in interwar Poland, who joined the kibbutz for a short while. Mentioning the group's leaders by name, he recounted stories about how mutual assistance had kept the group alive in Auschwitz.

When our librarian at the Holocaust Institute, Menachem Eldar, mentioned offhand that his name had been Englard before he Hebraicized it, I recognized it as one that my father had mentioned. "Have you ever heard of Rivka Englard?" I asked him. "You mean my cousin?!" he answered, giving me her phone number. That evening I spoke to Rivka (Englard) Hoffman, the mythological dormitory advisor at a nearby Beth Jacob school, and learned about the *Zehnnerschaft*, the group of ten Beth Jacob "girls", some related, others friends, who remained together throughout the war in Plaszow, Auschwitz and Bergen Belsen. Nine were still alive, and during the next two years I interviewed them, along with the daughter of the tenth member who had recently passed away.

The *Zehnnerschaft's* experiences fascinated me. They awakened memories of stories I had heard from my parents' women friends and relatives who had survived the war. Realizing the importance of salvaging women's Holocaust testimonies, in 1988 I had my students interview women who had worked at the "Canada" sorting barracks at Auschwitz. The result was a booklet entitled "Voices of Commando Canada".

Documenting testimony is the basis of scientific inquiry, but not enough to make one's mark in the field. For that I needed to know its movers and shakers, conduct cutting-edge original research, and publish my results in major journals. To succeed I needed not only enthusiasm and ability, but also connections and friends. At the time I was editing a book in a series edited by Henry Friedlander and Sybil Milton. Sybil, a pioneer in women's Holocaust studies, was extremely supportive of my work, encouraging me to explore the world of women's Holocaust experiences as she had recently done. Through her, I began corresponding with scholars who had made forays into the topic: Marion Kaplan, Brana Gurewitch, Atina Grossmann, Joan Ringelheim. I also met Esther Fuchs and Sara Horowitz who were probing a similar path. The connections that I forged with them and other gender scholars, reassured me that I was not alone in wanting to train my energies on that field.

Although my teaching schedule was grueling, my scientific work was exhilarating. It was a challenging field, in many ways still unknown. In writing about women's mutual assistance during the Holocaust I hoped to map out significant factors that distinguished it from its male counterpart. By doing so, I was shaping a new field of scientific inquiry that emphasized how bonds among Jewish women were not necessarily "deeper" or "stronger" than those among men, but certainly "different". Those differences, and the reasons behind them, became the crux of my research.

It was the early 1990s. I had just published my dissertation on refugee children as a book, and was working on two other volumes: Kibbutz Buchenwald, and Prayer during the Holocaust. What made me suddenly decide to recalibrate my focus and specialize in women's Holocaust studies? At the time my personal and professional life was in flux. I was my family's major breadwinner with several jobs, rarely seeing my daughters awake other than on the Sabbath. I lacked a strong university mentor who could storm the barricades to get me a tenure-track job. While writing an article during my graduate years I had already experienced what happens when a more senior scholar felt that I was stepping on his professional toes. "Women in the Holocaust" was uncharted territory in the Israeli academic world and appeared to be an up-and-coming topic worldwide. There I couldn't be accused of stepping on anyone's toes, at least in Israel. Could this be the niche that would help me make my name in the academic world, enabling me to finally find a full-time position?

There was also the personal aspect. Although my father had given me a male Holocaust perspective, for years I had been drawn to the stories of my female relatives and friends who had experienced the Nazi cataclysm: my sister, great aunts, and mothers of friends who had shared their stories with me. It was my grandmother Esther in that unforgettable dream, who had entrusted me with the task of ensuring that "they won't forget us". Was it her story that I had to tell, that of women during the Holocaust? Had the choice of topic actually been made for me long ago?

Although women's Holocaust studies were new in Israel, they already existed elsewhere, and I had a lot to learn. The first step was to locate my research on the broader playing field, and I spent months learning the basics of women's studies. These were the last years of second wave feminism, before the days of intersectionality and "micro-politics" that began in the early 1990s. I immersed myself in feminist theory, refrained from internalizing outmoded gendered stereotypes, and applied my theoretical insight to the *Zehnnerschaft's* practical cohesion during the Holocaust. The result was a series of articles about the group, using them as an example of women's agency and survival strategies in crisis. From there I branched out to other aspects including women's Holocaust heroism, women's post-war commemoration, women among the DPs, and women's Holocaust memory.

During those years I also began teaching the subject, offering the first course in Israel on women in the Holocaust. By then I had a part time tenure-track position at the University of Haifa, far from Bar-Ilan where I had reached a professional brick wall despite my extremely robust list of publications. I was still working at their Holocaust Institute, but knowing the lay of the land and the personalities involved, I realized I had nowhere to progress and looked to teach elsewhere.

The Institute's director, my former thesis advisor, supported my desire to focus on women, unlike some senior colleagues who were skeptical of the topic. Even those who cared about me didn't understand my choice. When Yisrael Gutman of the Hebrew University and Yad Vashem, who had always been sympathetic, learned of my interest in the topic, he turned to me with concern: "What will be with you *maydaleh* [little girl]? Instead of writing about *veibers* [women], maybe find a serious topic like uprisings or partisans. Otherwise, how will they take your seriously?!"

There were also pleasant surprises. Yoav Gelber of Haifa University stated that although he couldn't understand why anyone would want to specialize in women during the Holocaust, he would defend my choice with all his might. In 1995 Dalia Ofer and Lenore Weitzman conducted a scholars' workshop in Jerusalem on women's Holocaust studies, giving me an opportunity to meet other academics interested in the field. Unlike some, after the initial opposition I encountered when colleagues discovered my choice of topic, it was basically accepted without discussion. Was this due to the nature of Israeli academic culture, or the fact that as a historian, my analyses were source-based, not empirical or drawing on radical feminist theories? I will never know.

From then until the end of the decade I continued exploring different aspects of women's Holocaust experiences, but my research began taking a somewhat different turn. In 1993 I had been invited to participate in the Annual Symposium of Jewish Civilization sponsored by the Klutznick Chair at Creighton University in Omaha, Nebraska. That year's topic was "The Hero in Jewish History". "I don't really do heroism", I remarked to the Chair's incumbent, who had become a colleague of mine in Haifa. "Why don't you talk about Hannah Szenes", he suggested, referring to the famous WWII Yishuv parachutist, knowing that I researched women in the Holocaust.

I prepared the lecture, found it fascinating, and soon found myself writing a book about the parachutists' mission, charting its commemoration over half a century. The book began my transition from Holocaust studies to Israel studies. Although I published a volume summarizing my examination of Jewish women during the Holocaust,[2] and continued writing articles about Jewish women DPs, by the late 1990s I was firmly entrenched in Israel studies, emphasizing gender and commemoration.

Why did I move from women in the Holocaust to women in Israel? There was little academic opposition to Holocaust studies in Israel compared to the situation in American universities. Israel had no Gabriel Schoenfeld (the editor of *Commentary* who began a public polemic on the topic), and unlike my colleagues in other countries, I never encountered opposition among the general public to the idea of women's Holocaust studies. One might even say that the parachutists' mission was a bridge between Holocaust studies and Israel studies, the two pillars of American-Jewish identity on which I had been raised, allowing me to remain in both topics.

But that wasn't "the way it really happened", to use Ranke's terminology. In the late 1990s my department in Haifa got a new Chair who claimed to

---

2 *Double Jeopardy: Gender and the Holocaust*, London: Vallentine Mitchell, 1998.

oppose Holocaust studies, but in truth opposed me, an Orthodox Jewish woman trained at a religious university. "Religious scholars can never be critical thinkers as they uncritically accept God's will", he would say, alluding to me. When he became Chair I was still untenured and had just begun a three-year contract which I was told would not be renewed. From the lack of department opposition to his decision I realized how few friends I had in that department, something I had sensed after my father's death in 1993, when only one colleague from Haifa had made a *shiva* visit to my home.

Once again I felt the lack of a powerful mentor whose very existence would have deterred the new Chair from trying to harm me professionally. I also realized that my days in Haifa were numbered and I must find a job elsewhere. Although never stated outright, knowing the lay of the land in Israeli Holocaust studies I realized that no matter what aspect I would choose, there was a major player in the field who would not be happy to have me as competition. Israel Studies, an up-and-coming subject in Israeli universities, was a safer topic in which to get a job.

My father used to say that in life one needs 90 % *siata dishmaya* (Heavenly assistance) and 10 % good luck. However luck can be a two edged sword and one person's misfortune may be another's fortune. My job offer in Haifa had been the result of a colleague's sudden demise, and the same thing now happened at Bar-Ilan University. When a professor in Zionist studies passed away in June 1998 I was offered his job, but the search committee, and particularly my former thesis advisor, insisted on dividing the position between me and another female candidate, having us "fight it out" for a year, with the best woman being chosen at its conclusion. It was an unnecessary and exhausting battle which I won against the good friend pitted against me, primarily due to my rank as a senior lecturer, allowing me to advise doctoral students which she could not. She and I are still close friends, but those years, and particularly the unnecessary gladiator contest, took its toll on my health as I would soon find out.

Back to the Future (1999-present)

In October 1999 I began a full-time tenure-track position in the Department of Jewish History at Bar-Ilan University. At forty, I could finally quit the half-a-dozen adjunct positions I had juggled for over a decade. The department's "old boys club" had retired and my colleagues were friends. My students enjoyed my classes, particularly those dealing with women and gender, and I delighted in teaching them. Promoted to Associate Professor, I was granted tenure the next year as my sympathetic Dean understood why I feared postponing the tenure procedure and wait to have it linked to my next promotion.

Having finally attained professional security, I began to pay the price for the years of stretching myself too thin in order to support my family. My children had paid the price for my absence, and my physical health had deteriorated over the years, as did my marriage which now ended by mutual consent. I began a new chapter in my life, and a year-and-a-half later married a colleague who well understood the tensions of academic life. Like my mother before me, this time I married the boss. My husband was my sympathetic former Dean, Joshua Schwartz, also divorced. Together with our children, we built a marvelously blended family that surpassed our highest expectations.

All, however, was not well in paradise. Although I taught both Holocaust and Israel studies, I focused my research primarily on the latter for the same reason I had chosen it in the first place: a desire to escape the glass ceiling that a certain colleague in the field had set for competitors. I didn't attribute that ceiling to my sex but rather to my existence, assuming that junior men would have been treated the same way. As I battled through my final promotion, encountering some of the nastier aspects of academic life on the way, I swore that when it was over I would become the kind of mentor students dreamed of. One who would be there for them through thick and thin, fiercely protecting them according to the maxim of "an eye for a fingernail": you touch my fingernail (i.e. my students), I take out your eye!

Meanwhile, though, it was still far from being over. As the battles raged I forged on. I taught, wrote, advised, and held fulfilling administrative positions chairing the Graduate Program in Contemporary Jewry, the School for Basic Jewish Studies, and the Heller Center for the Study of Women in Judaism. But the tensions took their toll, and health issues from the past began popping up. Family, friends, and graduate students kept me going during those difficult years, but it wasn't enough. To clear my head and heal my soul, my husband suggested combining my two loves, family and history, to literally fulfill my grandmother's last wishes and write the story of my family so that they would not be forgotten. Roots. Understanding the past in order to build the future.

I began by writing my late father's biography which spanned almost a century and paralleled much of what European Jews experienced during that time. Deeply rooted in the Holocaust and rebirth of the Jewish people, it was gendered history from a male perspective. Several years after my successful promotion, but during another difficult professional period, my husband suggested documenting my maternal grandmother's life and her generation, the young Jewish female immigrants who came to America in the early 20th century, leaving their families behind. This was definitely women's history, including women's Holocaust history, as my description of her family's wartime tribulations in Transnistria was based on her youngest sister's testimony.

One book begets another, and I began sketching my 95-year-old mother-in-law's experiences, those of the immigrants' daughters, and the events that shaped their lives. Next came a book about my late mother, an unexpected chance to honor her and fulfill the fifth commandment for a last time. History. Love. Family. Women. And even Holocaust. The winning combination. My figurative cup runneth over.

An End that is a Beginning

My mother would often say "what goes around comes around" and the older I get, the truer it seems. In October 2018 I was appointed Director of the Finkler Institute of Holocaust Research at Bar-Ilan University, the place where it all began. The time had come for an interim summary as a new chapter in my life was about to unfold. After years of writing about other gendered topics I could return to my first choice with a lighter heart. What aspect of women's Holocaust experiences did I want to explore? Which angle drew me most? As I pondered those questions, I realized that more than anything I wanted to create "communities", multi-disciplinary forums of Holocaust-related scholars\activists under the Institute's auspices, giving them the framework and support I had craved throughout my career. Memories of all I had gone through flooded through me. Topics I had written about. Women I had interviewed. Colleagues, competitors, glass ceilings, choices, decisions.

Before I could face the future I had to set the past to rest. Speaking to friends from women's Holocaust studies, I realized how many women from my academic generation had similar stories and experiences, each with a different twist. Experiencing a sense of solidarity as we shared anecdotes and described choices, the words "in unity there is strength" came to mind. "You have a task", my grandmother had said.

How could I compile these stories to show the next generation of researchers what we had accomplished and save them from the problems we experienced? Should I create a website? Start a blog? Perhaps I should collect our stories in a book? How should I begin? Maybe with something that connects all of us. Here goes:

"Many of us have made the choice..."

Pascale R. Bos

Once More, With Feeling: Personal Positionality and Generational Conflict within Feminist Holocaust Studies

This essay recounts some of the intellectual conflicts I encountered in working with other feminist colleagues when I first entered the field of Gender and Holocaust Studies, and retrospectively reconsiders those conflicts from both a theoretical and, more importantly, personal vantage point.

1992–3: Reading myself into the field

I am a first year PhD student in Comparative Literature and Gender Studies at the University of Minnesota and have spent several months doing research on the topic of gender and the Holocaust. By searching through bibliographies and library catalogues and using interlibrary loan, I have been able to collect almost everything published on the topic thus far except for a few out of print memoirs. Without efficient internet and search engines, tracking down sources is tedious, but satisfying. It is exciting to be able to survey a relatively young research field in its entirety. Moreover, I have come to the United States to do precisely this. After writing an MA thesis at the University of Amsterdam on the literary work of a survivor and now seeking to write a dissertation on survivor memoirs by female authors, specifically German Jews, I have left the Netherlands, as pursuing interdisciplinary Holocaust Studies is not yet possible there. Meanwhile, scholars in the United States are publishing cutting edge new research on (Holocaust and other) trauma and memory, work that I am hoping to be able to use in my analysis of gender in Holocaust memoir.

By the Spring, I write a seminar paper on my early findings with a summary of the state of the field on gender and the Holocaust up to that point. I also articulate a short methodological critique of the prior publications, as the kind of sophisticated gender analysis that I expect to find in this work is mostly absent. I learn much from these publications about the historical circumstances under which Jewish women lived and died under Nazi rule, and the specific challenges they faced due to both their different pre-war socialization (and associated roles and expectations) and some of the Nazi regulations that affected them adversely. However, I am surprised to see a kind of naïve biological essentialism in some scholars' work, and by the tendency to valorize or even celebrate certain charitable or heroic behavior of female victims under Nazism as "typically feminine." Certain gendered patterns of behavior described by female survivors in memoirs or interviews such as the use of caretaking behavior from prewar life (cleaning, preparing food, providing emotional support for others) while in the ghetto or concentration camp, are interpreted as part of an innate and "natural" female essence, rather than a product of gender socialization. Some of this early scholarship seems to conclude that caretaking is what women naturally excel at, and moreover, that it helped women to survive, perhaps even "better" than men. One of the pioneering scholars in the field – in an unprecedented self-critical and revelatory analysis of her prior scholarship – has already identified and criticized the problematic propensity of a certain (cultural) feminist approach to essentialize and valorize the behavior of women survivors. However, this tendency still lingers on in many studies. Such scholars may now conceive of gendered behavior as socially or culturally constructed rather than as biologically determined, and thus see the self-described gendered survival skills of female survivors as a product of their prior socialization. But in their attempt to highlight such skills so as to show that women were not merely passive actors in history, and to correct what they see as much of the prior male dominated historiography of the Holocaust, they at times still come close to glorifying women's superior skills.

Coming from a background in literary theory and philosophy, and trained to think of gender as permeating cultural and individual discourse, I hone in on the representations and language that produces these gender differences. I understand the importance of gender socialization in survivors, not just in terms of the different roles men and women may perform, but also in the gender constructions internalized by survivors that influence *how* they represent themselves in testimony. Thus, I see the work of the scholar of Holocaust testimony as one of historical analysis of representation, of memory narratives that are active reconstructions of the past, rather than as an attempt to retrieve historical reality outside of, or unmediated by, language. In my observation of this same testimony or memoirs, I find myself intrigued but skeptical when gendered patterns emerge that overtly serve as justification or a teleology for the author's survival. I note that some female survivors state that their gendered caretaking skills helped them survive, sometimes described in contrast to more selfish and helpless behavior of male inmates. But I see such patterns more as suggestive of female survivors' internalization of the feminine gender norm, rather than as evidence from which we can derive conclusions about either men or women's "natural" tendencies or of their socialization. Instead, I conceive of such testimony or memoirs as gendered memories that conform to internalized gender norms.

In part, I realize, my critique reflects a disciplinary or a generational conflict: the task of the memory or literary scholar after the poststructuralist turn differs from how earlier historians or literary scholars thought of their work. I take the language of the testimony or the memoir and make that discourse the object of careful analysis, rather than seeing those narratives as offering evidence of what is presumed to be a reasonably accessible history of gender differences. There are, however, more than disciplinary differences at work: as a scholar whose mother and grandmother are nearly the only survivors of a large Dutch-Jewish family, I also have a deep personal investment in understanding how female survivors, in particular, recount their traumatic past. I am especially interested in how this recounting serves them in making sense of their experiences and possibly helps them gain some form of psychic integration.

I present my seminar paper at a regional women's studies conference. It is well received by an audience of interested feminist scholars whose work has no relationship to the Holocaust.

1997: Encountering Conflict

During the next few years I work on my dissertation and find that I have difficulty integrating the sophisticated scholarship on autobiography and gender and on trauma and testimony with the existing research on women and the Holocaust because these fields are, for the most part, still speaking a different theoretical language. I return to it for a panel on "Women's Voices in the Holocaust" at the Annual Scholars' Conference on the Holocaust and the Churches in 1997.

In this paper, I try to move beyond a critique of this earlier work and attempt to explicitly postulate a different model from which to conceptualize the relevance of gender during the Holocaust. I suggest that gender matters not only, and not always primarily, in empirical terms, such as how Jewish men and women were treated differently by the Nazi regime, or how they responded in different ways to this persecution based on gender, i.e. women's specific vulnerabilities and strengths. Instead, I argue that we ought to look at how gender profoundly inflects our sense of self, of self-definition. We internalize gender scripts, unconsciously for the most part, and this affects every part of our daily lives. We experience, perceive, recall, and express ourselves within and against deeply internalized, and thus normalized, culturally proscribed conceptions of gender. As deeply gendered human beings, men and women tend to experience and interpret the same events differently, recall such events along gendered lines, and speak or write about them in ways that conform to gender norms.

In short, I argue that while gender is extremely important as a category of historical analysis, it is significant not necessarily only for the reasons suggested in much of the earlier literature, but because nothing the survivor remembers, and therefore what we as audience learn from their testimony about this experience, can be separated from the lens of gender. I argue for a discursive gender approach to Holocaust testimony that pays more close attention to what language, images, and tropes male and female survivors use to describe themselves, others, and the world at large, and how this discourse is gendered.

I am aware that my approach challenges some of the established scholarship, but at this point I am impatient with what I consider the strong empiricist bent within the field, and feel ready to make a bold statement about the role of gender in memory and representation. Moreover, my concern is that unless we make our study of gender and the Holocaust methodologically more sophisticated, with less of an apparent agenda to have it serve as a historical corrective which valorizes women's behavior, this important work will continue to be dismissed by male colleagues as scholarship primarily driven by political activism.

Once I see the conference schedule, however, I get a bit nervous. My paper is scheduled as the second of four, and from the title of the first paper by a senior female scholar I fear that it will be an example of the kind of work my paper will be critiquing: emphasizing women's specific gendered victimization while simultaneously celebrating "female coping skills." Anticipating a possibly unpleasant confrontation, I suggest that my paper be moved to be either first or last, but my suggestion is dismissed by the chair, an esteemed scholar in the field. The room fills up almost exclusively with female scholars and a few survivors and the first presenter offers a fairly traditional paper. I notice some of the audience's impatience. Nervously, I go next and hardly look up from my paper. Once finished, I receive a standing ovation from a large part of the audience, something I never experienced before nor have since. I feel both relief and elation.

This marks an important moment, I realize. I see the applause as not necessarily about me but as a reflection of a shared eagerness of other (feminist) scholars to see the field pushed forward in a new direction, to see a more complex analysis. Whereas I am glad to have done my small part, this moment of appreciation also leaves me in an awkward position vis a vis the senior scholar on the panel and other pioneering scholars work whose work I implicitly critique. I sense that they find my attempt at intervention disrespectful, my call for "a new focus" overblown. I am adamant, however. I want the field to change course so that—with a more solid methodological foundation and more sophisticated, critical use of gender that includes men—it will be less marginalized and become an integrated component of Holocaust Studies.

It is the first of several personal confrontations, sometimes publicly, in which I feel a difficult tension between myself and some of the established scholars in this field, a tension that seems to be as much generational, and about respect and feminist solidarity, as it is supposedly about intellectual disagreement. Yet it also feels quite personal, something I can't yet put my finger on.

2001: Confrontation

I am an Assistant Professor at The University of Texas at Austin, working on Holocaust related projects on postmemory and second generation Holocaust literature. I include my work on gender in two courses, "Women and the Holocaust" and "Holocaust Aftereffects", but do not return to it until I am asked to submit an essay for a volume on gender and the Holocaust. I am excited to be able to revisit the material and to integrate several new publications. I note that the field is expanding; there are both a host of new scholars and approaches. Some of the established scholars have published new work as well, yet in much of this material I note the same methodological issues I encountered in the mid-1990s. I now use this essay to lay out such issues and make an impassioned case for what should happen next.

Memory research suggests that men and women do not differ in overall memory ability but that each gender makes assumptions about distinct sex differences in memory. It also claims that such assumptions, coupled with the strong but usually unconscious desire or need to conform to society's sense of what is gender-appropriate, affects what men and women recall when asked about their memories. If, as I argue, gendered patterns of socialization lead women and men within Western culture to perceive the world differently, experience it differently, remember experiences differently, and recount them differently, then looking at the stories of both women and men becomes imperative in both our research and teaching on the Holocaust. I make the case that the propensity towards gender conformity is not less, but possibly even greater, in cases of extreme experiences such as the Holocaust that assault the individual's identity. I also state that the sharing of memories, bearing witness, can have an important function for survivors in reasserting subjectivity and agency. In Holocaust memoir and oral testimony, I argue, the narrative functions both to make sense of one's past, and to justify and normalize it. Because "normalizing" strategies rely so heavily on normative discourse, and because traditional gender roles are such a central yet usually implicit part of this discourse, the perspective from which one speaks or writes will also by necessity be gendered.

Once I hand in the essay, I receive a signal from one of the editors that the co-editor, another pioneering scholar whose work my essay critiques, is hurt by my essay. I receive a private email from her in which she appeals to our joint (Jewish) feminist sisterhood and requests that I tone down some of my critique. She experiences it as a personal attack. I try to be diplomatic, and move critical references that pertain to her work and that of other scholars into the footnotes. Instead, I speak of the issues in more general terms. The essay is approved. I am taken aback by the personal nature of her letter, however. I feel accused of being disloyal, which I find hard to stomach, as someone who grew up as a child of survivors in a left-leaning atheist household in Amsterdam in the 1970s and 1980s within a very politically engaged cultural environment. I had been passionately involved with feminism, anti-racism, anti-imperialism, gay rights, and other emancipation movements for years. My feminism had been as much personal as political, and I, too, had felt marginalized doing gender research at the university in the early 1980s. From that perspective, I had a keen sense of how difficult the path of other early feminist scholars must have been, and I felt a sense of solidarity with them. Yet, here I struggle with my own deeply felt need to do what I consider is most important, based on my personal family experiences, which is to try do justice to survivors' memories and agency. I want their texts and testimonies to be approached as changing, living, dynamic – rather than static – narratives that reveal an often hard-won sense of subjectivity, identity, and self-worth after the war. That is, as text or speech that seeks, rather than accomplishes, integration, and not only as historical material from which to draw straight-forward factual conclusions, or worse, as case studies in which the survivors are objectified. Clearly, my critique and concern is personal and based in my deep familial and communal connections with and concerns for Holocaust survivors. Yet, I avoid disclosing this background. It feels at once too personal, uncomfortable, and unnecessary.

I have another rather public clash that year when I present my work as a keynote at "Departures: New Feminist Perspectives on the Holocaust." A most prominent scholar is my respondent, and I am both nervous and honored to receive her feedback. Our exchange proves more contentious than expected, however. The organizers have anticipated this, and they hope for a provocative exchange that will move the field forward, but the experience proves quite fraught for me. She takes issue with my suggestion to approach survivor testimony as memory rather than as history, and with more skepticism in terms of the empirical gender differences it may convey, and the role that gender plays in self representation. Do I mean to argue, she asks me, "that survivors are lying?" Certainly not, I respond. I try to reiterate that we need to distinguish how survivors tell their stories from an assessment of "what actually happened." I argue that the conclusions we draw from testimony in terms of gender difference ought to be more nuanced, and that examining how Nazi policy that affected men and women adversely, and claiming that gender gets discursively internalized, are complementary, not mutually exclusive endeavors. I reiterate that testimony is as much about a survivor reclaiming some control over her life story as it is about "the truth." In response, she accuses me of not paying enough attention to historical gender differences. The moderator tries to help out by situating our conflict as part of the "discursive turn" in Holocaust and feminist studies, but to no avail, and the exchange remains adversarial.

The encounter leaves me feeling defeated. I am also confused. What is going on here? Am I merely experiencing pushback as a younger scholar entering the field who critiques earlier work? Or is this a turf war between traditional historical empiricist or positivist approaches to testimony, and a more theoretical literary critical or memory approach? And does this scholar really not see my point, or does she refuse to see it? Can we really not bridge this divide? Do we not share the same broader goal?

Reflecting back on these strong and seemingly generational responses that my work once evoked, I realize that some of the resistance I encountered was clearly both about tone and positionality: I was young, came from disciplines heavy on poststructuralist theory while most of the senior scholars did not. I suspect that they had gotten plenty of rejection from their male colleagues and other non-feminist scholars, and neither expected nor were willing to put up with an outright critical voice from within their ranks. And they appealed to me on the basis of this – we are all women, Jewish women, feminists, so why are you doing this to us? Who do you think you are?

Ironically, it never occurred to me to answer the implied question – who I was and where I was coming from – beyond the obvious disciplinary differences. What would have possibly bridged the gap is if I had been more open about what my personal investment was about, what my passion about Holocaust research was based on. But that felt very uncomfortable and I strongly resisted it. From a professional standpoint, I felt that my personal background as a child of survivors ought not to matter. My ideas should be able to stand on their own, and not derive either status or be dismissed on the basis of that proximity or familiarity. But I also did not want to disclose my background out of a deep sense of loyalty to my mother and grandmother, both very private people who never discussed their intensely painful wartime experiences publicly. Yet my role as interlocutor between my grandmother and mother in the past, and the changing nature of the testimony I heard from them over the years, plays a profound role in how I approach my scholarly work and how I look at gender, memory, and the agency of the survivors.

Where I Come From

Born in the mid-1960s in Amsterdam as the daughter and granddaughter of Dutch-Jewish survivors on my mother's side, I grew up in the 1970s and early 1980s in both a culture and a family that was almost entirely silent on the Holocaust. Of course, the Dutch national story on "the war" was omnipresent, but that public discourse did not match the deeply painful experiences of my (Jewish) family. The public narrative held that the Netherlands had been unexpectedly invaded in May 1940 which left the Dutch devastated, and unwillingly governed by the German National Socialists for the following five years. During this time, the story goes, the Dutch suffered greatly, fought back valiantly, and resisted the Nazis bravely.

From family stories and the more scholarly studies of Jewish historians that I would come to read later on, it was clear that this was a one-sided version of history. For the two most stunning facts that had come to light after the war were completely glossed over or even omitted: the number of collaborators and SS volunteers in Holland had been exceptionally high, and with the help of accommodating Dutch bureaucrats, police officers, train conductors, and so on, the Nazis had been extraordinarily successful in their hunt and deportation of Dutch Jews: over 82 % of the Jewish community had been deported to concentration camps, mostly to Auschwitz and Sobibor. Less than 5 % of these deportees survived, which led to an astonishing 75 % death rate of all so-called "full Jews" in the Netherlands, the highest relative Jewish death rate of any Western European country. Although these numbers were deeply disturbing, their implications would not be discussed publicly until the mid- to late 1980s. Instead, in the aftermath of the war, the Dutch government had cultivated a politics of memory that restored its self-image through a national myth of unanimous resistance. The Dutch national narrative, from history books to commemorations, claimed a history in which the nation as a whole had been the powerless victim of Nazi occupation, or, in a variation on this theme, had been actively involved in resisting the enemy.

For our parents, the Dutch-Jewish survivors, this interpretation of what unfolded during the war was clearly false. Nevertheless, with their families and the Jewish community as a whole decimated, assets confiscated, and faith in the tolerance of the Dutch nation deeply shaken, most of them chose not to speak up against it outside of family circles, fearing that their critique would lead to more antisemitism.

This then, was the social-political climate in which I and other Dutch children of survivors grew up in the 1950s, 60s, and 70s. We lived among a decimated Jewish community that remained to a large degree "in hiding." Unable or unwilling to pass on Jewish culture and tradition to us, intermarried in great numbers in an attempt to assure a measure of personal safety, many of our parents remained uncomfortable with their Jewish identity, and deeply marked by, yet absolutely mum about their war experiences and their difficult postwar adjustment. In some cases, however, they would open up to us, as my family, indeed, did to me.

Disrupted Family Narratives

Family stories are important: we emerge from within the family stories our parents and extended families create for us. For the first eight years of my life or so, growing up in Amsterdam, my family story was one that only encompassed my grandmother and our nuclear family: two parents, two daughters. The family narratives, anecdotes, traditions, celebrations, jokes, and names we considered "ours" were in fact all self-made, all "new." They were notable precisely because they were not passed on from generation to generation.

Of course, I wasn't aware of this at first. What I did notice once I was somewhat older, was that we had no photos at all of family members on my mother's side at home. My mother and grandmother seemed to have emerged from nowhere. This absence of photographs was noticeable, for as in other families, our family narratives, too, were created and sustained through the use of family photos (especially as my father and uncle were avid photographers). If, as Marianne Hirsch suggests, photography is "the family's primary instrument of self-knowledge and representation, the means by which family memory would be continued and perpetuated,"[1] then, clearly, something strange was happening in our family. If photos allow us to create and represent family narratives, it meant not only that a piece of our family narrative was noticeably absent, but also that my grandmother was the only link to this seemingly absent narrative as the few photos that I knew did exist she kept tucked away in a small black cardboard box at her home. The way the photos were kept might well serve as symbolic for what had happened to the memories of the murdered family members of our family: they were unmentionable, hidden away so effectively that hardly anyone knew of their existence.

Once I was old enough to resist my family's implicit imperative of silence, I began to ask my grandmother, with whom I had a very close bond, about our family. I did so as my mother was born in 1938 and survived the war in hiding as a young child, often claiming that she could not remember much

1 Marianne Hirsch "Introduction: Familial Looking." In *The Familial Gaze*, ed. Marianne Hirsch, Hanover, NJ: UPNE, 1999, 7

detail. From about age 14 on, I would visit my grandmother, and ask her to show me the pictures in the black box. She would tell me stories from before the war. We thus enacted a seemingly normal family ritual: a grandparent telling a grandchild about the family's origins. The pictures themselves are not at all unusual. They are in fact striking in their normalcy, typical of the kind of photographic family representations that most European middle-class families created of themselves. Pictures commemorating the passing of certain life stages: childhood; student life; engagement; marriage; motherhood. They depict vacations, family gatherings, and of course, children. Nothing in these photos suggests that there is anything unusual about this family. But the family's narrative recounted by way of these innocuous family photos, of course, is not normal. If these pictures represented my family, it meant that I came from a family that no longer existed, that I had never known. The lives of the people in these photos were cut short, they would forever remain children, or 30- and 50-, 60- something adults.

While the details about how their lives ended were mostly kept vague or avoided altogether in the conversations with my mother and grandmother, through my own research, I did eventually come to know in detail what happened to the immediate members of my family. I also found that quite a bit of what I discovered by way of archival research did not exactly match the stories I had heard. Details or dates were wrong. But doing the research and uncovering this history was an astounding, often nearly unbearable process, and it also suggested to me from where the silence in my family had emerged. The facts were chilling and the cumulative number of close relatives murdered mind-numbing. It demystified this horrible black hole that had been my family's past, but being able to reconstruct the stories of their persecution and murders did not normalize it, or make it less horrifying.

The silence surrounding this family, the absence of their photos from my mother's and grandmother's postwar lives had become more clear to me. I understand why my grandmother could not breach these thoughts without threatening to fall apart. Her husband had been gassed to death, and so had her parents, her in-laws, her brother and her sister, her nephew, her brother-in-law. Uncles and aunts and cousins were killed, not to mention friends and acquaintances. Once I came to realize the full extent of her loss and that of my mother, I came to acknowledge this as a personal loss as well: not to be part of a multigenerational family means the loss of family narrative, a loss of identity. Yet I also discovered, powerfully, that my dialogue with my grandmother restored some of this connection to the past, as it produced a present in which that past and our murdered relatives could be integrated, rather than remain silenced. By repeatedly speaking about her life, the "before" and "after" the Holocaust, her stories enabled her to reconstruct her own autobiography as a continuum and to normalize her life to a certain extent.

Yet the stories she told me over the years were not static. Her present perspective kept changing her narrative, and this suggested to me that the telling served her needs for the reconstruction of her life story at that particular moment. This dynamic retelling in connection to a family member, in order to restore familial connection and cohesion, is what moved me deeply with my grandmother and with other relatives. It continually showed me a very different side of working through trauma, and of reclaiming life in the present than the clinical discourse emerging from the 1980s on from within the public sphere and in academic writing on survivors suggested.

Survivors Objectified

By the 1980s, in the wake of the showing of the U.S. miniseries *Holocaust* in the Netherlands in 1979 and a host of WWII commemorations, there was suddenly a great deal of public interest in survivors. Much of it was couched in the objectifying language of psychopathology: the discussion of concentration camp syndrome, survivor guilt, attachment issues. In this discourse, the complex life experiences and rich stories and personalities of survivors were poked, prodded, and described as case studies: as something exotic. And the same was starting to happen with the so-called second generation, the offspring of Holocaust survivors to which my Jewish peers and I belonged. I did not recognize my relatives or myself in these semi-scholarly works that described mainly dysfunction and neuroses.

In this context, I began to advocate for having the personal stories both of survivors and of my peers seen as rich and complex answers to this kind of objectification. I now started seeking out these stories, first in my family and then beyond. Time and again I found that they were dynamic, changing narratives that were not that different from other forms of narrative life integration. It was that discovery that led me to study survivor memoirs in the late 1980s. Moreover, I found that they had a liberating, emancipatory potential. I felt adamant that survivors ought to be heard in their own words, ideally in situations in which they chose to speak/write rather than in a context in which they were interviewed/spoken to/evaluated. I felt strongly that the sophistication of their realities should be left intact, and I gravitated towards works that allowed for and displayed that kind of self-searching/self-defining (Grete Weil, Jean Améry, Charlotte Delbo, Primo Levi, for instance).

Gendered Memory

The emphasis on gendered memory of the Holocaust came about through a combination of my family's experience and my research on women's memoirs which I started as an undergraduate. I was intrigued with how the research showed the different ways in which women and men speak of their (war) memories, and disturbed by how these memories get solicited and then become "sanctioned" in divergent ways. I became particularly interested in how this pattern may become perpetuated within families of Holocaust survivors. What gender dynamics play a role in the transmission of stories generally, and in those of trauma specifically? Do men and women, fathers and mothers, pass on different kinds of stories? If so, why, and what is the effect of this? Who gets to speak, whose memories are represented, and to what end? What mechanisms play a role in the silencing of some voices, but not others?

Ironically, in my immediate family with only female survivors, the women were not the main story tellers. Instead, the non-Jewish males, men who had married into the family, were the voices of authority. If anything, the women survivors in my family carried the affective dimension of the family memory while the men were in charge of the historical "facts." While these patterns had become apparent to me as an adolescent, I had not yet thought of them as representative of a more structural problem, rooted in patterns of gender socialization. Instead, I considered it a result of traditional marriages in which husbands simply spoke for their wives, in particular in the case of men who were more (formally) educated than the women. This dynamic in my family furthermore conformed to a broader national memory pattern in which the stories of non-Jews overshadowed and even absorbed those of the Dutch Jews, and whereby the Dutch-Jewish experience of victimization came to stand in for that of the entire nation. Looking at these gender dynamics in a more scholarly fashion proved revelatory and relevant for me both personally and intellectually.

Full Circle

This journey, from silence to revelation, trauma to attempts at mourning and integration within my family and Dutch culture at large, is what brought me to the U.S. working on gender in Holocaust memoir in the early 1990s. What distinguished my approach to Holocaust testimony from the onset from more established colleagues was not just my particular academic training. Sure, I was not a historian. I came to the field with more skepticism about our ability to construct the historical past through narrative, and my academic work was informed by French feminist theory and poststructuralism. What also made what I did or do different, however, has been the deep personal awareness that survivors, children of survivors, and anyone of the postmemory generation are always constructing the past retroactively. For me, this made the question of what memory does, was, and is, of central importance.

Looking back on how I first ventured into this field, I can see how some of the conflicts with senior colleagues may have unfolded differently if I had disclosed my own background and personal investment more. I also see my insistence on a kind of theoretical rigor from a different perspective. Theory offered me an important concrete frame of reference that provided a bit of a buffer against the deep emotions I often felt about my family's experiences while working on Holocaust memoir. But I also insisted on the use of a more sophisticated methodology precisely so it would protect me from what I feared would be the accusation that I could not be sufficiently objective about this topic or material because I was too close to it. I indeed felt that to operate from my own very deeply held intuitions about and experience with survivors and their testimony was only possible if I found a way to do so by way of the language of theory, as I feared that disclosing this personal background would be seen as disqualifying. In the end, though, finding a theoretical framework that allowed me to investigate what I had observed from so close up and felt so passionate about, made it possible to integrate the two – lived experience and scholarship.

Insa Eschebach

From the 1970s Feminism to Gender Research at Ravensbrück: Autobiographical Considerations

Introduction

In the beginning there was Anne Frank. I read her diary in the late 1960s, when I was around 14 years old. In her book I encountered a dimension of unprecedented horror that continues to reverberate with me to this day. On July 15, 1944, a fortnight or so before she was deported, Anne Frank noted in her diary that, in spite of everything, she still believed that people were really good at heart, a phrase that had an impact on me, too. In my own diary at the time, I jotted down that I too wanted to fight for good in the world.

In the following years, this somehow universalistic view formed a peculiar amalgam with the American peace movement, the repercussions of which echoed as far as my home town of Emden in north-west Germany in the late 1960s; amplified by a Californian exchange student and the music of Bob Dylan, Donovan, Joan Baez, Peter, Paul & Mary, and others. I gave up my cello lessons and learned to play the guitar instead. My schoolgirl's intellectual world was shaped by reading Albert Camus, Jean-Paul Sartre, Wilhelm Reich and Simone de Beauvoir, wishing to get away as quickly as possible from the restorative climate of Germany's provinces. In London 1975/76 I came across the women's liberation movement, participated in the squatters' movement in Islington, and worked in a left-wing bookshop tellingly named "Rising Free". We danced to the music of Patti Smith, Ike & Tina Turner and Stevie Wonder. I told no one I was German, I said I came from Sweden.

Berlin

By the mid-1970s, Berlin – that "ruin of German history" – was the place to go. The vast windswept squares, the bullet-pocked façades, the rampant greenery that grew wild among the ruins of bombed-out buildings, provided something of a counter world to the historical amnesia of West Germany's reactionary and conservatively staid post-war society.[1] Studying philosophy

1 See Michael Rutschky, 'Panzerhaut der DDR. Die Ruinierung der Berliner Mauer', in: *Ruinen des Denkens. Denken in Ruinen*, ed. Norbert Bolz and Wilhelm van Reijen, Frankfurt am Main, 1996, 60.

and religion at the Free University under Professor Klaus Heinrich held the promise of insights into a founded social criticism. I engaged myself critically with the history of ideas of the Conservative Revolution, with nationalist (*völkisch*) thinking, with Martin Heidegger, Friedrich Nietzsche, Oswald Spengler on the one hand, and psychoanalysis, the Frankfurt School, French structuralism and post-structuralism on the other. My doctoral thesis was on the reception of Friedrich Nietzsche's *The Will to Power* in Germany and France. During the Third Reich this book had been widely regarded as a key work in Nietzsche's oeuvre, and the "will to power" had been read as a triumphant, domination-orientated declaration of intent. But the French post-structuralist reception of Nietzsche emerging at the time saw in it an ontology-critical concept; Nietzsche's work was being read as a manifestation of nomadic and subversive thinking.

My generation, that of the feminists born between 1949 and 1959, became active during the second phase of the new Women's Movement, i.e. from the mid-1970s onwards. We were engaging ourselves in the wake of the '68 generation, those who had been born in the 1940s and, in an explicit response to National Socialism, were demanding democratic and social rights for women too.[2] These founders of the new women's movement, who initially campaigned in favour of the politicisation of private life, albeit still in a Marxist sense, coupled their gender policy demands with the tolling of the 'death knell of capitalism'.[3] My generation, for its part, experienced the women's movement as an almost autonomous political culture. We rejected the separation of work and leisure, of the private and the public; we did not think along the lines of long-term perspectives; we thought about projects. The Cafe Mitropa, the Blocksberg, the Dschungel, and the Andere Ufer were all venues where social and cultural prospects were articulated.

In the early 1980s I met a group of Jewish American female artists, actors, singers and painters; one of them was the daughter of survivors. We went to the south of France together and wrote a play entitled *The Promise of Spring*. Back in Germany, we brought it to the stage at various venues in Berlin. The play was by no means about the history of Germany's crimes; its plot revolved around comedic scenes featuring women's nomadic existence. Nonetheless, our conversations about this historic chapter would prove to be of fundamental significance.

---

2 Irene Stoehr, "Feminismen und politische Kultur. Die westdeutsche Frauenbewegung als Generationenproblem", in: Heinrich-Böll-Stiftung. Feministisches Institut (ed.), *Wie weit flog die Tomate? Eine 68erinnen-Gala der Reflexion*, Berlin, 1999.

3 Stoehr, 157.

I spent whole nights with my friend Rosalyn Jacobs discussing our different backgrounds. We had both been raised by parents whose lives had been substantially shaped by Nazi policies. My father, a low-ranking member of the SS, was an architect. During the Second World War he was entrusted with building air-raid shelters for Emden's civilian population. He never spoke about it. By contrast, Rosalyn's parents had endured the genocide on occupied Polish soil, surviving ghettos and concentration camps. After being displaced persons for many years they immigrated to the US. Her accounts of her family's life, her community's social cohesion, the significance of the *Landsmannschaften*, in which she actively participated as a representative of the Second Generation, made a lasting impression on me. This encounter was to become a milestone in my own personal and professional development. Rosalyn remained committed to the subject of the Holocaust, as indeed did I. She co-founded an organisation called Memory Project Productions and created an exhibit with a multimedia installation titled "Finding Kalman. A Boy in Six Million". It revolved around the theme of Kalman, her mother Anna's younger brother, who as a little boy did not survive the Holocaust. All that remains is a photograph.[4]

Microhistory

In the 1970s and 1980s Berlin was a focal point of the history workshop movement. Besides criticizing the hierarchically structured scientific community, it was now a matter of taking a look at history of everyday life and social practices of people. Historical events could no longer be researched merely by approaches structured around the history of ideas and canonised writings; the call was for letters, diaries, photographs, objects of everyday use and, last but not least, oral histories that were now elevated to the ranks of historical sources. This new-found interest in the cultural history of everyday life also opened up a new perspective on locations themselves. Structural relics, for example, resemble storerooms that preserve the remnants of the past.

My professional life began in the mid-1980s, at the Kunstamt Berlin-Schöneberg, an institution of the Berlin Senate aimed at promoting cultural life in the district of Schöneberg. Its director, Katharina Kaiser, put the emphasis of her institution's activities on the everyday history of the district during the period 1933 to 1945. I had the good fortune of learning the craft of historical exhibitions and to work on the catalogues it produced. By then, my topics included the forced labour camps in Berlin-Schöneberg, the camps

4 Rosalyn Jacobs and Anna Huberman Jacobs, *Finding Kalman. A Boy in Six Million*, New York, 2012.

for displaced persons, letters and diaries written during the Second World War, etc. I recall how my perception of the district began to alter: Suddenly, I no longer saw bars, shops and apartment buildings, but restaurants and bowling alleys once frequented by the SS, apartments from which Jews had been deported, the park with benches Jews were forbidden to sit on, the cellar where a young Jewish girl managed to hold out until the liberation in 1945.

A special project was the installation of a memorial by the artists Renata Stih and Frieder Schnock in 1993 at the Bayerisches Viertel in Berlin-Schöneberg. Around 6,000 Schöneberg Jews had been deported from this highly residential quarter; around 10,000 Jews managed to escape. The memorial in remembrance of these events consists of 80 enamelled double-sided signs affixed at a height of three metres to lamp posts throughout the neighbourhood. The signs feature the regulations designed to marginalise, socially isolate, and ultimately dispossess the middle-class existence of particular individuals. They include only some of the 2,000 decrees in total designed to stifle the Jewish population socially, paving the way for the deportation and murder. While one side of these enamelled signs reproduces, verbatim, the versions of the decrees complete with date, the reverse side depicts various image motifs. While a pair of golden wedding rings tersely references the ban on marriages between Jewish and 'Aryan' citizens, a domestic cat signals the ban, forbidding Jewish citizens from keeping domestic animals. Jews were no longer allowed to use public transport; they were excluded from choral societies; their supplies of allocated foods were discontinued; they could no longer buy newspapers – all these oppressive announcements are displayed one after the other throughout the district.

In summer of 1993, after the memorial's inauguration, we set up a booth on Bayerischer Platz where colleagues and I handed out information leaflets on the new memorial and fell into conversation with today's local residents, which we recorded.

Jewish and Non-Jewish Voices Commenting on the Expulsion of Jewish Neighbours

In 1995 we opened an exhibition at the Kunstamt Berlin-Schöneberg to commemorate the deportations in Berlin-Schöneberg. The voices of Jewish and non-Jewish residents who had been neighbours in the Bayerisches Viertel during the Nazi era could be heard in playback in two opposite sections of the exhibition. It became clear that their shared past did not yield shared memories. The recollections of Jewish survivors were textured by the experience of persecution and the murder of their relatives and friends. Their stories were like a narrative flow, driven by the urgent motivation of wanting to bear witness.

By contrast, clearly audible in the voices of non-Jewish contemporary witnesses was the refutation of any knowledge of the ultimate fate of their erstwhile Jewish neighbours. Seemingly, they had "suddenly disappeared", according to a stereotypical response, or at best: "We parted on good terms". And yet, to quote a phrase coined by Peter Burke, there is such a thing as "unofficial memories", reluctant images, put into words only once a subject has been broached specifically and usually at odds with the exonerating discourse collectively rehearsed in post-war Germany. Suddenly, people did recall looking through the half-open door of their apartment and seeing their neighbours being rounded up; they did see the elderly gentleman from the third floor being beaten out onto the street and into a lorry.

These unofficial recollections seem to stem from a pool of memories that has endured, untapped, across the many decades, as if wrapped in a cocoon. Liselotte Simon, b. 1915, clearly recalled the Massow family being deported, how "they were all neatly dressed, as if in their Sunday best (...) And as they made their way down, they made this gesture (she places her finger in front of her mouth): in other words, don't make a fuss, don't be emotional (...) And these people were – I can still remember – they were in the stairway, and he says: ‚I'm going to sing 'O Deutschland hoch in Ehren'. To which she said: 'Fritz, for goodness' sake, be quiet.' "

It was not unusual to hear people say that it was the Jews themselves that had asked their non-Jewish neighbours to look on in silence and not intervene, to stop greeting them, etc. Again, even in Liselotte Simon's account, it's Frau Massow herself who, at the moment of her deportation, signalled to her neighbour that she should not 'be emotional'. One gets the impression the only reason Liselotte Simon remained standing in her apartment doorway was because that's what the deported themselves wanted her to do. Asked where she thought at the time the family was being taken to, she promptly answered: "To Poland, to be put to work. What else were we supposed to...".

"They knew enough to know it was better if you didn't know more," to quote David Bankier on the mindset of the German population at the time.[5] That blend of knowing and not knowing is all too apparent in the incomplete formulation cited above: "What else were we supposed to...". What they were unable to conceive is both stated and unstated subliminally in their inability to do so. None of those asked were willing to say anything

5 David Bankier, *Die öffentliche Meinung im Hitler-Staat. Die „Endlösung" und die Deutschen. Eine Berichtigung*, Berlin 1990, 157.

about the purpose of the deportations. The deportations they observed on the streets and in the stairways are described as the epitome of all that is fatefully horrific, but not the actual fact of the Jews' physical extermination, which as a rule went unmentioned.

The middle section of the exhibition gave visitors an opportunity to engage with realities all too foreign to them, in the form of letters written by survivors, documents and photographs that had been preserved. This section also documented the names of the 6,000 people who had been deported from the Bayerisches Viertel. More than 80 biographies of emigrants who had lived in the Bayerisches Viertel (Nelly Sachs, Else Lasker-Schüler, Leo Baeck, Albert Einstein, Wilhelm Reich, Billy Wilder, to name but a few) blend here kaleidoscope-like. Altogether, these memories form an archive that is to be used time and time again by each new generation.

After the Fall of the Berlin Wall

I remember that we felt rather sceptical about the fall of the Berlin Wall. It was embarrassing and ridiculous to see German politicians in front of the Schöneberg Rathaus singing the national anthem. Our fears were that an unbridled nationalism would erupt across Germany reunified. Nazi crimes would now be regarded as part of a horrific past, but one that had been overcome and therefore rendered acceptable, a backdrop against which Germany could now position itself, on the threshold of new era.

In fact, once re-unified, Germany declared that the public remembrance of the genocide was a national duty, but fortunately one that was orientated along civic lines. 'Remembrance Day for the Victims of National Socialism' on January 27 was introduced in 1995, with a proposal that same year to erect a 'Memorial to the Murdered Jews of Europe'. In the 1990s concentration camp memorials, which for decades had been irrelevant to the Federal Republic in its political representation, advanced to sought-after sites for commemorative ceremonies staging politicians. Addressing the subject of National Socialism had been the prerogative of a dedicated minority, but now the topic itself was shifting to the middle ground of society.

My friends and I explored the former German Democratic Republic by bicycle. And as we cycled along the cobbled pavements of sleepy villages and stopped in village inns that served traditional German food, it seemed as if we journeyed back into the 19th century. However, I became interested in various topics in East Germany's history: the East German uprising of 17 June 1953, for instance, which by 1993 had taken place exactly forty years ago. Once the uprising had been quashed by the GDR government, many male 'ringleaders' were executed, but also one woman. I was keen to know who that woman was. Supposedly she had worked as a female police officer in the Ravensbrück women's concentration camp and that, fascist that she was, she had conspired, on June 17, 1953, to topple the GDR government in the market square of the town of Halle.

I travelled to the Ravensbrück Memorial Museum some 100 km north of Berlin to research the case of the woman known as Erna Dorn. In 1993 the C.I.S. troops still occupied large sections of the historical site and had not yet withdrawn. The laundry of Soviet families fluttered on washing lines hanging between the houses in the former SS residential quarter; at that time the prisoner camp was not yet accessible to the public. In 1959, only a small section of the historical premises beyond the camp walls had been turned into a memorial site. The entire complex, but also the staff offices that exuded the distinctive smell of a cleaning agent frequently used in East Germany, reminded me more of the GDR than the Nazi era. However, I distinctly remember how frightened I felt sitting in the memorial archives, and how I could barely concentrate as my mind ran riot imagining what must have occurred back then inside these very rooms at the concentration camp. As Maurice Halbwachs remarks, "the image of the room alone, given its permanence, conveys the illusion (...) of rediscovering the past in the present".[6] The insight that 'this is where it happened', that this here was the nadir of our civilisation, was a realization that took my breath away. Places like Ravensbrück are places of mourning, but also places that radiate energy, that constantly raise questions again and again; they are places of creativity and communication.

Sigrid Jacobeit, head of the Memorial Museum, welcomed me to her office. When I asked her about Erna Dorn, she gestured amply at the former residential houses of the female SS-personnel outside her window and said there was still a vast field of research out there lying fallow. She added that, thus far, relatively little was known about the female camp supervisors at the Ravensbrück women's concentration camp. With the fall of the Berlin Wall, East German archives had become accessible. At the time I had no idea about the sort of pitfalls that lay in wait when working on the documents of East Germany's Ministry for State Security [MfS], which had devoted politically motivated attention to National Socialism. It proved virtually impossible to clear up once and for all the story of Erna Dorn, who was executed in 1953, due to the fact that her identity's paper trail had been exhaustively processed and obscured by the MfS. Her case was to have been used solely as evidence bolstering the absurd proposition that the 1953 uprising had in fact been initiated by fascists.

6 Maurice Halbwachs, *Das kollektive Gedächtnis*, Frankfurt am Main, 1991, 162.

Women's Studies and Gender Research on the Ravensbrück Women's Concentration Camp

The Ravensbrück women's concentration camp (1939–1945) initially accommodated 3,000 German female prisoners, but over the six years of its existence it expanded into a camp complex of some 200 hectares. By 1944 the camp also included a smaller men's camp, the 'Uckermark juvenile protective custody camp', a factory complex, production floors, and a prisoner camp for the company Siemens & Halske, the camp's *Kommandantur* compound, an SS children's home, and 44 satellite camps. Around 123,000 women and children from some 30 nations and around 20,000 men and 1,200 female juveniles were deported to Ravensbrück, including around 15,000 to 20,000 Jewish women and children. According to current estimates around 28,000 prisoners died of starvation, exhaustion, typhoid fever and dysentery or as victims of medical experiments. They were either shot or, in the final months leading up to the liberation, murdered in an improvised gas chamber. The first Red Army soldiers entered the camp at Ravensbrück on 30 April 1945.

Up until 1989 there had been only three scientific studies on the history of the women's concentration camp, two of which had been authored by the survivors Germaine Tillion, of France, and Wanda Kiedrzynska, of Poland. After the fall of the Wall, research into Ravensbrück began to gather pace. I, too, was involved in this trend, initially as a freelance member at the Ravensbrück Memorial Museum, then as part of two research projects on Ravensbrück at the Free University and at Humboldt University, and from 2005 as director of the Ravensbrück Memorial Museum.

The research on Ravensbrück owes much of its impetus to the field of women's studies and gender research. Gender politics under the Nazi regime, the subject of women's resistance, and the connection between gender and race were key themes of the 1970s and 1980s. The 1980s were dominated by the so-called female perpetrator debate, revolving around the role that German women played within the context of Nazi crimes and the share of responsibility they bore. The debate first came to a head following the publication of Claudia Koonz's book entitled *Mothers in the Fatherland* in 1986. The anthology published by Kirsten Heinsohn and others in 1997 entitled *Handlungsräume von Frauen im nationalsozialistischen Deutschland* put an end to the debate about female perpetrators, giving rise instead to the concept of agencies in the historical analysis of the social behaviour of women and men, a concept which in the following years did gain paradigmatic significance in research.

This trend is mirrored in the studies on female cohorts within the SS. Sociologist Gudrun Schwarz led the way with her work on female SS guards, which soon was followed by a series of studies orientated along lines of structural history, biography and post-war history. It soon became obvious that due to gender stereotyping, court records in particular could not be used as a source material without raising gender-specific issues. My first research project on Ravensbrück also focused on this particular field.

Of great significance for the further development of the Ravensbrück research was the establishment of the "Interdisciplinary Women's Research Group on the Memorial Museum Ravensbrück – Free University Berlin"(IFFG) in 1995. The aim was to initiate, supervise and co-ordinate research projects on all topics relating to the Ravensbrück. The IFFG played a prominent role in organising conferences and symposia; it also provided a range of platforms for discussions and exchanges to those who were working on the history of Ravensbrück in the broadest sense. The IFFG was awarded the Margherita von Brentano Prize for its involvement in, and dedication to, women's studies and gender research.

The institutional link between the Memorial Museum and the University was the necessary precondition for attracting funds from the German Israeli Foundation for Scientific Research and Development (GIF). This research project focused on the history of Jewish prisoners at Ravensbrück and was carried out in co-operation with the University of Tel Aviv (Dina Porat and Hanna Herzog), the Memorial Museum (Sigrid Jacobeit) and the Free University Berlin (Claudia Ulbricht), initially from 1997 to 2000, and then again, from 2001 to 2004 (Gisela Bock). Numerous academic papers and individual studies were produced, as a result of which Jewish prisoners, as overlooked for decades, can now be regarded as relatively well researched. However, the Ravensbrück research focused initially on those groups of prisoners who had long been excluded from public remembrance in western and eastern Europe. For decades, women who had been persecuted for political reasons and honoured as resistance fighters had taken centre stage at the commemorative ceremonies. So there was certainly much catching-up to be done in this particular area.

Gender Matters

For the Ravensbrück women's concentration camp as a site of exclusion, extreme social control, and violence, gender as a category is of crucial importance, in at least three important ways.

Firstly, with regard to the gender politics of the Third Reich. These manifested themselves in the organisational structures of SS personnel and the gender-specific concept and operation of the camp, as well as the construction of socially, politically and racially defined enemy stereotypes. There are countless examples of misogyny, homophobia and constructs of deviant femininity to be found in the camp's history. The Nazi regime's gender policy categories were pivotal to the criminal prosecution of women. The criminal trial records of the women held prisoner at Ravensbrück provide images of supposedly inferior – and therefore often also sexualised – femininity in the Third Reich.

Investigative approaches structured around gender history are also indispensable when it comes to studies of 'prisoner communities' (Maja Suderland) in the broadest sense: whether discussing the 'families' that women frequently formed for mutual support, reasons for persecution, biographies or issues of forced labour, cultural and social practices, repression measures, even execution practices – without the gender category they cannot be adequately comprehended.

Thirdly, there is the issue of gender stereotypes, historical-political representations and gender-specific symbolisations within the realm of public commemoration, which are of crucial significance for Ravensbrück remembrance both in Germany and internationally; the works of Sybil Milton, Sarah Horowitz, Marianne Hirsch, Joan W. Scott, Judith Tydor Baumel-Schwartz, Silke Wenk, Christina von Braun and others have been, and still are, trendsetting pioneers.

I would now like to give an idea of the iconographic programme of the Ravensbrück Memorial Site, another one of my main areas of research. For the Ravensbrück Memorial Museum inaugurated in the German Democratic Republic in 1959 the image of a solidary community of prisoners long held sway. Remembrance activities revolved around the women who had been imprisoned for political reasons. Already in the early post-war years the image of the peace-loving, desexualised woman and mother was a key figure of the Ravensbrück commemoration ceremonies. Accordingly, the two memorials at the site, specifically the *Tragende* [Burdened Woman] (1959) and *Müttergruppe* [Group of Mothers] (1965), depict the former prisoners performing selfless charitable work.

However, the image of the mother engaged in charitable activities is the expression of a politically motivated and idealised fiction that is founded on the excluded, and the unnamed. Those who were not meant to be part of the socialist community of the GDR were denied access to Ravensbrück's history. These elements were not only deleted from national associations of prisoners; they were wiped clean from memory. So-called 'asocial' prisoners, lesbian women, criminals, prostitutes, Jews, Sinti and Roma, Jehovah's Witnesses and many others were part of Ravensbrück's history that was left blank; they became the reverse side of the camp and were certainly not meant whenever the talk was of women and mothers.

It was only in the 1980s that a change of direction first became noticeable in both German post-war societies, a shift towards those previously marginalised victims of Nazi persecution. That's when attention was first drawn to the sheer actual diversity of the prisoner groups held in Nazi camps. In 1984 a group of women from East Berlin sought for the first time to offer a public commemoration for lesbian prisoners in Ravensbrück. This group of women, who had convened under the roof of the Gethsemane Church in Berlin, was subsequently put under close surveillance by the MfS. The records show that new wreaths and garlands were to be "placed over the top of the relevant wreath", once the lesbians had left and that their dedications were to be removed from the visitors' book so the act of commemoration of the dead could be undone.

In the 1990s the site of the former 'Uckermark juvenile protective custody camp' also became a focal point of greater public attention. At the time some 1,200 girls regarded as 'wayward' were housed in this camp established in 1942, right next to the Ravensbrück women's concentration camp. From January 1945 the same camp was used as a death camp for the sick and elderly prisoners of Ravensbrück, who in the language of the SS were deemed 'bedridden cripples', 'unfit for work', 'unfit for marching', and 'rejects'. After 1945 the Uckermark camp had no group to lobby for the site's multifaceted history.

Today, there is nothing left to see in the rough terrain, of the historical topography of the 'juvenile protective custody camp'. Since 1997, 'anti-fascist feminist work camps' have been held there annually, implementing creative designs for the site, such as 'Maschas', airy and filigree figurines fashioned out of wire mesh ('Maschendraht'). More artistic activities were to follow, for example the installation of a wind chime made from fragments left behind by the Soviet military forces. Temporary installations such as those described are highly innovative and, unlike more conventional forms of memorials, act as a catalyst for people to engage critically with the site. Creativity and diversity of form are important achievements in contemporary monumental art inasmuch as they counter, with scepticism, the 'authoritarian scale of monumental sites' (James Edward Young), which reduces the visitor to the role of passive bystander.

However, even the current discourse surrounding Uckermark is marked by gender stereotypes. According to Christina von Braun, perceptions of the female body play an ambivalent role. On the one hand, the feminine symbolises all that is clean and pure and holy, in any case all that is inherently one's own; on the other, the female body also always represents the soiled and sordid 'other' and therefore 'that which has to be excluded'.[7] Accordingly, dichotomous constructions of femininity are noticeable even

7 Christina von Braun, on the notion of purity, in: *metis. Zeitschrift für historische Frauenforschung und feministische Praxis* 5 (1997)19.

in the history of remembrance of the Ravensbrück concentration camp and the Uckermark camp. The topos of the peace-loving woman and mother outlined above, which for decades was the focal point of the Ravensbrück commemorative ceremonies, is now being contrasted with the previously 'second-rate' figure of the Uckermark prisoner. While the former is all about the 'pure woman', the helpless victim, the mother as embodiment of all that is ultimately good, the latter is about images of 'inappropriate' femininity. 'Marginalised for failing to conform' and 'socially undesirable': these are the terms used by female activists, who bear in mind the continuity of marginalisation to this very day. What becomes clear is that deviance is now situated within a new constellation of identity politics. This is made possible against a backdrop where society's fear of deviance and homophobia appears to be diminishing, in an increasingly pluralistic political culture.

Nonetheless, both images of the prisoners at Ravensbrück and Uckermark – namely the conforming and adapted and the non-conforming and non-adapted woman – are based on an effective strategy of simplification. In both stereotypes, programmatic desires for homogeneity are expressed by de facto highly disparate social groups. And both of these gender stereotypes are the product of an extremely de-differentiating view of the camp's history.

Postscript

I would like to give a survivor of the Ravensbrück women's concentration camp the last word. Annika Bremell is one of the survivors who have enriched our lives and our work through their visits, by taking part in educational events, and through the sheer warmth of their personalities. Annika Bremell remembers how, in April 1945, as she stood for roll call for the last time, the camp gates suddenly opened and 'dashingly handsome young men' walked in, wearing the uniform of the Swedish Red Cross. They were the bus drivers who had come to evacuate the women from the camp to Scandinavia. Like many of her fellow prisoners, Annika Bremell had had her head shaved multiple times, and yet she described how, in that instant, her hand instinctively 'went up' to check her hair. As she became aware of that gesture, she realised she had managed to remain a woman and that her looks were still important to her.

Matthias Heyl, Head of Educational Programmes, occasionally tells this story on his guided tours as the groups reach what was once the *Appellplatz*, in clear sight of the camp gates. He has even on occasion caught himself 'reaching up' with his own hand, by way of illustration, when retelling the story. And he mentions that there have been times, when making this rather feminine gesture, that young lads in the group have been somewhat put off. He has, on such occasions, heard spontaneously uttered mumbles like 'bit gay'.

Clearly, the history of the women's concentration camp and the work of the Ravensbrück Memorial Museum today are inconceivable without gender sensitivity, which is why the category of gender plays such a big role in our education work. Today, concentration camp memorial sites are increasingly faced with the difficult expectation that a visit to these sites can give young people orientation, and help them gain the right ethical convictions. And yet we live in a world in which the 'unimpeded advance of liberal-humanist values' which our generation once held to be self-evident, is increasingly being cast into doubt.[8] We can draw attention to the fact that ideological paradigms, racist fantasies of affiliation and belonging, and handed-down gender stereotypes are able to endure. In our work, we can show that there are affinities with our present-day thinking and with present-day societal practices. That is how I would describe the horizon of our possibilities.

And so, as I reach the end of my essay written here on the island of Öland in Sweden, I wish to say that it has been an honour and a pleasure to contribute to this anthology. But writing it has also been a challenge when you consider that every autobiographical text is of purely constructive character. However, it has taught me to appreciate my good fortune and the role serendipity played in getting to know wonderful people, who time and time again have provided me with new insights into the difficult history that continues to cast a shadow over us, to this very day.

---

8 See Kazuo Ishiguro, *Speech on the occasion of the awarding of the Noble Prize for Literature*, 7 December 2017, Svenska Akademien Stockholm.

Esther Fuchs

Three Beginnings: Feminist Scholarship and Holocaust Studies

Introduction

Thinking about my scholarly engagement over the years with the Shoah, it seems to me that no other field academic interest presented as many professional challenges and obstacles. In hindsight, it is legitimate to construe these challenges as an ideological resistance to feminism as an inappropriate approach in Holocaust Studies. On the one hand, the field shares much in common with other areas to which I contributed over the years, Hebrew Literature, Biblical Studies, Jewish Studies and Israel Studies. All these fields were to some degree resistant to the concepts, paradigms, questions and critical analyses I introduced, and developed over the last four decades. However, while the other fields eventually opened up to them, and even encouraged research on women and gender, in Holocaust Studies the subject remains marginal. Though included in some anthologies, and while "exceptional" researchers are recognized and even endowed with institutional authority, it lags behind other academic fields.

I began to engage professionally with Holocaust scholarship in the late 1990s. By this time, most fields have crossed disciplinary boundaries to borrow from and communicate with Women's Studies. There was very little I could refer to as precedent, or model. A handful of essays, and a very small number of monographs. In Women's Studies representation has become a central subject of debate, while in Holocaust Studies the primary and almost exclusive scholarly discourse was historiography. What I wanted to do was to bridge the chasm between the fields, to create interest in gender by focusing on Holocaust films, many of which have become cultural icons, and to bring the Holocaust to the attention of students and faculty in Women's Studies, and to scholars of feminist theory.

I cannot claim much success in my venture. Guest lectures in colleagues' courses were limited to the "Holocaust," rubric; scholars invited from other universities to teach year round courses on the Holocaust (for the most part historians) did not show any interest in gender, or feminism, invitations to conferences about women in the Holocaust required the usual commitment to submit my presentation for eventual publication. The much needed conversation about shared pedagogic concerns, interests, and priorities was neither initiated, nor instituted. National and international conferences on the Holocaust do not appear to promote specialized panels on women or gender, and the Holocaust has not emerged as abiding focus of interest at the National Women's Studies Association.[1]

It is possible that the Holocaust remains to this day marginal in Women's Studies because it is framed as a disciplinary area of specialization, appropriately located in Departments of History rather than in interdisciplinary area studies. Yet, in the last three decades Holocaust Studies emerged as an interdisciplinary field in its own right. One of my primary concerns was to demonstrate that the Holocaust was as much deserving of discussion by literary, film and cultural critics as gender has been. This was indeed the main goal of the anthology I published, *Women and the Holocaust: Narrative and Representation.*

It is possible that gender remains marginal in Holocaust Studies because it is misperceived as a category of analysis that distracts from the primary category that is shared by all scholars who are actively involved in it: race and racism, specifically the anti-Semitic construction of a Jewish "race" and the racist genocide that included both men and women, heterosexual and homosexual. One may argue that recent work on gender and sexuality may yield important insights into the genocidal fervor of the persecutors. The fear that feminism promotes revisionist anti-historiographic theories that may support Holocaust deniers is also unfounded. Feminist theorists have for the most part been concerned about the constructions of women as embodiments of gender inferiority, in much the same way that Jews have been constructed by anti-Semitic ideologues as embodiments of a racial inferiority. And yet the fields remain almost entirely separate from each other.

It is possible that the earliest publications that appeared throughout the 1980s are held as exemplary of feminist Holocaust scholarship in general. These publications were to some degree reductive and simplistic distinctions between men and women and their different experiences during the Holocaust. Some publications argued that women suffered more than men, and suffered greater humiliation and sexual trauma. Some argued to the contrary, that women were equipped with domestic and social skills that helped them survive. These gendered differentiations, however, cannot be taken as exemplary of the entire venture. They cannot and should not be taken as paradigmatic of feminist work in Holocaust Studies. Yet the suspicion that feminism is irrelevant to say the least remains strong.

1 My observations are based on my tenure as Assistant Professor at the University of Texas (1979–1985) and as Associate Professor and Full Professor at the University of Arizona in Tucson 1985–2010.

To this day Women's Studies and Holocaust Studies are rarely theoretically or even institutionally or organizationally intersected. They are broadly perceived as two entirely distinct specializations. While the former is focused on an ongoing attempt to understand power, privilege and hierarchy, the latter is mostly interested in producing ever more nuanced and comprehensive historical narratives about the Holocaust. With the growing availability of sources, archives and personal narratives representing the Holocaust accurately becomes an ever more daunting task. It is reasonable to suggest that the feminist focus on theory and analysis may in fact help further sharpen the lens on the historical, social, economic and ideological causes of the Holocaust. And yet, little has so far been done on the Shoah by feminist historians or theorists. Even as acclaimed a feminist thinker as Judith Butler, who published profusely on gender and sexuality, sheds little light on the relationship between these discourses and scholarship on the Holocaust, Zionism and Jewish Identity.[2]

Of my three critical engagements with the Shoah, the first one, the most direct personal articulation of what I continue to consider as its core affective meaning, was the most difficult challenge. I began to write when the concept of "second generation testimony" and "post-memory" were not yet familiar in Shoah literature, scholarship and cultural life in general.[3] To venture into an area naturally reserved for those who had the authority of experience, those who witnessed and survived Auschwitz, seemed to me both morally untenable and discursively impossible. Immoral because it felt like an appropriation of my parents' story, the story of their generation. The second beginning was less difficult because it was scholarly, and required a reassuring academic distancing from myself. The difficulty here was the need to pave a new path, a feminist approach to cultural popular representations of the Shoah. The lack of previous models was a challenge I could not easily overcome because gendered literary and cultural representations of the Shoah have not yet been considered as worthy of scholarly critique. The third beginning, feminist Holocaust theory is also, in many ways, a first step for me and the field as a whole. If the cultural representations of the Holocaust may potentially bridge the gap between Holocaust and feminist studies, which is centrally focused on questions of representation, feminist Holocaust theory has the potential to resolve the current tension with

2 Judith Butler, *Parting Ways: Jewishness and the Critique of Zionism*, New York: Columbia University Press, 2013.

3 Marianne Hirsch, *Generation of Postmemory: Writing and Visual Culture After the Holocaust*, New York: Columbia University Press, 2012. See also *Family Frames: Photography, Narrative and Postmemory*. Cambridge, Mass.: Harvard University Press, 1997.

Holocaust studies, where feminism and gender remain a highly marginal topic of interest. This suggests to me that to some extent my personal three beginnings then refer not only to my own life story, but to the trajectory of the field.

The Personal: A Daughter of Shoah

I belatedly understood that selecting Jewish studies as an area of concentration for my undergraduate degree at the Hebrew University was neither unique nor extraordinary. As a daughter of survivors my choice was typical among what has become defined as "the second generation" of academics, intellectuals, writers, and artists in Israel. Focusing on the history, culture, literature and language that was almost wiped out globally, and that was already erased in Europe, was both a gesture of solidarity with those who did not survive, and resistance to the Nazi master plan. I rationalized it as intellectual curiosity at the time, hoping to find in this field ideas, traditions or personalities that may have served as provocation for the intense hatred that consumed the Nazi leadership with such murderous rage. Needless to say, I did not find any answers to this question to this day.

The Shoah was visibly etched on my father's face, a frightful scar that required multiple futile plastic surgeries, an embodied memory left by the shooting liquidation of the last surviving prisoners marched from the Stutthof concentration camp. With my mother it was her dentures, having lost her teeth in her early thirties for lack of adequate food and vitamins in the barn where she spent two years hiding from the Nazis. I do believe that in our home, the daily reminder of the Shoah did not require words, though it was loud in my father's silence and my mother's unceasing lament for our dead relatives. The creative work of second generation writers reveals the deeper meaning of survival, beneath the veneer of normality and adaptation, of living with the embodied memories of the first generation.[4]

Having graduated with my BA summa cum laude from the Hebrew University, I was granted the privilege of proceeding directly to my doctorate. But when it came to my receiving a scholarship, I was informed that it had been granted to a male student who intended to focus on Talmudic studies for his doctoral degree. As my plan was to focus on Modern Hebrew Literature, he stood a better chance of securing the full financial scholarship.

---

4 Esther Fuchs, "Second Generation Holocaust Poetry in Hebrew," *Shofar* 18/3 (2000), 64–76. Eva Hoffman, *After Such Knowledge: Memory, History, and the Legacy of the Holocaust*, New York: Public Affairs, 2004; Ronit Lentin, *Israel and the Daughters of the Shoah: Reoccupying the Territories of Silence*, London and Oxford: Berghahn Books, 2000.

The reasoning seemed odd, as it was the grade point average and general academic excellence that served, at least as officially, as the primary standard for granting a doctoral scholarship. The preference for Talmudic studies over Hebrew literature was also an odd explanation. I did not want to compromise, as some students had to do, I wanted to devote myself full time to my academic studies.[5] Nor could I rely on my parents' financial support. Despite the belated state and German restitution payments, they struggled economically to make ends meet, as did many survivors at that time. It would take another decade for me to realize that what was at work was gender discrimination. Jewish studies was dominated at the time by senior men and the preference for male straight graduate students. What I did not realize then was that my return to the Hebrew University, or to any other Israeli academic institution would be foreclosed by this decision, as even after earning my degree from Brandeis, I would find that all the Hebrew Literature Departments were headed by a young crop of heterosexual men, and in some rare cases by married women.

I noted earlier that pursuing an academic degree in Jewish Studies was common among the Second Generation, at least as an undergraduate pursuit. What was unique, however, was completing an advanced degree in Hebrew literature, a language so intimately and inextricably interwoven with my consciousness outside of the obvious context, guaranteed to nurture creative as well as academic writing on the Shoah. For many years, writing the Shoah in any other language was unthinkable for me, as its most immediate associations were articulated in Polish and Yiddish, certainly not in English. Even after earning a doctoral degree, years ahead of the other graduates, I published my poems and stories in Hebrew, during my frequent personal and professional visits to Israel.[6] Much as I was keen to join other Hebrew second generation writers, to follow the creative afterlives of and critical responses to my publications, and maintain the vibrant personal links that were forged early on with publishers, reviewers and anthologizers, leaving the country disconnected me from the intimate daily contact required for authentic literary engagement. Even more difficult, both morally and personally, was the growing distance from my aging parents, my direct access to their *Khurbn*.

---

5 Though I do not go into personal details, I discuss the masculinist frame of the Hebrew literary critical establishment at the time in my introduction to *Israeli Mythogynies: Women in Contemporary Hebrew Fiction*, 1–12. On similar problems in the Humanities and Social Sciences I wrote in my introduction to *Israeli Women's Studies*, 1–32.

6 Esther Fuchs, *Li asur lehitabed* [No License to Die], Tel Aviv: Ecked, 1983; Tsaleket [Scar], Tel Aviv: Ecked, 1997.

For years, I considered my departure for the United States as a temporary detour, and could not bring myself to admit that I left because of institutionalized gender discrimination that was rampant in the early 1970s in all major Israeli universities. It took me years to realize that I was one of numerous casualties of gender discrimination, young women who left the country in search of equal opportunity elsewhere. The Israeli Women's Movement was only just emerging, and issues of discrimination in the workforce in general have not yet come to the fore. Academic publications about the problem began to appear a decade later, documenting the inequality that shaped not only academia and the workforce, but the family, the military, and political life. Sexual harassment was also a concept that has not yet emerged as a legal and institutional problem. It was pervasive at the Hebrew University, and I thought I could escape this climate by immigrating to a truly democratic country which upholds the rule of law and protects students, and young professionals of all genders from harassment by professors, advisors, colleagues, and even leading Hebrew authors and poets. When I was invited to write about gender, exile and dislocation, I tried for the first time to link Holocaust post-memory to Israeli politics, and to my own personal story. These invitations provided me with the opportunity to think about my own life as a symptom of a much broader social and political context. Though I later published about this context professionally and academically, the personal remained submerged.

The grant that I received from Brandeis University released me from economic pressures, but I would soon learn that sexual harassment and gender discrimination, though not as pronounced and intolerable, did not disappear despite the stronger institutional and legal American commitment to equality and fairness. As an immigrant to a new country, in many ways I was not familiar with the unspoken gendered codes that structured Higher Education, even in my exile and adopted country. I would soon learn that gender bias, sexual harassment, professional retaliation, and discrimination are global and transnational problems. Though I completed my dissertation ahead of the doctoral candidates at Brandeis, I was neither rewarded nor recognized for it, nor offered a position in Jewish studies programs in the coveted Boston and New York areas, where Shai Agnon, the subject of my dissertation, and two subsequent books, did not require introduction, and where Hebrew literature was justifiably treated as a serious and exacting academic discipline.[7] The positions in Jewish studies that we, Brandeis

7 Esther Fuchs, *Omanut hahitamemut: al ha-ironia shel shai agnon* (Cunning Innocence: On S.Y. Agnon's Irony], Tel Aviv: The Institute in Literary Research at Tel Aviv University, 1985; *Aspectim komiyim beyetzirato shel shai agnon* [Comic Aspects in Shai Agnon's Work], Tel Aviv: Reshafim Publishers, 1987.

graduates, considered worthy of our academic degrees, would be offered to the male graduates and the married women who earned their degrees years after I left Brandeis.

Though the University of Texas in Austin prides itself on its Women's Studies Department and Jewish Studies Program, when I moved there in the early 1980s from Boston it had neither. Publishing on women and gender was risky for tenure track Assistant Professors like myself, though a small group of women faculty from the departments of French, English and German welcomed me as a fellow feminist critic, and cheered me on as I brought my book manuscript on the literary representation of women to completion.[8] As for the promotion and tenure process, it was a lonely and isolating experience, having had to omit from my file both the too "personal" Shoah texts, and the too "political" feminist manuscript. The departmental promotion and tenure committee consisted of senior men who claimed they protected me from unpredictable responses from the University-wide promotion and tenure committee, which also consisted of senior men, who judged junior professors by their ability to serve the stated academic, institutional and public mission of the Department. This mission did not include, apparently, gender concerns, nor did it include the Holocaust. Auschwitz was a European problem, unrelated to the departmental mission statement.

The Professional: Gender and Representation

As a tenured Associate and later Professor at the University of Arizona, in Tucson, I spent long hours, days and weeks insuring that junior women faculty, dependent on the approval of male supervisors, advisors, directors, and mentors, would not be vulnerable to thinly veiled anti-feminist. I was sustained in my formal and informal work by a network of women faculty across campus. Yet, I soon realized that even senior women, notably unmarried faculty and staff women, were just as vulnerable to sexual harassment as their younger cohorts. When it became clear to me that the dean of Social and Behavioral Sciences would appoint me as program director in exchange for sexual favors, I filed a formal intramural complaint. In 1988 the dean left (or was forced out) in the middle of his decanal term, a typical outcome which exported the problem to another University. For me, the repercussions were devastating, as few colleges were eager at the time to hire an activist feminist trouble maker.

---

8 Esther Fuchs, "Exile, Jews, Women, Yordim, I—An Interim Report, Chapel Hill and London: The University of Carolina Press, 1989; *Israeli Mythogynies: Women in Contemporary Hebrew Fiction*, Albany: State University of New York Press, 1987.

I was soon recruited to college and university wide committees charged with implementing anti-discrimination rules and regulations. Complaints about sexual harassment were routinely filed by students, and junior faculty who were preyed upon by predatory administrators charged with defending them. More often than not, the complainants moved on to other colleges and careers, and the files were buried in the archives of the Office of the Equal Employment and Opportunity Commission and the Committee on Academic Freedom and Tenure. No matter how many commissioned essays I was invited to contribute, or how many anthologies, no matter how many invited papers I presented, and despite repeated nominations by colleagues, the old guard duplicated its gender, politics and conservative academic philosophy by appointing compliant and grateful faculty. Senior feminist faculty like me were triply charged: with course work, committee work, and research work. In addition to assigned work, voluntary academic activism on behalf of egalitarian ideals often proved to be too heavy a burden for many who either left, burnt out, or opted for early retirement.

The excuse for postponing my promotion to full Professor was my multidisciplinary record which included "too many" areas of interest. I had to attach an explanation to my departmental file, clarifying that biblical literature is not a "new" area of research, but rather the linguistic, literary and cultural foundation of Hebrew literature, my original, doctoral area of specialization. There was little doubt in my mind that the reason for stalling, blocking and hindering the professional advancement enjoyed by male counterparts inside and out of the university, was the feminist approach I struggled with for over a decade to defend and legitimize feminism as a valuable scholarly discourse in biblical studies.[9] To my file, I added yet another explanatory note clarifying why interdisciplinary work should not be taken as a symptom of unfocused research. Crossing disciplinary boundaries was still a new concept in the 1990s, one I had to defend even in Jewish Studies.

Introducing Holocaust studies as a crucial scholarly subfield fell to me, when I organized the first and so far only interdisciplinary women's conference on Jewish studies. My paper focused on a problem that has become a central concern for both feminism and Holocaust studies: the problem of representation.[10] How to represent Auschwitz in post-Holocaust times has become a central concern for scholars who published on the representational

---

9 Esther Fuchs, *Sexual Politics in the Biblical Narrative: Reading the Hebrew Bible as a Woman*, Sheffield: Sheffield Academic Press, 2000; *Feminist Theory and the Bible*, New York and London: Lexington Books, 2016.

10 Esther Fuchs, "Images of Women in Holocaust Films," in *Women in Jewish Life and Culture* edited by Esther Fuchs (special issue of *Shofar: An Interdisciplinary Journal of Jewish Studies* vol. 17 no. 2; Winter, 1999), 49–56.

limitations of history, testimony, memory, literature, and film. My subsequent publications dealt with the tendency to idealize women who perished as disembodied, youthful, attractive, innocent, naïve, in some cases artistic and exceptionally talented. This idealization transformed the historical referents into two dimensional incarnations of European culture, whose passing the spectators were invited to mourn and grieve. The nostalgic, romanticized representation of a civilized world that fell to barbarism was the subject of European Holocaust cinema, which, for the most part focused on men as determined, clever, resilient survivors. This despite the growing testimonial literature by women writers, who survived and lived to tell their stories.[11]

I suspect that my critical analyses of Holocaust representations, had something to do with my intimate familiarity with my mother's story. It was etched on my consciousness since childhood. The sensationalist, eroticized, misogynous denigration of women survivors that often associates their survival with compromised morality and political indifference was personally offensive to me. I could not find my mother's story on the screen, even in literature. For years I implored her to trust her writing skills in Yiddish. It took four decades for her to finally publish her memoir.[12] The reluctance to share publically what she shared privately, is typical of women survivors, who feared not being believed, or worse, for securing their survival by exchanging sexual favors. In my anthology, I included a translated excerpt of the memoir. She did not live long enough to enjoy the release of the pressure that drove her to speak about it in person, phone conversations, throughout my childhood and after my departure. Her memory served her long enough to recall and describe in minute detail how she finally survived the terror, helplessness, humiliation, hunger, thirst, lice, unbearable cold, sweltering heat, in the dark, narrow, infested ditch under the wooden slats of a Catholic peasant's barn.[13]

My feminist deconstruction of popularized Shoah representation may have been motivated by personal indignation at the cinematic uses made of experiences of women survivors I knew well, including my own mother. As

11 Esther Fuchs, "The Construction of Heroines in Holocaust Films: The Jewess as Beautiful Soul," *Women and the Holocaust: Narrative and Representation* edited by Esther Fuchs, New York and Oxford: University Press of America, 1999: 97–112; "Gender, Identity and Family in the European Holocaust Film," *Life, Death and Sacrifice: Women and Family in the Holocaust* edited by Esther Herzog, Jerusalem and New York: Gefen, 2008: 287–305.

12 Zila Fuks, *Ze'akot lelo kol* (*translated from the Yiddish by Yosef Avni) Tel Aviv: I.L Peretz Publishing, 1988.*

13 Zila Fuks, "Life in Hiding: Razek's Barn: An Excerpt from *Silent Screams*," trans. and ed. by Esther Fuchs, *Women and the Holocaust: Narrative and Representation*: 127–134.

the generation of survivors dies out, and as women's memoirs are becoming increasingly consigned to literary and historical archives, it will be up to future generations of writers to reimagine and rewrite the Shoah. At the dawn of a new century, the work of daughters of survivors, like me are also decreasing in volume, accessibility and availability. What remains is women's scholarship, and here what matters is an awareness of generational continuity and difference.

The Theoretical: Feminist Shoah Scholarship

In the 2000s I began shuttling between Women's and Gender Studies conferences and national and international conferences in Jewish and Holocaust studies. Women and gender began to appear as a subject of interest in Jewish and Holocaust studies with some frequency, and several anthologies, including my own, were published on the subject. Similarly, Jewish identity and anti-Semitic racism were featured in a few panels at the annual National Women's Studies Association and less frequently in the flagship journals of the field. As a contributor to journals in both fields, I could not help noticing, and problematizing, the few theoretical linkages that had been essayed and the need for further and bolder border crossing between Holocaust and Women's and Gender studies. The main problem that concerned me was the lack of awareness in Holocaust studies of the multiplicity of genders and sexualities that have crowded out the stable, binary and largely heterosexist uses of "gender" in Holocaust studies, and the lack of awareness of the current meanings and political implications of the term. Simultaneously, I was astonished by the small number of publications devoted to the Holocaust in Jewish and Women's Studies, moving me to step outside both fields and to think about the problem theoretically[14]

It was impossible for me to outline a Jewish feminist genealogy of scholarship when I was invited to give a paper on Jewish studies at the conference on the Future of Women's Studies. For one thing, the terms of reference and areas of critical concern were so different. In many ways, the two fields were proceeding in opposite directions. "Gender" and "women" in Women's studies carried political meaning, and identified social conventions, processes and institutions that required reform and transformation. In contrast, at Jewish studies conferences on "Women in Judaism" or "Women in Jewish Civilization", the subject of inquiry and the exposition were disconnected

---

14 Esther Fuchs, "Jewish Feminist Scholarship: A Critical Perspective," *Studies in Jewish Civilization: Women and Judaism* edited by Leonard J. Greenspoon, Ronald A. Simkins and Jean Axelrad Cahan, Creighton: University of Nebraska Press, 2003: 225–246.

from present day political issues. The scholarly lens was trained on the past, for the most part on unearthing the histories of women in biblical, medieval and modern contexts. My presentation was critical of this depoliticized "objective" intellectualized practice of remaining blind to the social and political responsibility of the Jewish intellectual and the feminist scholar in particular.[15] Yet, though I outlined in general terms the way forward, highlighting Israeli-Palestinian relations, I did not provide a strategy.

In the same year, 2001, I gave an invited paper at an international conference in Oxford, England on "Remembering for the Future: The Holocaust in an Age of Genocide." The difference between the conferences was striking. While the women's conference was concerned with feminist theory, mapping trajectories for future research, the latter was eager to showcase the increasing areas of specialization, sources, archival documentation, statistics, data and information collected, catalogued, organized, categorized and labelled, with areas of specialization carefully outlined. Ghettoes, work camps, and extermination camps were differentiated and subjected to specialized scrutiny. Women too appeared as the subjects of an emerging disciplinary specialization. My paper focused on what has become my recognized professionalized area of academic specialization.[16] It was not understood as a critical intervention in the field at large, but rather as yet another example of the growing field of Holocaust studies. To the extent that this conference carried a broader message to the study of other genocides, it seems to have suggested that each genocide ought to be historicized and studied in detail.

As I continued to search for ways to link the political and the present with the academic and the past, I was invited to present a paper in yet another international conference on the Holocaust. It was there, in Dublin, Ireland in 2001, that I first presented an academic paper on my personal Shoah story. At that time the personal story was not yet considered an appropriate conduit of communication for scholars of Holocaust Studies. Once again I had no models, and had to invent a new genre as it were: the scholarly/personal essay. A genre in which the personal and the scholarly deconstruct each other, each questioning the other's positivist statements and propositions.[17]

15 Esther Fuchs, "Feminism, Anti-Semitism, Politics: Does Jewish Women's Studies Have a Future?" *Women's Studies for the Future: Foundations, Interrogations, Politics* edited by Elizabeth Lapovsky Kennedy and Agatha Beins, New Brunswick, New Jersey and London: Rutgers University Press, 2005.

16 "Women Holocaust Survivors in Cinema: The issue of Madness," *Remembering for the Future: The Holocaust in an Age of Genocide* edited by John Roth et al, London: Palgrave Macmillan, 2001.

17 Esther Fuchs, "Exile, Daughterhood and Writing: Representing the Shoah as a Personal Memory," *Re-Presenting the Shoah for the Twenty-First Century*, edited by Ronit Lentin, New York and Oxford: Berghahn Books, 2004: 253–268.

Even as I outlined what I believed to be unique to my story, I sought at the same time to embed it in the broader generational and historical context, much as I do here. As of this writing, however, I am much more interested in the theoretical implications of what I began to do over a decade ago.

In 2005 I introduced my recently published *Israeli Women's Studies* to the Israel Studies Association which accepted my invitation to hold its annual international meeting on the campus of the University of Arizona.[18] The point of the textbook, I argued, was not simply to demonstrate that vibrant academic programs on women and gender have produced important critical analyses in multiple disciplines. It was not simply that women and gender are a category that must be added to the Israel studies curriculum and to graduate programs. It was primarily to highlight the political engagement of this feminist scholarship with the Israeli Women's Movement, thus challenging the principle of detached scholarship, the legacy of European modernism, and the Enlightenment. Israeli feminist peace activism was based on the rejection of violence in all its forms, domestic, sexual, military and terrorist.

In the sequel to this textbook, I was concerned not simply with introducing Israeli feminist scholarship as a new discourse in Israeli Studies and Women's Studies. Rutgers University Press was interested in an anthology, but I felt that published essays have not yet gained recognition in these broader frameworks, and sought first to publish a collection of recently published interdisciplinary feminist work. In this collection, I included an essay on the Holocaust as well, which has been relatively under-theorized in most other contemporaneous anthologies on Israeli identity and politics.[19] The bifurcation of the Shoah and Zionism, exilic abjection and Zionist redemption, Diaspora and Israel, is a suggestive starting point for reflection on this complex issue. I therefore showcased this important theory as follows: "As representatives of effeminate exilic Jewry, the survivors were stigmatized against the norm of Hebrew masculinity. Stigmatized as outsiders, the survivors were understood as strangers, and excluded from privileged discourses of national heroism. The Shoah has become gendered as the quintessential representation of Jewish powerlessness, effeminate passivity and victimization. Powerlessness thus became associated with the memory of the European destruction of Jews, while masculinity defined the very essence of Zionism."[20]

---

18 *Israeli Women's Studies* edited by Esther Fuchs, Brunswick, New Jersey: Rutgers University Press, 2005.

19 Esther Fuchs, *Israeli Feminist Scholarship, Gender, Zionism, and Difference*, Austin: University of Texas Press, 2014.

20 *Israeli Feminist Scholarship*, 10.

To Be Continued

The beginnings I outlined in this essay as phases in my personal academic trajectory correspond to three feminist discourses that have barely just begun to emerge in Holocaust Studies. The workings of post-memory in second generation women poets, writers and artists have not yet been examined, neither in the context of Hebrew, nor in any other language. In this essay I did not make claims for gender differences in post-memorial literature, but in the personal essay I published a decade ago, I do. In "Exile, Daughterhood and Writing" I focus on the complex relationship between my story and that of my parents. At the time, it was crucial for me to point to the difference between the experiences, and the stories. With my parents' passing, and the generational passing of all those who could actually recall the Shoah, texts are inevitable replacements. Writing, however, may not be enough, as I note in my most recent theoretical book.[21] Reading what other feminist scholars have done, thinking about it, and theorizing the Holocaust as a feminist problem remains today as much of a challenge as ever.

21 Esther Fuchs, *Jewish Feminism: Framed and Reframed*, New York and London: Lexington Books, 2018.

Myrna Goldenberg

The Journey

The Origins

Incident 1: Bella in the College Bookstore

She tapped my shoulder as I browsed in the College bookstore very early in the semester. I turned and she said, "We're going to charge you rent." I recognized her as a student in my day class on Holocaust literature but couldn't understand why I owed her rent. She explained, "On Tuesday night, Hank and I talk about what you taught in the Tuesday morning class, and on Wednesday night, he tells me what you talked about in his Wednesday. We talk all night long and again on Thursday after he comes home from work and again you're in our conversation through the weekend."

> "I'm flattered, I think," I said.
> "You see," she went on, "we're both survivors and we took your class to make sure you taught it right."
> "And should I assume you both would speak up in class if I made a mistake and you'd set me straight, right?"
> "So far, so good. But we have to charge you rent because we live with you almost all week—or maybe you live with us!"

And so began a ten year close friendship between Hank, Bella, my husband and me. By extension, Bella's younger sister Irene—also a survivor— and her husband Carl became our close friends as well.

No more than five feet tall, Bella was a bright, very active, well-dressed blonde who appreciated and bought good clothing, jewelry, and dinners, and enjoyed theater, concerts, and a good party. Born in Lodz in 1922, she and her father tried to escape into the Soviet Union in 1939 when the Nazis attacked Poland. In their flight, they accidentally separated. She ended up in Oshmiany, at that point, under Soviet control, and got a clerical job with a Soviet officer who helped her learn Russian. She settled into her new community. Nearly two years later, on Sunday, June 22, 1941, on a bike ride with a friend, she heard the news that the Nazis broke their treaty with the Soviets and invaded the Soviet Union. Everything changed. Soon after, she was caught in a roundup and sent to Kaiserwald. In May, 1945, after incarceration in Kaiserwald, Stuthof, and Magdeborg, she escaped to the American side of the Elbe River, where she was liberated.

She always laughed when she spoke of seeing GIs throwing a small ball to one another. It seems so incongruous, she thought. "These tough American heroes playing ball like children."

She told her story to audiences at the United States Holocaust Memorial Museum (USHMM), colleges, other public venues, to school children, to anyone who was interested. Hank, on the other hand, had never spoken about his wartime experiences until he came home each Wednesday night and told Bella what we covered in Wednesday class. Bella said that he couldn't stop talking about his life under the Soviets and Nazis. His whole family had been deported from Riga and murdered. He had been a budding violinist who later saved his own life by claiming he was an electrician, a trade he assumed would be useful to the Nazis. He, too, was liberated from Magdeborg by the GIs.

Bella's and Hank's experiences inspired me to dig further for more information from survivors.

Incident 2 - Annette's Interviews

After about seven hours of talking about her experiences during the War, Annette excused herself to prepare dinner. She went into the kitchen while I pored over her bookcase and found *Le Memorial des Infants Juifs Deportes de France* by Serge Klarsfeld, the acclaimed book about French children who were deported and murdered because they were Jewish. I flipped through the pages and stopped suddenly when I recognized a familiar face (p. 804). There was a photo of a woman who reminded me of my mother! Of course, it couldn't be. My mother immigrated to the US as a toddler in 1908, along with her mother and 3 brothers and 1 sister. (The rest of her siblings were born in the US.) My grandfather, who had come to America several years earlier, had saved money to bring his wife and children to him. Grandma's sisters and brothers stayed in Tulchin, only to be murdered by Einsatzgruppen C, probably in 1941. The young French woman in the photograph was my mother's first cousin, named Fanny. She, the woman in the photo, bore a strong resemblance to my Mother who had occasionally spoken about her cousin. I now own a copy of that book, which has a prominent spot in one of the bookcases in the den and reminds me of my deep roots in the Shoah.

Annette, the subject of my interviews, prepared a remarkable French meal and insisted that I take a copy of the book home to my mother who confirmed that my identification of Fanny was right. She explained that Fanny's parents left Tulchin for Paris early in the century to flee the pogroms and to build a better life for their family. Most of that branch of the family did not survive the War.

My mother became sad when she talked about her mother's family. Her father, she said, was a tailor who sewed tunics for the czar's army. He also sewed shirts for his sons and, to save money, always cut them with no room to spare. As my uncles grew, the eldest handed his shirt down to the next son who did the same to the third son, and so on. As a result, uncle Harry, the oldest, wore shirts that were usually too tight and short for him.

My meetings with Annette, however, came to a bitter ending. I wrote the article about her that I expected to submit to a feminist journal and sent her the polished draft. She was indignant and even angry. That took me by surprise. Her rejection of the piece was based on her judgment that I hadn't exposed enough of the evil of the Nazis and didn't convey the horrors they inflicted on her and her family! In my defense, I explained that I didn't need to condemn the Nazis in so many words; my narration of her ordeal in Birkenau would lead the reader to that conclusion. She threatened me with a lawsuit if I published what I had written. I had shared the article with colleagues and even with a lawyer, all of whom said the article brought them to tears. The article remains in my desk drawer.

Incident 3: Bubbie's Scream

During the War, my Bubbie [Yiddish for grandmother], whose apartment was located one floor below ours, kept a close ear on the news from Europe in Yiddish. She was focused on Ukraine, her birthplace and still home to most of her cousins. Her youngest daughter, my aunt Annie, lived with Bubbie. One of her sons lived in a similar apartment on the floor below and another lived on the same floor. Her daughter, my mother, lived on the floor above. Thus, Bubbie was surrounded by four of her eight children. Two other children lived close by and a seventh was hospitalized. On Sundays, the "boys" straggled in, usually with a grandchild or two in tow, to pay respects and to give her a weekly allowance. Bubbie was free of financial worries, but not free of family worries. Most of her large family never left Ukraine, Tulchin or Odessa, to be specific, and she often sat in a world far away as she recalled them.

One Sunday morning, while I was upstairs listening to the Jewish Theological Seminary radio show "The Eternal Light" and my uncles were visiting with Bubbie, we heard a scream. Sure that it had come from Bubbie's kitchen, we raced downstairs to witness my grandmother sobbing and shaking. Her sons had given her the news that her siblings and extended family had been murdered by the Nazis. Whether it was weeks or months after the actual murder, I can't now know. Bubbie's generation is long dead, my uncles', aunts', and mother's generations as well. I know that some were murdered at Babi Yar; others, more likely in their villages.

My Bubbie's scream sears some of my quiet moments. At that time, I was in kindergarten with no knowledge of the War except that three of my cousins were serving in the military, two in the Navy and one in the Army, all in the Pacific. I did know that Bubbie's scream signified a tragedy. Within just a few years, I learned the nature of that tragedy.

In 1946, in that same kitchen, we welcomed my sixteen year old cousin Jean. With the help of HIAS (Hebrew Immigration Aid Society, now known by their initials), the family brought him over from Paris after the War. His parents had left Ukraine early in the century and settled in Paris. He knew very little English, had grayish teeth, and guzzled a quart of milk straight from the bottle when offered a glass of milk. Jean adapted to Brooklyn without trouble although it was clear that he missed his older sisters, who had chosen to remain in Paris. After his parents were deported when the Nazis took over the city, he was hidden in a sub cellar for three years; Hence, his decaying teeth. With help from various Jewish social service agencies, he flourished and went on to Ohio State to study architecture.

Incident 4: Mauthausen

Nearly forty years ago, I accompanied my husband on one of his business trips to the International Atomic Energy Agency (IAEA), housed in Vienna. I had never been to Vienna, so here was an opportunity to visit the sites and the coffee houses, known for their specialties *mit shlag*. It was mid-February and very cold but clear. Neal worked during the day, and I explored the city and the Schonbrunn Palace, the Belvedere, St. Stephen's, and the cafes. With other tourists, I enjoyed the fabulous Anker clock and was even invited to the opening of the opera by a distinguished looking gray haired British gentleman, who told me where I could rent an appropriate gown for the opening of the opera. Instead of the rental store, I walked to Freud's apartment, inhaled his presence, and stayed awhile. In fact, Vienna felt so hostile that I returned to the comfort and safety of Freud's apartment twice more. I was met with cold stares and ugly remarks during that week. When I attempted to buy a pack of cigarettes in a tiny newspaper/tobacco shop, my German sounded too much like Yiddish to the shopkeeper. She spat at me and turned her back. Too many neighborhoods were decorated with anti-Israel posters and anti-Jewish graffiti, all of which discomfited me.

I was ready for something different. I was not prepared for horror. Vienna was not far from the Mauthausen concentration camp, so we planned an excursion. On our way to Mauthausen, in a car borrowed from the American Embassy, we drove past thick beautiful forests of tall evergreens and planned where we'd stop for coffee on the return trip.

We pulled into Mauthausen in upper Austria and used the American Ambassador's briefing book to guide us through the newly opened camp. It was eerily quiet. Besides the staff, we were the only ones in the camp and walked through somberly. At one point, we followed different hallways. I didn't know where Neal was, but I found myself in a rectangular shaped white tiled room. Parts of the walls were streaked blue. I looked up and saw shower heads; I looked down but really didn't expect to find drains. There weren't any.

I heard myself scream but remember nothing else until I was aware that I was in a different building, tiled but not scary, in a bathroom stall. Nevertheless, I feared leaving the stall, sure that there would be a fierce woman guard waiting to take me back to a barracks.

Of course, there wasn't. Nor did we stop for coffee on the way back to our boarding house in Vienna.

Sleep eluded me. When I closed my eyes, I was back in that white tiled room —the gas chamber. After many sleepless, restless nights, I needed to control the experience rather than have it dominate and paralyze me. So, I immersed myself in every book in English that dealt with the Holocaust and was available to me to prepare myself to teach a course on Holocaust literature. Books written by men were generally available and became my bedrock for firsthand accounts of what happened until I met Sybil Milton and Joan Ringelheim, both of who worked at the United States Holocaust Memorial Museum (USHMM) and asked the question, where are the women?

That was a tipping point for me. I searched for and found the titles of Holocaust memoirs written by women. Most were out of print, so I shopped second hand book stores for women's Holocaust memoirs. So did other feminist scholars of Holocaust history. What we found, we shared. And, when possible, we mimeographed copies of the originals and shared those. Charlotte Delbo's remarkable memoir in play form, "None of Us Shall Return" was my introduction to women's Holocaust memoirs. Our private and collective libraries grew, as did our participation at various scholarly meetings. We knew we were having an impact when Gabriel Shoenfeld, editor of *Commentary* magazine, sent me the issue that included his article, "Auschwitz and the Professors," which was essentially a diatribe against the formal study of the Holocaust in academe. He particularly targeted articles and books written by women about women. When I was named as one of the six or seven offenders (all of us women), I felt assured that I was in the right discipline, doing important work. We countered his nasty remarks with accounts of the work we were doing. Much to my surprise, he apologized to me for taking my comments out of context.

The Effect

What's the point of recounting these events? To begin this essay, I thought about my journey to this point of my professional life. Except for my husband and Joan, just about everyone involved in these incidents is dead; the events, though, are fresh in my memory, active in my dreams, and raise questions and comments that can't be answered readily or easily answered but, at the same time, questions that I can't refrain from asking. Upon reflection, I ask myself whether my preoccupation with the Holocaust was inevitable. I think I've seen dozens of movies that deal with the Holocaust, from the very good ones like **The Pianist** to good ones like **Schindler's List** to very bad and misleading ones, like **The Boy in the Striped Pajamas**.

Clearly, my professional journey moved from an intense focus on American literature to an even more intense focus on Women's Studies to an exclusive focus on the Shoah. Has that journey changed me? Now that I'm thinking about it, of course. I see that I'm influenced by many sources and fiercely anti-war, yet I know that I can easily rationalize and justify defensive wars. I have a gut feeling that the atrocities I have read about beginning with but not ending with the Holocaust have given me a palpable horror of war. In fact, my studies have surely made me more considerate of others and impatient with bullies and liars and egotists.

As I read about the Holocaust and began to teach it, I became aware of the moral burden it brought. The purpose of teaching the subject is far more than the transmission of a set of events even though the Holocaust, in my opinion, is unique and a valuable subject in and of itself. I felt that teaching the subject was urgent. Students needed to be aware of the vulnerability of democracy, needed to understand, value, and protect freedom of thought and action. We all need to learn to recognize early political movements that challenged these freedoms.

While my research focused and still focuses on women's experiences, I found the earmarks of what constitutes moral behavior on the individual and collective levels. Clearly, just plain luck was the major factor in survival. The randomness of survival could not be the only factor. To survive, a prisoner also needed kindness, friendship, help, and compassion from fellow prisoners. Whether one argues that we are either born with such characteristics or not, we can learn them and by doing so, give the comfort that strengthens the will to survive. Women, particularly in the early and mid-twentieth century, were expected to take on these roles. Many transferred what they had routinely done for others before the Holocaust to the camps, in essence, caring for someone else, usually at a great personal risk. Neither sex is born with a "caring" gene, but women were more practiced in the caregiving role than men. By virtue of the social and political systems, men were expected to be independent and strong and able to provide for others. "Providing for" is a subset of caring, but in the ghettos and camps, caring carried more weight than providing. Caring, then and now, includes providing for another, but providing for may not be a caring or compassionate action.

The unique biological vulnerabilities of women were not addressed by my male colleagues. Yet surely pregnancy and sexual victimization were elements of survival and death. Pregnant women were deported and imprisoned and gave birth to babies who were often smothered, or otherwise killed (usually to save the mother's life). The Third Reich would not tolerate more Jews, so they were often killed as a way to keep their bodies from the Nazis who might have used them as subjects of inhumane experiments or as a reason to murder both mother and baby. Women were vulnerable to rape; Jewish women more so, considering that they were in no position to fight back, but rape by Aryan men constituted race-mixing, or *rassenschande*, deemed serious criminal behavior by the Nazi regime. At a conference, when I explained the issue of rape and its consequences to the victim and the perpetrator, one of my colleagues interrupted my talk to shout, "...couldn't have happened. It was against the law." When the laughter of the class abated, we talked about the preoccupation of the Nazis with sexuality and rape.

In the mid-1960s, we moved to Montgomery County, Maryland, just a few blocks from the DC border, and I became active in civil rights causes. I hardly missed a major or minor protest in support of civil/women's/human rights. I suppose that at least two sentences from favorite authors are chiseled in my brain: "Injustice anywhere is injustice everywhere" by Martin Luther King and Margaret Atwood's "War is what happens when language fails."

I don't "see" the Holocaust everywhere, but I unconsciously consider it a basis by which to measure political leaders and their behavior, including those in the United States and Israel. The rise of white supremacy in the United States has unmistakable connections to the Nazi era. It reminds me of the 1930s in Germany and frankly scares me. Indeed, although I have stopped wondering which of my neighbors would hide me in the event of a pogrom, I still think about my options if the unthinkable should occur. I also try to remember what Nesse Godin, survivor from Shaulai, warned me: "Go to all the camps and murder sites that you want, but remember [and here she always shook her finger at me] after living with the grim history all day, go out for dinner with your husband and dance and have fun. If not, you will be giving the Nazis a victory."

The study of the Holocaust has influenced my life in other ways. Specifically, I'm a better teacher—more sensitive and compassionate. I was teaching Holocaust literature to an undergraduate class and noticed that a young man who had had perfect attendance was missing from a session or two. As was my habit, I phoned him to find out whether he was ill. His mother answered the phone and apologized to me, explaining that the family was ethnically German and the course affected him deeply. He was a Vietnam War veteran and a recovering alcoholic. When he became aware of the roles of his extended family members, still in Germany and what he perceived to be their complicity because they never expressed a rejection of Nazism, he was crushed. He "fell off the wagon," said his mother and he couldn't return to class. Guilt ridden, I then apologized to her. "Not my fault," she insisted repeatedly. Yet, that experience made me re-think my Holocaust courses. I never again assumed my students would not be both intellectually and emotionally affected by my lectures and assignments.

I questioned my exclusive focus on Holocaust victims and survivors and began to discuss choices made by the perpetrators and bystanders. The issue of choice sparked a great deal of interesting discussion and journals. I assigned journal writing as responses to the reading assignments and classroom discussions to better understand the effects of the course content on my students. I noticed two effects: students read the books more closely and they felt free to express their feelings as well as their text-based commentary. Their responses reinforced issues that challenged me; their journal entries suggested that teaching any facet of the Holocaust led to multi-disciplinary aspects of the Holocaust. Teaching the Holocaust involves teaching its history as well as its philosophy, political science, drama, literature, music, and the visual arts. Some students raised the role of God, at which point I usually answered by asking questions of the student. Teaching the history was clearly necessary to contextualize the memoirs and important but not sufficient.

When I became a docent at the USHMM, guiding visitors through the permanent exhibition on the history of the Holocaust and through another exhibition, "Some Were Neighbors," I had a somewhat unnerving experience. After some of the tours, a Museum visitor from my group would stay behind to tell me that her or his grandparents had been Nazis but had never talked about their roles in the War. Their inevitable question was whether they should confront those elders. "To what end?" I would ask. If they had a close or good relationship with the grandparent, what purpose would a confrontation with an 80 or 90+ year old serve? I was never confident that the answer was the right one, but I felt and still feel that grandparents who never talked about the War and especially about the intention to kill all Jews would either lie about their role in the War or become angry at the grandchild. On the other hand, I encouraged the questioners to talk to their parents about Germany's aggression that began the War.

At this point of my life, I buy fewer books about the Holocaust than I used to. Yet, because the Holocaust seems to be of interest to most people and because most survivors will be dead within a few years, I accept invitations to speak and visit more and more exhibits on the topic. I wonder what to do with my extensive Holocaust library. Even the most casual visitor to my home can identify my pre-occupation with the subject. I am trying to wean myself from the topic, but I confess to being drawn back to this field and enjoy being an active part of this remarkable community of feminist scholars. I think back to the early 1980s and the isolation so many Holocaust academics faced; usually, we were the only faculty members in our schools whose research focus was the Holocaust. We met with our peers at conferences, built long lasting friendships, followed one another's progress and papers, and nurtured these connections, but usually gained promotions and tenure based on our work in other fields. That has changed, to be sure. AMEN

Sara R. Horowitz

Working the Margins

Introduction:

As a literary scholar, I inhabit a peculiar place in the field of Holocaust studies. In an area of study dominated by historians, looking at the Shoah through the lens of literature has long occupied a small, contested, and marginal space. To put it baldly, most historians don't know what to make of it. Even though by the 1990s there was a recognized canon of Holocaust literature and quite a number of universities offered courses in the area, many historians of the Holocaust did not see literature as a serious path to knowledge about the Shoah. At best, they saw it as a sentimental genre for those not quite up to the rigors of historical study. At worst, its imaginative license posed a threat to a commitment to uncovering the truth about what happened to the Jews of Europe. In a sense, if you centered your research on literature of the Shoah, you worked at the margins, a bit of an outsider in the field.

There is a price, of course, for working at the margins. But there are also distinct advantages. You learn to trust your intuition, your intellectual labor, your analyses. You take for granted the skepticism of your audience. You see every article, every conference presentation as an opportunity for education, for persuasion. Those factors were important, as well, as I engaged in work pertaining to women and the Shoah. When I became interested in writing about women and the Holocaust, most of the leading scholars in the field were dismissive. Employing gender as a category of analysis was misguided, many insisted. At best, it was irrelevant; the Nazi genocide was enacted on the basis of "race," gender simply did not matter. At worst, they warned, it was dangerous, distorting history for ideological purposes. The adamance of these critical voices made clear that thinking about women was relegated to the margins of the study of the Holocaust. But I had already determined that the margins could be a productive place.

Literature and History

Although my interest in Holocaust literature and my interest in women during the Shoah did not arise simultaneously, the trajectories are intertwined, and I can't map one without also mapping the other. If the ritual of the dissertation defense marks the official beginning of an academic career, then the particular challenges that shaped my career were present from the onset.

As anyone with a PhD knows, the composition of the panel of examiners at a dissertation defense always has an element of fraught unpredictability. In addition to the PhD candidate's supervisor and dissertation committee, there are examiners with whom the dissertation writer has no history, no relationship. Depending on the university and the department, someone will be charged with representing the institution and ensuring that institutional standards have been met. And then there will be "outsiders" – arms-length professors from other departments or other institutions, whose expertise and objectivity ensure that the work has merit in the field. In my case, although my degree was in comparative literature, because my dissertation focused on certain aspects of Holocaust literature, a distinguished historian was invited to be the outside evaluator.

As often happens, the questioning follows a particular order. The examiner most distanced from the PhD candidate begins, followed by those less distanced, and ending with the candidate's supervisor. At my defense, the courtesy of beginning the examination was accorded the historian. We had never met, and he had seen my dissertation only as a completed project. He began by describing his experience reading the dissertation. Effusive with praise, he called it fascinating, moving, beautifully written. Then came the kicker. "But," he said, "I just can't see the point of work like this. What use it is? How is it relevant? It's not history." I was, I admit, caught by surprise. As an opening gambit, it struck me as, well, undermining the entire worth of my dissertation. His demeanor was genial, but the challenge was real. I was surprised, but I was not unprepared to answer. By then I'd been to enough conferences and read enough articles to have encountered that attitude, and to have developed some responses. I took a breath. I think I even smiled. I'm glad you asked that, I began.

In essence, I treated it as a teaching moment, although that term was not yet current. Here was someone who simply did not yet understand. My task was to educate. I'll never know whether I succeeded in turning him around in his heart of hearts – that is, whether my argument persuaded him of the contributions of literary studies. For the purpose at hand – a dissertation defense – it sufficed. In the aftermath, my advisor tried to diminish the attack. "Well," he said, "you know, he felt he had to say that. As a historian, of course." In other words, the attack was not personal. Rather, my interlocutor acted as a representative of one discipline, marking its turf against an interloper. While it certainly felt "personal" at the time, the distinction that my advisor drew proved useful. Strategically, I find it helpful to consider attacks on one's academic work not as a weapon aimed at my person, but as an invitation to debate, to argue, to demonstrate, to persuade. Even – perhaps especially – on those few occasions when there was a personal element. I'll come back to some of those occasions later.

Thinking about Women

As anyone whose research centers on the Shoah knows, the subject takes hold and overwhelms. While my early writing focused on representations by and about both men and women, it was not until I began teaching Holocaust literature that I began to think actively about gender. It was the first time I had taught the course, and we were approaching the mid-semester point. Several of my undergraduate students asked me why so few of the course readings were by women. The question caught me by surprise. In preparing the syllabus, I had been attentive to the variety of experiences during the Shoah, and had purposefully included a wide range of sources. I thought about genre, geography, social and religious strata. My students were reading diaries, memoirs, fiction, and poetry, things written during and after the war. The works they read were written by victims who did not survive the Nazi genocide, as well as by survivors who had been in ghettoes, in labor camps, or in hiding; writers encompassed children, adults, religious, secular, eastern or western European, Jewish, not Jewish. But it had not occurred to me to pay attention to the gender of the writer, or to include gender at all as a factor in class discussions. After all, as everyone in the field at the time seemed to agree, it was racial ideology, and Jewishness in particular, that propelled Nazi ideology, targeting Jewish men and women equally for death, as Jews.

So my students' question caught me short. Because if, as the scholarly consensus had it, the horrors of the Shoah affected women and men alike, how had my list of primary readings turned out to have such a gender imbalance? Why were we not reading many women authors? Not because women were not important, or didn't write; not because their writing didn't measure up. But many works by women survivors had gone out quickly of print and so were not easy to assign as class readings. More importantly, scholarly work in the field that had shaped my thinking about how to teach Holocaust literature discussed the writing of women victims and survivors with far less frequency than that of men. And when they did discuss women, they tended to cite them as illustrations of suffering and victimization, but rarely as subjects, as thinkers, as interpreters of experience – such as Primo Levi or Jean Améry or Elie Wiesel – who not only experienced, but reflected on the implications of their experiences and the historical phenomena that enfolded them.

I began to wonder whether reading works written by women victims and survivors, alongside those by men, and paying attention to gender, would reveal different sets of experiences, different perspectives, different interpretive prisms, different aftereffects. If so, I wanted to know, what might those differences be, and what might that teach us not only about women's experiences during the Shoah, but about the Holocaust more broadly. This was the mid-1980s, and little had been published about women's memories and experiences during the Shoah. But a handful of scholars working out of several disciplines, and largely independently from one another embarked upon research projects that engaged the subject of women in the Holocaust. After all, by that time virtually every discipline had been influenced by the insights of women's studies. We understood that gender was crucial to understanding human experience. We knew it had to be significant in thinking about inhuman experience.

My engagement with literature and with women in the context of the Holocaust was not only sequential, but interrelated. When I discussed the way historians refused to countenance literature as a serious vehicle for reflecting on the Shoah, the late Paula Hyman would often remind me, "Not all historians, Sara. Not all historians." Of course, she was correct. In my experience, women historians tended to be more receptive to the insights of literary studies. I attribute that to the interest of many of them in social history – attending to daily life in a range of socio-political contexts. Literary writing helped establish that broad context, and the perspectives of individuals caught up in it. Even more importantly, at a time when many historians of the Holocaust regarded with suspicion, if not outright rejection, personalized sources such as oral testimonies and memoirs, literary theory had already developed an arsenal of tools to understand them. Many of the historians who laid the foundations for Holocaust history were reluctant to accept the first-hand accounts of Holocaust survivors, preferring instead to build historical knowledge from "official" sources – in large measure, documents produced by perpetrators and abettors of the Nazi genocide. Survivor accounts, many historians believed, were too subjective, too limited, to prone to factual error. They were considered unreliable as evidence in reconstructing an accurate picture of the past. When historians did cite memoirs, oral or videotaped testimonies, it was primarily to provide a cogent and moving illustration of a set of facts that had already been determined from other, more "reliable" sources. And when survivor testimony conflicted with official documents, the testimony was always thought to be in error.

Literary scholars were among the first to take seriously the first-hand accounts of Holocaust survivors, reading memoirs and listening to taped accounts to better understand the inner landscape of those who suffered under Nazism, and to gain a more complex understanding of the past and its impact on the present. By the early twenty-first century, attitudes shifted, and important historical projects relied heavily on testimonies and memoirs. But well before that, people doing research on women during the Holocaust understood how valuable such sources were – crucial to developing a broader understanding of women in a variety of contexts during the Shoah. In my conversations with women historians working on issues of gender and the

Shoah, their focus was not on guarding disciplinary borders, but on mining the porousness of disciplinary boundaries for the insights that could yield.

Marginal Yields

My first academic position was in an English literature department at a state university in the United States. My colleagues there could not understand the fuss made by leading historians of the Holocaust about the incompatibility of history and literature. After all, my colleagues reasoned, we studied literature of the French revolution, of the Civil War, of the Russian revolution, of World War I – and countless other cataclysmic historical moments. Why not literature of the Holocaust? I believe that the attitudes of the first generation of Holocaust historians (and many later ones) were tinged by the argument of the uniqueness of the Holocaust, that what pertained to other historical phenomena could not be neatly overlaid on the study of the Nazi genocide. But they also reflected an opposition of imagination to facticity, and an insistence on the scientific rigor of history vis a vis the play of literature. I often though of the distinguished Jewish historiographer Yosef Hayim Yerushalmi's statement about history and literature of the Holocaust. He observed that, notwithstanding the abundant research about the history of the Holocaust, he had "no doubt whatever that its image is being shaped, not at the historian's anvil, but in the novelist's crucible."[1] Many historians understood him as bemoaning the trivializing impact of genres of the imagination on the general public. But Yerushalmi was a historian who was drawn to literature. He was thinking not so much of the ability of literary writing to bend facts out of shape, but its proclivity to probe their meaning, to ask difficult questions about the human implications of history.

Although my departmental colleagues supported my work on Holocaust literature, and encouraged me to develop undergraduate and graduate courses on it, my status at the university was precarious. I had been hired to fill a position owned jointly by the English department and the university's Honor Program. The Honors Program offered special courses open to the top 5 % of the students. Classes were small, the students bright and motivated. The Honors Program was often referred to as an ivy league education at state university tuition rates. For those of us hired to teach in it, it was an exciting and privileged kind of teaching. But there was a down side for us. To resolve a turf battle between the Honors Program and the departments when the program was first inaugurated, it had been decided that such joint

1 Yosef Hayim Yerushalmi, *Zakhor: Jewish History and Jewish Memory*, Seattle: University of Washington Press, 1982, 98.

hires would be limited to four-year non-renewable contracts and not eligible for tenure. While my English colleagues were genial, I did not have a vote at department meetings. I told people I held a folding chair at my university.

Not long after I began teaching there, several colleagues across the university asked if I would help establish a Jewish studies program. Although my cohorts at other universities cautioned my against investing energy in an institution where I had no future – energy that could be turned towards publishing that would further my career – I was excited by the prospect of making real institutional change, something that could have an impact beyond my own classroom. I reached across disciplines to find colleagues to teach a range of new Jewish studies courses. Working to marshal broad support for the program, I forged alliances between Jewish studies and other nascent programs – what we then referred to as programs of the "other." I brought in donors to help anchor Jewish studies. The university soon found a mechanism to shift my position to a tenurable line.

By that time, the gender wars that roiled American universities were still ongoing, but the casualties had diminished. In other words, at least where I taught, many male colleagues would make snide offhand comments about academic work focusing on women, but this deprecating attitude towards women's studies no longer posed a barrier to tenure. As my work increasingly engaged women and the Holocaust, I found common ground with colleagues in English, in women's studies, in history, in African American studies, and other programs and departments. As for Jewish studies – an area notably slow to incorporate women's and gender studies – well, I had founded our university's program and served as its first director. From the outset, work done under its aegis integrated the lens of gender.

You could say that I benefitted precisely from working at the margins. Unlike colleagues in Jewish studies at many other institutions, my tenurability was not impeded by conservative trends in the field. Unlike my colleagues in history at other many other institutions, who bore the consequences of entrenched biases against applying the lens of gender to the study of the Shoah, working on women in the compass of literary studies did not pose a threat in my home institution. I never worried that the focus of my research would play a negative role as my department considered me for tenure.

Of course, our academic work does not live in the confines of our institution. While my university colleagues did not view as controversial the way that my work engaged the Holocaust through the prisms of literature and gender, in the larger arena, each of those approaches were embattled. Pioneering studies in Holocaust literature felt the weight of that marginality, the suspicion of irrelevance or subversion. In anticipation, their authors and editors often argued explicitly for a place at the seminar table, acknowledging the sheer horror of the events of the Shoah, and the responsibility not to trivialize or "academize" them. Similarly, as the work on women and the Holocaust developed, researchers labored against the accusation that a focus on women would ultimately eclipse the Holocaust, subverting its irredeemable horror to a more domesticated *histoire des femmes*. Editors of an early anthology on women in the Holocaust took pains to assert, in their introduction to the volume, that "asking questions about what happened to women in the Holocaust" does not "in any way minimiz[e] the horror of what the Nazis did to all Jews."[2] Defending the book – and gendered approaches more broadly – against harsh criticism, former director of the U.S. Holocaust Memorial Museum Michael Berenbaum insisted that such scholarship "has respect for its craft, fear and trembling for the event it studies, and a sensitivity for its victims."[3] These very defenses, of course, demonstrate the embattled positions that these two areas of inquiry – literary studies and gender studies – continued to occupy in the study of the Holocaust.

Battle Scars

Because I so clearly saw a parallel between the ambivalent place of literature in Holocaust studies and the embattled place of women's studies, and because my home department supported my work along both of those approaches, I anticipated that more established scholars who wrote about literature and the Shoah would encourage my work on women. But that wasn't always the case. When I began developing ideas about women and the Holocaust, I corresponded at length with a distinguished colleague whom I had come to regard as a mentor. He tried to warn me away from pursuing that line of inquiry, pointing to several early articles about women during the Shoah that he found deeply flawed. I expected him to urge me to make sure to be thorough, rigorous, to do better. To my surprise, he told me he believed I was on the wrong track altogether. Although he wished me well, he feared for me professionally – feared that the quality of my work would deteriorate if I focused on women. His was not the only friendly warning I received. Several other senior colleagues who had been supportive of my work reiterated what they saw as the pitfalls of paying attention to gender. They offered cautionary advice not in response to anything I'd written – my work was still at the conceptual stage – but simply in response to the idea of looking at women, at gender as a factor. Although in their own work they

2 *Women in the Holocaust*, ed. Dalia Ofer and Lenore J. Weitzman, New Haven: Yale University Press, 1998.

3 *Commentary* (August 1998).

made important distinctions, looking at such categories as nationality, religious observance, age, social strata, or political ideology—they somehow believed that paying attention to gender as a factor would result in distortion or trivialities.

I believe they meant it kindly; they were trying to save me from what they saw as a career-killing mistake. I felt disappointed but not threatened by their response to the ideas I had floated to them. The relative equanimity of my reaction to these warnings does not mean that I did not feel – that I do not feel – passionately about my work and about what is at stake in it. But it would be fair to say that these responses evoked in me a certain mixture of obtuseness and obstinacy. I regarded their hesitations as an opening – you might even say an imperative – to educate, to persuade, to turn them around. Sometimes I succeeded, and sometimes not.

Only on a few rare occasions did I encounter something different from a fair and tempered scholarly disagreement. In 1995, Dalia Ofer and Lenore Weitzman convened an International Workshop on Women and the Holocaust in Jerusalem. Those of us who participated remember it as intense, stimulating, challenging, and productive. As part of the workshop, I was invited to deliver a public presentation on women in Holocaust literature at Yad Vashem. By that time, I had published several articles women in the Shoah. I had been recently tenured and promoted to associate professor, and I directed my university's Jewish studies program. I felt deeply honored to speak at Yad Vashem, and to be, in a sense, the public face of the workshop.

When I arrived at Yad Vashem the evening of my talk, the organizers told me that there would be a "respondent" to my presentation. The daily format of the workshop had not incorporated formal responses to papers. Rather, all participants engaged in discussing one another's papers. So I was surprised to see that format introduced for my public lecture. Even more irregular, the respondent was not a participant in our workshop. A senior and influential scholar, he had approached the organizers and said he wanted to comment on my presentation. They felt compelled to agree.

It was the only time in my professional life that I was cut down in public. My respondent tugged at threads in my argument, mischaracterizing things I said. Although I had never met my critic before, this one felt personal. I later learned that he had been one of the evaluators for a manuscript submitted to a university press that contained an essay I had written on Spielberg's film, *Schindler's List*. My essay looked at the representation of women in the film, and the ways in which gendered representations shaped the film's import. I focused on the way that the film reproduced gendered European antisemitic stereotypes, undercutting its own critique of Nazi ideology. The essay suggested that Spielberg had set up the film as a contest of masculinity between Amon Goeth, the Kommandant of Auschwitz, and Oscar Schindler, the heroic rescuer. The evaluator gave the manuscript a mixed review, liking some of the essays in it more than others. He had singled out my essay as particularly problematic, I later learned, for "taking feminism too far."

Although it felt personal, I decided to play it as though it were not. After he finished, I walked back up to the microphone. I thanked him publicly for his attention to my presentation. I told him I had found his own work on Holocaust literature important. And then I said I needed to correct some the ways he had misunderstood my presentation. I laid out, point by point, why his objections were misguided. Truth to tell, I don't think I persuaded him. But neither did I allow him final say, nor let his comments bend my arguments out of shape. (My niece, then in her early twenties, was in the audience. "You told it to him, *doda* [aunt] *sara*," she told me later.) I spoke to my respondent respectfully because I wanted to coopt him, and also because I chose to model a different kind of discourse.

Controversies

The dimensions of this hostility towards women's studies in its intersection with the study of the Holocaust became clear in a public debate I engaged in on the pages of the literary journal *Prooftexts*. In the late 1990s, the journal editors invited me to contribute to a special issue whose focus was "Reading through the Lens of Gender." At their request, I explored what the perspective of gender contributed to the study of the Shoah. In my article,[4] which was published in 2000, I incorporated some readings of texts by women and by men, as illustrations of how the lens of gender might make us notice things we had not seen before, or understand them differently. More broadly, I discussed the impediments to having work on women taken seriously in the field of Holocaust studies, and the misconceptions that I believed led some of its staunchest critics to reject it as a productive avenue of inquiry. I mentioned in passing an article that had just appeared in *Commentary* and had been excerpted almost immediately in the *Wall Street Journal*. The article began by criticizing the academization of Holocaust studies – its "stultifying terminology" and "dispassionate" discourse. As the article progressed, it became clear that what rankled its author most of all was the consideration of gender in the Holocaust. This, he insisted, was a "voguish endeavor," "the worst of sins" and "the worst excesses of all." Women – feminists – who worked on aspects of gender or women's experiences during the Shoah,

4 Sara R. Horowitz, "Gender, Genocide, and Jewish Memory," *Prooftexts* 20 (January 2000) 1:158–190.

he argued, did so not to further an "honest understanding" of the events but to promote a "naked ideological agenda" to "target the male sex" and to perform "consciousness-raising."[5] They were poor writers, far worse than their male colleagues. In their scholarship, these women enacted a "macabre sisterhood with the dead Jewish women of Europe." Although I did not discuss the *Commentary* article at length, in a footnote I referred to it as "ideologically driven," and an "extreme example" of how a hostile reader "willfully misreads" the target of his ire.

The author of the *Commentary* article took issue with my article. One of the senior editors of *Prooftexts*, whom the author believed shared his views, agreed to publish his critique of my essay. In it, he accused me and unnamed "others" of "circl[ing] the wagon around some of the offensive rubbish generated by 'gender analysis.'" In particular, he challenged the way I had characterized his essay in my footnote. The editors invited me to respond to him, and the two pieces were published together in a later issue of the journal.[6]

The *Commentary* article bemoaning the outcome of "academizing" the Holocaust and laying its study open to "trendy" but ultimately dangerous new methodological approaches, such as focusing on women, staked out one side of a growing divide. It was one of several pieces that the magazine and other non-academic publications ran in the mid- to late 1990s decrying the "falsifying" and distorting incursion of women's studies into Jewish studies scholarship. While most of these articles grounded their arguments in close critical readings of particular books or articles they found flawed and problematic, they also made overarching statements about women's studies, feminism, and gender analysis. They saw its proponents as "progressive," often anti-religious, or anti-Zionist, or anti-Judaic. But in actuality, the scholarship – and the scholars – who were pushing to integrate the study of women into Jewish studies were philosophically and ideologically diverse – perhaps more so than their critics.

Listening to Women

I began my 2000 essay in *Prooftexts* with the following sentence: "Under the shadow of genocide, why gender?" That remains, for me, the most important question. What's at stake when we think about women in the Holocaust?

I've laid out the trajectories of my academic work on women in the Shoah and given it context, punctuating it with anecdotes that illustrate some of

5 Gabriel Schoenfeld, "Auschwitz and the Professors," *Commentary* (June 1998).

6 Gabriel Schoenfeld, "Feminist Approaches to the Holocaust," *Prooftexts* 21 (Spring 2001), 2: 277–279; Sara R. Horowitz, "A Response to Gabriel Schoenfeld," *Prooftexts* 21 (Spring 2001), 2: 279–283.

the challenges faced by those of us who insisted on bringing our questions about women into the ongoing conversation about the Shoah. I first came to write about the Shoah and its literary reflections not for familial reasons – my extended family left Europe decades earlier – but because it seemed to me to raise the crucial issues for our time. As a Jewish woman born after the war and a continent away, the fact that the Holocaust happened put on the line all certainties – about humanity and humanism, Judaism and the Jewish God, philosophical traditions and political ideologies. Most of all, the unspeakable devastation of human lives, people who deserve to be remembered, acknowledged, accounted for. What you read, what you hear, what you learn does not let go of you.

In outlining the pulls on my academic work, I skipped over one important set of interactions – my conversations with women survivors and their responses to my work. Several months after my 1995 lecture at Yad Vashem, I participated in a public event held at the U.S. Holocaust Memorial Museum in Washington that focused on American responses to the Holocaust. I was part of a panel discussing American literature about the Shoah. Although the panel was not about gender per se, my presentation explored the way that women were depicted in novels and memoirs about the Shoah that were written by men. My contention was that we should not read these as straightforward and accurate descriptions of women's experiences during the Holocaust. Sometimes the torment of women also functioned as a screen on which the author projected memories of his own humiliation and anguish, too painful to narrate outright. Some writing eroticized women, as victims or as perpetrators. I contrasted that with the way women write about themselves, or about other women. During the question and answer period, several men took issue with my focus on women. But several women survivors in the audience spoke out. They said they were heartened that young women scholars were paying attention to what happened to women, both during and after the war. They felt that so much of what they had endured remained unwritten, unspoken. Afterwards, more women survivors approached me to tell me their stories.

Over time, and especially when I began speaking in non-academic venues about my work, women shared memories with me. They told me stories, handed me scraps of memoirs, poems, letters. Once, after I spoke at a sisterhood luncheon at an Orthodox synagogue, a woman stood up and floored everyone by announcing, "Mengele was my first gynecologist." What she meant, we learned, was that she had been part of a group of adolescents in Auschwitz upon whom Mengele performed atrocious "medical experiments" on their reproductive organs. She talked about her fear – the shared fear of all the young women in that cohort who survived the war – that these torments had irreversibly damaged them – that they would not be able to bear children. She shared, too, the relief as one after another of those women became pregnant and gave birth.[7]

What I learned from women survivors – from personal conversations, letters, and interviews as well as from memoirs and testimonies – drove my academic writing. Their stories shattered gender stereotypes. As years went by, many women felt driven to leave a more complete account of what they had seen and experienced. They also devastated me, with accounts of sexual barter, assault and rape, infanticide – events almost too unbearable to think about. Their plunge into memory often cost them. They relived as they remembered.

How could we not listen?

7 I discuss this at length in Sara R. Horowitz, "Mengele, the Gynecologist, and Other Stories of Women's Survival," in *Judaism Since Gender*, ed. Miram Peskowitz and Laura Levitt, New York: Routledge, 1997, 200–212.

Phyllis Lassner

A Bridge to Build: Holocaust and Modern Cultural Studies

Introduction

They were only virtual boats – little destroyers, cruisers, battleships, and aircraft carriers – bobbing on ocean waves. The twelve inch TV that projected these images made their reality seem even more unreal, but the 26 episodes of *Victory at Sea* brought home the battles that in 1953, had been over for eight years.[1] Despite the distance of time and reprise of one fateful sea battle after another, there was an urgency in the sonorous voiceover and tense musical score that compelled us to watch. From beginning to end, the series' relentless rhythm ran parallel to the accretion of my knowledge: that victory on the Atlantic and Pacific oceans was never guaranteed just because it turned out that way. *Victory at Sea* was my initiation into a lifelong fascination with World War II. Every Sunday afternoon at 3:00, I would share our family room couch with my father, forging a common interest as a way of being close, but I also became captivated by the urgency of a victory that as the narrator intoned, with all its human and strategic costs, made us safe.

I should say kept us safe because there was never any sense in my family that we were ever in any danger. In the war's aftermath, even as newspapers reported the arrivals of war torn refugees, my parents never mentioned the Holocaust. All my grandparents immigrated to the United States at the turn of the century. My mother would occasionally mention a cousin, reputed to have been an opera singer, and who may have been trapped while performing in Italy. Besides this speculation, our cousin's presence is known only through her name, Regina, which my mother chose for my youngest sister. In retrospect, whatever problems afflicted our family, Nazi persecution wasn't one of them.

1 The series, created by Henry Salomon, a former US Navy Lieutenant Commander, narrated by Leonard Graves, with music by Richard Rodgers and Robert Russell Bennett, ran from October 26, 1952 to May 3, 1953, winning Emmy and Peabody awards for documentary public affairs programming.

Charting a Literary Journey to Holocaust Knowledge

Because it was through literature that the Nazi persecution of the Jews and the Holocaust entered my consciousness and then compelled me to learn its history and explore its representation, this essay will follow that course. It begins inauspiciously with my graduate work in the late 1970s that focused on the development of the English novel but, as I will explore, did not include the political or experiential realities of either the war or the Holocaust. How this recognition was impelled by feminist studies of literature and war constitutes another chapter in my story. The fact that this encounter coincided with my discovery of anti-antisemitic British women writers accounts for the argumentative position on which my journey pivots. For I also discovered that these courageous women writers had been overshadowed by Virginia Woolf as the iconic anti-war feminist, a position I then challenged in two research projects that I explore next and which facilitated my progress to studying women and the Holocaust. This progress was then expedited by serendipitous discoveries of women Holocaust writers whose lasting impressions on me I embed in analyses of their works. More directly, if I can't claim that I have built a bridge between modern cultural studies and Holocaust Studies, I conclude by arguing for its necessity.

The Lessons of Feminist Literary Studies

I don't think any war was ever considered more than a backdrop to the canon's aesthetic structures and eternal meanings. Likewise, it was only because of the influence of the women's liberation movement that Joanne Creighton, my dissertation advisor, observed that even those women writers who were considered exceptional barely squeezed into the pantheon of male greats. Mostly male critics assumed that the messages evinced from the lives of women writers and women protagonists did not rise above their domestic settings to the level of universally applicable wisdom. It was an act of cultural courage when Joanne created a seminar on American women writers. Feelings ran high as we struggled to identify criteria that would elevate Willa Cather and Flannery O'Connor to the canonical status of Henry James and William Faulkner. This struggle to read women writers from a feminist perspective led to my studying women in the Holocaust and continues through today. The timing was perfect, for by 1979, when Elaine Showalter's *A Literature of Their Own* appeared, I could count on unequivocal support for choosing to write my dissertation on a neglected woman writer. With great good fortune, this kind of support has continued throughout my career.

This is not to say that taking women writers seriously didn't face obstacles. Even today, feminist scholars contend with the damning category of middlebrow: meaning too popular, too accessible, and guilty of linear plotting. Nonetheless, these women writers had both shepherded me through my escapist adolescence and would become my research subjects. I remember the discussion that felt like a *coup d'état*, when aesthetics yielded analytical power to the social, cultural, and political contexts that shaped women's ability to become writers and that shaped us as readers. Such contexts allowed me to recognize that in the 1930s, economic depression and social injustice produced a politicized art that didn't make the grade for many literary scholars. Instead of paying homage to the cultural power of modernist narrative experiments, women writers were now focusing on social and political realities instead of interior consciousness. Among the 1930s women writers resurrected by feminist scholars from middlebrow oblivion was Edna Ferber, who had been found guilty of romantic resolutions and lack of narrative experiment. Although Ferber's novels and films were blockbusters, it was only as feminist studies gained momentum that she gained entry to graduate seminars. Until then, no one had noticed that her fiction opposed colonialism, slavery, and male-dominated American culture. My own appreciation of Ferber was inspired by learning that in the 1930s, her encounters with antisemitism made her increasingly aware of Nazism's threat.

Discovering Anti-Antisemitic British Women Writers

The modern persecution of the Jews found its way into my own literary consciousness when I chose my dissertation topic: the Anglo-Irish writer Elizabeth Bowen. Seemingly a far cry from women and the Holocaust, it was Bowen's astute recognition of the dangers of British antisemitism that became the cornerstone of my research on British representations of the Holocaust. Reading Bowen's 1935 novel *The House in Paris*, I was stunned by the narrative revelation that the half Jewish identity of Max Ebhart, the lover of the novel's female protagonist, makes him unwelcome everywhere and confirms the significance of his irrevocable anxiety:

> I looked back at my humiliations, my ridiculousness and self-deceptions, and dreaded Others. You do not know what is to be suspect and know why. What it is to have no wall to put your back against. (*HP* 177).

I quote this confession because its confrontation with antisemitism startled me into reading British literature as revealing the political and historical meanings of women's writing. My formative case is Bowen's elliptical style, which enshrouds her novel with dread as she builds an unmistakable portrait of antisemitic victimization: Max is perceived as having "that touch – Jewish perhaps – of womanishness," of marrying for money and social position, since "No Jew is unastute." When he commits suicide, I was not surprised; in fact it struck me that as I wrote in my 1998 book *British Women Writers of World War II*, his problem was "neither universal nor personal," but rather "the product of an historical condition that was already exploding outside and inside this novel" (*BW* 204).

I had turned to history as the source of the novel's psychological interest. Max's "movements in claustrophobic and unfathomable spaces are not so much gothic or modernist as they follow the trajectory of European Jews in the 1930s" (*BW* 203). Although Bowen's style has made her "hot" in modernist studies, I credit her writing for challenging me to recognize the historical urgency that drove the aesthetics of her fiction as well as the psychology of her characterizations. How she was situated in twentieth century literary movements came to matter far less to me than her sighting and analysis of the Jew's entrapment. I had no doubt that Bowen's menacing atmospherics was a prescient sign of worse things to come. I then learned that she was not alone in depicting the lethal implications of upper middle class British antisemitism in the 1930s.

Because my research on British women writers of World War II still infuses my work on women and the Holocaust, I'll discuss those who influenced me most. Among those I found revelatory was Stevie Smith, who strobe lighted antisemitism in her 1936 novel *Novel on Yellow Paper* in a sly monologue that "indicts all 'goys' who cling to a sense of their superiority with intolerance of Jews" (*BW* 197). That same year, Storm Jameson published *In the Second Year,* a dystopia imagining the consequences of an Oswald Mosley look-alike who becomes Britain's Fascist dictator. With political realism, Phyllis Bottome's 1937 novel *The Mortal Storm* features a scientist who is stripped of his university position, incarcerated, and murdered for debunking Nazi racial ideology and being a Jew. The 1940 MGM movie adaptation became a blockbuster and inspired me to combine literary with film studies. Katharine Burdekin's 1937 *Swastika Night*, a precursor to Margaret Atwood's *Handmaiden's Tale,* imagines the incarceration of women in breeding cages as the logical outcome of seven hundred years of Nazi victory. None of these writers was known in America, much less taught or researched in the late 1970s and early 1980s. It became clear to me that no one had noticed that like canonical modernists, these women experimented with narrative structures but emphasized their political moment. They galvanized my intellectual and political development because they dramatized the consequences of ambivalent official and popular responses to the escalating dangers of home grown antisemitism commingling with the expansion of Nazi power. With rhetorical strategies of their own, they reconfigured the aesthetic purposes of imaginative fiction by interweaving anti-fascist polemics.

Although my graduate studies included psychoanalytic theory, a path-breaking approach in the 1970s, I found that instead of privileging individual consciousness, there were British women writers who wrote polemical and dystopian fictions that imagined and dissected the consequences of Fascist domination on fragile democratic beliefs, structures, citizens, and refugees. I also wondered then and even more today, if the warnings of these women writers about unstoppable Fascist power would be taken seriously. As I wrote, these writers granted "women the moral energy to take responsibility for their complicity with oppressive power" that offers them "the alluring prestige of a privileged place" (*BW* 102).

Up Against Feminist Pacifism: The Case of Virginia Woolf

By the 1980s and through the early 1990s, it was difficult if not impossible to insert these anti-fascist writers into feminist theories dedicated to women as models of anti-war activism. Reading every feminist research I could find about women and war, I discovered that the pacifism of Vera Brittain and Virginia Woolf was considered exemplary in finding all wars unconscionable and driven by patriarchy. It was women's peace loving proclivities that would save us from fascist domination.[2] In particular, feminist studies of women and World War II preferred to focus on privations of the home front rather than the urgency of defeating the Third Reich. Aside from the writers I discovered, my research uncovered little scholarship about women's debates or support for the war and almost nothing about their responses to either home grown or European antisemitism.

The most startling example was Virginia Woolf. I find her a compelling subject because as a feminist anti-war modernist icon, she showcases questions about relationships between art and ethics. I continue to wonder whether it's possible to argue persuasively that her antisemitism should be integrated into celebrations of her writing. While her snide remarks about Leonard Woolf's Jewishness are sprinkled throughout her diaries and letters, instead of evincing a problem, they have been brushed off as typical

---

2 For Woolf as the foundational anti-war feminist, see Helen Cooper, Adrienne Munich, and Susan Squier, Eds. *Arms and the Woman*, Chapel Hill: University of North Carolina Press, 1989; *Gendering War Talk*, Miriam Cooke and Angela Woollacott Eds., Princeton: Princeton University Press, 1993. Sandra Gilbert and Susan Gubar's three volume *No Man's Land*, New Haven: Yale University Press, 1986-1994 links American and British women writers of World War I and II, eschewing all differences among wars and writers. Thanks to Margaret Stetz for reminding me that 1960s and 70s feminist anti-war thinking was influenced by resistance to the Vietnam War.

of her time and class. As Mia Spiro and I maintained in "A Tale of Two Cities: Virginia Woolf's Imagined Jewish Spaces and London's East End Culture," the antisemitic depiction of Woolf's Jewish character in her 1936 novel *The Years,* cannot, despite convoluted efforts, be explained away. That Abrahamson is as greasy as the ring he leaves in a shared bathtub, has been attributed to another character's perception, but our close reading reveals the author's imprint.[3] Woolf's writing, like that of other modernists, fails to recognize linkages between the antisemitism of Britain's Union of Fascists and Hitler's 1935 Nuremberg Laws. The significance of this today, as antisemitism is on the rise, is that Woolf studies also ignores this possibility.

Most shocking to me was a story that Woolf revised twice before the American *Harper's Bazaar* would publish it (May 1938). "The Duchess and the Jeweler" pivots on an offer by the Duchess of Lambourne to introduce the Jewish jeweler to her daughter, but only if he buys what turns out to be a fake pearl necklace. His name, Oliver Bacon, broadcasts his suspicious character which is confirmed by his Jewish nose, the length of which requires six lines of description to highlight its ability to "sniff out" hidden treasure. His nose also signals his unsavory sexuality and venality, illustrated by his passion for pearls and satisfied by "dabbl[ing] his fingers in ropes of tripe." Interestingly, Sander Gilman's seminal study of antisemitic representations, *The Jew's Body*, has not been cited in Woolf studies. The essay I published about the story, " 'The Milk of Our Mother's Kindness Has Ceased to Flow': Virginia Woolf, Stevie Smith, and the Representation of the Jew," concluded that "although Woolf pities the jeweler for being taken in by his desire for the golden Diana and her world, and satirizes the Duchess as […] the daughter of a hundred Earls," clearly she is "less at risk at any time than is any Jew in 1938."

Granted, the history of British antisemitism reveals a distinct political and cultural history and style, as Anthony Julius posits in his *Trials of the Diaspora: A History of Anti-Semitism in England*. I learned that in the twentieth century, a different antisemitism appeared, "an antisemitism of snobbery, of condescension, of partial exclusion, restriction, it was an antisemitism that kept Jews at somewhat of a distance, but it didn't really exercise as a constraint on our ability to prosper, realize ourselves as Jews as well as English men and women."[4] Julius distinguishes literary and social antisemitism from state sponsored persecution, concluding that "it would

3 In *The Woolf Studies Annual* (2013) devoted to "Virginia Woolf and Jews," with various perspectives but not links to Fascist antisemitism.

4 Anthony Julius, https://www.ushmm.org/research/scholarly-presentations/presentations-and-panel-discussions/new-antisemitism-in-britain

be wrong to interpret the one by reference to the other, so I suggest that it would be wrong to interpret any of them by reference to the Holocaust paradigm" (Julius, USHMM).

This insight led me to consider how Virginia Woolf's antisemitism and her death in March 1941 distance her from the Holocaust paradigm, as history. But reading her canonical anti-war treatise *Three Guineas* in tandem with anti-Fascist women writers showed me that there is a disconnect between her antisemitic representations and her pacifism. Reading Woolf's diaries and letters in tandem with Leonard Woolf's led me to the following argument. The fact that Virginia and Leonard both knew they were blacklisted by the Nazis because of both his Jewish identity and their antifascism indicates her recognition of the danger they and all English Jews faced if Germany were to invade Britain. Moreover, by November 9, 1938, when *Kristallnacht* exploded, it would have been difficult to ignore the peril facing European Jewry and dismiss antisemitism as parlor talk. But while Leonard raged against the Nazis' persecution of the Jews, Virginia remained theoretical. By the spring of 1940, when so much of Europe had been invaded by Germany and the Blitz on Britain began (the Woolf's London home was bombed), other writers, such as Storm Jameson and Rebecca West, found that it was impossible to sustain a pacifist position or to argue that all patriarchy was responsible.

Fifty years after the liberation of the camps and the trials of women guards, I found myself in opposition to many feminist scholars who clung to arguments for pacifism as women's ideological domain. Wendy Lower's *Hitler's Furies* showed that the reverse of this belief was equally anti-historical. As she observes, the brutality of German women guards was "portrayed either as appalling freaks of nature, or as naturally innocent and incapable of such monstrous acts. Intentionally or not, female defendants could exploit the latter prejudice to their advantage" (168). My personal encounter with anti-historical anti-war feminism occurred in 1990 at a feminist faculty seminar on women and war at the University of Michigan where World War II was granted little discussion and the Holocaust none. When I asked what difference it might make to consider women perpetrators and collaborators in feminist anti-war paradigms, the answer was dismissive: exceptional cases do not constitute an argument for the justice of any war.

The Lessons of Women Holocaust Survivors

At the time, I actually knew little about the roles and behaviors of women in the Nazi camps. The classics I had read, by Primo Levi and Elie Wiesel, recounted only men's experiences, but my serendipitous discovery in a used bookstore changed all that. The book was *I Was a Doctor in Auschwitz*, the memoir of Gisella Perl, a Hungarian gynecologist/ obstetrician who was sent to Auschwitz along with the other 440,000 Hungarian Jews. First published in 1948, it had been out of print for decades. Its publication in English encouraged me to write about it, whereas in the past, I felt that my lack of Central European languages was a serious impediment to working on women in the Holocaust. Perl's memoir also spurred my desire to bridge World War II and modernist cultural studies with the Holocaust, and so I published my first effort, "Race, Gender, and the Holocaust: Traumatic Modernity, Traumatic Modernism," relating Perl's memoir to Solomon Perel's *Europa Europa,* in a volume titled *Modernism and Race.*

Narrated as Perl's haunted memories *I Was a Doctor in Auschwitz* was her unapologetic, confrontational, and sometimes surreal voice that captured my attention

> Instead of the exhausted, tortured, but still self-respecting women who entered through [Auschwitz's] door, we were a heart-rending lot of crying clowns, a ghastly carnival procession marching toward the last festival: death. . . . (23)

As Danny Cohen, my collaborator on the new edition, and I wrote, Perl's writing grabs at the reader and doesn't let go. With graphic details and "unsparing soul searching, never letting herself off the hook," Perl recounts women's struggles to live another hour, of performing abortions and infanticide, and helping Josef Mengele's victims even as she was forced to assist him (2). Our research revealed that when Perl applied for US citizenship, her efforts to save women's lives was interpreted by an all-male immigration panel as collaborating with Mengele. That the panel would not allow themselves to believe her story attests to the persistent failure in many influential spheres to recognize the distinctive roles and responses of women in the Holocaust. *I Was a Doctor in Auschwitz* was my answer to the dismissive feminist scholars of women and war. Encouraged by the work of many women who have studied women in the Holocaust, Danny Cohen and I pursued the publication of a new edition of Perl's memoir. With its deeply affecting cover drawing by Ava Kadishson Schieber, the new edition made its appearance as I write this.

It was another fortuitous discovery, when I met Ava Schieber that emboldened me further. At a Rosh Hashanah lunch to which my husband and I were invited in 1993, I was introduced to Ava, a Holocaust survivor who at the age of fifteen, hid on a farm near Belgrade when the Germans invaded Yugoslavia. The shrewd irony with which she alluded to her experiences hinted at her artistic complexity, the fullness of which became apparent when she invited me to see her paintings. One in particular dramatized what she meant by "painting out her rage." Large, gangly, ungendered figures with oversized splayed feet and hands seemed to be storming out of the unframed edges of the canvas. Angry hues of yellow butted black and red splashes. Boldly confrontational, the painting shouted its unbridgeable distance from me as a viewer, an effect that never abated even though I've seen it so many times. When I asked Ava if she had written about her Holocaust experience, she showed me a typescript of a story, "The Party." Written in English, Ava's fourth language, after Serbian, German, and Hebrew, grammatical and syntactical mistakes were sprinkled throughout. Nonetheless, as I read, they failed to obscure the story's increasingly intense, circular interweave of loss and despair, memory and reflection. Because the story was so influential in my turn to study women and the Holocaust, I offer a brief discussion:

The story revolves around three incidents dramatizing Ava's social and psychological isolation. The centerpiece is a St. Nicholas (Slava) party where a momentary reprieve from loneliness becomes assaulting. Although the ravages of working as a farmhand protect Ava from detection, her appearance also exposes her to rejection when she's confronted by a young man who jolts her "into reality: Don't you have a toothbrush? Your teeth are half rotted away" ("The Party," 45). Startled by his cruelty, she retreats into her memory of being hit in the mouth by the rifle of a German soldier warding off an angry Serbian crowd. The palimpsest of incidents intensifies her feeling that there "was no place in my reality to feel sorry for myself" or for anyone else to offer consolation ("The Party," 47, 48). Intersecting with this emotional confrontation is another memory, generating a recognition of separateness and connection that pervades all of Ava's writing. On her initial walk to the farm, she had seen a horse, paralyzed with pain, standing in the road. Her reaction triggers her childhood fondness for horses, inspiring her to embrace the wounded one: "He was never going to gallop, trot, or even walk; I could never walk back into my life, the way it had been. I was crying for myself – sharing sorrow with this doomed animal. There was nothing I could do to ease its pain or my fears for my own safety" (48–49). As in many of Ava's stories, the cruel fates of animals reflect those of men and women, and result from human indifference, unintended, or intentional cruelty.

As Ava continued to write, each story challenged me with writing issues I had never considered as a literary scholar. The issues were never about the stories' content or structure, but rather concerned her English syntax and grammar, which were inflected with her other languages. As we negotiated where and how to make corrections, Ava questioned how we assess the integrity and authenticity of Holocaust writing. When I noted that readers might stumble over her phrasing, she insisted, "The road here is rocky and to stumble is the reality." With her canny input, I recognized that instead of an impediment to understanding, there were occasions when the language slippages in her phrasing both highlighted the drama and authenticity of her writing and challenged readers to recognize our distance from Holocaust experience. When I presented Ava's manuscript to Northwestern University Press, I argued that one of her great achievements is to draw attention to how survivors' languages and memories negotiate and transmit Holocaust history and responses across cultural and temporal boundaries. *Soundless Roar: Stories, Poem, and Drawings* was published in 2002. Her second book, *Present Past,* about life in the aftermath, was published in 2015, both at Northwestern University Press.

Ava's writing and art presented me with new ways of thinking about the distinctive but varied experiences of hidden children. Unlike so many who were too young to understand the circumstances and contexts of being hidden, as a teenager, Ava, like Anne Frank, could write with narrative self-consciousness and a confident sense of self nurtured by their prosperous, cultured families. As a survivor artist, Ava refracts her Holocaust experiences through interwoven perspectives and media. Translating her long ranging memories and responses into art, poetry, and stories, she conveys a wisdom that has affected so many so deeply. She taught me and the thousands of school children she continues to visit how to listen and how to read the Holocaust accounts so many, as I unfortunately have discovered, would prefer to avoid.

Ava's multimedia forms of expressing her Holocaust experiences glosses Myrna Goldenberg's observation that "hundreds of memoirs written by women survivors document'different horrors within the same Hell'." Although Ava endured the constant threat of arrest and starvation, because she was in hiding, she locates her plight in the "ante-room to Hell, not Hell itself."

Anglo-Jewish Women Writing the Holocaust

As I discovered while researching my 2009 book *Anglo-Jewish Women Writing the Holocaust: Displaced Witnesses*, like memoirs of the Kindertransport, accounts from beyond the ghettos and camps have only recently been integrated into Holocaust history and studies of memory and representation. *Anglo-Jewish Women* was the culmination of my intense interest in modern British culture and commitment to working on women and the Holocaust. The book brings together and analyzes novelists like Elaine Feinstein and Lisa Appignanesi, playwrights Diane Samuels and Julia Pascal, and Kindertransport memoirists such as Karen Gershon and Milena Roth. These women recount the experiences and responses of Jewish girls and women who found themselves in a culture that rescued them from being murdered and did not in so many cases know how to assimilate them while recognizing their Jewish difference. Such ambivalence is internalized by Samuels' protagonist Eva, in her play *Kindertransport* while Pascal's play interprets the lethal consequences of such ambivalence in her depiction of the Jewish women refugees who were deported from the Nazi occupied Channel Islands to their deaths. My goal for this book was to showcase Anglo-Jewish women writers who dramatize how Britain, the last democratic bastion against Germany's European blitzkrieg and the rescuer of imperiled Jewish children no one, including the United States wanted, illuminates the multifaceted voices of women who suffered even as they escaped the Holocaust.

Another serendipitous discovery on a bookshop remainder table challenged my thinking about the gendered shaping and reception to Holocaust escape stories. The title, *Some Girls, Some Hats, and Hitler: A True Love Story*, made me think, "Holocaust Chick Lit?" But Trudi Kanter's escape memoir turned out to be anything but silly. Veering between expressions of anxiety, biting humor, sentimentality, political savvy, and the lure of adventure, her multifaceted voice reveals an intrepid plan to escape. Kanter deployed her millinery talents to exploit Nazi wives' love of fashionable hats to forge an escape route for herself, her husband, and her parents, beginning in her workshop in Nazi occupied Vienna, extending to Paris and landing safely in London. Kanter's escape memoir sheds light on the aesthetic, social, and political meanings in her gendered work as a woman's designer. As artifacts and serving as an escape mechanism, hats became the key to understanding her identity as a survivor and her creativity as a writer.

From Women's Studies to Gender Studies

At the same time as my research became more informed by gender analysis, Northwestern University's Women's Studies Program became Gender and Sexuality Studies. My seminars focusing on women and war now integrated men's and women's Holocaust experiences. We examined how men and women perceived and remembered themselves differently, not only as victims and combatants, but also as bystanders and perpetrators. Although I can't claim that this integration attracted more male students, it certainly enlivened discussions and made them more comprehensive. Using gender to balance discussions of women's texts later motivated me to research Rachel Seiffert's 2017 novel *A Boy in Winter* and Pepe Danquart's 2013 film *Run Boy Run* and how their constructions of boyhood masculinity in the Holocaust challenge the classic boys' adventure odysseys into self-determination and disenchantment. My essay, "Jewish Boys on the Run," argues that "The world confronted by the Jewish boy escapees has foreclosed their social development by rejecting them along with their cultural traditions which have been erased."

If gender analysis of war, genocide, and trauma has become a cornerstone of twentieth century cultural studies, the insights of Holocaust Studies are rarely considered. While my observations are based only on my experiences at modern cultural studies conferences, they raise significant questions about the wider impact of Holocaust Studies. To start, from their note taking and occasional nods, I sensed the interest of my audiences when I discussed the innovative narrative strategies of Gisella Perl, Ava Schieber, and other Holocaust writers. They were taken with resemblances to modernist non-linear plotting, dissonant linguistic patterns, and fragmentation. Interest faded, however, when I posited that these same Holocaust writers and artists challenged the modernist mantra to "make it new." The urgency to remember, to memorialize, and to bear witness to the Holocaust past did not resonate, even with analysis of experiences and memories as gendered. That the horrors of this historical past enriched our understanding of modernist disenchantment was noted by some, but also resisted on the grounds that Holocaust Studies is a separate field.

The Holocaust and Modern Cultural Studies

Although relating modernist writers to the Holocaust is now of interest,[5] what remains disturbing is an overall lack of interest in Holocaust writers and artists, despite the proliferation of scholarship and lessons of all the Holocaust museums, conferences, and mandated curricula. By contrast, I'm extremely fortunate to have had the unwavering support of Bob Gundlach at Northwestern University, who for twenty-five years encouraged my research and seminars on World War II and the Holocaust. Henry Carrigan, editor-in-chief at Northwestern University Press, asked me to create and edit a series based on my interests. The result was "Cultural Expressions of World War II and the Holocaust," which created the bridge between the two subjects I have increasingly believed was necessary. Over five years of the series, we published eleven outstanding books, several of which won prizes in their fields. What I find most challenging, even with all this encouragement, is the unending need to argue elsewhere, why Holocaust history and representation are crucial to studying twentieth century culture.

Conferences that include Holocaust Studies are now my scholarly home, but I would still like to persuade others that the historical, cultural, and ethical relationships between Holocaust, World War II, and modernist studies are inextricably intertwined. Although modernist studies is committed to

---

5 See Joanna Rzepa, "The 'demonic forces' at Auschwitz." *Modernism/Modernity* 26:2 (April 2019): 329–350.

representing the multifocal cultures of modernity, the Holocaust is rarely to be found. What is so disturbing is the prevailing neglect of this cataclysmic event. For as Timothy Snyder and others demonstrate, "the Holocaust has come to be seen as the central event of modern European history" ("Commemoration," 77). The integration is easy if it is accepted that the responses of men and women writers and artists to the disillusionments of the twentieth century and those who endured the Holocaust share not only aesthetic, but political and ethical concerns. I would hope that Zygmunt Bauman's declaration might make a difference: "*The Holocaust was born and executed in our modern rational society, at the high stage of our civilization and at the peak of human cultural achievement, and for this reason it is a problem of that society, civilization and culture.*"[6] As I write this, safe at home in Evanston, Illinois, in April 2019, there has just been a shooting by a white supremacist who intended to murder all the Jews at a Chabad synagogue and the invasion of a bookstore, where psychiatrist Jonathan Metzl, was discussing his book, *Dying of Whiteness: How the Politics of Racial Resentment is Killing America's Heartland* by a bunch of American Nazis chanting "This land is our land." So I can't help thinking that studying modern culture ought to remind us of our responsibility to confront, not dismiss, the problem that continues to stalk us.[7]

---

6 Bauman's italics, *Modernity and the Holocaust*, Ithaca, N.Y.: Cornell University Press, 2000: x.

7 My gratitude to Margaret Stetz, Vicki Aarons, Ravenel Richardson, and Penny Hirsch for their incisive reading of this essay.

R. Ruth Linden

Never Again Is Now

Introduction

I moved to San Francisco in November 1978, the week that Supervisor Harvey Milk and Mayor George Moscone were assassinated. The candle-light procession of mourners that snaked along Market Street from the Castro, the center of The City's exuberant gay life, to the site adjacent to the double murder, is among my first memories of the place I still call home. By chance, several years later, I met a charismatic documentary producer from Western Public Radio, Lani Silver, who had begun interviewing Holocaust survivors two years earlier at the World Gathering of Jewish Holocaust Survivors, in Jerusalem.

A second, chance meeting between Lani and me, in 1983, led us to begin working together on her documentary series, "Children of the Holocaust." Lani invited me to join her as an interviewer at the inaugural meeting of the American Gathering of Jewish Holocaust Survivors for which she had assembled a team of reporters to help expand her collection of oral histories. I could not resist this opportunity of a lifetime. The experience culminated in my writing *Making Stories, Making Selves: Feminist Reflections on the Holocaust*,[1] a project I was immersed in for a decade.

The timing of the American Gathering was propitious. I had just completed a fellowship in bioethics at U.C. San Francisco, and the dust-ups over the book I had recently edited on an unrelated subject, *Against Sadomasochism: A Radical Feminist Analysis*,[2] were sufficiently resolved for me to refocus my attention. I was hungry for purposeful work and a new intellectual project.

I was particularly interested in bringing a feminist prism to our survivor interviews and eager to hear women's stories. I would learn that in the month before the American Gathering, the "Women Surviving the Holocaust" conference was held in New York City. I soon connected with Joan Ringelheim and discovered I was not alone in asking feminist questions about the Holocaust.

---

1 R. Ruth Linden, *Making Stories, Making Selves: Feminist Reflections on the Holocaust*, Columbus: Ohio State University Press, 1993.

2 Robin Ruth Linden et al., eds., *Against Sadomasochism: A Radical Feminist Analysis*, San Francisco: Frog in the Well, 1982.

Lani and I interviewed attendees at the American Gathering from dawn until nighttime. We returned home feeling exhilarated by the survivors we had met and the stories they shared, brimming with ideas about the projects we would undertake, from conducting more interviews with San Francisco Bay Area survivors, to transcribing the interviews, editing a book, producing a radio documentary series, and designing a traveling museum exhibition in collaboration with two photographers who had set up a studio adjacent to our post at the conference. I wrote a proposal for a planning grant to the California Humanities Council and the California Public Broadcasting Commission, which was awarded. But several weeks after we received notification of our grant, California's Republican governor cut the funding agency from the state budget.

I quickly grew impatient with collecting oral histories and trying to raise funds from a Jewish community uninterested in supporting our work. Instead, I wanted to study and write about the survivors I had interviewed and their stories – activities that would require me to return to school. To my surprise and relief, my nagging uncertainty dissolved about the field of graduate study I would enter and the institution and faculty where an autodidact like me would find a hospitable home.

The next year, I moved to Cambridge, Massachusetts and began graduate school in the Department of Sociology at Brandeis. I recall these years as one of the richest and most complete times of my life. I was finally pursuing the degree I had dreamed of in an academic department where I found professors who embraced me, recognized the value of my research, and endorsed my plans to study with anthropologists at MIT and Harvard. In addition to my enduring bonds with faculty, classmates, and several writers and scholars affiliated with the department, Regine Winder Barshak who had been imprisoned in Drancy, the transit camp outside of Paris, whom I had interviewed at the American Gathering, became a cherished friend. In 1989, I completed my doctoral thesis. Soon after, I won the Helen Hooven Santmyer Prize.[3]

My path to the study of women in the Holocaust was unorthodox and chancy. Indeed, my book about my encounters with survivors and their narratives stands apart from most, or all, of the contributors to this volume. *Making Stories* is an experimental book that explores the interconnected processes of remembering, storytelling, and self-fashioning. I wrote it at an

3 The Santmyer prize was awarded for the "best book-length manuscript on the contributions of women, their lives and experiences, and their role in society." "Professional Notes and Comment," *PMLA* 105, no. 3 (1990): 562, *JSTOR*, 462905.

intellectual moment when ethnographers and other social scientists, troubled by the conventions of positivism, sought to break free of our disciplines' epistemological foundations, rhetorical strategies, and narrative strictures. By reflecting self-consciously on my postionality as interviewer, researcher, data analyst/interpreter, writer, and active-knowing subject, I acknowledged my place in the production of knowledge.

As such, the book juxtaposes autobiography and ethnography. It reflexively examines its own means of production, akin to M.C. Escher's famous lithographs, "Drawing Hands" (1948) and "Print Gallery" (1956). My beloved professor and friend, the late Irving Kenneth Zola, presented me with a poster of "Print Gallery" while I was writing my dissertation, a gift that confirmed his appreciation of the epistemological problematic at the heart of my work. The poster hangs in my home today.

In *Making Stories*, I explored what I called the "phenomenology of surviving": how agency was exercised in the ghettos, camps, resistance, and on the Aryan side. I wanted to understand how individual women carried on day to day *in extremis*. My epistemological position led me to begin the book by positioning myself in the context of my assimilated Jewish family, where the Holocaust had been shrouded in silences. Early chapters were entitled "My Grandmother's Samovar," "We Don't Believe in Organized Religion," "Coming of Age as a Feminist," and "Reinventing Ethnicity."

To Be an Assimilated Jew in the Late Twentieth Century

As I wrote in the book's prologue:

> Over and over again, I have examined the impress of the Holocaust on my Jewish consciousness. My self-reflections became an integral component of my research, inseparable from the book "about" Holocaust survivors I had initially planned to write. This process transformed my Jewish identity, and the book tells that story as well.[4]

In the book's early pages, I situated my Jewish identity within a family history I cobbled together using citizenship and related documents about my grandparents and great-grandparents, who immigrated to the U.S. in the late nineteenth century. Written prior to the current wave of Jewish genealogy and the availability of electronic databases, my account was cursory and incomplete, and doubtless contains more than a few errors. But no matter; producing an exhaustive family history was never my intention.

4 Linden, *Making Stories*, 2.

In "My Grandmother's Samovar," I recounted the death of my maternal grandmother, whom I called Nana, on Thanksgiving morning of the year I began interviewing survivors:

> Several years after Nana's death, my mother and her sisters broke up her apartment. In one of our weekly long-distance telephone calls, Mother and I were discussing which of her sisters had staked a claim on Nana's brass samovar. Although I had never actually seen it used, for as far back as I could remember, the samovar had sat majestically on the china cabinet in Nana's dining room. Always polished to a high sheen, through my child's eyes it had been the centerpiece of her apartment.
>
> Mother and I speculated on the samovar's origins. I assumed that Nana's mother, my great-grandmother Leah, had brought it with her from Russia, but Mother thought not. 'Daddy [my grandfather, Louis Berry, né Berezniack], used to bid on odd pieces at auctions. He loved antiques. One evening, he brought the samovar home to Mother.' 'Besides,' she added, 'Mother was born in this country. After all, she never spoke with an accent.'
>
> We argued back and forth about where Nana had been born and I recalled the Russian pogroms I had first heard about from her as a twelve-year-old, writing a report on American immigration for my eighth-grade history class. But Mother had no memories of the conversation that had taken place between her mother and me more than fifteen years earlier. She viewed her mother's nationality as one hundred percent American. Indeed, along with many Eastern European immigrants of her generation, Nana had successfully assimilated.
>
> 'The *unspoken*...becomes the *unspeakable*;...the nameless becomes the invisible,' wrote feminist poet and essayist Adrienne Rich. It is likely that Nana never spoke to her daughters about leaving Russia or the transatlantic voyage to America. Had she deliberately buried these memories or were they washed away by time? Perhaps the shock of settling in a new land and, later in life, bearing six children, had blotted them out.[5]

* *

"We Don't Believe in Organized Religion" was my mother's explanation to my sister and me while we were growing up of why our family didn't attend synagogue.

> The world of my youth, Los Angeles's West Side, had a dense Jewish presence. My parents were atheists, although I do not recall their using that term to describe themselves. For years I was perplexed by the idea of 'organized religion.' What was disorganized religion? I wondered.
>
> Yet every year without fail, Mother kept us out of school on the first day of Rosh Hashanah. How ironic that we marked the Jewish new year with our annual visit to the eye doctor!
>
> We never attended *shul* as a family. In fact, I don't believe I ever even entered a synagogue with my father. (The young rabbi who officiated at his memorial in 1969

5 Linden, *Making Stories*, 21.

had never met him.) On only a handful of occasions had my mother and I attended synagogue together...for a family bar mitzvah...and memorials.

Beginning when we were young girls, my sister and I spent part of each summer at Jewish camps. More than any other childhood experience, this nurtured my Jewish identity and love for *Yiddishkeit*. At camp we sang Jewish songs, learned Israeli folk dances, and observed *shabbos*. Friday night supper was a special meal, for which we would dress in crisp white shirts and navy-blue shorts.

We learned [an idealized version of]...Zionism and about the founding of the state of Israel and the Holocaust. We were taught to identify with *Eretz Yisroel* – the Jewish state. I was astonished to learn that the Law of Return automatically granted us Israeli citizenship, simply because we were Jews. For the first time, I saw footage of the liberated death camps. My stock images of the Holocaust – piles of emaciated corpses at Dachau and Bergen-Belsen, and children packed into cattle-car transports – date from the summer we were shown the film "Let My People Go."[6]

* *

"Coming of Age as a Feminist" recounts the identity work of becoming a feminist in the 1970s and early 1980s. I use the term identity work to refer to the commitments, alliances, and conflicts I negotiated as a young woman struggling to chart a life course that expressed my personal values, vision of social justice, and emerging understanding of being an actor in history.

I came of age in the second wave of the women's movement.... During and after college, I embraced several different feminisms: socialist feminism, lesbian feminism, lesbian-separatism, and radical feminism. Distinctions among feminisms were of the utmost significance to us, for the women's movement of the 1970s was ideologically segmented. We defined ourselves by what we didn't believe, as much as by our principles, values, and praxis. Making The Revolution was a serious commitment....

At U.C. Santa Cruz, I was a member of the Thorn Collective, a women's group whose name underscored our commitment to being a thorn in the side of the university. Nearly half of the Thorn women were Jews, but I don't recall a conscious sense of Jewish solidarity among us. Only one occasion comes to mind when we spoke of being Jewish. Feminist constructions of identity were singular and one-dimensional. Our individual identities were rooted in the [women's] movement; thus, any distinction that might have set women apart from each other could have been viewed as divisive – a betrayal of sorts. We believed that we were women "first," then Jews and lesbians, students and mothers, and so on.

I have few Jewish memories from the 1970s although the campus was an assimilated Jewish community of sorts.... As I came of age as a feminist, my connection to Judaism and Jewish culture was suppressed. Still, as a metaphor for genocide and terror, the Holocaust lingered at the surface of my consciousness. In 1978, after reading Philip Levine's poem, 'For the Poets of Chile,' I wrote the following passage in my journal:

6 Linden, *Making Stories*, 26–28.

> The coup, 11 September 1973, has been an important political lesson for me. It is a frightening reminder of the phenomenology of terror – like the destruction of six million Jews but different because it is happening right now, in the present. And no matter how much money I send, how many letters I write, signatures I gather, or *peñas* I attend, people are being tortured and murdered daily. And there is really nothing that I can do to stop the killings.
> 'Someone must remember it over and over…' Levine is talking about a kind of resistance – the dialectic between the burden of remembering and the recognition that we must remember.… We all must remember so as to carry on, to resist, to survive.[7]

* *

In 1982, the year before the American Gathering of Jewish Holocaust Survivors, I began calling myself Ruth and asked my friends and family to do the same. Ruth is the middle name I was given at birth in memory of my father's first cousin, Ruth Serwer, who, at age 17, married an artist, moved to Paris, and died of the flu in the winter of 1928.

> In traditional cultures, many life transitions are marked by taking a new name. Similarly, in our own time and place, rites of passage may be accompanied by namings: births, christenings, confirmations, marriages, divorces, and so on. By taking the name Ruth, I signified to myself and others my desire to explore what it means to live consciously as a Jew.[8]

In doing so, I reinvented my ethnicity.

Wandering in the Academic Wilderness

It was my good fortune that finding a publisher for *Making Stories* proved to be effortless. The Santmyer Prize carried a contract with the Ohio State University Press and my editor deemed the manuscript in need of only perfunctory revisions. I edited *Making Stories* between moves to upstate New York and around New England for one-year teaching stints offering courses on HIV/AIDS, women's narratives, and science studies – nothing, that is, related to the Holocaust. I can still summon the dread I felt as a knot deep in my chest during the summer leading up to the first Gulf War, listening to the news in the background as I edited my manuscript.

On the other hand, finding a permanent job was an overwhelming obstacle. In its heyday, the Sociology Department at Brandeis was renowned for minting maverick feminist scholars, several of whom had been my mentors and professors when I was an undergraduate. I had anticipated following in their footsteps. But the department left me ill-prepared for the bitter

7 Linden, *Making Stories*, 34–36, 43.
8 Linden, *Making Stories*, 53.

demographic reality of the academic job market for peak birth-year baby boomers in the last decade of the twentieth century.

And, so, I wandered in the academic wilderness for two decades. After a string of year-long teaching appointments, I couldn't face packing up one more time to move to a new city. When my house in Watertown, Massachusetts was sold out from under me, I decided to return home to San Francisco. I applied for and was awarded an Andrew W. Mellon Postdoctoral Humanities Fellowship in the Program in History and the Philosophy of Science at Stanford. There, I tried to relaunch my academic career on new terrain.

In the 1990s, I turned my attention to the problematic of cancer. Several close friends had recently received diagnoses – two were misdiagnosed in their forties, resulting in delayed treatment and premature death – and I wanted to bring a sociological lens to the issue. Breast cancer and the history of breast imaging became the focus of my research on what I called the "biopolitics of breast cancer." I soon came to understand that mammography was the wrong tool for the job of imaging women's dense breast tissue. As I delved deeper into the history of mammography, I discovered that no clinical trials had ever been conducted to establish the technology's safety or efficacy in reducing breast cancer mortality before its introduction as a population screen in 1972. I became intrigued by the debate about the age at which women are advised to begin having regular mammograms. I was soon swept away by the rhetoric surrounding breast cancer screening, which I referred to, ironically, as *semiotic hyperplasia* (overgrowth of meanings).[9]

While engaged in the biopolitics project, I was approached by a group of breast cancer activists to collaborate on a novel initiative. Genentech, the biotechnology giant, was launching clinical trials of the first ever personalized cancer therapy – the biological agent known as HER-2/new that had shown promising activity in a sizeable fraction of women with metastatic breast cancer who overexpressed the HER-2/neu gene.[10]

Expanded access would offer women with metastatic disease, who did not meet the strict eligibility criteria of the clinical trials but had exhausted their treatment options, one last chance to receive potentially life-extending therapy outside the trials' strict framework.[11] It would also represent a

9 R. Ruth Linden, "Writing the Breast: Screening Mammography's Contested History, 1976–1999," unpublished manuscript, 2002.

10 HER-2/neu is an oncogene that plays an important role in the development and progression of 25% to 30% of certain aggressive types of breast cancer. The therapy won FDA approval in 1998 under the generic name trastuzumab and is marketed under the brand name Herceptin.

11 Expanded access is sometimes referred to as compassionate access.

form of compensation to the affected community in exchange for individual women having put their lives on the line as research subjects. But Genentech refused to provide the therapy to the women whose lives it might have extended. Using the direct-action model of ACT-UP, the activists sought to change the company's mind and, eventually, they triumphed.

The activists who would write the expanded access protocol – the road-map for implementing the trial – asked me to serve as their bioethics consultant. This was a role for which I was ideally suited by virtue of my earlier training as a bioethicist and my commitment to justice for patients with life-limiting illnesses.

Genentech accepted our protocol as the framework for the trial, the first ever expanded access arm of an oncology clinical trial, to which 300 women eventually gained access and received drug. It turned out that data from subjects in the expanded access arm actually helped HER-2/neu win FDA approval. The next year, I was invited by the FDA to testify at a hearing about the place of expanded access in cancer clinical trials and offer recommendations for implementing guidelines. Ten years later, federal regulations on expanded access to investigational drugs were approved.[12] Expanded access arms have since become a routine component of late-stage oncology clinical trials.

Finding a home in science studies didn't work out as I had hoped though my Stanford courses were extremely popular and deeply satisfying to teach. I continued to write occasional journal articles about the Holocaust. In "Troubling Categories I Can't Think Without: Reflections on Women and the Holocaust,"[13] I described two early projects exploring women in the Holocaust in which I participated: an experimental course taught in 1984 in San Francisco by historian Konnilyn Feig and a dialogue on the topic initiated by feminist artist Judy Chicago in 1988. In "Deportations and Discursive Displacements,"[14] I explored the rhetorical linkage between the

12 U.S. Department of Health and Human Services, Food and Drug Administration, Center for Drug Evaluation and Research (CDER), Center for Biologics Evaluation and Research (CBER), "Expanded Access to Investigational Drugs for Treatment Use – Questions and Answers, Guidance for Industry," (June 2016, Updated October 2017 Procedural), retrieved on 7 August 2019 from https://www.fda.gov/media/85675/download.

13 R. Ruth Linden, "Troubling Categories I Can't Think Without: Reflections on Women and the Holocaust," *Contemporary Jewry* 17 (1996): 18–33.

14 R. Ruth Linden, "Deportations and Discursive Displacements," *Sociological Research Online* 4, no 2 (1999), http://www.socresearchonline.org.uk/socresonline/4/2/linden.html.

war in Kosovo and the Holocaust, which loomed large in the U.S. at the time of the Kosovo War.

I retooled again, this time, as an academic administrator. First I was a dean at an idealistic but academically anemic institution that I planned to satirize in print (as a sanity-maintaining strategy) as Camelot U. and, later, in the field of medical curricular reform. Once again, I found a temporary home at Stanford. My appointment carried an attractive compensation package, an assistant, and my own conference room but only for one year. As Director of Curricular Reform, my major triumph was including students and junior faculty of color in the curricular reform initiative. This earned me some wrath from the dean, who had appointed a steering committee for me to lead composed of more than a dozen tenured, white male professors and one white woman, the wife of Stanford's then president, a psychiatrist.

I had my last hurrah at a community-based research institute studying diversity in health professions education, where I directed a grant funded by the prestigious California Endowment. Then, in 2008, came the Great Recession. Hiring freezes followed at the University of California and Stanford, the largest employers of the reserve army of academic laborers like me. Although I was short-listed for a number of research and administrative positions, the economic downturn threw me into the abyss. I collected unemployment insurance benefits for three years.

In 2012, I stopped submitting job applications and, instead, applied for admission and a scholarship to an online certificate program at UCLA. Next, I enrolled in a "mini-MBA" course for entrepreneurs in preparation for starting my own consultancy as an independent health advocate. At this writing, I am entering my sixth year in practice. My work is deeply satisfying. I love taking care of my clients, many of whom have been failed by the healthcare system. Still, I miss the pleasures of discovery conferred by conducting research and writing.

Never Again Is Now!

Making Stories, Making Selves was an early contribution to the now robust body of scholarship on women in the Holocaust. My research and writing in the field spanned a relatively short period of time at the beginning of my career as a sociologist, and ended as the possibility dwindled that I could sustain a research program without a steady paycheck.

Two decades have passed since my last Holocaust-related publications. I sometimes reflect on the direction my research might have taken had I continued to explore the trove of survivor narratives that Lani Silver and I collected under the aegis of the Bay Area Holocaust Oral History Project. During my writing years, among the broad concerns that most engaged me were Jewish women's agency *in extremis*, narrative "vs." historical truth, autoethnography, social memory, the rhetoric of the social and human sciences, and comparative genocide studies. Had I continued to enjoy the luxuries afforded by life in academia, my research would likely have continued on the unconventional course I had charted.

But, instead, as my dear friend, the late Tillie Olsen, wrote in *Silences*, "Compared to men writers of like distinction and years of life, few women writers have had lives of unbroken productivity, or leave behind a 'body of work.' Early beginnings, then silence; or clogged late ones (foreground silences); long periods between books (hidden silences); characterize most of us."[15] I am one such writer-scholar, whose career was quashed by socially-determined silences. I am awed by the tenacity and accomplishments of my friends who built productive careers as independent scholars and writers with nominal support, and often hostility, from the academy, sometimes while facing life-limiting illnesses and caring for partners, parents, and children.

Of all the unasked, and therefore, unanswered questions stimulated by my research, a deeply personal one weighed on me early on, during my immersion in interview transcripts: What would I have done, as a Jewish woman living under Nazi occupation when the Nuremberg Laws were passed, or when Jews were ordered to register, or when the borders were sealed? Would I have fled in the early-1930s, joined a resistance group, or gone into hiding? Would I have sought to buy or otherwise obtain illegal documents?

I could never imagine a scenario for myself, my own "path through the Holocaust."[16] Not Susan Cernyak-Spatz' path from Vienna to Prague, to Thereseinstadt ghetto, to survival in Auschwitz;[17] nor Leesha Rose's path as a resister in the Dutch underground;[18] nor the path of my dear friend Vera Obermeyer, whose mother fled Berlin in 1938 with her in tow, leaving behind Vera's father, an attorney, who believed his prominence would ensure his family's safety. The possibility of state terror was unfathomable to me, not intellectually of course, but viscerally.

But, since the 2016 presidential campaign and inauguration, my ability to imagine state-sponsored terror has sharpened. In the current political moment, I have no doubt that, as a Jew and a lesbian, I am a potential target of white nationalist terror.[19] Certainly, we are not living in 1930s

15 Tillie Olsen, "Blight—Its Earliest Expression," in *Silences*, New York: Delacorte Press, 1978: 178.

16 Linden, *Making Stories*.

17 Linden, *Making Stories*, 84–112.

18 Linden, *Making Stories*, 113–146.

19 The 2018 mass shooting at Tree of Life – Or L'Simcha Congregation in Pittsburgh, PA, killing 11 people (including two members of my wife's extended family),

Germany. My rational mind tells me that I will not be taken into "protective custody" because of who I am, who I share my life with, the petitions I sign, or the social media articles I post and comment on. Still, my wife and I have renewed our passports, even though neither of us has traveled abroad for almost two decades nor has future travel plans. We no longer attend the synagogue where we feel most at home because its weak security makes us uneasy.

We frequently discuss "what if?" scenarios. What if the president is elected to a second term of office? What if we suddenly have to leave the U.S. and abandon our home and bank accounts with only a few suitcases and the clothes on our back? What if the next executive order targets us? What if martial law is declared? I wonder how many tens of thousands of German Jews asked these same questions after Hitler was appointed Chancellor in 1933?

* * *

In the 35 years since I began my work with Holocaust survivors, I have had many opportunities to reflect on the lessons of the Holocaust for our own time. At my more cynical moments, when the media and popular culture were awash with sanctimonious representations and rhetoric, I have even wondered if there were any lessons at all to be learned. But, today, with the rise of fascism in the U.S. and globally, the most trenchant lesson the Holocaust can teach is expressed in a twist on the cry, Never again is now!

This slogan sounds a warning that Jews will not stand on the sidelines while one minority – ethnic, national, religious or sexual – is stripped of its civil rights and liberties. Our recent and distant history, as well as our Prophetic tradition, mandates us to act. It matters not whether Jews are among those targeted or whether Latinx, undocumented foreign nationals, documented immigrants, Muslims, or LGBTQ people are singled out. We have learned from the destruction of European Jewry that our silence will not save us.

On any given day at the end of the second decade of the twenty-first century, in the U.S.-Mexico border cities of El Paso and Clint, Texas, 2,000 migrant children, separated from their parents, are locked in cages at detention facilities. They languish in government custody with neither the surety of a release date nor sufficient drinking water, sanitation facilities, adequate food, nor the ability to keep themselves clean. Alongside these material privations, these children are denied a "place in world [a political space] in

---

increased my sense of vulnerability. As it happens, Tree of Life is the name of my health advocacy firm. For several months after the shooting, my website bore a banner expressing solidarity with the synagogue and the victims of the hate crime.

Hannah Arendt's words."[20] U.S. Congresswoman Alexandria Ocasio-Cortez (D-NY), following her visit to the border, referred to these facilities as concentration camps, sparking a fiery debate about whether use of the term was an affront to Holocaust survivors, victims, and the wider Jewish community.

For dispassionate reflection on concentration camps, I turned to Arendt, who was herself imprisoned in a French internment camp before landing in New York Harbor in 1941. Arendt viewed concentration camps as the instrument used by totalitarian regimes to control national (or ethnic) minorities. She recognized statelessness as the most obdurate and enduring problem of her time, one that has only grown graver and more intractable in the intervening eighty years. Arendt noted, with due sarcasm, that becoming stateless was a process in which a "new kind of human being [was] created by contemporary history," the kind that "are put into concentration camps by their foes and into internment camps by their friends."[21] But what of we actors in history who are not stateless – Arendt's friends and foes? Morally and ethically, who do we become as this new kind of human being is created?

The lessons we distill from the Holocaust, whatever they may be, are embedded in national laws and boundaries, international compacts and treaties, and supranational bodies. They are also inscribed in survivors' memories and narratives and on their bodies. Following Faulkner, who wrote, "The past isn't history. It isn't even past," the lesson I take from my research on women in the Holocaust is that not to act in light of the past is to mock the past. Never again is now.

20 Elisabeth Young-Bruehl, *For Love of the World*, New Haven: Yale University Press, 1982: 257.

21 Young-Bruehl, 152, citing Arendt, "We Refugees," *Menorah Journal* 31 (January 1943): 70.

Dalia Ofer

Why Women – and What That Means for Me as a Historian

I will begin by expressing my gratitude to two women who granted me the privilege of conducting research on women in the Holocaust. The first is my colleague and dear friend Lenore Weitzman; the second is Cecilia Slepak, a woman I know only through my historical imagination. Her scattered manuscript in the Ringelblum Archives guided me in understanding her mind, her sense of social justice, her emotions and vision.

However, before elaborating on this dramatic statement I shall explain why I studied the Holocaust, and end by asserting the enormous advantage I gained by extending my research to gender and women.

Some Biographical Facts

I was born in Jerusalem in 1939. My childhood in Palestine (pre-State Israel) was overshadowed by the Second World War. Not that I personally experienced any difficulties of the war, nor did I feel threatened by it. I do not even remember my parents talking or sharing concerns about their families in Poland and Latvia. However, I do remember the pain I felt when my friend Gili, who lived upstairs and wanted to scold me, would call me Dalia Italia (Italy in Hebrew, and it rhymes with my given name), which was a great insult, as Italy was an ally of Hitler. And even more vividly I remember the day when I was out in the yard, Gili was again scolding me, and I proudly retorted that Italy is no longer an ally of Hitler in the war.

The arrival of relatives, Holocaust survivors, in early 1946, made the war and our relatives' experiences a subject of conversation of my parents in their secret language, Yiddish. My parents often sat together with friends and neighbors while my sister and I were sent to our room. However, the small apartment enabled us to hear the tone of their talks and here and there scattered sentences. Our curiosity and some anxiety increased upon hearing the sobs accompanied by *oi vei* and we sensed that something agonizing was in the air. In order to understand from the few words I was able to catch, I had to use my imagination, which did not follow any historical facts of a sound narrative.

I recall a visit by a beautiful young woman who came with a tall and ugly red-headed man. She was introduced as Naomi and the man as Yitzhak, two Hebrew names. My father was very emotional when meeting them. The woman was unable to speak Hebrew but the man spoke fluent Hebrew and brought us a domino game. He loved to play with us while Naomi talked at length with my parents. My father explained to my sister and me that Naomi was his cousin who had just arrived from Poland, and that he remembered her as a little girl in 1932, before he immigrated to Palestine. He also told us that she, together with her older brother and his children, had lived for months in the forest, when they were fleeing the Nazis. She was able to tell him about his family and hometown, but he did not disclose any details to us, nor did we ask. He proudly told us that Yitzhak had served in the Jewish Brigade and when he left his unit to go his hometown, he met Naomi, her brother and his family, whom he remembered from before he immigrated to Palestine shortly before the war. He helped Naomi to immigrate illegally to Palestine by pretending that she was his wife. (They did marry shortly after.)

This story fired my imagination. The words "forest," "snow," "and "escape" that I picked up stirred my mind. Forests and escapes were scenes of childhood legends, such as Snow White and Little Red Riding Hood. For a seven-year old who lived in the bare Judean Mountains and for whom the ample stony fields of Jerusalem served as playgrounds, imagination played a major role. The story of Naomi's *aliyah* with false documents was no less heroic for me, if one bears in mind the struggle against the British Mandate, of which immigration was a central issue, often in the news, spoken about in public—and always on our minds.

In my mind, these stories were the foundation that designated Holocaust survivors as heroes. Other family survivors came for short visits; some had children younger or older than me. At first, we did not have a common language in which we could communicate, but it was soon the summer vacation months during which one visited aunts and uncles. By then we all spoke Hebrew and compared our suntans. I, the Jerusalemite, usually lost.

In school, we never studied the history of the Holocaust. Nor did we discuss the Holocaust in our youth movement or participate in commemorative ceremonies.[1] At least I am unable to recall any. In elementary school

~~1 In 1979, the Ministry of~~ Education decided to make teaching the history of the Holocaust mandatory in high schools and started to implement the program in 1980–82. Only in 1983 was a textbook for the high schools published: Yisrael Gutman and Chaim Schatzker, *The Holocaust and Its Meaning*, Jerusalem, 1983 [Hebrew]; a second edition was published in 1987.

however, teachers spoke to us about the major current events, such as the forced return of the *Exodus* from Haifa harbor to Germany. All the narratives we heard were very emotional and ideologically loaded.

The War of Independence was the foremost experience of my childhood. Living in Jerusalem and in a sector that was heavily shelled by the Jordanians, it left a strong imprint upon me. Its connection to the Holocaust was a non-issue at the time,

When I was in high school, my sister married a Holocaust survivor from Hungary. He had immigrated in 1946, was deported to Cyprus, released and arrived in time to take part in the War of Independence, and was wounded in one of the major battles to relief besieged Jerusalem. His older brother, who had protected him in Auschwitz, was killed in March 1948 defending the village of Atarot, north of Jerusalem that had to be abandoned. The retreat from Atarot one month later, in April 1948, was fresh in my mind, since my parents took in a family from that village for the duration of the siege of Jerusalem that lasted for four weeks.

I was fourteen when I first heard my future brother-in-law's biography and the tragedy of his late brother. It was a difficult story to bear. On the one hand, it reinforced the sense of heroism about the survivors of the Holocaust. On the other hand, it revealed the boundless tragedy of survivors who came to Israel and experienced such a great loss, as did my brother-in-law.

I remember thinking at the time that at some point in my life I have to try to gain a better understanding of this tragedy and learn how the survivors were able to cope with the routine of daily life, family, and the demands of society after such losses. I was still too young to plan an academic education, but history was my first love in school. So, in some respects, ignorance rather than knowledge, emotions rather than reason, were the imprint of my childhood and adolescence in relation to the Holocaust.

When I recall these experiences of childhood and adolescence, I wonder to what extent they accounted for my academic preferences and my intellectual development. Perhaps I am constructing a narrative to support my field of research? Were the memories and the determination to understand the survivors' return to life a genuine motivation when I decided to focus my graduate studies on the Holocaust period, a goal I set before I began undergraduate studies in history and the Bible? Moreover, my research topics display a progression from what I would identify as the fringe of Holocaust events and geography—Istanbul as a center for rescue efforts, and illegal immigration to Palestine—to the core of the tragedy, the life of the Jews in east European ghettos.

When Did Women Become Part of My Research or: But Where Are the Women?

Prof. Lenore. J. Weitzman (Lenore)

I shall now turn to the first of the two women mentioned in my opening statement, to my friend and colleague Prof. Lenore Weitzman. There is a song by the famous Israeli composer and poet Naomi Shemer: "It's all because of a small nail". My small nail was a brief meeting with Prof. Weitzman in Jerusalem. She spent one year in Israel researching Jews who survived the Holocaust by passing as non-Jews and then moved on to study the *kashariyot*, the women couriers of the underground movement. I was on a sabbatical that year in Washington, DC, devoting my time to writing a large article about the memory of the Holocaust in Israel, and planning to continue with a monograph on the mass immigration to the State of Israel during the first decade of the state. I actually thought to abandon research of the Holocaust for some time, feeling that it was too trying.

The meeting with Lenore ignited a new passion. She told me about her research and how she had created a brand new data set from the Yad Vashem testimonies archive. She shared her thoughts about the fact that women *kashariyot* did not receive the acclaim that men did. I doubted her statement. In Israeli culture, I claimed, women in the underground such as the *kashariyot* were recognized as central leaders no less than men. I cited the example of Vitka Kovner and Haika Grossman. I went on to argue that in Israeli Holocaust memory, women and men in the underground, in partisan units, or in ghetto fighting were equally esteemed. To reinforce my (incorrect) argument (as I now know better), I stressed that I grew up with the sense of complete equality between men and women. If I remember correctly, I even cited my aunt, my mother's twin sister, telling me as an adolescent and young adult to remember the achievements of great women such as the Romanian foreign minister Ana Pauker, Golda Meir, and Rosa Luxemburg. In my aunt's mind, these were models of women's achievements.

Lenore disagreed, and widened her claim to include Holocaust research in general, saying it was not gender free and conceived men's experiences as universal. This led me to ask myself where the women were. I promised Lenore to think about the subject and returned to Washington and to my unfinished projects.

Well, those who know Lenore will agree that she never gives up. A short time later, she contacted me in Washington and informed me that she had obtained some money for a conference on women in the Holocaust, and asked if I would cooperate in finding additional resources. I suggested that we organize a workshop, feeling that we were not yet ready for a conference.

And all the rest is history, and our volume *Women in the Holocaust* was the result of this workshop.

I started to look for funding and approached Yad Vashem and the Institute of Contemporary Jewry at the Hebrew University of Jerusalem where I taught. My close and dear friend and colleague, the late Yisrael Gutman, whose work and personality were a source of inspiration, supported my request. However, in a fatherly manner he let me understand that only because of his appreciation of my research was he prepared to support funding the endeavor. Personally, he thought that the subject of gender and women did not really matter; what mattered was Jews. Nevertheless, during our conversation he told me how different his father and mother were after the occupation and the move to the ghetto. His father lost his job and fell into a state of helplessness, remaining at home not knowing what to do and how to react. His mother, on the other hand, was invigorated to support the family and take care of her teenage son and young daughter. When I hesitantly commented that his story is a good reason to study women's responses, he answered that it is well known that women are stronger than men, and I should beware of banalization. It was an important warning.

My "Meeting" with Cecilia Slepak

I now had to decide what would be my presentation in the workshop and how to embark on new research. My best advisor was the Ringelblum Archive. I read Yosef Kermish's introduction to the selection from the archive, *To Live with Honor, to Die with Honor* (Jerusalem, 1986) and learned that as part of the archive's research plan to cover "two years of occupation, one year of ghetto," Ringelblum commissioned a study about women. I was surprised for two reasons. First, that I did not notice it years ago when I read the introduction, and second, that I did not recall any of it in the collection which I used extensively in my teaching in Israel and abroad. So I consulted the table of contents and, to my amazement, nothing of this report appeared. What does that mean, I wondered: was the report not good enough, or was it in the part of the archive that was not found? The next step was to look for the report, which was listed in the catalogue, and not long afterward, it was in my hands. My own voyage had begun.

To my surprise, I found sixteen narratives based on interviews with women from all walks of life. The diversity of these women and the richness of the narratives was gripping. However, before narrating my personal journey with women in the Holocaust, I will share with you the limited knowledge that we have about Slepak.

Cecilia Slepak was a journalist and translator who lived in Warsaw. One of her major projects was the translation into Polish of the twelve volumes of

Simon Dubnow's *World History of the Jewish People*, which was published posthumously in 1948. She was part of the intellectual Jewish elite immersed in secular Jewish culture and the YIVO Institute, while also integrated into Polish culture. Slepak's home was a meeting place for Jewish intellectuals and had the reputation of being a pleasant venue for cultural and social discussions. From one description by Rachel Auerbach, we learn that she still hosted friends in her home for a four o'clock tea in the spring of 1940. The description lends itself to a typical middle-class afternoon of leisure in a home space that had already been looted by the Germans. Her husband was an engineer; she had two children, a girl and a young boy who were send to Treblinka during the great deportations of 1942. Auerbach wrote that her husband survived.

We know very little about the Slepaks' life in the ghetto. Rachel Auerbach testified that she met her in the self-help organization in the ghetto, and thought that her questions about the soup kitchen hinted at her being part of the Oneg Shabbat archival team. Commissioned to write about the life of women, Slepak interviewed sixteen women, a cross-section of those in the ghetto. As far as we know, her previous writings were not about women and we have no information about her being active on behalf of women's rights.

Let me return to the women and the interviews. They were unlike the women from the underground whose stories I knew, nor were they women who were known for their contribution to art or the theater before the war. They were a mix of "ordinary" women: a cashier, a corset maker, a housewife, a librarian, a person active in Toporol (Towarzystwo Popierania Ropnictwa, a society to promote agriculture among Jews), a small vendor, a wife of an artist, etc. She juxtaposed women with formerly unacceptable occupations such as a thief, a woman reduced to prostitution to make a living, and a beggar, alongside those engaged in traditional "women's work" and new occupations for women. Each presented her particular story, responding to questions about her life before the war's outbreak, the weeks of the hostilities, the year of Nazi occupation before the move to the ghetto, and life in the ghetto.

Slepak's narrative was so compelling that it filled my days and nights. For days I lived with these women, and at night I followed them in my dreams. Slepak did not mention their names, but only wrote the letter of what I thought was the woman's first name. I wanted to give them names, but did not dare to invent any. I was happy when I was able to track down the librarian, Batia Temkin, the only woman interviewed by Slepak who survived the war as far as I know. I had endless dialogues with the women, and particularly with those upon who I had focused in my first article about the report—and with Slepak herself. Naturally, these dialogues existed only in my mind, where I asked and responded and told and retold their stories for months on end.[2]

It was so clear to me that these women had their story, one comprised of a world of daily, seemingly banal, issues that did not receive meaningful attention during my long years of studying the Holocaust. It was the story of love for a husband and admiration of his artistic talent which compelled the wife to assume all responsibility for providing the basics of living; or a story of devotion, or of a mother rescuing herself and her child and escaping with that child to Warsaw in the hope of a better chance to survive. But it was also a story of a woman whose husband escaped just a few weeks after her wedding and wanted her to join him, an adventure that failed, leading her to develop a relationship with a Volksdeutsche who assisted her and her parents to maintain a restaurant before the move to the ghetto, and even for some time in the ghetto. Her parents encouraged this relationship, and when it ended, she did not hesitate to develop another, this time with a Pole who helped her smuggle food, thus enabling her to save herself, her brother, and her parents from starvation.

Slepak also included a narrative of a woman prepared to manipulate to get a job as a building superintendent in her apartment building, even at the expense of another family. What I want to stress is that these were not heroic stories, or stories of success or despair. Of course these were terribly sad narratives, but the efforts and hopes to survive the hardship of ghetto life, the creativity and endless manipulation of those who failed and those who partly succeeded, and of the woman who was murdered after being caught smuggling—all these were among the sixteen. I tried to delete from my mind the knowledge of how these women ended their lives, and instead continued to walk with them through the ghetto trails that Slepak had opened up.

Having read Slepak, I now read the classic diaries such as those of Chaim Aron Kaplan and Peretz Opoczynski very differently. I absorbed all details about women in Ringelblum and Huberband, and the many diaries that had been part of my reading for years.

Before starting to write my first draft, I studied what I thought was the classic Holocaust and gender literature of that time: Sybil Milton, Joan Ringelheim, Roth and Rittner's collection, Marion Kaplan, and studies of women in the Third Reich. I began developing my historical approach, yet

2 "Her View through My Lens: Cecilia Slepak Studies Women in Warsaw," in *Gender, Place and Memory in the Modern Jewish Experience: Re-placing Ourselves*, Judith Tydor Baumel and Tova Cohen (eds.), London and Portland, OR: Vallentine Mitchell, 2003: 29–50.

many questions arose concerning the exclusion of women from the overall story, and about similarities and differences between women and men.

I started to look back on the writing about women in different periods of Jewish history and received great inspiration from the works of Natalie Zemon Davis, Paula Hyman, Moshe Rosman, and others. It was, as Natalie Davis wrote, in the margins; however, it set a great intellectual and methodological challenge to social and cultural history. Issues of methodology were also central, with microhistory, biography, narrative analysis, and social history standing firmly in the center. All charged my historical imagination.

The workshop "Women in the Holocaust" conducted in Jerusalem in 1995 was another important stage of opening horizons and raising questions. It was the first workshop on the topic in Israel, and except for those who presented papers only a small number of scholars were invited. Judy Baumel (Schwartz) was the first in Israel who had done substantial work on the topic. There were those who doubted whether the subject could contribute to the understanding of the Holocaust, among them Laurence Langer and Ruth Bondy, who presented papers, and Yisrael Gutman who participated in the workshop but did not present a paper. In a discussion following the only public lecture in Yad Vashem on women's writings from the Holocaust, critical voices were heard relating to the core issue: the particularity of women's voices. Among the critics was Sidra Dekoven Ezrahi, a pioneer scholar on the literature of the Holocaust.[3]

The second important stage in my development was working with Lenore on editing the book and writing the introduction and conclusion. Our work together gained a lot from Lenore's training in sociology and mine in history. Each of us had quite strong opinions on many issues and great respect for each other. We thought a lot about methodology and writing about the Holocaust. For two weeks we sat in Lenore's home in Virginia, reading and discussing the final drafts of the articles. We debated how to problematize major issues and keep them in context. One of my main concerns was how to integrate women's history of the Holocaust into the Holocaust's metanarrative. I agreed that in order to move the women from the margins to their rightful place in the narrative of the Holocaust, a separate study had to be devoted to the subject. However, the main goal, I thought, was to integrate their narrative into overall writing about the Holocaust.

The book's success was encouraging, and the fierce criticism that followed by those who resented the discussion about women proved how important it was.

---

3 Sidra DeKoven Ezrahi, *By Words Alone: The Holocaust in Literature*, Chicago: Chicago University, 1980.

Teaching was an important part of my professional life. I started out as a high school teacher and later moved on to the university. Having the privilege to teach mostly MA students, I was able to make my research topics the subject of the courses. In this respect, the seminars were very much research seminars, and I opened the way for women and gender to be an important topic of students' research papers. Unlike my naive approach to women's equality, the younger generation expressed feminist ideas and their analysis was embedded in theories of feminism. This created a dialogue that was not always appealing to me, but was an educational experience. The fact that each generation reads history through its contemporary lens was certainly evident in those conversations. We intensely negotiated methodology, choice of documentation, and the imperative of contextualization. Was the behavior that my students interpreted as sexual abuse understood in the same way by the women we were studying? How should we interpret the information that Rachel Auerbach provided about men who substituted younger girls for their wives? Or what about Huberband's charges about women's conduct in the forced labor camps? And the popular songs cited in Josef Garr's books on Kovno, "*Yeder Yaleh hot sein Kalleh, un polizei hot Zwei*" - "A man with means can have his pick of women, and if he's with the police—he can have two!"[4]

While the issue of ideology and the writing of history is a major one to deliberate with, students, feminist theories and the writing of history ignited heated debates which served for good discussions and challenged interpretations. My students wrote on different subjects, and a few devoted their research to women, to families in Transnistria, and to everyday life in the ghettos and other countries under Nazi occupation.

The next stage of looking into women's Holocaust history followed almost naturally. In a passing conversation with my colleague Peter Medding, he told me that the issue of the annual, *Studies in Contemporary Jewry* that he was editing would be focusing on the Jewish family. Without a moment's hesitation I told Peter that I wanted to write about the family in the ghetto and asked if I could contribute an article to the annual.[5]

Armed with Selpak's interviews, in which a number of women spoke about their families, I embarked upon a new research project focusing on gender

---

4 Joseph Garr, *The Destruction of Jewish Kovno* (Yiddish), Munich, 1948: 410. I would like to thank my colleague Prof. Eli Lederhandler for the English translation.

5 "Cohesion and Rupture: The Jewish Family in East European Ghettos during the Holocaust," in *Coping with Life and Death: Jewish Families in the Twentieth Century*, Peter Y. Medding (ed.), Studies in Contemporary Jewry, 14, New York: Oxford University Press, 1998: 143–65.

rather than women. Reading the sources, mothers and fathers together with brothers and sisters enabled me to imagine endless conversations and troubled arguments between couples, children and parents, daughters and sons, and more. I looked for diverse documentation which combined the personal and the public, diaries and chronicles from the ghettos, youth movement publications, and police accounts. I was confronted by endless encounters that enriched my approach to everyday life, helping me return to—and better understand—women of different classes, causing me to ask over and over again how to define class in the ghetto, without reaching a satisfactory conclusion.

I learned in first person about the desire to live, the despair and helplessness caused by extreme poverty, mothers who lost their spouses, and fathers left alone with children, mothers who put their hungry children on the doorsteps of an orphanage, and the disintegration of refugee families in the *punkten* (centers in Warsaw where refugees were housed). Despite the number of articles that I published on the family, and the different areas in eastern Europe that I studied, I still have a long way to go. I now understand better how important and difficult it is to present an integrated narrative, and I now study masculinity and its effect on Jewish males when reading the pioneering dissertation of Anna-Madeleine Halkes Carey, "Jewish Masculinity in the Holocaust."

As I mentioned above, one of my main research goals is to understand people's lives before and during the ghetto period, to be able to understand how they thought, how they managed to evaluate the present in view of the past, and whether they were able to envision a future. I want to be able to touch upon some of the moments when thinking was no longer possible, when intuition or instinctive reaction was the only way to function. Indeed, I know that this is impossible. I realize the gap between here and there is unbridgeable and endless! To construct a bridge to enable that crossing is an unmanageable wish. Nevertheless, I am satisfied even if I captured just a touch of the human condition and of the women's emotions. I also truly know and understand that it is all for the better that I cannot bring myself to imagine that I was really there. However, whenever I watch the films that depict a little girl with hair ribbons knotted like a butterfly on her head, my heart skips a beat. Is it me, celebrating the ribbon that my mother used to put in my hair for holidays or Sabbath of which I was so proud?

Conclusion

At my university and in my close academic circle I felt both support for and doubts about my choice to study women. The comments I received expressed doubt regarding the contribution the subject could make to meaningful understanding of the Holocaust. Some even said bluntly that it is a fashion in historical research, and that in regard to the Holocaust it misses the main points and would fade away in time. What about the banalization of the Holocaust? What about relativization of the suffering, are you not making women better than men and create new heroes? What about essentialism—the statement that women are more connected, more emotional, more dedicated to their family just because they were females? I know that many encountered such comments at some point. When the book was published the conceptual framework of the introduction brought some of my colleagues to have second thoughts and there were those who encouraged me, many from other departments and disciplines. However, I never sensed any disrespect or attempts to let me down. Those who did not agree commented, asked questions—but always to the point, never in a degrading manner.

My studies on the family received across-the-board favorable reactions. Gender and women were of course a major factor. However, although an article I published on motherhood received a comment as to whether focusing on mothers expressed a feminist bias, I did not hear such a remark about my article on fatherhood.[6] I should, however, note that it was published much later, when the issues of gender and women were already part of the consensus.

Therefore, recently I was quite surprised when during an interview of Prof. Yehuda Bauer that I conducted together with a colleague, she asked if the issue of gender and women in the Holocaust is not exaggerated by women scholars. Bauer responded in short: Not at all, and just look at the work Dalia did. How could you write about the family and everyday life without these concepts?

In many respects I feel that I have reached a point of satisfaction. I fear that due to personal reasons I will not be able to complete my monograph on the family, but I am sure that other scholars will continue my work and contribute their own findings. After all, our contribution should be planting some seeds for further deliberation, to agree, to expand, to provoke, and to contest. Each is important and follows the right trail of historiography. I learned lately, when writing a review of Zoe Waxman's book *Women in the Holocaust: A Feminist History* (Oxford, 2017), that I underestimated the issue of sexual abuse. Yet, I was not sure that I agreed with its centrality

6 "Motherhood under Siege," in *Life, Death and Sacrifice: Women and Family in the Holcoaust*, Esther Hertzog (ed.), Jerusalem and New York: Gefen Publishing, 2008: 41–67; "Parenthood in the Shadow of the Holocaust," *Theologie.Geschichte Beiheft* 8 (2013): 181–210.

as Waxman presented in her book. Is it because we are historians of different generations? I will leave that to history. Regardless of any other consideration, without the perspective I gained from the women I studied, my research would have been much poorer.

Melissa Raphael

The Why and How of a Gynocentric Theology of the Holocaust: An Autobiographical Essay

Introduction

By the closing decades of the twentieth century, women scholars had begun to join what had previously been an all-male religious conversation about the Holocaust.[1] Nonetheless, when I published *The Female Face of God: A Jewish Feminist Theology of the Holocaust* in 2003, it was the only monograph-length feminist theological response to the Holocaust. To date, it still is. The disciplinary settings of most gender studies of the Holocaust have been history, sociology, psychology, and literary studies. By contrast, Jewish feminists have, as Katherina von Kellenbach put it, 'remained reticent and refrained from systematically articulating the feminist theological implications of the Holocaust.'[2]

As specific a set of personal and academic factors came together to produce my book as it would anyone else's. It is to the personal experiences that were formative for *The Female Face of God in Auschwitz* and to my feminist theological positioning among women scholars of the Holocaust that I turn first.

A 'Non-Jewish Jewish' Childhood

I was born in 1960 into a London Jewish family whose social life was almost exclusively Jewish, whose Zionism was absent-minded, and whose religious observance was non-existent. Although one of my two grandfathers identified as Orthodox and the other as Reform, neither Shabbat nor any other festival was observed by my immediate family (other than entirely secular versions of Christmas and Easter). It was not until I went to university and joined the Jewish Society that I even became aware that Jewish women

1 E.g., Yaffa Eliach's pioneering 1982 *Hasidic Tales of the Holocaust*; Esther Farbstein's 2007 *Hidden in Thunder: Faith, Halachah and Leadership During the Holocaust*, and Isabel Wollaston's 2018 *Jewish Religious Responses to the Holocaust*.

2 Katharina von Kellenbach, 'A Roundtable Discussion on Melissa Raphael's *The Female Face of God in Auschwitz*: Introduction', *Holocaust Studies: A Journal of Culture and History* 15 (2009): 1–4, 1.

traditionally light candles on Friday evening. Whatever Jewishness I had absorbed had been through books and talking to my grandfathers. Judaism was something other, older, people remembered. While some children from observant homes rebel by protesting that, my own preoccupation with all things Jewish was an assertion of self that was greeted by my parents and siblings with more forbearance than appreciation.

Apart from eagerly anticipated family and friends' weddings and (boys') bar mitzvahs, my Jewishness was not a festive affair but a morose diet of expulsions, pogroms, and the Holocaust. I was under-informed about Jewish life, and over-informed about Jewish death. And even my relation to the latter was uncertain. I was a Jew, but an outsider to Judaism; as an Anglo-Jew, I was and was not a European Jew. My grandparents and parents had been born in Britain: a small island about twenty miles distant by sea from the fate of European Jewry. Most of my close relatives left London at the beginning of the war and moved to the comparative safety of the coastal towns of Brighton and neighbouring Hove. Brighton and Hove would have been in the front line in the event of a German invasion, and like other towns along the British South Coast, they were vulnerable to attack by German bombers, as on 25 May 1943, when 22 bombs were dropped and the streets strafed with machine-gun fire. Yet, as it turned out, my maternal grandmother's only personal brush with danger was when she risked smuggling a large bar of black-market chocolate under her mink coat past a local policeman. The upheaval and privations of anywhere in wartime were too much for her sister, my great-aunt's, nerves. She spent the entire war in the calming environment of an establishment in Surrey's Walton-Upon-Thames that, with its rose gardens and manicured lawns, combined the benefits of a hotel and a convalescent home.

In short, my parents and grandparents, uncles and aunts, had lived in the eye of the Holocaust's storm and emerged quite unscathed. I recently watched a home movie of a family wedding in London in the early 1950s and was struck by how *everyone was there*, waving off the bride and groom as they got into a car and drove away for their honeymoon. None of my four grandparents ever referred to the Holocaust in any of the many lively discussions we had around their weekend dinner tables. To have raised the issue of the Holocaust, and by implication the great good fortune of their exemption from the fate of the rest of European Jewry, would have seemed a kind of bad manners. Their Jewishness was not of the abject sort. My maternal grandparents walked out of the cinema where *Fiddler on the Roof* was playing when it came out in 1971: it was too 'brown' (depressing) in its visual palette. They were not cold-hearted people. Unstintingly loving to us, their grandchildren, they did not, even so, put themselves through the unnecessary upset of reading a book or going to see a film about the Holocaust.

My mother was less reticent about the Holocaust than her parents. By the time I was about seven or eight years old, before the debate between intentionalist and functionalist historians of the Holocaust had entered educated consciousness, she would alarm me with talk about Hitler as if he had been a kind of serial killer personally responsible for the death of six million unsuspecting Jewish victims. She also liked to speculate about who of our non-Jewish acquaintance would hide Jews and to identify people who might be Jewish by no more than a sadness in their eyes. These deliberations may have given me the kind of nightmares that continue to this day, but my childhood perspective on the Holocaust was not at all that of the so-called Second Generation. It was more a mood of profound disquiet and distrust of the wider world I had been born into than an object of knowledge or historical enquiry.

If my eventual study of the Holocaust used the methods of narrative theology, it was not only because the idea of redemption is itself a theodramatic representation of history, but also because by the end of my childhood and well into my teenage years, the Holocaust was mediated for me, as it was for so many others, by popular male storytellers such as Leon Uris; Ira Levin, and William Styron. Only later did I graduate from what were essentially Holocaust thrillers to Etty Hillesum's diaries and letters, George Steiner's reflections on language and the Holocaust, Claude Lanzmann's cinematic masterpiece, *Shoah*, and books by Primo Levi; André Schwarz-Bart, and Tadeusz Borowski.

A lifelong habituation to Judaism as less a community of people than of words shaped my approach to Holocaust studies. Had I grown up surrounded by women who had survived the Holocaust, ordinary proximities would have made it difficult or even impossible to theorize their experience under the methods, categories and narrative forms of a more theoretical feminist theology. But as I did not, it was almost inevitable that I would eventually engage women's Holocaust experiences from a literary distance. I listened to the women of the Holocaust not by the empirical method of interviewing survivors, but silently, inwardly and meditatively, through the correlation of Jewish theological and scriptural texts; of women's Holocaust memoirs and a then limited secondary literature on the Holocaust written by feminist historians.

In the summer of 1979, less than a year after my mother died, I had, in fact, got to know two Jewish women who had survived Auschwitz. One was a sales assistant in the Designer Room at Harrods, the department store where I had a Saturday job, and the other ran the laundry at Kibbutz Afek, near Haifa in Israel. With motherly warmth and kindness, both showed me the ropes of, respectively, selling and sorting clothes. I was keenly aware of the numbers tattooed on their forearms, but too diffident, too fearful of prying, to ask them anything at all about their experiences. It would be over thirty years of academic study until I was ready to write, as it were, to these and other women survivors, asking the questions of their experience that I could not ask then.

Some Formative Academic and Spiritual Experiences

The first admission of women to Trinity College, Oxford was in 1979. I matriculated a year later, when Trinity awarded me an Exhibition (a kind of scholarship) to read for a degree in Christian theology. My apparently eccentric choice was simply a consequence of being an assimilated, twentieth-century Jewish girl in search of some means by which address a sense of cosmic crisis for which she had no Jewish name. With no background or intention of converting to Christianity, I may well have been the first Jewish woman to study Christian theology at Oxford. There, I studied a revelation history played out between men and an exclusively male God. Women's religious agency was never discussed, not even that of the catastrophic Eve or the sexless Mary. I studied works written only by men and was taught by exclusively male tutors. My diligence was rewarded with a University prize for meritorious work. But I had, effectively, excelled as an honorary male student. I had no concept of a female religious voice, let alone my own. By the time I graduated in 1983, the foundations for religious feminist scholarship and spirituality had been laid by Judith Plaskow, Carol Christ, and a number of others, but I had no knowledge of it. The female faces of God were not merely unknown to me, but literally unimaginable.

Similarly, when I spent a preparatory day or so in 1989 being trained by the oral historian Paul Thompson to interview Holocaust survivors for the British Library's National Sound Archive, I do not remember gender-difference informing the methodology or the questions I was given to ask survivors. I interviewed several women survivors for the project, but I had no means of prompting them to reflect on how their being girls or women had shaped their experiences.

It was a postdoctoral appointment in 1990 to teach theology and religious studies at a college that would later become the University of Gloucestershire that first awakened me to the absence and silence of women in Abrahamic religious institutions and their canons. Many of the modules I taught were, crucially, shared with the women's studies department. Learning how to use gender as a category of analysis, I was now able to understand that traditional theistic religion is both oppressive and liberative of women. It is at once the ideological root of discrimination against women that permits only men to be the full normative subjects of their own religious experience, and it is the foundation of a prophetic ethic that countermands the sexual-political status quo: an engine of liberation for those whose gender and sexuality has left them estranged from the patriarchal divine.

My embarking on a gender-critical study of Holocaust theology at the turn of the twenty-first century was a chance event: browsing at a study of religions conference book stall, I picked up, and of course bought, a copy of John Roth and Carol Rittner's recently published 1998 collection of pioneering essays, *Different Voices: Women and the Holocaust*, which included now-classic essays by Myrna Goldenberg and Joan Ringelheim. I cannot describe the intellectual and spiritual effect of reading this book without descending into cliché. But the most immediate trigger to my constructive feminist theological response to the Holocaust was a set of several striking articles written by Judith Tydor Baumel, the editor of the present volume.[3] Her research on the sustenance of relationship between *Lagerschwestern* (camp sisters) was, in all senses of the word, a revelation. Judy (and Myrna's) work suggested to me that the narratives of presence that so often underpinned the women's memoir literature could be understood and (re)told through a feminist ethic of care and a modern Jewish (Levinasian) theology of face or presence to the suffering other that was itself derived from the rabbinic literature on the Shekhinah, the indwelling presence of God.

A hermeneutical circle could be drawn to link the women's memoir literature, the early feminist historiography of the Holocaust, and a covenantal theology of relation. Far from the perpetrators making Auschwitz a 'no-go' area for God, as most post-Holocaust theologians had inferred, the maintenance of relations of obligation; of the powerless power of presence to the other in the women's camp in Auschwitz seemed to me to have sanctified it. Auschwitz was absolutely and definitively inhospitable to the human, but in resistant moments of common humanity it could nonetheless be hospitable to God. Not dissimilarly to Emil Fackenheim's interpretation of small gestures of humanity as redemptive acts of mending or *tikkun*,[4] Auschwitz could be read, from a post-Holocaust perspective, as witnessing not the dereliction of history by God, but God's presence within its very trauma. The name for that presence is the Shekinah: the 'female' figure of being-there to the need of the neighbour and stranger that has long been invoked in the classical Jewish literature.

3 These publications include 'Social Interaction among Jewish Women in Crisis during the Holocaust', *Gender and History* 7 (1995), 64–84; 'Women's Agency and Survival Strategies During the Holocaust', *Women's Studies International Forum* 22 (1999), 329–47 and parts of Judy's 1998 book *Double Jeopardy: Gender and the Holocaust*.

4 *To Mend the World: Foundations of Future Jewish Thought*, New York, Schocken, 1982.

It is important to emphasise that not all women could or did care for others in the many different periods and settings of the Holocaust. But it seemed possible to me to argue that when Jewish women performed acts of loving kindness, whether religiously motivated or otherwise, they fulfilled the people Israel's priestly vocation to make this world a sanctuary for God; to purify or wash the world by love of the neighbour, of the stranger, of God. As one woman reached out to another in friendship and care she drew God's image back into a face that Auschwitz existed to erase. When one woman in any sense lifted up another woman from the mud and excrement of Auschwitz, she raised the standard of a messianic peace and justice that is always on its way and carried it through the fiery darkness of Auschwitz.

Teaching religion and gender, feminist ethics, and Christian and Jewish feminist theology had equipped me to embark on a feminist theology of the Holocaust. But an intrication of academic and personal motivations also drove the project. I gave birth to my daughter, Verity, in 1993. She would be my only child. I began to study and write about the Holocaust not least because I did not want her to be told that, in extremis, the Jewish God could abandon her, as post-Holocaust theology and other literatures of divine hiddenness had once seemed to tell me. While patriarchal Jewish theology protested God's apparent incapacity or unwillingness to intervene in innocent Jewish suffering, my daughter and her generation's protest would, I thought, be better levelled at a patriarchal model of God whose projective omnipotence had failed him and us, than against the impotence or injustice of God as such. I also wanted to say to my daughter that women's testimony matters as decisively as men's.

Laura Levitt is right that Jewish narratives of ordinary traumatic loss, and extraordinary, holocaustal, loss are not the same but are mutually interpreting.[5] I can see now, years later, that, conversely, I did not want the God of the Holocaust to be left as abandoned as 'he' had been by my grandfather, Jack Shaffer, when his only daughter, my mother, died of lung cancer at the age of 42. His first child, Jonathan, had died in the early 1930s, within weeks of his birth. After his prayers for my mother's survival were also left unanswered and she died within a few months of her diagnosis, my grandfather spurned God. Embittered by what he perceived as an all-powerful God's betrayal of his loyalty, he neither blessed us nor laid tefillin ever again. It was only when drafting the present essay that I became conscious that a dialogue with my grandfather that I had never had was buried somewhere in my theoretical engagement with divine omnipotence. At the same age as my mother

5 Laura Levitt, *American Jewish Loss after the Holocaust*, New York and London, New York University Press, 2007, pp. xvi-xvii, 2 and *passim*.

was when she died, I was trying, at least in part, to write to my long-dead grandfather of another God of Israel: one who was a mother-God as much in mourning for her children as he was of his.

After the Publication of *The Female Face of God in Auschwitz*

Quite apart from any intrinsic merit in its argument, the book attracted attention in so far as, published in 2003, it appeared at the close of the post-Holocaust period and was the only full-length work of post-Holocaust Jewish theology to be written by a woman in a canon dominated by figures such as Elie Wiesel, Richard Rubenstein, Emil Fackenheim, Eliezer Berkovits, Arthur Cohen, Yitz Greenberg, and Hans Jonas.

Within a short space of time, excerpts from an early article I wrote proposing a Jewish feminist theology of the Holocaust,[6] as well as from the book itself, were published in several readers, including Dan Cohn-Sherbok's 2001 *Holocaust Theology: A Reader* and Steven Katz, Shlomo Biderman and Gershon Greenberg's 2007 *Wrestling With God*, a magisterial anthology of Jewish theological responses written during and after the Holocaust. In both of these readers, mine was the only piece written by a woman. That my work had been published and then selected for re-printing suggested that a discursive shift was underway: even those who did not question the androcentric character of the Holocaust and post-Holocaust religious canon had come to see that a feminist perspective on Holocaust theology would be of interest to readers, if only for its novelty.

Not long after *Female Face* was published, I began to receive invitations to participate in events such as the 2004 Stockholm International Forum on the prevention of genocide, at which not only academics but representatives from 58 governments were present. My paper on women and genocide was briefly cited by Carol Rittner in the closing plenary speeches of the forum. That same year I was interviewed and appointed as the Academic Representative of the British Government's Foreign and Commonwealth Office Delegation to the intergovernmental Taskforce for International Cooperation on Holocaust Education, Remembrance and Research (now known as The International Holocaust Remembrance Alliance) to replace the historian David Cesarani who had stood down from the role under pressure of work. As is the way with these things, I had been appointed not only on the strength of my contribution to the Stockholm Forum, my book, and my professorial status, but also because my connections in Holocaust Studies

6 'When God Beheld God: Notes Towards a Jewish Feminist Theology of the Holocaust', *Feminist Theology* 21 (1999), 53–78.

were something of a personal recommendation. (I was the then partner of one of the Holocaust historians who had been instrumental in the establishment of the Taskforce in 1998).

My experience on the Task Force was rather different to that of the Stockholm Forum. The Task Force was, at that time, dominated by two groups. The first was made up of almost exclusively male historians whose perspectives and methodologies were androcentric by default. The second, still predominantly male, constituency was made up of diplomats keen to smooth ruffled governmental feathers as evidence of economic and other complicities with the Nazi regime, not least those of the so-called neutral countries, was becoming ever harder to ignore. Women's experiences during the Holocaust, and even more so, feminist perspectives on those, were a matter of (women's) "special interest", if they were of interest at all.

Meetings of the Task Force's panel for academic research were chaired by Professor Yehuda Bauer, who was of the view that a gender perspective was, if not beside the point, then of peripheral interest: Nazi Germany's policies to the Jews did not differentiate between the ultimate fate of women and men. Admittedly, important studies such as Rochelle Saidel and Sonja Hedgepeth's 2011 *Sexual Violence Against Jewish Women During the Holocaust* had yet to be published, but Dalia Ofer and Lenore Weitzman's *Women and the Holocaust* had been out for some years and Nechamah Tec's *Resilience and Courage* had been published in 2003. Even so, familiarity with, let alone enthusiasm for, feminist historiography could not have been less apparent.

While it was understandable that historians would suspect theologians of using the Holocaust to lend moral and spiritual leverage to separate contemporary debates,[7] I was not persuaded that historical analysis alone was capable of explaining or responding to Nazism. I shared the prevailing academic view that Auschwitz is un-mendable, but was frustrated by the way that any stance other than a secular, anti-redemptive one was, a priori, excluded from discussion. One eminent Holocaust historian, who was still closely associated at that time with the work of the Task Force, would make humorous, if condescending, remarks about the 'soft' Holocaust Studies practiced by feminists, artists, religionists or anyone contributing anything other than the 'hard' historiography of the 'archive rats' whose knowledge and understanding of the catastrophe was derived almost exclusively from Nazi documents.

7 David Tollerton, 'Was Jewish "Holocaust Theology" ever really about the Holocaust? Assessing the roots and implications of a recurring critique', *Holocaust Studies*, 22 (2016), 125–139.

If they were considered at all, religious responses to the Holocaust were assumed to be Orthodox and indifferent to the historically unique and unprecedented aspects of the Holocaust. There seemed to be an assumption that any Jewish theologian would be incapable of understanding the Holocaust other than under a typology of Jewish suffering operative since the destruction of the First Temple. Jewish feminist theological perspectives were obscure to the point of even deeper irrelevance. I resigned my post after four years, not only because of the logistical difficulties of combining its regular meetings in foreign cities with lone-parenting and full-time work, but also because the Jewish religious and gendered subjectivities at the centre of my work were procedurally ignored.

The Academic and Popular Reception of my Book

Nonetheless, the wider reception of my book was, and has remained, good. It has not only been read by general readers, it has been shared from the pulpit by (mostly liberal) Jewish and Christian ministers, and taught and debated in seminaries and universities all over the world. Its argument, whether considered alone or in relation to other Holocaust theologies, has been examined in relatively large numbers of undergraduate dissertations and postgraduate theses.

Academic books are seldom prominently displayed in bookshops and are now almost invariably bought online, but soon after its publication, copies were spotted in the window of Foyles on London's Charing Cross Road; on the shelves in the Jewish Museum New York's gift shop and, my personal favourite, on a tartan-draped table in a tiny book shop in one of the more remote Scottish Isles. The book also lay behind an invitation to give a (Jewish) Lent talk for the BBC and it was shortlisted for the Koret Jewish book award in 2004 under the category of Jewish religious thought (Daniel Matt's new translation of the Zohar took the prize).

One of great compensations for the sheer drudgery of drafting books while other people are relaxing or asleep are the kind emails later sent by their readers. Whatever the critical reservations some Holocaust scholars might have about feminist historiography or redemptive readings of the irredeemable, many of the women who have written tell me, not that it has resolved anything about the Holocaust itself, but that the book has helped them feel spiritually closer to female relatives who died in or survived the Holocaust. Or again, one woman wrote to me by email just a few weeks ago saying 'this text helped shift my paradigm to one in which I could breathe again… I am a different person because of work you created.' I list these outcomes not in self-congratulation, but to confirm that there is a need and demand for gender-focussed studies of the Holocaust.

However, it is also the task of the academy to subject new arguments to critical analysis. At the 2009 Annual Meeting of the American Academy of Religion a panel was convened to discuss *The Female Face of God in Auschwitz*. Of the five papers presented, two notable critiques of the book were offered by Ellen Umansky, a historian of Jewish women's spirituality, and Isabel Wollaston, who lectures in Holocaust Studies, with a particular interest in the post-Holocaust theological canon.

Ellen Umansky regarded the book's critique of patriarchal models of God's sovereign will and purpose during the Holocaust as a 'major contribution' to the body of theology that was written in response to it. But she also thought that the work romanticized femaleness in general and motherhood in particular; that it reaffirmed a highly traditional Jewish belief in a God who is not accountable for human evil. She felt that the book's emphasis on female care and grieving motherhood gave a gender-essentialist account of both women and the divine, reinforcing binary associations of the feminine with powerlessness, compassion, and love in the sphere of the everyday or immanent, and the masculine with sovereign transcendence, law and commandment. Moreover, she noted an element of anachronism in the book: the *Shekhinah* reclaimed by Jewish feminists in the late twentieth century did not feature historically in women's piety and prayer. During the Holocaust, Jewish women would have called upon a male, monarchical Lord of history, not a maternal one immanent within it.[8] At that time, Umansky pointed out, the *Shekhinah* was a somewhat ambiguous masculine idea of the divine feminine that may have been prevalent among a kabbalistic elite but was seldom found elsewhere.

Isabel Wollaston pointed out that, as a theology of redemption, my book 'scarcely mentioned' the 'testimony of radical negation' embodied by the so-called *Muselmänner* - the walking dead. She also criticised the book's methodology, wondering whether I was using women's testimonies as 'proof texts' for my own theology. She found it difficult, at times, to distinguish between my post-Holocaust voice and that of the cited Holocaust testimony upon which it mediated.[9]

This essay is not the place to enter into an intra-disciplinary debate. Suffice to say that (as Wollaston acknowledged) I had anticipated most of these criticisms in the book itself. I was not trying to tell anyone anything

---

8 'The Presence of God at Auschwitz: Theological Reflections on the Work of Melissa Raphael', *Holocaust Studies: A Journal of Culture and History* 15 (2009), 5–12, pp. 9–10.

9 'Swimming against the tide: Melissa Raphael's Contribution to the Study of Jewish Religious Responses to the Holocaust', *Holocaust Studies: A Journal of Culture and History* 15 (2009), 28–46, pp. 37, 40.

about the historical experiences of women in the Holocaust that feminist historians did not already know. I was emphatically not trying to speak for, or over, the dead or those that survived. Indeed, well before I finished writing the book, I had become acutely conscious of all these dangers, not least after receiving an email from a woman survivor of Auschwitz who had heard about my research. She told me, quite without rancour, that she herself had never had any sense of the presence of God in Auschwitz but was always "willing to learn". This woman's great humility had confronted me with the breath-taking presumption of my project. I could not continue writing the book without reminding myself that I had no desire to arrogate the meaning of any woman's suffering to another purpose. I wanted only to see if one generation of women's stories might not have died with them, but could live in and through the stories of the next.

I was writing with a modern religious conviction that God's speech is our hearing; God's witness, our seeing. My approach was midrashic: a commentary on women's Holocaust narratives written only for the living. Unapologetically dependent on Levinasian ethics, the book offered an account of the human as created in God's image in ways that bind God and humanity together within the space of welcome made in the going out of one to greet or hold the other.[10] My aim was not to replace any tradition, sacral or historiographical, with a different one. It was rather to allow different Jews access to these traditions, and to at least oxygenate what seemed to me to be a stagnant post-Holocaust theodical discussion that laboured under an a priori profession of the necessity of divine omnipotence over history, rather than the transformative power of love. Women's testimonies and memoirs had provided a kind of evidence (not-unmixed with counter-evidence) that violence or other kinds of utter relational numbness were not paradigmatic of the entirety of the individual and collective Jewish condition in Auschwitz. Read through the lens of a feminist ethical theology of care, women's testimony suggested that trust in God's faithful and uninterruptable presence in the entire history of the people Israel, its women as well as its men, could still, after Auschwitz, be professed.

It is not that theological truth claims have any permission to transcend the detail of historical actualities. But their scope and perspective are different. What I wanted to do was to offer an orative reading of women survivors' memoirs which, correlated with classic Jewish texts and the secondary feminist historiography of the Holocaust, could be contemplated until their testimony to sustained relations of care opened an aperture, no more than that,

10 *The Female Face of God in Auschwitz: A Jewish Feminist Theology of the Holocaust*, London and New York, Routledge, 2003, p. 42 and *passim*.

onto the sphere of the holy.[11] Women's deaths during the Holocaust were not what individualistic western thought would consider good or noble deaths, nor were they usually sanctified by the ecstatic spiritual focus associated with Jewish men's sacrificial *kiddush Hashem*. Yet it seemed impossible to read women's Holocaust testimonies and leave a western philosophical and Christian theological imaginary predicated on death and violence, rather than on natality and its bonds of care, unchallenged. There was enough, if only just enough, in women's Holocaust experience, as much as there was in men's, to return beauty for its ashes (Is. 61: 3).[12]

Postscript

I continue to teach about the Holocaust in a variety of Higher Education institutions, including Leo Baeck College, a liberal and reform rabbinical seminary, to the present day. In whatever setting I have taught Holocaust Studies, gender and the Holocaust has usually been the way into its difficult territory that students most readily engage and grasp.

Yet after the publication of *The Female Face of God in Auschwitz* I stopped writing about gender and the Holocaust. This was, in part, so that my heart would not, eventually, break in sorrow, to borrow a phrase from André Schwarz-Bart. It was also because I have long been preoccupied not so much with the Holocaust itself, as with a phenomenological theology of the image of God in the human as it enters history. Perhaps, though, no Jew who has thought and written about the Holocaust ever stops thinking and writing about it. In one way or another it has always been, and remains, implicit in all my books, whether on the visualization of Judaism; on holiness; idolatry, or on the ideology of femininity. Emotionally and intellectually, the Holocaust casts a shadow that is always longer and heavier than one's own.

11 Melissa Raphael, 'From Historiography to Theography: Reflections on the Role of Theological Aesthetics in *The Female Face of God in Auschwitz*', *Holocaust Studies: A Journal of Culture and History*, 15 (2009) 47–56, p. 48.

12 My thinking is indebted here to Grace Jantzen, *Violence to Eternity*, Routledge, London and New York, 2009, esp. pp. 59, 141–3.

Dr. Rochelle G. Saidel

Why I'm Not Painting Flowers in the Garden

Introduction

I consider Remember the Women Institute's 2018 exhibition, *VIOLATED! Women in Holocaust and Genocide,* the culmination of my work on women and the Holocaust—at least as I write these words. The artworks that curator Dr. Batya Brutin and I chose for this exhibition at the Ronald Feldman Gallery in SoHo, New York City, echoed what I have written and spoken for decades.

It took many years and some detours for me to arrive at my focus on women during the Holocaust, with the specific topic of sexual violence beginning to solidify in 2006. When Jewish feminism began blossoming in the 1960s I was not on the scene. I had married young and was living in Albany, N.Y., with my daughter Esther born in 1967 and my son Daniel, in 1970. I caught up at the end of the 1970s, especially after I met and became friends with Aviva Cantor, one of Jewish feminism's founders. Both Holocaust Studies and Women's Studies had begun, but they had not yet come together. For me, and probably in general, this merger took place in 1983, a year before I moved from Albany to Manhattan. My journey to the topic of women and the Holocaust began with the issue of Nazi war criminals in America in 1977, developed as a result of my visit to Ravensbrück women's concentration camp in 1980, and was also connected to my work on museum exhibitions. After women and the Holocaust became my academic subject, I founded Remember the Women Institute in 1997, and most recently have focused on sexual violence during the Holocaust.

I am not a child of survivors and was born in the small Adirondack city of Glens Falls, N.Y. in 1942, statistically the worst year in the history of the Jewish people. My grandparents had immigrated to America from Lithuania/ Poland at the beginning of the twentieth century. I don't remember hearing much about the Holocaust at home or in Hebrew school, with two exceptions. My father, Joseph Saidel, became more religious over the years and transformed from a practicing Conservative Jew during my childhood into an Orthodox Jew by the end of my adolescence. He said that Hitler had made him religious. His mother, my grandmother Esther Saidel, received a letter in the early 1950s from her niece, Yenta Beker, in Lithuania. She had been caught by the Nazis in Kovno, imprisoned in the Stutthof concentration camp, and had barely survived. She was living in Vilna after the Holocaust and needed medicine. No one else in my grandmother's extended family had survived, but she never talked about it. Yenta and her family arrived in Israel in the 1970s, and I heard firsthand (in installments) about her ordeal and the murder of the rest of the family.

Nazi War Criminals in America

The specific catalyst for my professional and personal interest in the Holocaust had nothing to do with family losses. The 1977 deportation case against accused Latvian Nazi war criminal Vilis Hazners in Albany brought the Holocaust directly home to me. The Special Litigation Unit of the United States Justice Department, the precursor of the Office of Special Investigations, initiated this case against Hazners, accused of lying on his entrance papers about being a policeman in the Riga ghetto. I was volunteering with the local Jewish Federation, and the region director of the Anti-Defamation League asked me to monitor the hearing.

When I attended, I learned that witnesses had been brought from Israel to testify. They were asked to relive the most horrible period of their lives, and the government had not given them any social, psychological, or other support. Rabbi Paul Silton, a local Conservative rabbi, and I decided to try to alleviate their isolation by arranging for local Jewish families to host them for Shabbat meals. Several witnesses joined my family for dinner, and one woman said at the table: "Vilis Hazners beat my sister-in-law bloody in the ghetto while she was holding her baby. I never saw either of them again." Perhaps this statement was the beginning of my interest in the experiences of women during the Holocaust. However, I didn't realize it for some years.

The issue of Nazi war criminals in the United States did lead to my working on women and the Holocaust, albeit in a roundabout way. Because I was covering the Albany hearing, I offered to send articles to the Jewish Telegraphic Agency (JTA). As a result, I became a freelance journalist for JTA, working with editor Murray Zuckoff and writing on varied subjects for many years. Soon after I met Zuckoff, he introduced me to his wife, pioneer Jewish feminist Aviva Cantor.

As I continued writing about Nazi war criminals in the United States, I met journalist Charles R. Allen, Jr., who was an expert. With his encouragement, I wrote my first book, *The Outraged Conscience: Seekers of Justice for Nazi War Criminals in America* (SUNY Press, 1984). The book detailed the efforts of individuals in the United States who had been devoted to the issue when the government and most of the organized Jewish world were in denial. Allen and I also created a series of videos and a booklet on the subject. I was producing and hosting a television program called *Heritage and Destiny* for the Albany Jewish Federation, with Allen and Nazi hunter Simon Wiesenthal among my guests.

Allen had contacts in the German Democratic Republic (GDR), and through him, I was invited there to write about the Jewish community for JTA. Two other journalists, Aron Hirt-Manheimer, editor of *Reform Judaism*, and Harvey Rosenfeld, then editor of *Martyrdom and Resistance*, were also on this 1980 trip. In retrospect, I understand we were invited to be shown that there was no antisemitism in East Germany (unlike in West Germany), which could ultimately encourage trade between the GDR and the United States.

Ravensbrück Women's Concentration Camp

Ravensbrück women's concentration camp was not on the itinerary. With her encyclopedic knowledge of women's issues, Aviva Cantor told me that if I was in the GDR, I must visit Ravensbrück. Like most Americans in 1980, I had never even heard about this concentration camp behind the Iron Curtain. Trusting Aviva's instincts, I pushed our GDR hosts hard until they finally brought me, along with Aron Hirt-Manheimer, to the Ravensbrück memorial. Aron later jokingly said I went crazy that day, and maybe, in a sense, I did. This was surely a turning point in my devoting myself to women and the Holocaust.

This first visit to Ravensbrück shocked me. I had not realized there had been a camp specifically for women, where so many suffered, were murdered, or died of starvation, disease, or neglect. Moreover, something was missing from the picture painted by our Communist survivor guide. She never mentioned any Jewish women prisoners. Even though I had no factual information, it seemed logical that a Nazi concentration camp probably had held Jewish victims. I finally asked her, "Weren't there any Jewish women here?" Hardly deviating from her narrative, which mirrored the concept of the camp memorial as a Communist shrine, she answered: "One German Communist political prisoner, Olga Benario Prestes, was also Jewish."

This was the impetus for the research that led to my 2004 book, *The Jewish Women of Ravensbrück Concentration Camp* (University of Wisconsin Press, with Hebrew and Portuguese editions). Beginning with random contacts and interviews as they became available soon after 1980, I found and interviewed Jewish survivors, most in the United States and Israel. My organized research and writing became possible after 1995, when I met Jewish survivors at the camp memorial's ceremonies marking fifty years of liberation. After being told for fifteen years (often by people who should have known better) that I should forget my research because there was no Jewish story for this camp, I knew for a fact that unfortunately there were thousands of Jewish victims.

By 1995 the Berlin wall had fallen and Ravensbrück had moved west without budging an inch. I had visited a year before and observed the memorial being transformed. After hearing for years that the Jewish presence was negligible, I was surprised at the 1995 ceremonies to discover a good-sized delegation of Israeli survivors. There were also Jewish women from the United States and several European countries. I interviewed as many women as I could and gathered contact information. The questionnaire that I developed after the 1995 ceremonies even reached survivors in Australia, via a survivor in California. The United States Holocaust Memorial Museum helped by sending my letter to survivors in their registry.

The Museum of Jewish Heritage and the New York State Museum

In addition to working on Ravensbrück, I was also pursuing other projects. In 1992, at age fifty, I received a PhD in Political Science from the City University of New York Graduate School and University Center. I had originally wanted my dissertation to be about the Jewish Ravensbrück victims, but my advisor, Prof. Asher Arian, discouraged me. He suggested that I stick to a subject closer to home that didn't require a foreign language, and then I could go back to work on Ravensbrück. My dissertation was about the politics of memorialization, specifically the case of the creation of New York City's Museum of Jewish Heritage – A Living Memorial to the Holocaust. My book on the subject, *Never Too Late to Remember: The Politics Behind New York City's Holocaust Museum*, followed (Holmes & Meier, 1996). While the book was not about women and the Holocaust, I did unsuccessfully try to use my connection with the museum's creation to encourage the mostly male power structure behind it to include women's experiences.

My connection to and knowledge about the museum's creation were based on my employment (1981 – 1990) as a special assistant to then New York State Democratic Leader Manfred Ohrenstein. Representing or accompanying him, I was present at the meetings of the executive board that created the museum. There were few women on the board, and women's experiences were never on the agenda.

In the early 1980s, through Senator Ohrenstein's office, I also helped to create a permanent exhibition in the New York State Museum in Albany, *Bitter Hope: From Holocaust to Haven*. While working on the exhibition script, I participated in a 1982 Yad Vashem summer seminar for educators. (Women and the Holocaust was not part of their syllabus.) The *Bitter Hope* exhibition, which opened in 1984, depicts how journalist Ruth Gruber brought Holocaust survivors from Italy to Oswego, N.Y., to the only refugee camp created in the United States during World War II. The exhibition has a section on Holocaust history and another about life in the Oswego camp. Ruth Gruber was a feminist ahead of her time, and I am glad that the exhibition documented her role in this remarkable rescue.

Women and the Holocaust Becomes My Academic Subject

Meanwhile, I had the opportunity to attend part of an eye-opening conference at which women and the Holocaust was very much the focus. The first public event that addressed women, gender, and the Holocaust took place in March 1983, when Dr. Esther Katz and Dr. Joan Ringelheim organized the groundbreaking *Conference on Women Surviving the Holocaust* at Stern College in New York City. Sexual violence was not on the agenda, and I observed how some Holocaust survivors who were present became enraged when an audience member asked about sexual experiences in concentration camps. This pioneering conference brought together female survivors, academics, and feminists to discuss various aspects of women and the Holocaust.

By 1990 I had left Senator Ohrenstein's office, remarried, and moved part time to São Paulo, Brazil. My husband, Guilherme Ary Plonski, a professor at University of São Paulo and a child of a Holocaust survivor who immigrated from Germany to Brazil, encouraged my work on women and the Holocaust. I completed and defended my dissertation while continuing my limited work on Ravensbrück. I also found a new home for my research, becoming a senior researcher at NEMGE – The Center for the Study of Women and the Social Relations of Gender at the University of São Paulo. As part of my research there, I developed a project to interview Jewish women who had immigrated to São Paulo because of the Holocaust. I have used the material for a number of academic papers, articles, and lectures, and still hope to organize it into a book. I represented NEMGE and spoke about women and the Holocaust at a conference in connection with the 1995 UN Fourth World Conference on Women in Beijing, as well as a Women's World Conference in Tromso, Norway, in 1999.

In 1996, while I was working on my Ravensbrück book, I was accepted for a National Endowment for the Humanities (NEH) summer seminar at Brandeis University. Prof. Alan Mintz led the seminar about the Holocaust and the culture of memory in the United States and abroad. He, along with two other brilliant men who influenced my academic work, all about my age, died much too young. My dissertation adviser Prof. Arian died in 2010, my dissertation reader and mentor Prof. Marshall Berman, in 2013, and

Prof. Mintz, in 2017. Their loss was personal, and also deprived the world of their wisdom, creative thinking, and intellectual brilliance.

The 1996 NEH seminar at Brandeis was a big step forward for me regarding women and the Holocaust, because some of the colleagues I met there influenced my work. Among them were Prof. S. Lillian Kremer, who later edited *Women's Holocaust Writing: Memory and Imagination* (University of Nebraska Press, 1999) and Prof. Sonja M. Hedgepeth of Middle Tennessee State University. The connection with Sonja continues until today, and we have cooperated on many projects, conferences, and writings over the years. We've had work-related adventures together around the United States, as well as in such countries as Israel, Russia, Poland, Germany, and Austria.

Creating Remember the Women Institute

In 1997 I founded Remember the Women Institute, a not-for-profit organization based in New York City, in order to further research, publishing, and cultural activities that contribute to including women in history, especially Holocaust history. By the 1990s a core of books had been published about women's experiences during the Holocaust, but sexual violence was absent or not emphasized. For the first time in its then 29 years of conferences, in 1999 the Annual Scholars' Conference on the Holocaust and the Churches presented a plenary session on women and the Holocaust. As co-chairs of this plenary, Dr. Myrna Goldenberg and I decided to feature recent scholarly books on the subject, with the session entitled "Women's Holocaust History: Books in Print." The occasion was remarkable not only because the subject was deemed worthy of a plenary, but also because by early 1999, there was such a core of books.

I curated an art/history exhibition for the Florida Holocaust Museum in 2001. The *Women of Ravensbruck – Portraits of Courage: The Art of Julia Terwilliger* exhibition featured mixed media panels by the late artist, along with photographs and biographies of a diverse sampling of the female victims and history panels about the concentration camp. I also created a catalog for the exhibition which traveled to Houston, Pittsburgh, Detroit, and elsewhere, and has been remounted at least twice at the Florida Holocaust Museum. In most cases I was invited to speak to the public, docents, students, or educators.

In 2007 I created another exhibition, this time for Hebrew Union College – Jewish Institute of Religion in New York City, *Fiorello's Sister: Gemma La Guardia Gluck's Story*. On view from September 2007 through January 2008, the exhibit was organized for the 125th anniversary of the birth of New York City Mayor Fiorello La Guardia. Based on my book of the same name, the exhibit described the life's journey of Fiorello's sister Gemma, who had been arrested in Budapest and incarcerated as a political hostage in

Ravensbrück. I had learned about her and included a chapter about her in my Ravensbrück book. An out-of-print memoir, edited by S. L. Shneiderman and published in 1961, was the basis for that chapter. With more research, new information, and contacts with her family, I was able to augment and document Gemma's original memoir in the new version that I edited (Syracuse University Press, 2007).

Gemma is one of my personal heroes, women whose stories I have written and whom I would choose to invite for lunch, if I could. Others include two Ravensbrück Jewish political prisoners murdered in the Bernburg euthanasia facility in 1942: Olga Benario Prestes and Dr. Käte Leichter. Olga was a German Jewish Communist who fell in love with Brazilian Communist leader Luís Carlos Prestes and was deported from Brazil to Nazi Germany. Käte was an Austrian Social Democrat and member of the resistance who had been a pioneering social scientist. To round out my table, I would invite Haviva Reik, a British Mandate parachutist from pre-Israel Palestine who was sent to Slovakia in the midst of World War II. She was murdered there, while trying to save downed Allied airmen and remnants of the Jewish community. Although I can't chat with them over lunch, I envision creating new plays, programs, or films to honor them. I am pleased I had a role in the 2016 correction of Haviva's birth and death dates by the Israel Ministry of Defense on her gravestone on Mt. Herzl, in the Jerusalem cemetery for Israel's heroes.

Focusing on Sexual Violence during the Holocaust

My husband and I had officially made aliyah by 2001, and I began spending more time in Israel, based in Jerusalem. At around that time, Dr. Batya Brutin and Prof. Esther Hertzog were organizing the first international conference in Israel on the subject of women and the Holocaust, held in 2002 at Beit Berl Academic College, The Ghetto Fighters' House Museum, and Beit Terezin. I'm not sure whether I was at their first conference, but I was there for the second, in 2003, the third, in 2005, and others, as part of the organizing committee.

I met Nava Semel at one of the early organizing meetings. She was wearing one pink and one purple Croc, along with two different earrings. I didn't know much about her or her work then, but I immediately knew that I liked her. We kept in touch and saw each other in Tel Aviv and New York, working together on conferences and projects. Nava was especially helpful in discussing sexual violence during the Holocaust with Sonja Hedgepeth and me for our anthology, *Sexual Violence against Jewish Women during the Holocaust* (Brandeis University Press, 2010). We wrote a chapter on Nava's works, and she spoke brilliantly in New York for some of the book launch events. When Remember the Women Institute organized a 2012 symposium on sexual violence, along with USC Shoah Foundation and Equality Now, Jane Fonda read, crying, from Nava's *And the Rat Laughed*. Nava died on December 2, 2017, at age 63, a deep loss for all of us who loved and worked with her. Remember the Women Institute and the Arnold and Leona Finkler Institute of Holocaust Research, Bar-Ilan University, organized a conference in her memory in January 2020.

Sonja Hedgepeth and I were together in 2006 at the Yad Vashem Holocaust memorial in Jerusalem when the idea began percolating for our 2010 anthology about sexual violence. At an international conference for educators there, we organized through Remember the Women Institute a workshop entitled "Beyond Anne Frank: Teaching about Women and the Holocaust." During my presentation about Ravensbrück, a prominent Holocaust scholar rudely interrupted me to challenge my statement that some Jewish women had been raped. He insisted, even at that late date, that Jewish women were never raped during the Holocaust. This encounter became a call to action for Sonja and me, and the result was the book we edited on sexual violence. It took until 65 years after the Holocaust ended for the first book on the subject to appear.

When I began doing research about Ravensbrück in the 1980s, I thought that sexual violence during the Holocaust was rare and affected only a small number of female victims. Any information I gleaned from the many interviews I did with Jewish survivors into the 1990s was minimal, almost by accident. In those days, interviewers seldom pressed the question, and such information was rarely offered. By now I have changed my mind completely. After years researching and writing about this specific aspect of Holocaust history, as well as learning from victims, witnesses, documents, and other scholars, I no longer think that sexual violation was isolated or unusual. Instead, I am confident that in one form or another, to one degree or another, most women must have suffered from sexual abuse during the Holocaust—from humiliation to outright rape. As Nava Semel noted, the very induction into a concentration camp was sexual violation. Within the Jewish population destined for extermination, women and men had different experiences. Among these differences, women suffered from sexual violation particularly designated for women.

After our book about sexual violence against Jewish women came out at the end of 2010, Sonja and I participated in many conferences, panels, and lectures. We were the first to make presentations on the subject at the World Congress for Jewish Studies, the Association for Jewish Studies, the Scholars' Conference on the Holocaust and the Churches, and other conferences in the United States, Israel, and Europe. I wrote another book during that time, *Mielec: the Shtetl that Became a Nazi Concentration Camp* (Gefen, 2012). While this book was more general, my research revealed that a Nazi agent in Mielec, Poland, used a Jewish woman as his sex slave, a job description that included cleaning his home while naked. Along with other information about women's experiences, this is part of the book.

Two Moving Events

I have organized panels, attended international conferences, planned events, created exhibitions, participated in films, and presented lectures as part of my work through Remember the Women Institute. Among these activities, by now countless, two instances stand out as moving in both senses of the word: they moved me emotionally and moved the topic of sexual violence forward intellectually. The first event was a March 20, 2011, *Panel and Speakout on Sexual Violence during the Holocaust and Other Genocides* at the Brooklyn Museum's Elizabeth A. Sackler Center for Feminist Art. A discussion about whether understanding sexual violence during the Holocaust could decrease or prevent it during other genocides took place among Equality Now founder Jessica Neuwirth, Shalupe Foundation founder Maman Jeanne Kasongo L. Ngondo, Nava Semel, feminist activist Gloria Steinem, Sonja Hedgepeth, and me.

The highlight for me came during the subsequent audience participation. A long line formed on both sides of the big auditorium, with people asking questions and commenting. At the end of one line stood Consolee Nishimwe, a Rwanda genocide survivor whom we had asked to join our panel. She had refused after much deliberation, saying she just couldn't do it. And then suddenly there she was, announcing publicly for the first time that she had been raped at age fourteen. She was crying and we were crying, as was most of the audience. Since then my courageous friend Consolee has become an accomplished speaker, published author, and activist, telling her story to keep the memory of the horrors of the Rwandan genocide alive as a deterrent for the future.

The second event, which could be described as historic, was a symposium on sexual violence during the Holocaust, held in Los Angeles in November 2012, co-sponsored by Remember the Women Institute and the USC Shoah Foundation. The meeting of some twenty invited academics and activists who had worked on this issue was held at University of Southern California. Participants spent two days reflecting on the evidence that points to sexual violence, its place within genocidal processes, and how genocide is shaped by gender. We then drafted a statement of purpose for going forward: "Evidence, information, and scholarship are emerging that sexual violence, long largely ignored, was an integral part of the Holocaust in many forms. Absence of acknowledgment of this reality has not only harmed survivors but also the understanding of and efforts to prevent genocide, and efforts to stop sexual violence in genocide, war, and every day. We hope that increasing awareness of this subject, obscured by shame and denial, will bring recognition to the victims, many of whom did not survive, rectify this omission from history, and support the work of those who oppose these atrocities." Jane Fonda read Nava Semel's description of a violated girl in *And the Rat Laughed* during the public event connected with the symposium.

Genesis of the *VIOLATED! Women in Holocaust and Genocide* Art Exhibition

In 2013, among the conferences where we presented information about sexual violence, Sonja Hedgepeth and I were at the Israeli *Women and the Holocaust* conference, where Remember the Women Institute coordinated the session entitled "Sexual Violence against Women during the Holocaust: Ways to Consolidate and to Reveal the Personal Narrative." The Institute had paid the expenses for an independent Polish scholar to be part of our panel. Because she and Israeli artist Gil Yefman had a mutual friend, Gil attended our session. As I sat on the panel I was distracted by a young man who was sitting in the front row crocheting.

This was Gil Yefman, and the beginning of our friendship and cooperation. His extraordinary artistic creations, often crocheted, include the theme of sexual violence during the Holocaust. When he had a solo exhibition at the Ronald Feldman Gallery in New York in 2016, Sonja Hedgepeth and I participated in a panel discussion and met the gallery owner of the same name. We also wrote an article for Gil's Tokyo exhibition catalog, translated into Japanese. Gil introduced us to the Kuchinate Collective in Tel Aviv, founded in 2011 by clinical psychologist Dr. Diddy Mymin Kahn, working with Aziza Kidane, an Eritrean nun, to help African refugee women. I visited the workshop several times along with Batya Brutin, and we saw how the women socialized, ate meals together, and crocheted baskets to earn a small income. We decided that Yefman would create giant baskets along with the women, as part of our *VIOLATED! Women in Holocaust and Genocide* exhibition. Their handwork recalls their suffering in their homelands, followed by their horrendous trip toward freedom, sometimes held captive by Bedouin traffickers and raped in Egypt's Sinai Peninsula. In December 2018 Gil Yefman had a solo exhibition, *Kibbutz Buchenwald*, at the Tel Aviv Museum, and both Diddy Mymin Kahn and I participated in a panel discussion.

Women, Theater, and the Holocaust

I began a new project through Remember the Women Institute in 2015, not specifically related to sexual violence. We created our first *Women, Theater, and the Holocaust Resource Handbook*, which I edited with Karen

Shulman. This on-line free PDF, now in its fourth edition, is available from www.rememberwomen.org. The 150-page handbook includes an introduction, six scholarly essays, and annotated lists of plays by and about women, as well as a bibliography and a lesson plan. In connection with the launch of the handbook's editions, the Institute has held five annual programs of dramatic readings in New York City on the theme of *Women, Theater, and the Holocaust.* In 2018 the performance took place at the Ronald Feldman Gallery during our *VIOLATED! Women in Holocaust and Genocide* art exhibition. The readings and the artworks combined to powerfully bring the theme home.

Since the inception of this project about theater, I have worked with two outstanding, talented, and devoted partners, Dr. Meghan Brodie and Cynthia L. Cooper. I met Meghan in 2014, when she was directing her University of Southern Maine students in a production of *In the Underworld*, an English language translation of the dark operetta that Ravensbrück prisoner Germaine Tillion wrote in the camp. I attended a dress rehearsal and spoke with the actors. For five years afterward, Meghan Brodie, now a professor of theater at Ursinus College, has brought her students to perform in all of our readings programs. In 2019 two of the students I had met at her 2014 production, now professional actors, performed an excerpt from *Claude & Marcel,* Meghan's play-in-progress.

I met Cynthia L. Cooper at around the same time and she, too, has worked with us since the beginning of our theater readings project. She is a prolific playwright, and we have presented a number of her plays. In 2019 she wrote an original short play for the event, *The Box*. For our spring 2016 program, she surprised me by writing and presenting *The Spoken and the Unspoken*, a play based on the work of Remember the Women Institute and the resistance we have faced in bringing the subject of sexual violence into the open. Although she had informally interviewed me beforehand, I didn't know she was going to have one of the actors quote me saying something like it would be nice to "paint flowers in the garden and enjoy my grandchildren" instead of struggling with this subject. While I do enjoy my four Israeli grandchildren, I have not yet made any new flower paintings and the work goes on. This play was also performed at the Actors' Temple and the Museum of Jewish Heritage, New York City, and at our exhibition in 2018.

Creation of the *VIOLATED! Women in Holocaust and Genocide* Art Exhibition

Other important possibilities and projects continue to crop up even as I am writing this, but I would like to focus on the 2018 exhibition, *VIOLATED! Women in Holocaust and Genocide*, which I consider the high point of my work until now. I had majored in art with an emphasis on art history for my bachelor's degree, earned a master's degree in art education, and taught art in public and private schools for eight years. But that was ancient history that had seemed to evaporate as my interest in the Holocaust and women developed and became my life's work. Nevertheless, adding art as a third component of my focus on women and the Holocaust was not without foundation. The exhibition was an outgrowth of the *Sexual Violence against Jewish Women during the Holocaust* book and subsequent discussions that co-editor Sonja Hedgepeth and I had with our friend Batya Brutin, Israeli art historian and curator. Batya became exhibition curator with me as coordinator and Sonja, Karen Shulman, and Rebecca Pristoop on the exhibition team. When Ronald Feldman agreed to hold the exhibition in his SoHo gallery, we gained not only a wonderful exhibition space but also his wise counsel.

The 47 artworks by thirty artists in our April – May 2018 exhibition reflected the artists' deep convictions that such atrocities occurred, both during the Holocaust and later genocides. This is also demonstrated through the accompanying artist statements in the catalog that Batya Brutin and I co-edited (available from Amazon.com or as a PDF from www.rememberwomen.org). The international group exhibition included many Israeli artists, most of them children of survivors. Gil Yefman's Nazi bordello sex slave sculpture was prominently featured. We were fortunate to borrow a half-size study, still twelve feet long, of Judy Chicago and Donald Woodman's *Double Jeopardy* from their *Holocaust Project: From Darkness into Light*. Other well-known artists included Nancy Spero, Boris Lurie, and Safet Zec. There were also two extraordinary drawings done in camps during the Holocaust, and one done immediately afterward. We are seeking to mount the exhibition again in other venues.

This exhibition uses artistic expression to reveal some of the objective facts about sexual violence that we have become aware of over the decades. By now I would like to hope there is no dispute that sexual violence was prevalent during the Holocaust. Nevertheless, I will summarize here some of the various forms: the system of official Nazi brothels "staffed" by women prisoners forced to be sex slaves; personal sex slaves; the rape of women about to be murdered in killing fields; sexual abuses accompanying the camp entry process and *Appell* (roll call); forced exchange of sexual favors for bread or another necessity for survival; and "medical" experiments related to fertility and pregnancy. Even some Jewish ghetto leaders were complicit, giving the Nazis young women for their pleasure in order to stave off a general deportation. People hiding Jews should have tried to protect them, but there are accounts of so-called righteous gentiles who required sex as payment.

I believe that one reason that the fact of sexual violation is now generally, if sometimes reluctantly, accepted is the revelations of sexual abuse during later genocides. Because sexually abused women have been in headlines about later genocides, one can see the link to what happened to women during the Holocaust. The later genocides or ethnic cleansings that our team studied in preparation for our exhibition took place in Bosnia, Darfur, Eritrea, Guatemala, Iraq (Yezidi), Nigeria, and Rwanda, as well as in Cambodia, Congo, and Myanmar (Rohingya), and we were able to include art from all but the last three. There are, of course, differences. Rape and sexual violence were not part of the Nazis' weapons of war as they have been in later genocides. However, during the Holocaust and later, such violence has been part of some women's experiences, with the same result of violated, shamed, and often dead women. We wanted the exhibition to make that connection clear.

I had the opportunity to learn details about the Bosnian and Rwandan genocides when Sonja Hedgepeth and I represented Remember the Women Institute at the Salzburg Global Seminar entitled *The Global Prevention of Genocide: Learning from the Holocaust* in Austria in 2010. Because of this conference, I by chance met Karen Shulman when I returned to Jerusalem. Soon afterward, then in her twenties, she began working with me at Remember the Women Institute. We need dedicated colleagues in younger generations to ensure that our work on women and the Holocaust continues into the future.

Lenore J. Weitzman

How Reading Women's Holocaust Testimonies Helped Me Cope and Then Changed My Life

My Life Was Falling Apart and I Did Not Know How to Cope

It felt like my life was falling apart: my mother had a stroke, then broke her hip, and was living alone in Florida. She needed my help and I wanted to be with her. But I was an Associate Professor of Sociology at Harvard University, coming up for tenure, and I had to finish the book I was writing. I didn't know how to cope with these two urgent but conflicting needs.

I knew my mother had to come first and I asked for a leave of absence for the next semester to take care of her. I wrote a long letter explaining what had happened, why I needed the semester to be with her, and argued that it was similar to the leave they granted new parents who had additional family responsibilities. I asserted that taking care of an aging parent who was seriously ill was even harder than childcare because there were fewer institutional supports and it was a downward trajectory, in contrast to the upward trajectory of continuous growth in child care.

At that time my field was sociology of law. I had written an award-winning book, *The Divorce Revolution: The Unexpected Social and Economic Consequences for Women and Children in America,*[1] and I was teaching a large course on "Women and the Law" with over 200 students. I was keenly aware of the ways in which women's roles in the family, and, specifically, their taking care of vulnerable children and elderly parents, disadvantaged them at work. I urged the university to adopt a policy that would help mitigate those disadvantages.

It didn't help.

The Dean said "no." Harvard would not approve a family leave to care for a parent. I heard the Dean was afraid it would set a dangerous precedent and be too expensive.

I then thought of taking an unpaid leave and talked to several senior members of my department. They made it clear that would "not be wise": it would be seen as a sign of my lack of commitment to my profession. One told me, as an example of what he thought one's priorities should be, that

1 *The Divorce Revolution: The Unexpected Social and Economic Consequences for Women and Children in America*, New York: The Free Press, 1985.

he was proud of the fact that he did not attend his father's funeral because it conflicted with a class he was scheduled to teach.

I was appalled. But despite their dire predictions of how taking the leave would jeopardize my career, all I could think about was what was happening to my mother. Whatever the costs, I knew I could not abandon my mother. Today, as I write that sentence, I immediately think of how often I encountered those very words in women's Holocaust memoirs and the vivid descriptions of daughters clinging to their mothers.

I took the unpaid leave and spent most of the next six months with my mother. That time saved her – and me. Even though I could not find a single doctor who was willing to operate on her hip (because they said she was too old and it was too dangerous), and even though they told me she could never walk again, we proved them wrong. My mother got through those excruciating months with an amazing group of therapists, and we both cried when she took her first steps without assistance.

In hindsight, those difficult months also turned out to be equally valuable for me because they brought me to the Holocaust and to a new field that changed my life. It was a circuitous path. At first, I dutifully carried scholarly articles for the book I was supposed to be writing to the waiting rooms of the endless doctors, hospitals, and rehabilitation facilities we visited. But I found I couldn't focus on anything academic. As someone who had been such a strong advocate for women to persist in other spheres, I felt that I had lost my ability to formulate a strategy to get my own life back on track.

I decided I had to find out how others had faced difficult situations, ones much worse than what I was facing, so I could learn how to cope. The worst situation I could imagine was to be a Jew trapped in the Holocaust. So I turned to Holocaust memoirs for lessons.

By chance, Leesha Rose's book, *The Tulips Are Red*, had arrived just before I left for Florida and I had taken it with me in case I needed a break from "real work." Leesha was a nurse in the Jewish hospital in Amsterdam who became a courier for the Dutch resistance during the Holocaust. I had ordered her book after interviewing her when I was in Israel for an International Conference on Women. When a friend told me about Leesha's experiences passing as a non-Jew, I was immediately intrigued: I had no idea it was even possible for Jews to pass during the Holocaust. At the time I thought I might use her story of how she created a false identity in one chapter of a book I was writing on social identity.

I remembered being inspired by Leesha's amazing coping skills. Here I was searching for a strong female role model, and her book provided the perfect place to start. It led me to seek out and read every survivor memoir I could find. I became obsessed.

Although it may seem counter-intuitive, these memoirs changed the way I looked at and felt about my situation. When I compared my situation to what Holocaust victims had endured, my "problems" became minor. And when I read about their courage and determination, I felt as if I was gaining strength from them.

By the end of my six-month leave I had decided to change the focus of my academic work – and my life – and to study the Holocaust. It was an enormous decision because I had no scholarly credentials and had just begun to read the literature. I would have to become a "graduate student" again and would need several years to catch up.

I was fortunate to be awarded a Fulbright fellowship in Israel for research at Yad Vashem, The Holocaust Memorial Museum and Archive in Jerusalem. At the same time, the Sociology Department at the Hebrew University invited me to join them, and arranged an apartment in university housing in Jerusalem. My former colleague at Stanford, Professor Marilyn Safir, made plans for me to teach a course on "Women and the Law" at Haifa University, and convinced me it would be an easy commute from Jerusalem and I would get to see the country. And then I, being totally unrealistic and optimistic, also enrolled in the Ulpan at the Hebrew University in Jerusalem.

A year after my mother died, my husband, William J. Goode, and I arrived in Jerusalem. He had been a chaired professor in sociology at Columbia University and had many close friends and former students who were now themselves chaired professors throughout Israel. We were warmly welcomed "as family" in a way that seemed possible only in Israel. By chance his son, Erich Goode, had a Lady Davis fellowship at the Hebrew University that year, and Erich's wife, Barbara Weinstein, had a Fulbright fellowship, so we were surrounded by and embedded in family. It turned out to be an enormously productive and personally fulfilling year.

I write this because instead of becoming depressed by the subject of the Holocaust, as some of my Harvard colleagues predicted, I began my new career with the support and encouragement of a wide circle of friends and family in Israel. I doubt that would have been possible anywhere else at the time. In fact, when I returned to Cambridge for a brief visit in the middle of that year, I ran into a Harvard colleague I considered a friend, and was happily sharing my excitement with him. He looked surprised and warned me that it would be "crazy" for me to specialize in the Holocaust because the Holocaust would never be considered a legitimate area of study. It was "just an historical event" and had "no theory." Besides, it was too depressing. He urged me, for my own good, to stop and reconsider what I was doing — because he cared about me.

In contrast, my former colleagues in the legal and feminist communities in Israel, especially Frances Raday and Alice Shalvi, strongly supported my new interests, and I fondly remember Alice including me in what was my first all-women's dinner in her sukkah shortly after we arrived.

Background: The Absence of the Holocaust

Unlike many of my Israeli friends who worked on the Holocaust, who had survivor parents, relatives and neighbors, both of my parents were born in the United States. Their parents had left Bialystok and Letichev (Western Ukraine) in the late nineteenth century. I did not know any survivors when I was growing up in Brooklyn, even though I went to a Jewish day-school. Nor do I remember any talk of the Holocaust or Holocaust memorials.

One of the great surprises of my year in Israel was meeting "new cousins" who had recently arrived from the former Soviet Union. They had been young children during the Holocaust but had vivid memories of their escape from Novograd Volinsk, Ukraine, ahead of the mass killings, and their experiences of displacement. I remembered my father telling me about his cousins in Russia and how, in the 1950's, they had asked him to stop writing to them because it was dangerous for them to get letters from the United States. Almost 30 years later, shortly before my father died, one of these most emotional experiences was finally receiving a letter from his cousins. Now I also had cousins who had experienced the war firsthand, and who were willing to stay up all night to tell me about it. It added a portrait of the Holocaust that was vastly different from the Polish experiences I had erroneously assumed were universal in Eastern Europe.

The Challenge of Research at Yad Vashem: Finding the Testimonies of Jews who Survived by Passing as Non-Jews

I planned to answer two questions by drawing a random sample of Jews who had passed as non-Jews from the testimonies at Yad Vashem. First, I wanted to find out how many of the Jews who survived the Holocaust had been passing as non-Jews. I believed this previously ignored group of survivors was larger than scholars had assumed, and that their experiences would add a new dimension to our understanding of the full range of survival strategies during the Holocaust. Second, I wanted to compare the experiences of Jews who had passed in different countries during the Holocaust and examine the influence of the larger society in creating opportunities for, and constraints on, those who were pretending they were not Jewish.

But first I had to do more background reading on the Holocaust and asked Professor Israel Gutman, my academic sponsor and mentor at Yad Vashem, for a reading list. He must have been shocked by how much I did not know, but he was gracious, and gave me a list that consumed my first month.

I had foolishly assumed that I would be able to draw a random sample of survivors who "had passed as non-Jews" from the Yad Vashem archives. I was therefore surprised and dismayed when I found out that that the archives were not computerized, and there was no "master list" of testimonies that I could use to draw a random sample or to do a key word search. I was told that the only way to find testimonies of those who had passed would be to examine each of the 6,500 testimonies in the archive. I calculated that even if I could look at 10 testimonies a day, 6 days a week, it would take me more than two years to do that. In addition, because the testimonies were in the language of the survivors, they were in 12 languages, and I would have to read testimonies in languages I did not know.

Responding to my panic, Professor Gutman suggested I hire a research assistant, and that we begin reading the testimonies to figure out a new plan. He introduced me to a young woman, Neta Frishman, who helped me recruit a team of 17 researchers, working in 12 languages, to examine the 6,500 testimonies.[2] Many of those Neta recruited were her friends and friends of her friends who had been working as flight attendants for Delta airlines and had been temporarily laid off after the busy season around the Jewish Holidays. They were all fluent in several languages, interested in reading the testimonies, and enthusiastic about my project. We devised a coding sheet to record the results of our search for testimonies that mentioned any of my keywords – "passing, false papers, forged documents, living illegally or living on the Aryan side" – in any Nazi-occupied country in Eastern and Western Europe.

I was excited to find what I considered a significant percentage of Jews who had survived by passing. There were more than 800 testimonies, about 12 % of the testimonies in the archive, that discussed passing.

But, at the same time, I was overwhelmed by the challenge of exploring their experiences in 11 countries. When I looked at the distribution by country, I found that about half of the testimonies of those who passed were from people who had lived in Poland. That led me to decide to begin by focusing on Poland. I drew a random sample from the list we had compiled of all the Polish Jews who passed, selecting slightly more than half of the Polish testimonies, a total of 248 testimonies, to read more thoroughly and to systematically code for further analysis. The results of that statistical analysis were reported in my article, "Living on The Aryan Side in

2 Gali Avrahami, Na'ama Begin, Gabriel Bar-Shaked, Emmanuel Darmon, Karen Dengler, Neta Frishman, Vardit Hortman, Aryeh Julius, Bluma Lederhandler, Karen Margolet, Iris Mazel, Margoret Melchior, Eugenia Prokop-Janiec, Julia Vercholantsev, Ella Walner, Olaf walner, Eva Weitzman, and Maria Westerman.

Poland: Gender, Passing and the Nature of Resistance" in the book that Dalia Ofer and I edited on, *Women in The Holocaust*.[3]

I also began interviewing survivors who had "passed" in Poland and who were then living in Israel. I started by contacting survivors suggested by Professor Gutman, who remained a generous source of contacts and advice. At the end of each interview I asked if they knew other survivors who had survived by passing and soon ended up with what sociologists call a "snowball" sample (which is often used when one is interested in talking to people who are otherwise hard to locate.) It was exciting to set out to meet survivors in their homes in different kibbutzim, towns and cities throughout Israel. It gave me a chance to see the country, and to have the luxury of time to linger over tea and warm hospitality. Israel is a small country and return visits and follow-up questions were always within reach.

In the following years, I interviewed additional survivors who passed in Poland who were then living in the United States and England, and also interviewed survivors who had passed in France and Germany. I was then able to return to my original aim of comparing those who passed in different countries, and compared those who passed in Poland with those who passed in France and Germany.[4]

Why Women?

In retrospect it may seem odd, but when I started working on the Holocaust I assumed I was working in an entirely new field and had put aside my focus on gender. I wanted to be totally and completely grounded in the Holocaust. But as soon as we started getting preliminary results, it became obvious that gender was the single most important variable in determining who passed and how successful they were in passing.

In the Yad Vashem testimonies of Polish Jews who passed, more than two-thirds, 69 percent, were women. There were several reasons for that. The first was that it was more dangerous for Jewish men to pass because they were circumcised and could be easily identified as Jews. Whenever a Nazi or a Pole suspected a man of being Jewish, they told him to drop his pants. A second factor was the psychological effect that circumcision, or lack

---

3 Lenore Weitzman "Living on the Aryan Side in Poland: Gender, Passing and the Nature of Resistance", in Dalia Ofer and Lenore J. Weitzman, *Women in the Holocaust,* New Haven and London: Yale University Press, 1998: 187–222.

4 Lenore Weitzman "Masks for Survival: The Experiences of Jews Who Passed in Poland and Germany During the Holocaust" in *Remembering for the Future: The Holocaust in an Age of Genocide*, John Roth and Elisabeth Maxwell, eds., Oxford: Palgrave, 2002, v.1: 589–609.

of it, had on men and women. Because men knew they could be identified, they were more fearful of passing to begin with, and less likely to try it. In contrast women could be confident that they could not be unmasked by a physical exam.

A third explanation for the larger number of women who passed was the greater cultural assimilation of Jewish women in Poland before the war. As Gershon Bacon noted, Jewish girls, even those from Hasidic homes, were more likely than Jewish boys to attend regular Polish schools and become familiar with Polish literature, customs and fashions, something that would help them pass in the future. Boys, however, were often sent to heder and yeshiva which gave them a superior Jewish education but limited their contact with Polish culture and non-Jewish Poles.

Ironically the "inferior non-Jewish education" that Jewish girls received provided them with the ability to speak colloquial Polish, and contacts with non-Jewish classmates to whom they might be able to turn to for help.

Finally, another explanation for the predominance of women among those who passed was the type of sex role socialization that girls received at that time. Girls were encouraged to behave in ways that provided them with social skills that were useful in passing – to be sensitive to the feelings of others, pay attention to the social sphere, and to adapt and fit in, all of which were critical to passing. In contrast, none of these traits were encouraged in boys.

The Deviant Cases – How I Discovered the Kashariyot

After talking to many survivors and reading hundreds of testimonies, I thought I understood what it was like to be a Jew passing in Poland. It was a life of endless strain and fear, knowing that any slip, or any chance event, could lead to being captured or killed. While most Jews who were passing described those anxieties, my research assistants and I started to notice a very different "tone" in some of testimonies from young women who had been passing. They described themselves as bold, confident, and defiant. These young women, who came to be called kashariyot (connectors, because they were the couriers between the ghettos), rarely talked about trepidation, or apprehension. Instead their interviews focused on plans to outwit the Nazis, thwart the Germans, and help other Jews. For example, Bronka Klibanski, who smuggled guns into the Bialystok ghetto said: "I wasn't afraid, I was determined to do something to take revenge for what the Germans were doing. And it gave me strength."[5] When Bronka spoke she was relaxed and

5 See Lenore J. Weitzman, "Kashariyot (Couriers) in the Jewish Resistance During the Holocaust," in Paula Hyman and Dalia Ofer, eds., *Jewish Women: A*

smiling, with a twinkle in her eye, seeming to enjoy her memories of all the times she had outsmarted the Nazis.

At first I was hesitant to accept what I assumed was just bravado. I believed that every Jew who was passing in Poland had to be fearful of being unmasked, and I knew these young women were constantly exposed to non-Jews who might detect that they were Jewish. But when I began focusing on their testimonies, I became convinced that they were, indeed, different from all the other Jews who were passing – i.e. different from both Jewish men and other Jewish women who were not Kashariyot.

I soon understood why they were different. They were all members of a Jewish youth movement that was part of the Jewish resistance. That emboldened them. It also gave them strong social support and a deep sense of the importance of their mission. The movements to which they belonged ranged from Zionist youth groups such as Dror, Akiva, and Hashomer Hatzair, to the Bund youth organization, Tsukunft, and the Communist youth, the Komsomol.

These movements provided them with an ideology and a network of support. Their ideology defined their mission as critically important and inspired their courage. Their network of members and friends sustained and supported them. They were eager to take advantage of every chance to outwit and frustrate the Nazis. Instead of seeing danger, the kashariyot saw opportunities. Their attitude was surprising because it was at odds with objective reality. They were actually in much more danger than the average Jew who was passing because their missions involved smuggling weapons, bluffing their way through border controls and rescuing other Jews, all blatantly anti-Nazi acts. While they used false papers to conceal their Jewish identities, as did most Jews who were passing, these young women were much more likely to have direct face-to-face contact with Nazis. How could they not be afraid?

I wanted to know more: How had they become involved in the Jewish resistance? Why were they willing to risk their own lives to warn and save other Jews?

Once I had published my work on passing, I turned to a more comprehensive study of the Kashariyot. I was excited to find that many Kashariyot were still alive, living in Israel, and willing to talk to me. My repeated interviews

---

Comprehensive Historical Encyclopedia, online version; http://jwa.org/encyclopedia/article/kashariyot-couriers-in-jewish-resistance-during-holocaust. See also Lenore J. Weitzman, "Women of Courage: The Kashariyot (Couriers) in the Jewish Resistance," in Jeff Diefendorf, ed., *Lessons and Legacies*, Evanston, IL: Northwestern University Press, 2004: 112–152;

with them extended over a period of more than 15 years. I returned to Israel many times to continue those interviews and to visit them. Some, like Bronka Klebanski, Bela Ya'ari Hazan, and Liza Chapnik, also became life-long friends. I also found a few former Kashariyot who were living in the United States. Access to them, especially to Vladka Meed and Leah (Lodzia) Silverstein (whom I visited and interviewed over many years) greatly enhanced my research. The untold stories of these brave women who were Kashariyot are told in my new book (forthcoming, 2020.)

Meeting Dalia Ofer: Within an Hour We Were Planning an International Conference

Throughout my year in Israel, whenever I would meet with Professor Gutman, he would tell me how much he wanted me to talk to Dalia Ofer, a Holocaust historian. What a shame, he would say, that she was away in Washington DC for the whole year that I was in Israel. But Dalia returned just before I left and we arranged to meet for a quick lunch.

Within an hour we had agreed to work together. This was in spite of the fact that we did not initially agree about the role of gender in the Holocaust. I was sure that there were systematic differences in the way women experienced everything, while Dalia was hesitant. I was also convinced that men's experiences during the Holocaust were defined as normative and universal, while Dalia was skeptical. And when I told Dalia I was distressed because the women I most admired as heroes, the kashariyot, were neglected by Holocaust scholars, Dalia was sure that those in Israel had been recognized and treated as equals.

But it was so refreshing to talk to Dalia about the issues that had been swirling in my consciousness all year, and, at the same time to observe her encyclopedic knowledge of the field I was just learning. I suggested we find a way to work together and to explore when gender mattered, and under what conditions. We agreed to do that, hoping, and already knowing, that we would both flourish from combining our divergent training in history and sociology. We also talked about what then seemed like a wishful fantasy: organizing an international conference on Women in the Holocaust.

Then we got lucky. I asked a friend who worked for a private foundation if she knew anyone who might fund our conference. She thought her foundation might be interested and told me to write a one-page letter, with a budget. Not really believing it would happen, I didn't want to bother Dalia, so I just wrote the letter and asked for $10,000. A week later, they accepted my proposal.

When I called Dalia, she sprang into action. During the next few weeks, every time I talked to Dalia she announced that she had found another source of support. I don't know how she did it, but I remember she kept adding funds until we had "real money," a staff (of one), and a host (the Hebrew University.) We were not only hearing back from scholars we had invited, but also from others but who wanted to participate. At the same time, some scholars who thought gender was irrelevant wanted to come to present that view. We welcomed serious scholars like Lawrence Langer, who wrote a strong paper with that perspective, and stimulated a lively dialogue.

For me, the most interesting responses came from women like Ruth Bondy, who told us that she did not believe that men and women were treated differently or had different experiences in the Holocaust, but she wanted to come to the conference so she agreed to write a paper. But then, when Ruth described the lives of men and women in Theresienstadt, she ended up writing one of the most detailed and persuasive papers on the importance of gender differences. Drawing on Ruth's experience I naively believed that simply asking and answering questions about what happened to men and then, separately, what had happened to women, would lead everyone to see the importance of gender.

After the conference, which most participants considered a watershed event, we faced a different challenge when we turned to crafting a book. At that point we wanted to go beyond "simply" presenting the best scholarship from the conference: We also wanted to lay out the structural sources of gender differences and the theoretical basis for gender-based analysis.

That was the hardest part of writing the book and why I am most proud of the "Introduction" where we addressed these issues. In the Introduction, "The Role of Gender in the Holocaust", we developed four structural sources of gender differences during the Holocaust – a model which I am happy to note has been widely used – and asserted that a focus on gender leads to a richer and more finely nuanced understanding of the Holocaust. That essay also anticipates and addresses the resistance of some Holocaust scholars and survivors to gender-based research. It has been re-printed many times and I believe it still holds up as a fundamental introduction to the field.

After the initial process of editing the conference papers and writing the Introduction while living 6,000 miles apart, Dalia and I spent a few intense weeks at my home in Virginia, re-writing everything in the book, with breaks for long walks in the woods. My husband, William J. Goode, who had a well-deserved reputation as a gourmet cook, was especially generous in making sure we were well fed and cared-for, which clearly enhanced our productivity.

Of course our book also generated some critiques, but I believe those debates helped us by stimulating more interest in our work and more support for our perspective.

Although I have devoted more space to our early days and early work, I want to note that Dalia and I have continued to collaborate over the years, while also working on our individual projects. We recently developed a new model, what we call a sequential model of women's coping strategies during the Holocaust.[6] It offers another way to analyze gender that takes into account responses to changing conditions over time. It thereby encourages more dynamic and fluid analyses of changes in gender roles during periods of war and social upheaval.

My Gratitude to my Colleagues and Survivors Who Were My Mentors, and to Dalia Ofer

I cannot end this essay without mentioning the extent to which my work on women in the Holocaust has also been enhanced and sustained by my colleagues in the United States and my experiences in working with survivors in teaching graduate courses on the Holocaust.

I met my first American mentor, Michlean Amir, an archivist at the US Holocaust Memorial Museum in Washington DC, when I had a fellowship there in 2002. Michlean was the only person on the staff of the library who could read Hebrew and Yiddish, and she guided my quest to find the interviews and documents I needed. As a child of survivors and a child-survivor herself, she also introduced me to many of the survivors in the DC area and then became a cherished friend and my personal mentor for the next 18 years.

I am also grateful to Professor Zvi Gitelman, of the University of Michigan, for his sustaining collaboration on a project we thought would be just "a few" interviews with Noach Roitman, a survivor from Baranovich, and ended up continuing over the course of the next 10 years. After writing a book on Roitman's experiences in the resistance in the ghetto,[7] we addressed the more general academic question of why there was resistance in some ghettos but not in others, in several papers.[8]

---

6 Lenore J. Weitzman and Dalia Ofer "The sequential development of Jewish women's coping strategies in ghettos during the Holocaust "in Andrea Peto, Louise Hecht and Karolina Krasuka (eds.), *Women and the Holocaust: New Perspectives and Challenges*, Warsaw: Instytut Badan Literackich Pan Wydawnictwo, 2015.

7 Lenore J. Weitzman and Zvi Y. Gitelman *Noach Roitman: From Baranovich to the Partisans*, Forthcoming.

8 See, for example, Zvi Gitelman and Lenore J. Weitzman, "Jewish Resistance in Ghettos in the former Soviet Union during the Holocaust," in Wendy Goldman and Joe Trotter, eds., *The Ghetto in Global History*, Routledge, 2018: 148–168.

Over these years Zvi has also been my mentor in Jewish history and culture. He has been enormously helpful in my work on the kashariyot and has introduced me to materials he translated from Russian, Polish, Hebrew and Yiddish, most of which I would have never seen. He always enlivened our work as an all-time great story-teller.

My other vital colleagues were the Holocaust survivors who participated in my graduate courses on the Holocaust and taught me the unparalleled value of learning about the Holocaust through the personal experiences of survivors. I now believe that the most meaningful way to teach courses on the Holocaust in the United States, where most of my students are not Jewish and have no "personal connection" to the subject, is to pair each graduate student with a survivor. A special bond is usually formed as the student then helps the survivor by preparing background materials (such as maps and family pictures) to show when the survivor speaks to the class about his/her experiences during the Holocaust.

These survivor's presentations to my graduate class, many of which were later shown on cable TV in the Washington DC area, covered a wide range of countries and experiences. Hearing a survivor talk about "life in the Lodz ghetto", "arrival at Auschwitz", "the Kindertransport" and "hiding in a convent" made these topics come alive. For example, none of my students will ever forget hearing Leah Silverstein, a former kasharit who lived in nearby Maryland, describing her experiences passing, especially on the day she was almost caught for stealing a gun from a German officer. Many of these survivors kept returning to my classes, year after year, as both teachers and friends.

While I am enormously grateful for all of these cherished mentors, it feels most appropriate to end this essay with a tribute to my first and life-long mentor-colleague-and friend, Dalia Ofer. I never would have been able to embark on this path without Dalia: she was not only my intellectual guide, but also the encouraging and supportive friend willing to wait for me to "catch up," and sustain me when I doubted that I could ever become a "Holocaust scholar." I have gained so much from our collaboration and friendship and am so very thankful that she has played such an important part in my life.

Part III The “New Voices”

Natalia Aleksiun

Conversations I Missed: Asking Other Survivor Grandmothers

In January of 1946, Hieronim Majzlisz recorded his testimony at the Jewish Historical Commission in Kraków, Poland. Barely thirteen at the time, he recalled in a matter-of-fact tone his own survival in Lwów (today Lviv in Ukraine) and the death of his family members.[1] Among the most remarkable details was his memory of being thrown out of the train to Bełżec in November 1942. He jumped following his mother Cecylia, who had asked other men and women in the cattle car to help her son through the window. His pious maternal grandmother said she would rather meet the fate of the rest of the Jews and stayed on the train. Wounded in the head, Hieronim spent time cared for by the Jewish community in Żółkiew (today Zhovkva, Ukraine), a town not far from Lwów. There, a nurse, Pepka Fisz, organized a Sanitary Commission – local Jews who looked for "jumpers" along the train tracks who survived the jump but were wounded and unable to run away. Hidden among Żółkiew Jews, they were nursed back to life and sent to their hometowns. Hieronim was also reunited with his mother and was able to return to Lwów.

Sometimes, those whose lives make history and their stories do not seem completely real to those of us who write history. Other times, their stories come into focus. In the fall of 2019, I returned to Hieronim Majzlisz's testimony because of his connection to Żółkiew, a town near Lwów, I was working on. I simply wanted to clarify a footnote about the Sanitary Commission there and fill in details that this survivor's account contained.[2] But it was hard to forget this remarkable child survivor with a self-assured voice, I thought I could almost hear. This time, I read the pages scribbled in Polish differently and noticed actors that had eluded me before. In her pioneering essay Judith Tydor-Baumel framed her research question as "an attempt to locate, explore and understand the role of women during the Holocaust".[3] I guess I was looking for women in Hieronim Majzlisz's personal accounts.

---

1 Archives of the Jewish Historical Institute in Warsaw (furthermore AŻIH), 301/1652. See also Archives of Yad Vashem (furthermore YVA), 0.3/8498.

2 Gerszon Taffet, *Zagłada Żydów żółkiewskich*, ed. Natalia Aleksiun, Warsaw 2019, 46.

3 Judith Tydor Baumel, *Double Jeopardy. Gender and the Holocaust*, London and Portland OR: Vallentine Mitchell, 1998: 3.

Indeed, his story rendered a new gender-sensitive reading of memory, with women who played both direct and indirect roles in his survival. There was his encounter with a woman he did not have a prior connection to: a nurse, Pepka Fisz, who organized medical assistance for Jews in Żółkiew. Hieronim's female relatives – grandmother, mother and aunts – cared for him and organized his escape from the ghetto in December 1942. In his grandmother's former apartment, Hieronim found temporary haven outside the ghetto. His grandmother's former servant agreed to hide the boy and his mother, aunts and uncles after their escape to the "Aryan side". Emil Wawrzycki, a non-Jewish man who was to marry his aunt, provided Hieronim with food and hid him in his apartment until the arrival of the Red Army in the summer of 1944.[4]

The most dramatic event recalled in Majzlisz's testimony also concerned women. His mother's and aunt Mania's suicide on 27 June 1943 was the date he would "never forget". In her last words, Cecylia Majzlisz beseeched her son "to study, [and told him] that he had a life ahead of him and to go with open eyes through life".[56] In his later oral testimony, recorded in Hebrew under a new Hebrew first and last name, Hieronim recalled his mother and aunt getting tipsy before they left the hiding place to take poison on a park bench in their hometown. "It takes courage to do such a thing and Mother got drunk to get the courage," he explained in his interview for Yad Vashem in 1994.[7] Still he neither understood nor explained her decision, only implying that she had no place to hide and possibly hoped that her son alone would be taken care of by her family's Polish Catholic friends.

A close reading of these two ego documents of the same survivor – a child's testimony written down in Polish and an oral interview given in Hebrew - reveals the centrality of gender in interpreting daily lives, survival strategies, and networks of help. A careful analysis of these two sources confirms what historian Zoë Waxman has argued: "We have to reassess what we mean by the Holocaust, acknowledging that it was not a totalizing event, but was rather of different – and differently experienced – events."[8] Hieronim Majzlisz recalled different Holocaust stories of his grandmother, his parents and his own, with gender and class defining individual and familial responses. Reading these two texts together, I was confronted with

---

4 A note from Elhanan Ben-Nun (Hieronim's Majzlisz), dated September 5 2019, in the author's possession.

5 AŻIH, 301/1652, p. 2.

6 AŻIH, 301/1652, p. 2.

7 YVA), 0.3/8498.

8 See Zoe Waxman, *Women in the Holocaust. A Feminist History*, Oxford, Oxford UP, 2017: 8.

a realization that it was a very personal and emotional experience. I was angry at his mother for leaving the boy behind and choosing to die when a new route of escape through the border to Hungary proved deadly for her family. I also wondered what happened to Hieronim and if he followed his mother's ethical will of sorts, which in the context of Lwów in 1943 seemed so out of place. Cecylia's voice was missing and only available to us through her son's account. But her experience as a mother, sister and daughter was still distinct.

For my generation, scholars interested in the modern Jewish experience and trained in the late 1990s, at least those who received their graduate degrees in the United States, asking about women's experiences and analysing gendered expectations in familial and communal contexts has become a path opened by scholars such as Judith Tydor Baumel, Dalia Ofer, Marion Kaplan, and Atina Grossmann.[9] I read their works as a doctoral student at New York University and discussed their scholarship as one of the important new perspectives on the Holocaust.[10] Tydor-Baumel's *Double Jeopardy: Gender and the Holocaust* was suggested to me as an additional reading in preparation for comprehensive exams. Yet it took a lot longer to turn the interest in women and gender into the central lens. Some of the scholarship mentioned above examined the German Jewish experience and therefore seemed not directly pertinent to my work, and most importantly, they wrote about the Holocaust. Not the history I wanted to research myself until much later. Emotional investment in the implications of the Holocaust seemed too steep.

Discovering Jews

Growing up in Poland of the 1980s, I felt jealous of my classmates who all seemed to have large families and family graves to visit. On November 1, the day of the Dead, in Poland called All Saints' Day, the sense of missing out on something important was particularly strong. Entire families went to cemeteries which, by the evening, looked like seas of light with candles burning, and where neighbours and friends met and exchanged pleasantries. The dead and the living seemed to have enjoyed the solemn atmosphere of the occasion. But for me, this day felt uncomfortable, making

9 *When Biology Became Destiny: Women in Weimar and Nazi Germany*, ed. Renate Bridenthal, Atina Grossmann and Marion Kaplan, New York: Monthly Review Press, 1984; Tydor Baumel, *Double Jeopardy. Gender and the Holocaust*; *Women in the Holocaust*, ed. Dalia Ofer and Lenore J. Weitzman, New Haven: Yale UP, 1998; Marion Kaplan, *Dignity and Despair. Jewish Life in Nazi Germany*, New York: Oxford, 1998;

10 Tydor Baumel, *Double Jeopardy*; Atina Grossmann, Marion Kaplan

me different. Nobody could brag about family plots yet – after all this was Wrocław, which until 1945 was Breslau – and the traces of the war were still very visible in the cityscape. My classmates and I were born in Wrocław, but our parents and grandparents were all newcomers. Why didn't we have graves to visit? This was not a question I remember asking, just hoping that at some point we would. It is at times difficult and at times amusing to connect myself today to the child yearning for family graves to visit.

But the dead of our family were not completely absent from our lives. Occasionally, my grandmother would make comments that suggested she carried a lot more memories than she was willing to share. They crept up on her, it seemed, and forced themselves to the surface, but always in fragments, incomplete sentences, inevitably fractured. We were peeling potatoes for lunch and she told me that during the war her starving nephews sneaked out to villages and brought back home potato peels to cook. She stopped there, without mentioning any names or places, almost certainly not uttering the word "ghetto". She never mentioned her siblings were Jewish; the word "Jew" was unmentionable and the language she argued in with my grandfather was introduced to me as "a bad local variety of German used by people in Łódź before the war". What she conveyed was that I was lucky not to starve and sneak to villages or cook potato peels. But I do remember being perplexed by the image of these children with whom I was somehow connected. My grandmother Helena, turned out to have a different name at birth, a different date of birth, different names of parents than those I saw in her Polish ID, and a different first language than the one in which she didn't tell me about herself. I was interested in the Second World War and taught about the suffering it had brought upon Poland. Somehow, I could not place the children trying to find peels in the stories I knew from school ceremonies, curricula, and television. The school curriculum did not lack details about the cruelty of the German occupation and the heroism of Polish society. Sometime in fourth grade we read Janusz Korczak's *King Matt's the First* –a much loved children's novel on responsibilities of making the world a better place. Eager to please the teacher I volunteered to prepare a short presentation on the author, a Polish Jewish pedagogue and physician. I read his bio in the encyclopaedia and even cut his picture out as illustration prompting a lengthy discussion about the respect for and integrity of books. But what I remembered best was the story about Korczak's decision to "accompany his children", the orphans he was taking care of, "to their deaths". Neither the encyclopaedia article nor our beloved teacher mentioned Korczak or the children being Jewish, or the Warsaw ghetto, or Treblinka.

Discovering the Holocaust

Drawn to history, I was first interested in the nineteenth-century Polish struggles for independence, seduced by the imagery of the artist Artur Grottger and his series of drawings titled "Polonia". In Communist Poland, history was part of a counter culture with books, and articles published underground, tape recordings by intellectuals active in the political opposition. It felt only natural that even in the 1990s "real" Polish history was the normative experience of heroic men and that it belonged to male historians and to serious topics: if not war and battles, then at least parties and movements. Indeed, I entered the University of Warsaw's History Department to study the topic with the then leading Polish historians. I dreamed of becoming a historian of the Polish January 1863 failed uprising against the Russian Empire. This was an exciting time for Polish historiography – archives were opened, new journals founded, and university libraries slowly began purchasing books in English. Also, new questions could be asked openly.

Historians wrote extensively on new topics, especially studying daily lives in the People's Republic of Poland. That new Polish historiography turned also to Polish-Jewish relations, before, during and after the Holocaust. These were the thorniest, most hotly contested and possibly feared questions, but the difference between then and the silence of the previous decades made it all a rather optimistic enterprise. Barbara Engelking and Małgorzata Melchior published their first books, introducing me to the wealth of details one could glean from oral interviews with survivors and their children.[11] This was also the time when diaries and memoirs of Polish Jews began to appear in Polish translation or original. They even made it into university curricula: in the course of our seminars we read Janina Bauman's *Winter in the Morning* and Mary Berg' *Diary*.[12] Young historians were also beginning to tackle the experience of Polish Jews during the Holocaust, writing primarily about the destruction of individual communities, Jewish survival strategies, and assistance given to them by non-Jewish Poles. All this was

11 Małgorzata Melchior, *Społeczna tożsamość jednostki (w świetle wywiadów z Polakami pochodzenia żydowskiego urodzonymi w latach 1944–1955*, Warsaw, 1990; Barbara Engelking-Boni, *Zagłada i pamięć*. Warsaw, 1994.

12 Janina Bauman, *Zima o poranku. Opowieść dziewczynki z warszawskiego getta*, Kraków, 1989; Mary Berg, *Dziennik z getta warszawskiego*, Warsaw, 1983. Some of the key Holocaust studies and diaries began to be published in Polish even before the political change see Adama Czerniakowa dziennik getta warszawskiego, ed. Marian Fuks, Warsaw, 1983; Emanuel Ringelblum, *Stosunki polsko-żydowskie w czasie drugiej wojny światowej. Uwagi i spostrzeżenia*, Warsaw, 1988; *Pamiętnik Dawida Rubinowicza*, Warsaw, 1987.

before the publication of Jan Gross's *Neighbours*, the book that precipitated a crisis in popular and scholarly understandings of Polish national identity.

Still, traces of the Holocaust were hard to miss in Warsaw, even in the early 1990s when the large empty square in front of the Monument to the Ghetto Heroes designed by Nathan Rapoport and unveiled already in April 1948, was used for sunbathing and dog walking. The windows of my studio overlooked the Jewish cemetery and the bus that took me to the University drove through the streets of Nowolipki and Anielewicza, Tłomackie, all of which had been part of the pre-war Jewish district and the wartime ghetto. Studying Jewish history or studying Polish history through studying Jews was still almost unthinkable. Just like studying women. In April 1993, a massive commemoration of the Warsaw ghetto uprising took place in Warsaw. The city was paralyzed with security blocs and traffic jams on streets leading to the Warsaw Ghetto Memorial. Fellow passengers on the bus complained bitterly: "If they want to celebrate their uprising, let them do it in Israel!" The Holocaust, or even the loaded subject of Polish-Jewish relations during the Holocaust, was hardly the center of scholarly creative efforts, not really considered part of Polish history, something that has not changed until today. It is important to Poland's collective sense of agency and victimhood and yet it is still about what Catholic Poles witnessed and not about the death of Polish Jewish citizens.

While I read all that was available in Polish libraries and book stores, my own work kept a safe distance from the topic that just seemed all too consuming. And so I took on the political choices of survivors in the immediate postwar period in Poland as my focus. I visited numerous archives in Israel and read reports written down by leaders and members of various Zionist parties and youth movements, assessing the strength of their group, and ideological commitment of their members, not realizing that what I researched belonged very much to the field I still tried to avoid. However, my actors were all survivors who joined political movements, expressed political opinions and voted with their feet, leaving Poland in two large emigration waves: following the Kielce pogrom of July 1946 and the creation of the State of Israel.[13]

Discovering Women

One particular account made a deep impression on me at the time. In his postwar memoirs titled *A Surplus of Memory: Chronicle of the Warsaw*

13 Natalia Aleksiun, *Dokąd dalej? Ruch syjonistyczny w Polsce 1944–1949*, Warsaw, 2002.

Ghetto Uprising, Yitzhak Zuckerman "Antek", one of the leaders of the Jewish underground in the Warsaw ghetto and on the so-called Aryan side, described the joy of finding a group of young female survivors in Częstochowa. He saw in them the hope for national rebirth.[14] At the time, I looked for ideological discussions and party conventions but also lacked the scholarly context to fully appreciate what this happy confession revealed about gender relations among survivors. I noted that the majority of survivors, Jews who had survived under the German occupation, were young men and that women, children and nucleus Jewish families returned to Poland from the Soviet Union only in the spring and summer of 1946, much like my own grandparents. While I understood that the prevalence of men among Polish Jewish survivors supported the idea of "double jeopardy" of being Jewish and female, it was still marginal to my research which moved from postwar survivor political agencies to Jewish historiography.

Until I witnessed an intimate and playful conversation of two elderly survivors. It was Passover in Israel when I was invited to my husband's family. It was a happy multigeneration occasion on which *gefilte fish* made from scratch was served proudly while Israeli born grandchildren tried to avoid eating it and be polite at the same time. Between courses, I overheard two elderly survivors giggling in Polish about their experience in the bunker. They were teenagers then and went into hiding with their pious parents and future husbands. While their parents pretended not to see, they had experienced their first intimate moments and something in the festive family gathering triggered their memories, memories of transgressions that their parents tactfully chose to overlook in the forest bunker near Borysław (today Ukraine) in Eastern Galicia, in the last months before their liberation in the summer of 1944.

Many years later, on a different continent, I was interviewing a survivor from Rawa Ruska in Eastern Galicia. I was beginning to collect oral testimonies from survivors who had been willing to talk to me. Still unsure about the direction in which I was going to take my interest in surviving the Holocaust in Eastern Galicia. My interviewee was a man who escaped from the ghetto with a group of teenagers and survived hiding in a forest. "What was your mother's maiden name?" I asked him as he mentioned the death of his mother. His voice trembling, "Why do you want to know?" he asked me with suspicion. Why did I want to know? What was the importance of the name of the woman killed in 1942? Why do you want to know my mother's maiden name? I ended up explaining rather naively that I was making up for

14 Yitzhak Zuckerman, *A Surplus of Memory: Chronicle of the Warsaw Ghetto Uprising*, Berkeley, University of California Press, 1983.

the questions I did not ask of my own family, especially of my own grandmother. He was right in his suspicion and a sense that intimate memories of his mother who had not survived and whose memory he was the only person to carry at this point, belonged to him. Yet, I was taken aback by his resistance and repeated efforts in the course of our conversation to tell me an authorative history of the Holocaust rather then share details about his mother's death in one of the round-ups in Rawa Ruska, after she told him she was too tired and too old to try and hide among the peasants.

Pieces Coming Together

Whom do we study when we research and reflect on the fates of the Polish Jews during the Holocaust? How do we write that history from below, to include a vast variety of communal, familial, individual responses? And since scholars have long argued to expand our notion of resistance beyond the armed resistance, what do we gain in pushing women to the center of the picture? I believe, it invites one to develop a more nuanced understanding of the dynamic between individual decisions and social and cultural identities, one that leads to and result from the privileging of individual testimonies.

Noticing (Jewish) women and the idiosyncrasies of their experience during the Holocaust has led me to realize how central gender was for understanding the Holocaust. It made me appreciate the scholarship that I began to read as one of the possible approaches and I began to embrace it as my own. It also allowed me to explain and contextualize many childhood recollections and treat them as a starting point for a discussion about the fractured lives of Polish Jewish survivors. What links me to that past is the conversations I did not have and questions I did not ask. But I can and will ask other grandmothers.

Batya Brutin

Treasure Inside the Drawer – Objects That Led Me to Research about the Holocaust

My Personal Connection to the Holocaust

In my desk drawer there are three objects. The first is an Iron Cross, awarded to my mother's father, Friedrich Fritz, for his heroism in World War I as a soldier in the German army.[1] The second is a yellow Star of David with the word "Jude" in the center, which my mother, Ruth (Fritz) Fersht was forced to wear by the Nazis during the Holocaust. The third is an old, worn, 1936 Polish passport shared by my father Zvi Fersht (Ferszt) and his parents Hinda and Aron. These objects, which have accompanied me since my childhood, have influenced me, first unconsciously, and later with great awareness.

I grew up in a home where the Holocaust was an integral part of daily life through conversations between my parents, relatives and friends, often openly, and sometimes secretly. My mother often told my sister, my brother and I, about her childhood in Germany before the Nazis came to power, and about her experiences in the orphanage in the Netherlands. In December 1938, shortly after Kristallnacht,[2] she aged 11, her older sister Hennie, and her younger brother Bernard were sent by their widowed mother to an orphanage in order to get them out of Nazi Germany. She also talked about what happened to her during the Holocaust when her mother was reunited with her children after more than a year, moving with them to occupied Amsterdam. There, as a young girl, my mother had to deal with refugee living conditions, fear of being captured by the Nazis, and almost a year of hiding from them in a bow of a ship.

On my father's side the story was different. Prior to the war his three siblings had immigrated to *Eretz Yisrael* (pre-State Israel, then under a British

1 The Iron Cross (German: Eisernes Kreuz) is a former military decoration in the Kingdom of Prussia, and later in the German Empire (1871–1918) and Nazi Germany (1933–1945). Emperor Wilhelm II reauthorized the Iron Cross on August 5, 1914, at the start of World War I. My grandfather was awarded an Iron Cross 2nd Class for his bravery as a German soldier in World War I. He was born and raised as a Christian Evangelist who converted to Judaism in order to marry my grandmother in 1914.

2 Kristallnacht - November 9–10, 1938, when hundreds of synagogues and Jewish businesses in Germany and Austria were vandalized or destroyed by the Nazis.

mandate) with different Zionist youth groups. In 1936, at age 14, he also immigrated there with his parents. Two brothers were left behind in Łódź, Poland. One was hospitalized in a mental hospital in Warta, Poland, and was murdered in April 1940. The other was shot by the Nazis in Wolności Square in Łódź, in 1941. His wife and two children's fate are unknown to me, the assumption being that they perished in Chełmno extermination camp in Poland. Other members of my extended family died in the Łódź Ghetto and in Chełmno.

The trigger to my engaging with the topic of women and the Holocaust began with my mother's yellow Star of David, which for me symbolized her female experience during the Holocaust. I went through several stages until I become engrossed in this subject. These included a general interest in Holocaust events, teaching the subject in the Israeli educational system, organizing educational trips to Poland for my students, and composing study programs on art and the Holocaust. Later, when it became my academic practice, I organized and headed international conferences on women and the Holocaust, and I wrote academic studies on the subject. Currently I am focusing on researching sexual violence against Jewish women during the Holocaust and I have already curated an art exhibition on this topic.

Teaching about the Holocaust

My decision to choose the Holocaust as my central topic of research was triggered by a joint Israeli-German seminar that took place in Poland in 1993 where scholars from Beit Berl academic college (where I used to teach for many years) met with their counterparts from Wiesbaden, Germany and its vicinity. Each of us was required to present a lecture or a workshop on the Holocaust. As an art historian I chose a workshop on Holocaust Art. The seminar was exciting, enriching, and most of all shaky for me. It had a decisive influence on my continued occupation with the Holocaust. I understood that this is the subject I want to engage in both in research and education, in order to influence future educators.

After returning from the seminar, two significant things happened. First, Beit Berl Academic College established a Holocaust teaching center for the Education department's students directed by Prof. Ofer Shiff. In 1994, based on my multi-year experience of teacher's training, I was chosen to be the center's pedagogical coordinator. Second, I decided to make a drastic change in my academic studies. I began a new research project focusing on Holocaust art and the Holocaust's visual commemoration in Israel and throughout the world. I clearly remember two opposite reactions. My mother responded harshly and said: "the materials are so difficult to deal with, and the entire subject is so sad. Will you have the mental strength to withstand it? What do you need it for?" On the other hand, my university advisor embraced me and offered me all the support necessary to "jump into the waters".

In 2000, after Professor Shiff left Beit Berl Academic College, I was appointed the director of what became *The Holocaust Teaching in Israeli Society Program*. The program aimed to train future educators to teach Holocaust history while imparting the Holocaust's historical, moral and educational significance, both Jewish and universal.

It was not easy to convince the college authorities to adopt this direction as the Holocaust was not an independent discipline but was being taught as part of history curriculum. I made two major changes in the program to help it succeed. The first was to compose a curriculum that would teach our students about the Holocaust through an interdisciplinary approach based on historical events. The curriculum included art, literature, music, film, popular culture etc. The second was to adapt a suitable curriculum for each training department: early childhood, elementary school, junior high school, special education, informal education and youth advancement, in order to make Holocaust teaching more effective.

In addition, to assist our students in teaching the Holocaust using an interdisciplinary approach, I conducted a comprehensive and thorough survey of educational materials used in teaching the Holocaust throughout the Israeli educational system. My results indicated a lack of materials for teaching the subject in various disciplines, such as art. Together with my colleagues and the Curriculum Design Center at our college, I therefore designed a number of study kits: *The Representation of the Holocaust in the Map of the State of Israel*,[3] *In the Artist Eyes: studying about the Holocaust through artworks*,[4] *In the Artists Eyes: The Story of Anne Frank*,[5] *In the Artists Eyes: The Story of the Warsaw Boy*.[6]

---

3 Batya Brutin and Alex Beck, *The Representation of the Holocaust in the Map of the State of Israel*, a learning kit, Kfar Sava: Beit Berl Academic College, 2002, (Hebrew and English).

4 Batya Brutin, *In the Artist Eyes: studying about the Holocaust through artworks*, learning program, Kfar Sava: Beit Berl Academic College with the support of the Claims Conference (The Conference on Jewish Material Claims against Germany), 2005, (Hebrew).

5 Batya Brutin and Avriela Amit, *In the Artists Eyes: The Story of Anne Frank*, learning program, Kfar Sava: Beit Berl Academic College with the support of the Claims Conference (The Conference on Jewish Material Claims against Germany), 2007, (Hebrew).

6 Batya Brutin and Avriela Amit, *In the Artists Eyes: The Story of the Warsaw Boy*, learning program, Kfar Sava: Beit Berl Academic College with the support of the Claims Conference (The Conference on Jewish Material Claims against Germany), 2009, (Hebrew).

I also started a tradition of offering an educational tour to Poland to students from the Faculty of Education, the Faculty of Art (from the Teacher Training department) and the Faculty of Society and Culture (from the Teacher Training departments) which ran until my retirement in 2018. It was influenced by my participation in the Israeli-German seminar in Poland in 1993 and by my father's Polish passport which evoked my curiosity and desire to learn more about the culture of my father's original home. The trip, entitled *Poland: History, Heritage and Culture*, took us to sites connected to Polish Jewry's history, and introduced us to remnants of the cultural and spiritual Jewish life in Poland before the Holocaust, as seen by sites and artifacts scattered across Poland in cemeteries and active and abandoned synagogues. We also visited sites connected to the Holocaust and its memory: death pits, sites of former concentration and death camps where we learned about their role in "The Final Solution"; monuments and memorial sites commemorating the Holocaust through which we learned about the way Poland commemorates the Holocaust and its victims, both Jewish and non-Jewish. We interwove those visits with sites connected to contemporary Poland in order to become acquainted with the culture, history, and daily life of the Polish people. Prior to the trip, students participated in a 28 hour preparation program, and two weeks after their return they held a concluding session.

After a few such trips I began researching my own family tree. I took a private trip to visit all the sites connected to my family, searched through archives and made a lot of discoveries along the way. I am still in the process of finding my Polish roots.

Academic Research, Activities and Publications

In order to "dive" into the Holocaust's multifaceted contents, I invested much time, thought, and energy to expand my knowledge on the field. Simultaneously, prior to my doctoral dissertation, I began a new research project about Holocaust commemoration as seen through Israeli monuments (1996–1998). In 2005, this study was published as a book.[7]

In 1993, after twenty years of extensive research, my PhD advisor Prof. Ziva Amishai-Maisels, published a book about Holocaust's influence on visual arts.[8] The importance of Amishai-Maisels's book lies in its broad scope and in the originality of its conclusions, which demonstrate the impact

7 Batya Brutin, *Living with the Memory: Monuments in Israel Commemorating the Holocaust*, Lohamei Hagetaot: Beit Lochamei Hagetaot, 2005, (Hebrew).

8 Ziva Amishai-Maisels, *Depiction and Interpretation: The Influence of the Holocaust on the Visual Arts* Oxford: Pergamon, 1993.

of the Holocaust on modern art. The pioneering nature of her work brought the topic to the attention of academics both in Israel and abroad and established a new area of research. A groundbreaking work, it is today the basis for all research on Holocaust art. She concludes her book by mentioning artists of the "second generation," children of Holocaust survivors. Amishai-Maisels is convinced that there is clear evidence of the Holocaust in works by children and even grandchildren of the survivors, who try to understand the Holocaust through both their personal experiences and their national history. She explains that she has not dealt with such "later art" as the different approaches and symbols of the "second generation" warrant separate research.

As a "second-generation" descendant of a Holocaust survivor, I decided to write my PhD dissertation on the responses to the Holocaust by Israeli "second generation" artists (1999–2006), thus continuing Amishai-Maisels's research. The "Second Generation" is a world-wide phenomenon, and although I limited the discussion to Israeli artists, it was clear that they are only part of a global phenomenon. Many members of the "Second Generation" imbibed a traumatic atmosphere of death and loss, which many of them have internalized. With the passing of time, it has become a central element of their identity arousing in them a desperate need to cope with its problems.

The research deals with topics common to several artists and discusses their artistic responses while preserving the special nature of each. On the one hand, "Second Generation" artists have continued along the route taken by artists of the Holocaust period with respect to subjects, images and style such as descriptions of the dead, the corpses, the sacrifice of Isaac and the number on the arm. On the other hand, they create their own images and style, which respond to the subjects, questions and problems preoccupying their generation. Through the artworks of "Second Generation" artists, we are exposed to a wide variety of subjects and questions which preoccupy them, and we see diverse ways of expressing what was happening in their Holocaust-affected inner world.

Based on this research, together with Irit Levin I curated an exhibition entitled, *Strata of Memory, Israeli Artists "Second Generation" of the Holocaust*, at the Artist's House in Tel Aviv in 2008.[9] With some modifications, this research was also published as a book, *The Inheritance: The Holocaust in the Artworks of Second-Generation Israeli Artists* in 2015.[10]

---

9 Irit Levin and Batya Brutin, *Strata of Memory, Israeli Artists "Second Generation" of the Holocaust*, Tel Aviv: Artist's House, 2008, (Catalog - Hebrew and English).

10 Batya Brutin, *The Inheritance: The Holocaust in the Artworks of Second-Generation Israeli Artists*, Jerusalem: Yad Vashem and Magnes, 2015, (Hebrew).

Since the 1990s, important and groundbreaking studies have been published on women's experiences during the Holocaust, such as *Different Voices: Women and the Holocaust* by Rittner Carol and Roth John (eds.) in 1993,[11] *Double Jeopardy: Gender and the Holocaust*, by Judith Tydor Baumel in 1998,[12] *Women in the Holocaust*, by Dalia Ofer and Lenore J. Weitzman (eds.) in 1998,[13] and others. Their existence indicated that the subject had become a central one in Holocaust studies. Subsequently, Prof. Esther Hertzog and I initiated an international conference on *Women and the Holocaust* in 2002, as representatives of Beit Berl Academic College and in cooperation with Beit Terezin and Beit Lohamei Haghetaot.

As this subject was totally new to me, I asked Prof. Hertzog for assistance, and she introduced me to the aforementioned studies. We later held five more international conferences: *The Family During the Holocaust – Gender Perspectives*, 2003, *Gender Issues in Holocaust Studies*, 2005, *Childhood and Youth Under the Third Reich – A Gender Perspective*, 2007, *Creativity and the Arts in the Holocaust - a Gendered Perspective*, 2009, *"Her Story": Transference Methods of Women's Biographies and Autobiographies from the Holocaust*, 2013. Each of the conference's three days took place in one of the three partner institutions, allowing for a varied view of the topic, influenced by each institution's unique character and activities.

Two books were published as a result of the conferences, based primarily on lectures delivered there. The first, *Women and Family in the Holocaust*, edited by Esther Hertzog, was published in 2006.[14] The second, *Sexual Violence Against Jewish Women During the Holocaust*, edited by Sonja M. Hedgepeth and Rochelle G. Saidel, appeared in 2010.[15] I had a great sense of satisfaction and accomplishment in directing these conferences, and helping turn women in the Holocaust into a mainstream research topic.

In 2007, while preparing for an interview for the Center for Educational Technology as part of the *second generation speaks* program, I came across

---

11 Carol Rittner, and John Roth, Editors. *Different Voices: Women and the Holocaust*, New York: Paragon House, 1993.

12 Judith Tydor Baumel, *Double Jeopardy: Gender and the Holocaust*, London: Vallentine Mitchell, 1998.

13 Dalia Ofer and Lenore J. Weitzman, eds., *Women in the Holocaust*, New Haven: Yale University Press, 1998.

14 Esther Hertzog, ed., *Women and Family in the Holocaust*, Petah Tikva, Israel: Otzar Hamishpat Publishing, 2006, (Hebrew).

15 Sonja M. Hedgepeth and Rochelle G. Saidel, eds., *Sexual Violence Against Jewish Women During the Holocaust*, Lebanon, NH: Brandeis University Press/ University Press of New England, Hadassah-Brandeis Institute Series on Jewish Women, 2010.

my mother's yellow Star of David with the word "Jude" in the center, lying in my desk drawer. It reminded me of a story she used to tell us about herself when we were children. Using a false identity, she worked as a seamstress in a small workshop in Amsterdam on Prinsengracht street where Nazi uniforms were sewn. One day, an event occurred in front of the workshop which everyone went out to watch, including my mother. A Jewish family was taken out of their hiding place, put on a truck and sent to a Nazi camp. My mother noted that it was clear to everyone where the Jews were being taken to. The workshop's manager, the only person there who knew that my mother was Jewish, asked her to quietly pack up her belongings, and leave the place permanently.

Along the way, a roundup of Jews took place and my mother happened to meet the son of Dutch acquaintances and asked him to help her get away. He took her to a hiding place in a boat his family owned, where she hid for several months. After reading the diary of Anne Frank, as an adolescent, I realized that my mother saw the Frank family being taken from their hiding place. Right after the interview I started to look for artwork in which Anne Frank's image appeared. I discovered that in many works of art she is portrayed wearing a yellow Star of David with the word "Jude" (in German) in the center, just as my mother wore. Although the German Jews lived in the Netherland, they wore the Germans badge in order to distinguish them from Dutch Jews. Looking at Anne's depiction with the badge, it reminded me of my mother's photographs with the yellow Star of David, and it strengthened my interest to research Anne Frank's description in artwork.

Fortunately, Beit Berl Academic College financially supported my research on Anne Frank's image in art. In the *Women and the Holocaust* international conference, *Childhood and Youth Under the Third Reich – A Gender Perspective*, 2007, I presented a paper on the image of Anne Frank in visual art. Based on this study, together with Avriela Amit, my colleague from the Curriculum Design Center at Beit Berl Academic College, I published a study program entitled *In the Artists Eyes: The Story of Anne Frank*, 2007–2008 with the support of the Claims Conference. In view of the paper and the study program's success, I felt confident enough to present the topic at two exhibitions. The first, *Anne Frank in the Artists Eyes*, was staged in honor of Anne Frank on her 80th birthday. Held in 2009 at the Rumbach Synagogue in Budapest by Peter Wilhelm Art Projects, it was created with the generous support of the Israeli Foreign Ministry and the Israeli consulate in Budapest.[16] In this exhibition we showed a wide variety of subjects concerning Anne

16 Batya Brutin, *Anne Frank in the Artists Eyes*, Budapest: Rumbach Synagogue by Peter Wilhelm Art Center, 2009, (Catalog).

Frank's image as portrayed by artists from around the world. This exhibition has a special personal meaning for me. My mother was born in Germany, fled to Holland, and lived in Merwedeplein, Amsterdam, just as the Frank family did before entering their hiding place. They all thought that everything will be over quickly, and they will be able to return home to Germany. But history told a different story, one of oppression, destruction and death. Unfortunately, Anne Frank, her mother Edith, and her sister Margot, perished, while my mother, her mother and siblings were fortunate enough to survive. I dedicated this exhibition to my dear mother who honored me, together with my two daughters Michal and Yael, by being present at its opening.

The second exhibition, composed of artwork by Israeli artists depicting Anne Frank, took place at the Yad Lebanim Gallery in Rishon Lezion, Israel, on Yom Hashoah (Holocaust and Heroism Remembrance Day) 2010. The gallery invited all junior high schools in the city to attend my lecture on Anne Frank, and I took them on a guided tour through the exhibition. I am satisfied to have passed on the legacy of the Holocaust through the story of Anne Frank to the young generation, so it will not be forgotten.

In 2002 I participated in a conference about *The Holocaust and the Arts*, at the European Parliament in Strasbourg. There I met Samuel Bak, a Holocaust survivor artist, who lectured about how his art was influenced by the iconic photograph of the little boy from Warsaw Ghetto in short pants, boots, coat and cap with his raised hands, and a Nazi soldier pointing his submachine gun at him. Many have claimed that they were the boy in the photograph, but since there is no conclusive evidence, we do not know his identity. I was very impressed by Bak's paintings depicting the Warsaw Ghetto boy and started to investigate other works of art using this image. I was very surprised to find that so many artists were influenced by this photograph and use it in their artworks. Marianne Hirsch described the photograph in these words:

> If you had to name one picture that signals and evokes the Holocaust in the contemporary cultural imagination it might well be the picture of the little boy in the Warsaw ghetto with his hands raised. The pervasive role this photograph has come to play is indeed astounding: it is not an exaggeration to say that, assuming an archetypal role of Jewish (and universal) victimization, the boy in the Warsaw ghetto has become the poster-child for the Holocaust.[17]

17 Marianne Hirsch, "Nazi Photographs in Post-Holocaust Art: Gender as an Idiom of Memorialization," in *Crimes of War: Guilt and Denial in the Twentieth Century*, eds. Omer Bartov et al., New York: New Press, 2002, 100–101.

Lucy Dawidowicz suggested a meaning in historical terms:

> Consequently, in the deluded German mind, every Jewish man, woman and child became a panoplied warrior of a vast satanic fighting machine. The most concrete illustration of this delusion is the now familiar photograph taken from the collection attached to Stroop's report of the Warsaw ghetto uprising. It shows uniformed German SS men holding guns to a group of women and children; in the foreground is a frightened boy of about six, his hands up. This was the face of the enemy.[18]

Like Anne Frank's image, the photograph of the boy from Warsaw Ghetto became famous worldwide as a document representing the Holocaust. Many artists adopted this photograph as a source of inspiration to express their feelings and ideas about the Holocaust in general and the fate of child victims in particular.

In 2005 I published the article "The Boy from the Warsaw Ghetto as Holocaust Icon in Art".[19] Based on this study and with support from the Claims Conference, together with my colleague Avriela Amit from the Curriculum Design Center at Beit Berl Academic college, I published a study program *In the Artists Eyes: The Story of the Warsaw Boy,* 2009.

As photographs of Anne Frank, a young girl whose life story is known through her diary and the Anne Frank House, and the unknown Warsaw Ghetto boy fascinated me, I continued studying the use of these two children's images in artworks. Eventually they were the basis of six chapters in my forthcoming book, *Holocaust Icons in Art: The Warsaw Ghetto Boy and Anne Frank*.[20]

Another gendered topic that attracted my interest had to do with sexual violence during the Holocaust. By the turn of the twenty-first century it was clear that women's experience during the Holocaust were different than those of men, and the issue of sexual violence deserved a more thorough investigation. After the studies about women's experiences during the Holocaust that I previously mentioned were published, along with the *Women and the Holocaust* conferences, and Sonja M. Hedgepeth and Rochelle G. Saidel's book *Sexual Violence Against Jewish Women During the Holocaust,* Dr. Saidel and I discovered that no art exhibition had been held on this topic. In 2016 we began working on *Violated! Women in the Holocaust and Genocide*, which was displayed by the *Remember the Women Institute* at the

---

18 Lucy S. Dawidowicz, *The War Against the Jews: 1933–1945*, London: Weidenfeld and Nicolson, 1975, 166.

19 Batya Brutin, "The Boy from the Warsaw Ghetto as Holocaust Icon in Art," *Ars Judaica* 11(2015): 55–78.

20 Batya Brutin, *Holocaust Icons in Art: The Warsaw Ghetto Boy and Anne Frank*, Berlin, Germany: De Gruyter, and Jerusalem: Magnes, forthcoming 2020.

Ronald Feldman Gallery in New York City during April-May 2018. There we exhibited artworks of an international group of 30 artists from Israel, the United States, and other countries, including Holocaust survivors, their second and third generation descendants, and others who portray sexual violation during the Holocaust, as well as artists (some of whom are survivors) who address later genocides and ethnic cleansings in Bosnia, Darfur, Eritrea, Guatemala, Iraq, Nigeria, and Rwanda. These artworks highlight the sexual humiliation, sexualized violence, sexual slavery, and rape that women have suffered during the Holocaust and later genocides.

This exhibition was very special for me on both the professional and personal levels. Professionally, as it was the peak of my academic and curatorial work so far; Personally, as my own mother was sexually molested by the son of the family hiding her during the Holocaust. I dedicated this exhibition to her and to all the women who were violated during the Holocaust and later genocides.

In 2016, Prof. Tamar Ariav, president of Beit Berl Academic College, introduced me to Sarit Zaibert, an independent historian conducting research about Jehovah's Witnesses during the Holocaust. Zaibert is the initiator and organizer of conferences about *The Non-Jewish Victims of the Nazi Regime*. Based on my teaching experiences with Jewish and non-Jewish students at the college, I told Zaibert how important the subject was. In addition, I believe that dealing with the non-Jewish victims of the Nazi regime will broaden our universal perspectives about the general context of the Jewish Holocaust. On a personal level, this subject also brought to my mind a thought I had for many years, regarding the fate of my converted German hero grandfather who was awarded with an Iron Cross (that I safely keep in my desk drawer), had he been alive during the Nazi Regime. Zaibert and I collaborated in organizing further conferences on this subject including a one-day conference, *Non-Jewish Victims of Nazism*, at Beit Berl Academic College for the I*nternational Holocaust Remembrance Day* on January 27, 2017. The conference dealt with the Nazi regime of terror throughout occupied Europe that also led to the persecution, torture and murder of racial groups such as the Gypsies and Serbs, social and ideological groups such as the Freemasons and Jehovah's Witnesses and social groups such as homosexuals.

Currently I am focusing on completing a study of the *Pictorial Testimony during the Eichmann Trial in Jerusalem in 1961–1962*, which I began in 2011 for the conference *50 years to the Eichmann trial, the event and its seal*, held under the auspices of Tel Aviv University, the University of Haifa and the Ghetto Fighters' House.

Eighteen drawings by four painters were introduced at the Eichmann trial in Jerusalem during 1961–1962. Pictures by Leo Haas, Ferdinand (Felix) Bloch, František Mořic Nágel and Yehuda Bacon, and one album with twenty drawings by Zofia Rosenstrauch (Naomi Judkowski) depicted scenes from the Theresienstadt ghetto and Auschwitz, some painted during the Holocaust and the rest soon after. The paintings were presented as part of three testimonies: one by Mordechai Ansbacher (session 38 on May 12, 1961), a second by the painter Yehuda Bacon (session 68 on June 7, 1961), and a third by Vera Alexander (session 71 on June 8, 1961). All were an inseparable part of constructing the comprehensive story of the Holocaust during the trial. I plan to discuss these works of art, not only in terms of what they portray, but to ask a number of questions. For what purpose they were presented? Who chose them? What is the degree of historical truth in the depictions compared to other types of testimonies such as photographs, oral and written testimonies? How did the audience and the judges react to their presentation? I will also refer to the reactions of artists who attended the trial. These artists described the course of the trial, the witnesses' responses, and those of the audience, the judges, the lawyers and Eichmann himself.

In 2018, the year that I retired from teaching, I received the Yad Vashem lifetime achievement award in the field of Holocaust education. Although I am very proud to have been given such an award for my achievements, I feel that there is so much that must still be done in the field of Israeli Holocaust education. In his 1943 poem *The Vow*, Avraham Shlonsky wrote: "I vowed everything to remember. Remember all and forget nothing." Currently, we have already reached the fourth generation born since the Holocaust and there are those who wish to reduce the scope Holocaust studies, teaching it as a chapter of general history. Because of the uniqueness and importance of the Holocaust, we must take the responsibility to continue teaching the Holocaust as a separate subject and continue researching it in depth.

The significance of the Holocaust's legacy for our generation and those to come, and the educational mission of preserving its memory, must be addressed as a living and relevant topic in Israeli society. The transformations that this topic has undergone in the Israeli collective memory and its influence on the Israeli cultural experience makes it imperative to continue studying it in depth as a separate and relevant topic. This includes highlighting its universal implications on public discourse, artistic creation and education.

In light of all the above, I plan to continue my studies of the many varied and fascinating Holocaust-related issues, such as artistic creation during the Holocaust and the Holocaust's visual commemoration. Above all, I hope to dedicate my time to researching various aspects of women's lives during the Holocaust, and creating exhibits that will focus on this important topic.

F. K. Schoeman

An Academic Autobiography in Seven Uneasy Vignettes

July 9, 2019. Husevík, Iceland

Monika, the young Polish emigrant who manages the most picturesque chalets complex of this famous polar island cheerfully entertains us during breakfast in the common dining area. My husband and I are the only people in the old-fashion Bergmanesque room with views over the glaciers and the ocean. On a napkin she draws for us maps of "secret" places unknown to tourists that we ought to visit. When the owner joins us to chat, she makes fun, in good humor, of his bad tastes in foods. It is the old jovial Icelandic man who enquires about our professions. Upon hearing of mine, he asks "Are you Jewish?" "Yes," we answer. "See?," tells him *Pani* Monika, "But they are nice."

Dear Next-Century Reader

I.

Society is history's midwife. Every historical event is born in the hands of very specific, and often old, societal dynamics which prepare and facilitate it.

I was born in Italy a couple of decades after WWII. Long enough to have directly suffered none of its effects, but near enough to be impacted by that same mentality that begot it in the first place. The nationalistic, corrupt, and bigoted world of Western politics and conformist social norms were alive and kicking. My country was in the chokehold of the Mafia, Red Brigades, rotten political turncoats, the long-reaching fingers of the Church, and foreign and national secret services spying on everybody's life and meddling in our elections. Women were furious at the powerlessness to which they were reduced. Everywhere, young people were marching, protesting, and burning anything they could throw a Molotov cocktail at. They were dismissed as agitators: Feminists were all "lesbo bitches," young men "faggots."

Rage has fashioned my character.

But I no longer rant. Instead, I use my writing to bear witness, even when I cannot be sure that there is someone else beyond the solitary confinement of academic life who will hear and carry my message outside.

I wish to use this essay to walk the reader through the most significant epiphany I had: the discovery that the voices of women victims of monstrous violence (especially on a mass scale) give us access to the frame within which to contextualize a focal event; that in order to understand the fate of Jewish women during the Holocaust one must critically look at the long-haul historical situation of women overall; and that *only* by doing so, we can gain a new understanding of how the Holocaust itself was possible. Of how, unless we intervene, history indeed *does* repeat itself: the first time as tragedy, Karl Marx said, the second time as farce.

II.

According to Mary McCarthy, "Every age has a keyhole to which its eye is pasted." This will be defined, for our age, by the global political moves to increase the power pressure against women. Historians, archeologists or filmmakers of the far future will enter this early 21st-century *Wunderkammer* and find an eclectic collection of tools by which every conservative rank attempted to turn back the clock on women's rights and freedoms; time and again cranking the breaking wheel to which we are bound a notch tighter, especially forcefully after every escape attempt. Far from being exemplary prisoners, we and our foremothers relentlessly turned to every instrument at our disposal to scrape, scratch, and dig little openings in the fabric of our social, psychological, economic, public or domestic prison cells. Had we always failed, civilization itself would be in a very different place. Luckily (though luck had nothing to do with it), our gender journey has seen incredible victories, forward leaps, and notably we have carried with us others who needed our support in liberating their voices and owning their choices—homosexuals, immigrants, and a variety of categories of *Mitmenschen*, co-humans (to use Primo Levi's word).

Women achieved a lot. A lot more is ahead of us. But cyclical reversals of fortunes of epic magnitude bring progress to a halt. And the first quarter of the twenty-first century is rife with such setbacks: it'll be remembered for its world-wide impetus to return to a chimeric *status ante*, nostalgia for a "safer" past when the margins were quieter and the hegemony undisturbed. This regressive outlook is invariably characterized by a hate for the "Other", a disintegration of diversity, an obsessive control over women's bodies. Could we have anticipated the socio-political and economic turmoil of our own era?

History can and ought to be anticipated. Unlike earthquakes, volcanic eruptions or tsunamis, societal shifts give us ample time to think, adjust, and act. Society breeds its own behaviors. There's nothing new under the sun, but the old is novel to each generation. A wave of political aggression against women may not be new as such, but it keeps occurring, partly because we refuse to see the connection between *it* and the ideology that presides over it.

Gendered violence proves time and again to be an integral division of other grand-scale forms of violence and abuses, among them, also antisemitism. Antisemitism and its apogee, the Holocaust, are not gender-neutral because war, not to mention genocide, is a gender issue. Gender oppression is political and works as the barometer for disparate versions of moral wrongdoings. It's the canary in the coal mine of world justice and equality.

Root Causes

I come from a good family, I was a good girl, and mine was a bourgeois upbringing steeped in an internationalist, humanistic, rationalistic atmosphere. My parents were lucidly political. They never did drugs, never smoked, never got even close to being drunk. I guess they were not fun people. They read more than one newspaper every single day. Where I come from, the heart of Rome, we used to have a myriads of dailies at the newsstands, and none was neutral. The paper you carried under your arm declared publicly what party you voted for. My parents were always a bit to the right of me: but I was so far left that, to an American, their more "centrist" position would still make them liberal extremists. Voting day was a family holiday: long before I could cast my own ballot, my parents would force me to accompany them to the voting precinct and instilled in me a permanent awe of the process. In 1970, they marched and protested for divorce to become legal, and in 1978 they were there to fight for the legalization of abortion. Unlike most families, in mine women dictated everybody's political positions. My father took his cues from my mother: and that was that.

My mother's archenemy was my only uncle, her brother-in-law. A strange complex character whose tragic war experience as a child made him a bitter and hateful adult, holding the most outdated and inexplicable ideals. When the extended family and friends gathered around the table, ferocious arguments would explode, so loud that you could hear them from two neighborhoods away. Everybody talked over everybody else's voice, punched their fists on the table, threw their arms up in the air, they cussed, and suddenly, just as thunderously, they laughed at the best-delivered satirical remark. But my mother and uncle seemed to want to kill each other. The main topics of discord: Women and world politics, specifically Israel. My uncle objected to his daughter attending university away from home (a battle my mother fought for her niece until it almost destroyed the family); he objected to my father's feminist conduct (my mother's fault), to my mother's liberal parenting (of me), to her advice to his second daughter to follow her dream of becoming a photographer; and he objected to his wife's every move. He hated the two "Austrian sisters"—as he called my mom and aunt (because of their Viennese origins). And then there was Israel, which my mother defended against his and everybody's criticism as if, as it happens, its life depended on it. Her love for Israel was irrationally Jabotinskian.

Fed by my mother's consuming passion for history and politics, I spent years gorging on material that should have been filed under the rubric "Evil" and set aside behind a locked glass case. One oughtn't allow such books in the hands of children. Instead our library was enormous, gorgeous, and at my disposal. Back then, the emphasis was on shielding children from sex, not genocides and tortures. My mother was insane.

Together with *White Fang* and *The Prince and the Pauper*, the bibliography of my childhood included illustrated texts on Nazi atrocities; diaries from Soviet prisons and gulags; accounts of the years of terror after the Bolshevik Revolution, the Chinese Revolution, the French Revolution, all religious revolutions, and every day in 1848. Bloodbath after bloodbath after bloodbath. I read them all.

But while I could count on nobody's direct knowledge of the bottomless cruelty of Genghis Khan's hordes or Chmelnicki's *pogromishtchiks*, pretty much everybody could tell me all about WWII and the Holocaust. The traces of the nearby past were still visible everywhere.

I was born in Rome, the last in the family, surrounded by older female cousins. Our parents' generation was uniformly born before the war. Our grandparents had all known, participated in, and in some cases died as a consequence of the Great War. Growing up in Europe meant growing up on the stage of the Holocaust. We were surrounded by people whose forearms bore tattooed numbers from the concentration camps they had survived: bluish, fading, never invisible nor hidden. We children were told transparently what they signified. Stories of atrocities were narrated plainly and as fully as emotions and decorum would allow. What we heard seemed both unfathomable and all-too plausible. The war was long over, but the dyed-in-the-wool anti-Semitism, which had paved the way to the Jewish genocide, was not. That we knew well.

Walking to the market place was an exercise in historical memory. Storeowners used to stand on the thresholds of their shops watching the neighbors flow by, and I remember my grandmother responding politely to their *Buongiorno* and then under her breath saying—maybe to God, maybe to five-year-old me, or her 60-year-old self—"Bloody collaborator." There was nothing she could do but speak that truth, *each time*, for the record. The record, I now understand, was me. She wanted me to know and remember.

Before Pope John Paul II and the progressive mayor of Rome Francesco Rutelli joined forces to clean up the Eternal City for the 2000 Jubilee of Christianity, walls of building after building everywhere were used as public billboards where part of the political fights between right-wing and left-wing factions played out. The right-wing vandals used black ink, their enemies sprayed in red. There were swastikas everywhere as well as hammer-and-sickle graffiti, in addition to various longer slogans—sometimes hilarious. But one common theme both factions shared was the "Jews into the ovens" theme in all its imaginative iterations ("Watch out, Jews, we'll finish up the job," "Jews, bastards," "Jews *raus*!" and so on). With the only distinction being that the red-ink muralist would spice up his Jew-hate with a dose of anti-Zionist poison ("Down with Nazi-Israel"). I remember reading the writings on the walls—literally and metaphorically—knowing there was nothing to be done about it, wanting so badly to run away.

It was not during Hitler's reign, but during my lifetime, that the two-year-old Stefano Taché was killed and over 30 people wounded when a bomb deposited by a Palestinian terrorist exploded in Rome's Great Synagogue in 1982. Only three years later, terrorist attacks at the ElAl and TWA terminals at Rome Fiumicino Airport murdered 16 people and injured almost a hundred. The desecration of Jewish cemeteries was *à l'ordre du jour*. The world in school, in the workplace, in recreational contexts (soccer arenas in particular) was unbearably inimical.

No one could deny it: yet Jews had to be careful not to make a stink of it. It would be bad form. The majority in the world did not appreciate being reminded of its execrable sins. Jews were allowed to talk about the Holocaust "educationally": it was marginally taught in school, just enough to recap for Christians what they had done, but not effectively enough to elicit a deep transformation of the national sense of self.

So one lived on, as if antisemitism wasn't the most dominant hate form in the public arena. Shadowed very closely by only another form of troubling ferocity: misogyny.

Red Stars

I.

At the age of 7, my uncle, who owned a distinguished jewelry store downtown, hung a golden Magen David around my neck, where I wore it since, proudly aware of what it signified. My mother glowed with pride at her child's courage.

One day, just outside the school building, a classmate, Mimmo L., two years older than I, charged against me full-steam with all the strength of his teenage testosterone-packed body: chest first, mouth bent downward like a maddened bulldog, forehead lowered to better aim at mine. "Ebrei di merda! Tutti ai forni!," he yelled. Dumb with equal parts surprise, curiosity at what was happening (as if to someone else) and terror, I watched his arm rise up in the sky, above both of us, thick and muscular like Michelangelo's

David. I did not see it come down. But I felt something clobber the top of my head so hard that I heard the inside of my cranium thud like a ripe watermelon. Mimmo was flogging me with a long black umbrella. It ended only when the umbrella broke. I walked back home, my hair all messed up in a cluster of dirt and blood.

As soon as I got home, the phone rang: "Mr. C., is Federica alive?" a tear-choked voice asked. "Yes, Mimmo," my father answered calmly: "But I don't know whether you will be after I'm done with you."

The following morning, when Mimmo saw me approach the school flanked by my parents, he burst out crying and ran away. My father had no intention to harm him; we were there to meet with the administration. Feckless, the principle leaned back against his chair and, with a pleased expression on his face, delivered his inspired insight into the situation: "It's very simple. Mimmo has a crush on Federica. This is what boys do to express their feelings."

On the way back, we were dead quiet. I could feel my mother's rage inwardly mounting. She knew there was nothing to do other than to teach me a lesson from this. (*Which?!*) Mine was not a society of legal actions: no one sued anybody. And most of all, it was still strongly held that hard life experiences were useful to toughen up children and it would be a parental mistake to indulge a child's propensity for overblown self-pity.

Truth be said, I myself wasn't feeling any self-pity. I remember distinctly being solely preoccupied with Mimmo's human profile. In our public school system, each classroom sampled the whole range of the social order: from the richest children to the poorest, we were all together. Mimmo's story was one of the saddest. He was the son of a laborer, who lived with his family in what was commonly referred to as a *baracca*, a makeshift shack of sort. It was rumored that this man not unfrequently beat everybody at home and had been known to chain his son at the dog's pole outside, as a disciplinary measure. So all we could talk about for days was our fear that Mimmo's umpteenth screwup could translate into some gory punishment by his father. In other words, I ended up feeling guilty.

Only today, with a forty-year hindsight, I size the event in all its distortions: the real focal point is no longer me nor Mimmo. But the indelible words of the school principle, a man: "This is what boys do." A grand cenotaph to his and his era's total acceptance of two inextricable positions: misogyny and antisemitism.

II.

In that same middle school, I was exposed to the teaching of an extraordinary woman: Professoressa Luisa Perego. Her bony body, slightly bent, was enwrapped in a sunburned, wrinkly layer of thin skin that made her look like a resurrected mummy whose only zoetic features were an enormous bramble of white hair and two spirited sapphire eyes. She had fought in the Resistance during WWII and hence earned the right to be defiant of rules and irreverent to all authority: she smoked in class, despite many parents' petitions for mercy. As she paced the room, front to back, lecturing, she unawarely turned the beautiful blue packet of Gitanes in one hand, while elegantly holding up in midair the filter-less fag in the other, bringing it, between sentences, to her long, receptive lips. I loved her, and was fully reciprocated. For her, I composed the most poignant essays. I read what she recommended, extra-curricularly, and ran to her to relate my impressions. She was the first woman to teach me about Feminism.

Truthfully, I must have often recycled stuff I heard from the adults at the dinner table and, with it, tested her ideals and pushed back on some of her assumptions. She must have known that I was simply parroting what my world was feeding me, yet without upbraiding me for my superficiality she would lengthily counter my parents' socialist beliefs with her Marxist-Leninist convictions. I concluded she was in the right camp. She won me and made me: I was hers; I wanted so much to be her one day.

Once the umbrella incident had secretly made the rounds, she approached my desk—in the middle of a lecture about universal suffrage and the socio-political dynamics behind the Great War—stood there, hard and fierce, and while still talking to the class, unclipped from her neck a chain with a golden Hammer-and-Sickle pendant and hung it around my neck, side by side with my Magen David.

Was she putting forth new availabilities for my worldviews? Replacing one creed with another? Proposing a belief system, Communism, that at least theoretically, is not programmatically against women—unlike most systems, the religious one *in primis*?

I kept wearing both pendants together for many, many years.

A Tale of Too Many Cities

I.

When it was time for me to choose the discipline for my degree, I went in search of the Jewish Studies Program at La Sapienza University of Rome. It was hard to spot. No one even knew if it existed. I eventually made it to the physical place where the one and only professor of this discipline held court. At the end of an infinite narrow corridor, in a Kafkaesque building designed by, as much as for, the Fascist mind, one small door opened into a cavernous, vent-less office room, curtains drawn to blind the only existing window, filled with cigarette smoke. Behind the only desk, sat an enormous man, so obese, I thought, that he could not have gotten up to greet me even if he wanted to. But he hadn't wanted to. He looked at me suspiciously, had me repeat my surname twice. *No one he knew*. What was I doing there? "I would like to work on the Jews of Poland…" "Let me stop you right there," he said as if to halt a criminal act in its tracks. "I have only four students" – *what about the way he said it made it so clear they were all males?!* – "and by the end of the four-year program we hardly make it to the Roman times. So, if you are interested in modern Jewish history, this is not the place for you." I was dismissed with the wave of a hand, like a fly, without being told what the place for me was and whether there existed one.

I sheepishly retreated and moved to Poland. And after five years there, I moved to Israel. From Israel I came to America. I have touched all the shores of Jewish geographies. I shared Candide's naiveté and Gulliver's growing spite for unquestioned customs and irrational yahoos.

II.

One night, upon returning to my apartment in Warsaw after a party, my boyfriend Tomasz, our best friend Paweł, and I found scribbled on the door the Polish equivalent of "We know who you are." Sobriety returned in a flash: within a couple of hours we had packed all my belongings into our Fiat 500 and I was moved elsewhere.

I went to study in Krakow and while there I fell quite ill and had to check into a hospital. I remember a large room with several beds in the exclusive company of women patients. I was immediately a sensation in the ward: the latest arrival, the youngest, *and* Westerner, fluent Polish speaker, *and* from Rome. The simple word *Rzym* (Rome) turned a Pole's knees to water. Those were Pope John Paul II years. Catholicism had just performed its greatest miracle yet: Poland had been freed! I got special treatment and worshipful admiration. Then at 5:30 am, the priest showed up to offer patients the sacrament of the wafer. I politely demurred. He pushed a bit. I again declined. Comes a third attempt, I state in flawless Polish, "I am not Christian." The room freezes over: my situation takes a sudden turn for the worse. Thanks to my parents, who urgently involved a friend—a Polish Jewish exile in Rome and a rather influent public figure—I am taken under my embassy's care and repatriated "Operation Solomon" style.

To my friends' astonishment, I decided to move to Israel, thus indelibly disappointing almost everyone in my social circles of prominent politically-active leftist intellectuals. *My* friends, people I loved, grew up with, worked with, shared my ideological stance with, hated Israel and everybody who associated with it.

On the other hand, my mother was ecstatic. The fear that I could die as a casualty of the First Intifada was in no way a spoiler. However, I disappointed her too when almost two years later I called from Jerusalem to announce my imminent departure, because I was admitted into the Near Eastern and Judaic Studies Ph.D. program at Brandeis.

I moved to America. Unbeknownst to me, I was not alone.

America

I.

A Jewish guy, who had been shipped to Israel by his wealthy New Jersey parents in hope that his *aliyah* would help erase all traces of some venial sins at home (a DUI arrest and enough other faux pas to embarrass the family in front of their gilt-edged friends), developed a crush on me while we were together in Kibbutz Ma'ale HaChamishah.

When I left Israel to come to Brandeis, he did too. He followed me: not just to America. He began to follow *me* around. He knew where to find me. He stalked me. He took over my life. First, he only hurt my things. Then he hurt me, which hurt my graduate career. And in the end, he tried to kill me. Twice. The recovery was so strenuous that many a time I found myself wishing he had succeeded.

I was among the very first women in America on whom VAWA (Violence Against Women Act)—a brand new act introduced by Senator Joe Biden to Congress and signed into law by President Bill Clinton—was tested. It worked. It saved my life.

I resumed graduate school and this time I chose Holocaust Studies.

II.

It is not something I experienced that brought me to Holocaust Studies so much as it was Holocaust Studies that made me realize what was wrong with everything I experience.

When I wrote my dissertation, and later my first book, about the Holocaust, I chose to write about women, because I realized that the female victims' situation could help me expose a broader endemic issue with the way in which dominant oppressive groups mastermind their targets. Gender violence is violence ground-zero. To get there, I had to forensically investigate an oppressed group (women), within an oppressed group (Jews), in a situation of ultimate oppression (genocide).

My brightest insights would come when I started teaching.

During my early years as an adjunct for City College in NYC, I focused my Holocaust courses on the canonic *Night*, *If This Is a Man*, and *This*

Way to the Gas, Ladies and Gentlemen. Rather than to shock students with graphic exemplifications of the infinite varieties of ways by which people kill people, I wished to make them grasp the catastrophe through an understanding of what is lost when people kill people. Perhaps, in truth, I also wished for them to take a tour of my own mind, to visit the places I knew, to hear the painful melancholy in the voices I had known back home in Europe, to walk through living rooms, market places, and courtyards that hosted a life that no longer exists. It wasn't long before I realized that neither Elie Wiesel nor Primo Levi nor Tadeusz Borowski were furthering my intent. Where were their families, their life before and after? What did they eat? What did they quarrel over with their siblings? Wiesel offers a tiny glimpse of the life before Auschwitz, but in such a stylized and mythologized way that it is more poetry than portrait, more fantasy than recollection.

I started adding new requirements to the fixed canon Wiesel-Levi-Borowski-Spiegelman. Enter: Edith Bruck, Ruth Klüger, Sarah Kofman, Charlotte Solomon, Anne Frank, Milena Roth, Anita Lobel, Bernice Eisenstein, and my beloved Natalia Ginzburg.

Suddenly the Jewish everyday world became apparent to my students. They learned more about the victims and what was lost with them. And for the first time, they encountered women as subjects of history. They saw history through a woman's eyes and realized it looks different from there.

These women's writings make women appear on the scene in all their depth, complexity, or even duplicity: mothers, sisters, female rescuers. And by focusing on women, who are traditionally segregated in the domestic sphere, they make family life relevant, and highlight the power imbalances that reduce the life of (Jewish) women to a subcategory of men's—crippling us privately and publicly. This gender story is larger than Jewish history, and Jewish history can be made sense of differently when understood as part of this story. (There's a reason why when people want to emasculate hated groups, they feminize them. It happened to Jews. It happens still.)

The stories of women are often denied or, at best, made disappear by encompassing them in the stories of men.

Western culture, I realized, starts off with the erasure of the Mother, the silencing of the female victim's voice: it starts with Zeus' lie to his daughter, Athena, as soon as she erupts out of his head, telling her that she has no mother, that she is his brainchild. Athena's mother, Metis, had been raped and swallowed by omnipotent Zeus: it was Metis who, while pregnant in the god's belly, had made the famous shield with the Medusa effigy for her child-to-be. Being denied a maternal story, Athena herself will never be mother.

How thrilling it was to discover that many women scholars had already blazed a trail for me! Joan Ringelheim said that for her generation applying Feminist theory to the Holocaust had been unthinkable. Then she proceeded to do the unthinkable: she connected genocide and gender! I wasn't alone, but I too was needed.

I brought these ideas to my dissertation director who proceeded to dismiss them. He volunteered an alternative topic: An examination of the private epistolary of 19th-century men of letters. I blinked. I attempted to negotiate: I offered a variant of my original idea; he refused and insisted on his choice; I said OK, because I feared for my graduate career. After a while, I returned to beg to be allowed to work on something more akin to my Jewish-Feminist Studies interests; the big-shot professor became hostile, veiledly threatened me, and I ran for shelter to Nancy's office.

With eyes as blue and fiery as those of my childhood teacher Professoressa Perego, she curiously stared at me, patiently listened to my ideas, and finally said: "Sounds great." Nancy K. Miller, Second Wave militant, scholar of autobiographies and writer of memoirs, fearless fairy godmother of numberless graduate students, my mentor, my friend. Once again, I was saved.

Since then my scholarship turned into an examination of, as much as a tribute to Jewish women in general and Jewish mother-daughter relationships in particular. I devoted my book, my articles, my film-script to undoing stereotypical expectations about these figures, set up as enemies by culture but bonded together by personal and historical experience. Holocaust women wrote about themselves and their mothers in ways that expose the psychological binds (inscribed by culture, not nature) that determine a daughter's loyalties and behavior, and about the macro *and micro* injustices that under the circumstances of genocide put girls and women at greatest risk, in ways ignored by canonic male authors. My body of work highlights how patriarchy at large, Jewish patriarchy specifically, and anti-Semitism, were *all* simultaneously at work in determining the way in which women reacted to the genocide and their chances to survive.

I obeyed Hélène Cixous' instigation: "Woman must write herself: must write about women and bring women to writing, from which they have been driven away as violently as from their bodies." And by this she calls *us*, scholars too, to action. We "must put [ourselves] into the text—as into the world" in order to undermine the phallogocentrism that denies us our strength and the strength of our foremothers. We remember. We remember women in the Holocaust, and we reclaim an *office of our own* within academia in which to protect ourselves and others (past and present) from the blows of a system which has grown quite old under the sun.

Lest We Never See Another Butterfly

In *The Human Stain*, Philip Roth writes: "We leave a stain, we leave a trail, we leave our imprint. Impurity, cruelty, abuse, error, excrement, semen - there's no other way to be here…" Is there really no other way to be here?

Maybe not. Yet, it's worth trying.

Personally, I decided to take everything I learned so far about antisemitism, the Holocaust, misogyny, and miscellaneous phallic destructiveness, and I am using it to establish a new offshoot of environmentalism: Jewish Ecofeminist Criticism. A 21st-century Jewish philosophy of nature, whose purpose is to upend the environmental crisis facing us, starting with the human crisis that underlies it.

The environment is a feminist concern. It is *my* concern. Ecology is a feminist battle, because hate for nature is hate for women (since always placed in the same metaphorical caldron by patriarchal discourse). Ecology and environmentalism are Jewish concerns: the language used to demonize, marginalize, inimicalize and eventually exterminate Jews is a "naturalistic" discourse that reduces the enemy to an inferior position on the biological scale (or, as in the case of the Jews and other historically oppressed communities, even non-biological)—thus making it possible for the perpetrators to conceive of their extirpation—and it is the same discourse applied to the conquest, exploitation and, if needed, obliteration of the nonhuman world.

Ecocide and genocide are underscored by an identical mentality of toxic aggressiveness, violence, and delusions of biological superiority—and this mentality has fashioned for itself a language capable of sustaining its crimes. Suffice it to think of the animal metaphors (visually exemplified in all sorts of propaganda posters) used to equate a target group (women, ethnic or racial "Other", war enemies, and so on) to undesirable or feared lower lifeforms (lice, leeches, rats, apes, etc.). Entomologists experimenting with poisons to get rid of insects at the beginning of last century created the term extermination which was quickly extended to include the "handling" of (undesirable) people as well. The language of ecocide *is* the antisemitic language of the Holocaust, and vice versa.

If we can conceive of exterminating animals, we are de facto already conceiving of exterminating people.

Just as Feminist historians revolutionized Holocaust Studies by programmatically treating women as a category onto itself within the broader victim rubric, our next step is now to propel the scholarship a new leap forward by including the environment as an additional victim category in its own right, one coequal with Woman.

I believe that the extermination of the Jews and the annihilation of the biosphere are associated, and I wish my research to expose how the chain that links them is the ancient and yet undefeated model of phallocentric supremacy and domination.

Unlike the male scholarly tradition that imposes a dignified invisibility on the writer, I decided to appear in everything I write and teach. I won't drown my personal experience in my own ink. Let Adrienne Rich's words be an inspiration for Jewish women in academia: "And sometimes I feel inadequate to make any statement as a Jew… Yet we can't wait for the undamaged to make our connections for us; we can't wait to speak until we are wholly clear and righteous. There is no purity, and, in our lifetimes, no end to this process."

I don't shut up when I disagree with someone, just like my mother wouldn't. Like professor Perego, I pace my classroom like a lioness, wearing my past, my scars and my ideals right on my sleeves, because I can only defend others by exposing myself.

Sarah M. Cushman

To Follow and to Lead – Feminist Mentorship in Holocaust Studies

Introduction

The question I aim to answer here is: what about my journey as a feminist Holocaust historian is unique and important to tell with regard to those who came before and those who follow? The answer has three parts that I will expand on below. First is my personal journey to studying the Holocaust, particularly women's experiences, and the location of my research in relation to that of others. Second is the role of mentorship by and support from other women. Lastly is my career path, which is unusual for someone trained in academia, but which may inform younger scholars as academic positions become scarcer.

Journey to Studying the Holocaust

I am trained as a Holocaust historian. My research centers on women's experiences during the Holocaust, particularly regarding the women's camp in Auschwitz. Many people wonder how I became interested in the topic, particularly when they learn that I am not Jewish and have no personal connection with this history. Unlike children or grandchildren of survivors who have entered the field as a way of commemorating family, and Jewish scholars who view the Holocaust as a Jewish tragedy, my interest in the Holocaust arose from trying to understand a pivotal moment in world history that had a devastating impact on humankind.

My first recollection of encountering the Holocaust is from childhood. My home was filled with books. We had two large bookcases that bracketed the fireplace in the den and to which I had free access. My parents did not restrict my reading; I was limited only by my ability to reach the shelves, which evolved, and my interests, which were broad-ranging. I remember seeing the name HITLER on a spine on the top-shelf and thinking that I must read the book. I was 11 years old and I could not easily reach the highest shelf. My imaginative memory has me scaling the bookcase like a mountaineer. The adventure probably involved a ladder rather than climbing, and certainly not crampons and rope. Still, it was a significant moment, which I recall more vividly than the book itself. My deep engagement with Holocaust Studies was still 20 years ahead of me; a future that I did not yet discern or imagine. I knew only that the Nazi regime was an interest that I pursued with determination.

It is only in retrospect that I see the thread connecting my interests over time. Questions about how and why people treat others terribly, and the impact of war and violence on women, have animated my curiosity about history. My (perhaps unwarranted) trust in the power of education has influenced my professional development and career choices. I am not sure precisely when these interests began, but my encounter with Hitler's biography definitely figures in the equation. Encounters with sexism and racism also fueled me, particularly with regard to the expectation of family and the behavior and attitudes of the community I grew up in.

My intense interest in history deepened in high school. I explored European history and African-American history. The latter "won out" in college. I undertook a major in history, where I explored literary perspectives on African-American women's history. My deep curiosity about the history of slavery and its legacy in the United States was fueled by questions about the spectrum of human unkindness. Why do people treat each other so terribly? Why do we view some people as less worthy? Can education about mass atrocity diminish its prevalence? Why has the history and legacy of slavery, particularly its impact on individuals and collectivities, been elided? Why do people see African-American history as pertaining only to African-Americans? Because my focus was specifically on the experiences of black women in America, similar questions about women's histories also drove my work. I came away from my college education with an appreciation for the ethnic and racial diversity of America and a commitment to race and gender equity. These commitments, however, did not manifest directly in my immediate post-college career.

I come from a family in which attending college was expected and graduate school encouraged. I felt pressure to pursue an advanced degree, but I wanted to be clear with myself about what I wanted to do with my life. I was, and am, privileged to choose a path that both called me and that I felt would serve others. Still, my path was unusual – it has had twists and turns and included many years away from academia.

With bachelor's degree in hand and a firm commitment to figure out what I wanted to do, I set off in an entirely non-academic direction. For ten years, I worked in bookstores and warehouses, in the trades as a carpenter and plumber, and then found what I thought was my true calling as a sea kayaking guide on the coast of Maine. I loved the work and the people I encountered. I love the ocean and the islands and the kayak itself. Travelling so close to the water in a self-propelled craft is truly incredible. These lovely boats allow one to approach coastlines in an intimate way. I experienced the joy of living outdoors for most of each summer. I witnessed the rapid recalibration of people who spent much of their time inside, sedentary, and stressed out.

I also worked with one of the best kayaking instructors in the country who gave me the opportunity to learn in exchange for work and then, as my skills increased, to become an assistant and then a lead guide. That was a magical time of life for me. Yet as the sea and my heart pulled me in one direction, my head and my heart pulled me in another. Practicality also figured. Life as a guide (physically, financially, and intellectually) was not sustainable in the long-term. My mind craved deeper engagement.

One day, I was paddling around exploring the familiar nooks and crannies of Casco Bay with a group of inexperienced kayakers. The sun shone in a blue sky and a light wind played across the water. A perfect day. A startling thought popped into my mind: "Holocaust and Genocide Studies." "What?!" I thought to myself. "Where did that come from and why?" I had a lot of thoughts in my years of paddling. Many were deep and many fleeting, but few had much of an impact on my day to day life as this one did. Over the next few months, I began to research the field of Holocaust and Genocide Studies, which at the time I did not know for certain was a field, and enrolled in courses in European history and French – a language I had studied in college. I began reading as much as I could on the Holocaust and genocide and looked at the universities where the scholars I was reading worked. I decided I wanted to go to graduate school and to pursue a degree in Holocaust and Genocide Studies.

This decision startled a number of people in my life. My family was perplexed. They wondered why on earth I wanted to spend my time and energy studying mass atrocity. This question persists in my life as I imagine it does for most in our field. The more unusual question I get, one I was never asked prior to studying the Holocaust, is whether I am Jewish. Now, many people simply assume that I am. This means that sometimes I have to "out" myself as Gentile, which has occasionally been uncomfortable – more so than outing myself as lesbian, something I rarely have to do these days.

I worked hard and a path opened. Over the next two years, I continued studying European history and the French language, as well as taking up German. I found four universities to which I wanted to apply, visited all of them in rapid succession, and submitted my applications. I enjoyed my visits to all four universities, but one in particular felt like a perfect fit. Apparently, they felt the same way. The Strassler Center for Holocaust and Genocide Studies admitted me the following year. Our mutual acceptance changed my life.

Mentorship

The importance of my decision became apparent shortly after my arrival on campus in September 2001. First, I met my mentor, Debórah Dwork, whose presence in my life has been pivotal. Second, a few weeks after classes began, terrorists attacked the World Trade Center in New York and the Pentagon near Washington, DC. With the first, I found a lifetime friend; with the second, I sadly became aware that my course of study would not become irrelevant, at least for the foreseeable future.

Dwork taught the first course I ever took that was specifically about the Holocaust. She integrated the experiences of women in ways that I had not encountered before. While I had read quite a few histories of the Holocaust in preparation for attending graduate school, most had either not included women's experiences at all, were specifically about women, or had a small section about women's experiences. While Nazism was a male-centered ideology, it certainly addressed the role of women in society and had a vast number of women supporters. Approximately half of those targeted by the Nazis were women. It made sense to me that women's experiences be integrated into a general history of the Holocaust. It also made sense that there were studies that focused specifically on women as their unique positions had been ignored and marginalized.

I began diving into women's Holocaust history straight away. I started with the foundational literature related to women and the Holocaust, which included scholarship by some of the women in this volume. At that time, the major objections that faced early feminist scholars had been voiced and responded to. Because of that, I felt secure in pursuing my work about women during the Holocaust. This was true primarily regarding the challenges and responses of women who had been targeted by the Nazis. I was curious about analyses of women's special skills that helped them cope with Nazi persecution, particularly with regard to the early years in Nazi Germany and in the concentration and annihilation camps. I was also drawn to studies of women affiliated with the Nazis. At that point, some feminist scholars had tried to demonstrate that women, even "Aryan" women, were victims of the Nazis. The argument went something like: Nazism was a masculinist ideology that considered women second-class citizens who should be relegated to the home. They should be absent from public life and should focus on raising the next generation of "Aryans." Their primary role should be in choosing "racially" appropriate partners and raising "racially" conscious children, while shopping with racial and national consciousness. Indeed, these were important roles for women according to Nazi ideology. With regard to those targeted by the Nazis, scholars suggested that Jewish women suffered due to the both racist and sexist ideology of the Nazis, as well as from sexism within Jewish communities.

In addition, the 1990s and early 2000s saw the publication of several monographs and edited volumes that dealt with women's experiences under the Nazi regime and during the Holocaust. These shaped my course of study and my scholarship. Among the most influential books for me were Marion Kaplan's *Between Dignity and Despair*, Dalia Ofer and Lenore Weitzman's *Women in the Holocaust*, Claudia Koonz's *Mothers in the Fatherland*, Renate Bridenthal's (et al.) *When Biology became Destiny*, and Carole Rittner and John Roth's *Different Voices*.

At the same time, I knew that women had been guards in concentration camps. Many of these women were violent and seemed to enjoy the violence, their power over others, and the opportunity to carry out Nazi racial policy in an overt way. I thought to myself that this was something worth exploring: the Nazi ideal of womanhood was just that, an ideal. Real women responded to the ideal, adapted it, or related to it in a variety of ways. We as historians could not assume that what the Nazis wanted was necessarily what the Nazis got. This was certainly true of their efforts to render Germany free of Jews. Historians had discerned a pattern of trial and error and an evolution that radicalized in fits and starts resulting eventually in "the Final Solution." It seemed there was significant space in which "Aryan" women could act, and that even for women targeted by the Nazis, some seemed able to carve out a meager space for response and resistance.

As I focused in on women's experiences during the Holocaust, I also began to explore dissertation topics. Dwork and I had numerous discussions during which I became aware that no one had written a history of the women's camp in Auschwitz. This was surprising for several reasons. A number of feminist scholars had explored how women prisoners responded to imprisonment in concentration camps and many of the testimonies came from women who had survived Auschwitz. Auschwitz, at that time, was understood as the center of the Holocaust and there had been little work done on women camp guards. Most scholars understood prisoner functionaries (kapos, block leaders, etc.) as coming primarily from the "criminal" (green) and "antisocial" (black) prisoner categories. This seemed like a great dissertation topic, one in which I would be able to explore three categories of women: guards, prisoner functionaries, and common prisoners, discretely and in interaction with one another. Individually, each was practically a new topic as was the women's camp itself. And it was just a few years later that Friedlander published the second volume in his monumental history of the Holocaust in which he called for "integrated histories" – histories that explored perpetrators, witnesses, victims, and others in a comprehensive and interactive way. What I was writing regarding the women's camp in Auschwitz was just that – an integrated history.

There were few objections to my course of study. In fact, I received a lot of support. Edward Kissi, then a professor at Clark, thought my work on women perpetrators would add an important new perspective. Robert Jan van Pelt and Thomas Kűhne were on my dissertation committee and both thought the topic worthy. One person commented that it was a wise decision not to bring my identity as lesbian into the topic; that I was not focusing on lesbians specifically because that could lead to a lack of objectivity and perspective. I found (and find) this statement perplexing. I think most scholars who enter the field of Holocaust studies do so because of identity – their families were targeted by or participated in persecution of Jews. And I do bring my full identity to my studies – I do not know how not to – not only that one aspect of it.

I also found support among a broader community of scholars. I had the great fortune to receive a fellowship at the US Holocaust Memorial Museum. There, I encountered colleagues who pushed me to think deeply about my arguments. I am most grateful for the friendship I developed with Monika Flaschka, whose research on sexual violence paralleled my own and broadened my perspective on the topic. I also conducted research in Europe and found several scholars to be most helpful. Gudrun Schwarz, who had brought to light the complicity of Nazis wives, helped me gain access to archives that I otherwise would not even have known about. Linda Appel and Christa Schikorra offered friendship, advice, and occasionally a place to stay. Beate Meyer and Frank Bajohr made themselves and their homes available to me at critical junctures in my research.

When I began my graduate studies, there was very little work on women's camps and virtually no work on women camp guards. In the ensuing years, a number of scholars asked and began to answer some of the questions I had explored in my dissertation. Their work has enriched the field incredibly and deepened my own understanding of the women's camp in Auschwitz, even as much of the work focused on other camps and regions.

In addition, a lot of work has been done about women's experiences during the Holocaust: sexual violence; women's roles in resistance, women's access to privilege in the camp system and individual camps; women in hiding and in the partisans; and more. Some of the work done more recently that has influenced my own includes: Wendy Lower's *Hitler's Furies*, Elissa Mailaender's *Female SS- Guards and Workaday Violence*, Anna Hajkova's "Sexual Barter in Times of Genocide," and Na'ama Shik's analyses of women prisoners in Auschwitz. I have had conversations with all of these women about the overlapping topics of our work and have come away from the encounters enriched and buoyed.

Now, in 2019, I am shaping my earlier scholarship into a book about the women's camp in Auschwitz, I see that my research sits solidly among the work of these four women and that of scholars who have explored the vastness of the concentration camp system and women's places in it, as well as micro-histories of specific camps. While much of that investigation focuses on perpetrators or victims, mine remains centered on integrating those histories and integrating the history of the Auschwitz women's camp with that of the larger Auschwitz comp complex, the camp system, and the place of Auschwitz in the Nazis' genocidal project.

Career Path

My life and career reflect a deep interest and focus on the lives of women in history and in the present. I was attracted not only to women's history, but also to women scholars whose work was to bring women's experiences to the center of Holocaust history.

Dwork was a model of both how to integrate women into Holocaust history and how to be a leader and mentor in the field. She served as the founding Director of the Strassler Center for Holocaust and Genocide Studies at Clark University, which remains the only PhD program in Holocaust and Genocide Studies in the United States. I was privileged to be among her first doctoral students and to be a part of the community of scholars she has mentored. As leader of the Strassler Center, she has brought visibility to the field and created a legacy of professional and scholarly excellence. Her students now hold important positions in the field as professors, researchers, and organizational leaders. She has shown that a small center can have a huge impact and that the field of Holocaust studies needs focused graduate study.

Dwork's scholarship is outstanding as well. She pioneered in exploring children' experiences during the Holocaust and tackled the daunting projects of writing a new history of Auschwitz and a comprehensive and readable single volume about the Holocaust as a whole. She has written about sexuality and sexual violence, refugees, resistance, and now rescue. In each of these roles, she has served as an example to me; and I carry her example with me. When she undertook to lead the Strassler Center, such a journey for an academic was rare. When I turned from academia to education and then back to a career that included both, as well as administration, such a journey was still unusual. Currently, with academic positions becoming ever more difficult to secure, our paths can perhaps be viewed as road maps or at least precedents for those who follow, particularly women.

I did not realize when I took a job at the Holocaust Memorial and Tolerance Center of Nassau County (HMTC, Long Island, NY) in 2007 that it would have such a big impact on my life. I trained as an academic and aimed to find a tenure-track position at a university after finishing my dissertation. I thought this job would allow me to finish writing and set me up for a university career. While at HMTC I became deeply engaged with Holocaust Education. I served first as the Assistant Director of Education and then the Director of Youth Education. In the course of nearly six years there, I had the privilege of helping to design the museum, develop and implement programs for children and teachers, recruit and train volunteer staff, and engage in community outreach. I loved the work; and I loved the teachers, the students, and most of the all the volunteers, who included a number of Holocaust survivors. I was thoroughly delighted to be in contact with non-academics who cared so deeply about the Holocaust and making sure that students learned about it. Theirs was a labor of love and my love for them and their mission grew. I was also fortunate enough to stay connected with university-level teaching through an adjunct position at Touro College, where I taught a small general survey course on the Holocaust.

While on Long Island, I finished my dissertation. I found that I needed some time and space away from the topic and I needed to find a new job. I was fortunate to find a position at the Strassler Center. I returned to Clark for three years, first as the Academic Program Liaison Officer and then as Head of Educational Programming, both with a special appointment as lecturer in the History Department. This job gave me the opportunity to engage with university-level Holocaust Education, organizing conferences and lecture series, and budget management and outreach.

Now a colleague of Dwork, I learned much about being a Director. This was an invaluable education, one that many in the field of Holocaust Studies never receive: how to run a non-profit; how to manage and supervise personnel; how to allocate and reconcile budgets; how to plan events, including paperwork, contracts, and visas for guest from near and far; how to help doctoral students navigate the hoops of bureaucracy that many find difficult, if not impossible. In short, I acquired and honed a number of skills that would put me in a great position to become the Director of the Holocaust Educational Foundation of Northwestern University (HEF of NU), a position I took in September 2016 and continue to hold in October 2019.

When the position at the Holocaust Educational Foundation came to my attention in early 2016, I was not looking for a job. I was engaged and thriving at the Strassler Center. Still, when I saw the job description, I thought it would be a perfect fit for me. It would allow me to use the skills I already had and challenge me to develop new ones. I saw that HEF of NU and I could help one another. One benefit of being in this role is that I am a woman in a leadership position in the field. This is important in and of itself. But I also bring a feminist perspective. For me it is critical to support women in the field not only by highlighting their scholarship, but by making sure they fill important roles in HEF of NU's programs and events and that they are among the beneficiaries of HEF of NU's programs and events.

Conclusion

As Director of the Holocaust Educational Foundation, I have a unique opportunity to influence the field of Holocaust Studies and Holocaust education.

While scholarship remains an aspect of my work, one that I hope makes a contribution to scholarship; the bulk of my daily activity is related to helping increase access to Holocaust education by students at the university level in the US and around the world. This is important work and my training at the Strassler Center and the Holocaust Memorial and Tolerance Center of Nassau County helped me gain the skills and vision necessary to carry this mission forward. A Claims Conference study from 2018 found that many people in the US know little or nothing about the Holocaust, yet understand that learning about the Holocaust is important.

The Holocaust Educational Foundation was founded in 1976 by Theodore Zev Weiss and his cohort. The Foundation has been pivotal in establishing the field of Holocaust Studies. Zev travelled far and wide encouraging professors to teach about the topic. He, in cooperation with Peter Hayes, Christopher Browning, Roger Brooks, and others, saw the need for a conference and training for professors and brought both to fruition in the form of the biennial Lessons and Legacies Conference and the annual Summer Institute on the Holocaust and Jewish Civilization, both of which remain staples of HEF of NU and the field of Holocaust Studies. Until recently, HEF's leadership has been primarily male. Still, over the years, HEF has highlighted the work of women scholars and has come to recognize the importance of women's experiences during the Holocaust. I hope to add to the expansion of women's roles in Holocaust Studies, not only by serving as a leader and (hopefully) a model for women in the field, but also by helping to advance the presence of women in settings and positions of importance and visibility. This is a work in progress, especially as women remain in the minority among leaders of Holocaust organizations both in the United States and abroad, particularly at the university level. There is work to do and I am honored to be a part of it. I look forward to welcoming ever more women to the field and supporting them as they shape Holocaust Studies in new and important ways.

Sharon Geva

My Unknown Sisters

Introduction

On September 2004, I met Ahuva Fried. We talked about her sister, Zivia Lubetkin, who had become a role model for Jewish Heroism during the Holocaust. Lubetkin was one of the senior fighters in the Warsaw Ghetto Uprising (1943), one of the leaders of the ZOB, the Jewish Fighting Organization (Zydowska Organizacja Bojowa). After immigrating to Eretz-Israel, she was among the founders of Kibbutz Lohamei Hagetaot. While Ahuva was talking about her, she used the present tense. Even though Zivia passed away in 1978, for her she was still alive. At that time, Ahuva's hair-style was the same as her sister's: short hair, straight, gray. She used to smoke too. For me, a close conversation with Ahuva was the closest I could get to approaching Zivia Lubetkin, not to mention talking to her. And I still have so much to ask.

Like many Israelis who grew up in the 1980s, I participated in Holocaust Memorial Day school ceremonies, awaiting the fearful siren at 10:00AM when everyone stood at attention. In sixth grade, we visited the Yad Vashem Museum in Jerusalem. In high school, we studied about the Holocaust and the Second World War for our history matriculation exam. The Holocaust was part of my family history. Nevertheless, no one spoke about it much. My grandfather's parents and two of his brothers died in the Lodz Ghetto. Grandpa made *aliyah* in May 1939, when he was twenty years old. He passed away when I was a young child, and as far as I know, he did not talk much about his lost family. In 1956, Grandma filled in a Page of Testimony at Yad Vashem, with details of his lost family members. Years later, I found these pages in in the Holocaust Victims Database on the Yad Vashem website. There was no one that could tell me anything more about them.

Like many Israelis who grew up during the 1980s, I read children's and young reader books about the Holocaust, such as *The Island on Bird Street* by Uri Orlev (1980), *The Cigarette Sellers of Three Crosses Square* by Joseph Zieman and of course, Anne Frank's diary, *A Diary of a Young Girl*. When I was in 12th grade, the First Gulf War (1991) broke out. Everyone was exhorted to carry gas masks at all times, and after dark we had to stay at home. Scud missiles were targeting Israel, and Israel took no military defensive measures. When there was a siren, we rushed to a bomb shelter at home.

I remember people talking; the gas in the chemical missiles was produced in Germany.

During my MA studies, I taught History in high school. According to the curriculum, we taught about the Nazi regime's policy against the Jews, focusing on the Nuremberg Laws and Kristallnacht, the Jewish life in the ghettos, and the Warsaw Ghetto Uprising. The last chapter of the curriculum was devoted to the history of the State of Israel during the 1950s and the early 1960s. Here we taught about the Eichmann Trial in Jerusalem (1961) and the main issue we discussed was how the trial changed the attitude of Israeli society towards the Holocaust. Teachers had to explain the trial's impact on the Israeli attitude towards first-person Holocaust stories, saying what was believed at the time: that during the 1950s Holocaust survivors in Israel were silent and passive. As a result of the trial, their personal accounts of Holocaust-related experiences entered the Israeli public discourse for the very first time.

A Beginning of a Conversation

In early 2002 I began my PhD studies in the Department of Jewish History at Tel Aviv University, under the supervision of Anita Shapira and Hannah Naveh. My motivation was to figure out how Israeli society defined heroism in the context of women. What did Israelis consider as heroism, with regard to women? From what I had known previously, the term related to women who belonged to armed resistance organizations, such as Sarah Aharonson (1890–1917), one of the leaders of Nili, the Jewish pro-British underground during WWI, who committed suicide; Hannah Szenes, a poet and paratrooper, who was executed in Budapest in 1944; Zivia Lubetkin, a senior member in the ZOB; Zohara Levyatov, a member of the *Palmach* (*Plugot Hamachatz*, The Striking Force), the enlisted brigade of the *Haganah*, and a pilot in the Israeli Air Force, who died in an airplane crash in August 1948.

The phrase "Holocaust and Heroism" (*Shoah ve-gvura*), well known in the Israeli public discourse, frequently appeared in that context. Holocaust Memorial Day (*Yom Hazikaron LaShoah VeLaGvurah*) is marked on the 27th of Nissan,[1] and was linked to the Warsaw Ghetto Uprising. The uprising was a source of pride and comfort for Israelis, a counterfoil to the destruction of the Jewish people in Europe during the Second World War. However, did the concept of heroism during the Holocaust have other aspects? What

1 *"Martyrs' and Heroes' Remembrance Day Law," Knesset website.* https://knesset.gov.il/shoah/eng/shoah_memorialday_eng.pdf

could be considered women's heroism during the Holocaust? What were the roles of Holocaust heroines?

Studies conducted by women researchers about women during the Holocaust became the foundation for my work and gave me food for thought. The title of Joan Ringelheim's article summarized the matter: We have to take the women into account.[2] Dalia Ofer and Lenore Weizman explained how a gender perspective contributes to a deeper and richer understanding of the Holocaust, and showed that women's experiences, which were different than men's experiences during the war, not only enrich the history of the Holocaust, but contribute to better understanding of it.[3] Their arguments became fundamental assumptions for me regarding Israeli society and the Holocaust. Viewed from the Israeli perspective, women's heroism during the Holocaust can enrich the Israeli perception of the Holocaust and of Holocaust survivors, and the general Israeli viewpoint regarding the status of women in the State of Israel. Judy Tydor Baumel(Schwartz) ended her article about female heroism in the Holocaust with questions.[4] One of the questions was how do Holocaust heroes differ from Holocaust heroines? I felt that this was the beginning of a conversation.

I started working on my research proposal while I was pregnant with my eldest daughter. Following conversations with my advisor, Hannah Naveh, who was then head of the Women's and Gender Studies Program at Tel Aviv University, the dichotomy "Holocaust and heroism" echoed the theory of Simone de Beauvoir (*The Second Sex*). Strong and active Sabras warrior, vis-à-vis weak and passive Diaspora Jews. I wrote my research proposal during my maternity leave, a period that made me think about myself as a woman, causing me to question my role in Israeli society, gender borders, and opportunities to cross them. How did Israelis view the concept of mothers and motherhood during the Holocaust?

Key sources for my research were the Israeli press, including testimonies from the Eichmann trial. The press reflects a certain reality: it compiles what it views to be new, significant and compelling. It also reports in accordance with what it believes its readers need to know, or want to know. It also represented a variety of views, as the newspapers at the time represented different political parties and movements. An advantage of this material is its

2 Joan Ringelheim, "The Holocaust: Taking Women into account," *Jewish Quarterly* 39, no. 3 (1992): 19–23.

3 Dalia Ofer and Lenore J. Weitzman, *Women in the Holocaust*, New Haven: Yale University Press, 1998: 1–18.

4 Judy Tydor Baumel, "'She Girds Herself with Strength': Holocaust Heroines in Collective Memory", *Dapim Leheker Tekufat Hashoa* 13 (1996):189–201. [Hebrew]

speed of response as opposed to textbooks or literary works, where immediacy plays little role. During the 1950s, the press was the primary media outlet in Israel. Relative to the number of potential readers at that time, Israeli produced a large number of Hebrew newspapers.

No archive of any newspaper has separately cataloged the subject of women during the Holocaust, and the cataloging of the Holocaust itself during those years was only partial. Databases and digital search engines did not yet exist. I spent three years next to a microfilm machine and volumes of newspapers, reading them page by page, searching for items which referred, directly and indirectly, to women in the Holocaust, in order to create an archive of my own. Alongside this, I collected items from the press connected to perceptions of the Holocaust, and items regarding the status of women in Israel.

Reviewers had initially expressed doubts about my research proposal. They were concerned that I would not find enough material in the Israeli press about women during the Holocaust. In view of the popular argument that the 1950s were a period characterized by silence vis à vis the Holocaust, the assumption was that very little had been written in Israel then about women in Holocaust. In fact, the opposite was true. At that time, the Israeli press published numerous articles about women during the Holocaust. These articles led me to additional documents. Consequently, I ended up with a large corpus of material: in addition to the daily press and magazines, women in the Holocaust were mentioned in pamphlets, brochures, speeches, protocols, reports, official and personal letters, chronicles and journals, testimonies, memoirs, eulogies, biographies, autobiographies, and more. Together, they provided a variety of images of women in the Holocaust in Israeli public discourse. Many were written and created by women. The shelves in my study at home began to fill up with these documents.

Day after day I read stories about women during Holocaust, their experiences, forms of coping and means of resisting. During that time, I gave birth to two of my three children. In the morning, I would read documents about women who were mothers during the Holocaust, such as the testimony of Rivka Yoselewska at the Eichmann trial.[5] The afternoon I spend with my children – a toddler and a baby. In retrospect, I was attempting to separate the hours during which I delved into the stories of these women from the hours when I cared for my own children. I had a daily routine: from 9:00AM

5 Testimony of Rivka Yoselewska, The Trial of Adolf Eichmann, vol. 1, session no. 30, *The Nizkor Project*, http://www.nizkor.org/hweb/people/e/eichmann-adolf/transcripts/Sessions/Session-030-04.html

until 3:30PM – work in a library or archive. Maybe it was a type of avoidance. Anyhow, it worked.

The sources taught me that the Israeli public's concept of heroism during the Holocaust was a broad one. Different types of women were presented as Holocaust heroines, and no particular weight was afforded to factors such as age, ethnicity, family status, occupation and education, political leanings or Zionist affiliation, external appearance and personality traits. The common element was the evaluation of each one as willing to engage in self-sacrifice: when she went out to armed battle; when she tried to free prisoners who were to be sent to the gas chambers; when a woman participated in piecing together a plan for mass rescue; when she exhibited tenacity in observing the mitzvoth; when she fought to continue drawing and painting; and when she defended her children to the death. According to Israeli society, heroines during the Holocaust were those women who were willing to make choices for the benefit of the other, even when that choice cost them their lives.

Sources have shown that without a doubt, stories of women during the Holocaust were an active, forceful and prominent part of the Israeli public discourse. They were central to the construction and preservation of national identity. Relative to the representation of men during the Holocaust, the image of woman during the Holocaust included different types of heroism, and not only the prototypical and classic one of weapon-in-hand. The 1950s were emphatically not characterized by silence or hushing. Every topic related to the Holocaust included a reference to women. I realized that what I taught only a few years earlier in high school was far from what actually happened.

Women's Talk

Sometimes I was asked if my research included interviews with women survivors. The answer was no. This was historical research based on documents from the period under study. However, the Holocaust survivors were still there, even though they were already very old. There were no interviews, but instead, conversations. The aim was to shed light on the findings that had already emerged from the documents and perhaps to reveal new ideas. Furthermore, I was curious. Looking back, these talks were a very important tool for me to formulate the argument.

All the women I talked to referred, directly or indirectly, to their identity as women during the Holocaust. Women who were members of the ghetto undergrounds and women partisans spoke about the advantages of having a woman's body during the war, their roles in the underground, and their struggle. They talked about women's dual struggle. First they had to prove to their commanders that they were worthy of carrying arms. They then had to prove themselves a second time when going into action. They all talked about a women's ability to survive, to bear suffering. They all stated that women were stronger than men were.

I met with Vitka Kempner-Kovner at her home in Kibbutz Ein Hahoresh. She was a member of the underground in the Vilna ghetto and a partisan, and the wife of Abba Kovner, a poet, writer and partisan leader. He was a public figure in Israel, and most of the time she tended to leave center stage to him. During the Holocaust, she said, a woman had to fight to have the opportunity to fight. When a woman had the chance to do so, she proved that she – and by that, other women – were capable of fighting. She told me what she did when she learned that Russian partisans stole weapons from her fellow partisans. "These guys did not dare defend themselves, and that made me very angry," she said. "I took a horse, and I said: Now we will go back and reclaim these weapons." And so it happened. Courage, she said, is not necessarily to carry a gun, but to insist on your rights.

Vitka Kovner did not speak of the concept of power in physical terms. Men are physically stronger, she explained, in terms of courage and torture, women are stronger than men. Mentally, she said, we are stronger. For young men, she said with a little smile, "food is a very important thing, right? Men must eat on time, we – women – do not. A woman can stay awake for 24 hours if necessary, right?" She spoke to me woman to woman, as if we were equals. At the time, as mother of a baby, I knew from experience how women could go without sleep for a night and day, not eat properly, and still function.

Chavka Folman-Raban, who was an underground courier (*kasharit*) in the ŻOB in Warsaw ghetto, also spoke about women's strength. During our conversation in Kibbutz Lohamei Hagetaot, she said: "Women always have more endurance, not only during the Holocaust. First, we give birth. Men couldn't stand it. They would stop having children. It's how we are made." She told me how having a women's body was an advantage in the ghetto underground, how women concealed weapons on their bodies, sometimes in undergarments. Pre-existing attitudes protected women. No one expected them to use weapons, so it was easier for them to pass roadblocks and checkpoints without being arrested. Physical strength was not crucial to success and above all, their Judaism was not marked on their body.

The women I met spoke not only about themselves, but were also eager to talk about their sisters-in-arms. Hela Schiffer-Rufeisen did not live far from Chavka Folman-Raban's home, in Moshav Bustan Hagalil. She was a fighter in the Krakow ghetto who smuggled the first pistols into the hands of the ghetto underground. She told me about her testimony at the Eichmann trial, and emphasized the heroic story of her friend, Gusta Davidson (Justina), who did not survive. At that time, a new edition of Justina's Diary had just been published in Hebrew.[6]

These conversations confirmed what I knew from research about women's perspective on events, and the power of sisterhood during the Holocaust.[7] The conversations also showed how fragile women's solidarity was. Fela Szapszyk-Finkelstein, a member of Betar and the Jewish Military Union (ŻZW) in the Warsaw ghetto, told me about Auschwitz. She talked about the solidary that existed among women in the block. How differences between women who were members of different political movements faded away. But it was temporary. When she spoke of the Warsaw Ghetto Uprising, she painfully noted the political divide between members of the ZOB and the ZZW. Thanks to her, I understood the magnitude of the political divide in Israel: Sisterhood could not overcome it.

Ruth Bondy, a journalist, author and translator, shared with me her initial thoughts on researching the Holocaust from the gender perspective, and her own doubts while writing an article for an anthology of women in the Holocaust.[8] "At first," she said, "I did not see a difference between men and women regarding Holocaust research. I may have been an unconscious feminist," she said, not without a sense of humor. We kept in touch. In 2014, her book *Not Only Kafka and the Golem* about Czech Jews was published. She gave me a copy, wrote a dedication and signed with the words: "Ruth Bondy, who did not deal with gender, even though gender defined her life."

Doubts about the relevance of the gender perspective to Israeli perceptions of the Holocaust also came up in conversation with poet and intellectual Haim Gouri. During the conversation, which took place in his home in Jerusalem, he mentioned stories about women in the Holocaust that had touched him. One was a story of parents who hid their daughter with a Polish family, and left her two letters. In her letter, the mother asked her daughter to forgive her for abandoning her. She pleaded with her to understand. "Next to such a letter, a novel that received a Nobel Prize is worth

---

6 For the English version see: Gusta Davidson Draenger, *Justyna's Narrative*, University of Massachusetts Press: Amherst, 1996.

7 Dalia Ofer, "Her view through my lens: Cecilia Slepak studies women in the Warsaw ghetto," Judith Baumel-Schwartz, and Tova Cohen (eds.), *Gender, Place, and Memory in the Modern Jewish Experience: Re-placing Ourselves*, Parkes-Wiener Series on Jewish Studies, London: Vallentine Mitchell, 2003: 29–50. Judy Baumel, "The 'Zehnerschaft' as an example of Mutual Assistance Among Women During the Holocaust", *Dapim Leheker Tekufat Hashoah* 10 (1993): 107–128. [Hebrew]

8 Ruth Bondy, "Women in Theresienstadt and the Family Camp in Birkenau," Ofer and Weitzman (eds.), *Women in the Holocaust*: 310–326.

nothing", he said. He found it particularly important that a woman had written it. "That's the point, she wrote it. She is in charge". My impression was that the gender perspective gave him food for thought. In retrospect, this conversation had a special power that strengthened me.

The granddaughters of Holocaust survivors had no doubt: being a woman played a great role in their grandmothers' lives, especially during war. Sharon Alexander, the granddaughter of Vera Alexander, who was a *Blockalteste* (block elder) and a *Kapo* in Auschwitz-Birkenau, remembered that her grandmother told her once: "You do not understand how much power you have as a woman, as you grow up, so you will understand and maybe use it". She said her grandmother explained that women could cope better with hunger, exhaustion and pain. The body, she told her, saved me. She was proud of her grandmother.

In a PhD dissertation, these conversations are usually located in the footnotes. The key sources were the documents, and I had plenty of them. Publishing my dissertation as a book[9] allowed me expand on these conversations. As for the manner in which the women were represented in the book, I had a dilemma. In primary sources women were frequently mentioned only by first name. This was common in the sources about the ghetto fighters. In other cases, women were portrayed as being related to a man. For example, Hansi Brand, a member of the Jewish Relief and Rescue Committee in Budapest, was presented as the wife of Joel Brand and sometimes as the lover of Dr. Rezsö Kasztner. On one hand, I felt that presenting them with their last names alone would be too formal, and on the other hand presenting them with only first name might reinforce their reduction. Therefore I presented them at all time with full names.

The book's distribution in 2010 showed that the acceptance of the legitimacy of historical research about women in the Holocaust was not self-evident. In one of the two largest book chains in Israel, the book was categorized under "women and relationships", not under "Holocaust" nor under "history". That is to say, bookstores categorized a book about women in the Holocaust and their image in Israeli society alongside self-help books for a better marriage, and guides on how to find a true love. An article about this appeared in the *Haaretz* daily[10] and was widely shared in social media. Women initiated a petition protesting the chain's cataloging method and shared it on Facebook. It was a warm-hearted expression of sisterhood. This

9 Sharon Geva, *To the Unknown Sister: Holocaust Heroines in Israeli Society* (Heb.), Tel Aviv: Hakibbutz Hameuchad, 2010.

10 Esti Aharonowitz, "Women, relationship and Steimatzky catalog system," *Haaretz*, June 17, 2011. [Hebrew]

inspired me when I launched my blog about women in history (December 2012) which I entitled: "towards a shelf of history books."

Although there was no change in the bookstores, I felt that I was not alone. It seems that marginalizing the issue of women in the Holocaust, in real and symbolic terms, triggered something wider. In retrospect, I saw how opposition can cause women to band together and work for change: when we confront an attempt to revoke our privileges as women, we are willing to fight.

We Are Not Alone

Since the academic year 2011–2012, instead of a taking test or submitting papers, students in my courses on women in Israel write encyclopedia entries about women in Israeli history and publish them online on Wikipedia.[11] The goal is to provide the public with reliable and up-to-date information in Hebrew about women in Israeli history whose search results in Google are few or nonexistent. Thus, students share what they learn in class in order to promote the public status of women who had made history but are still on the margins. The paucity of sources available online prompt them to act. They go to archives, libraries and contact the women's families, if there are any.

More than 100 entries on women in the history of Israel have been uploaded to the Internet, and significant portion of them are about women in the Holocaust. Among them are fighters in underground ghettos, such as ghetto fighter, partisan, political leader and Knesset member Haika Grossman, or artist and stage designer Esther Lurie (Shapira). Students wrote about non-Zionist women who were not familiar figures in Israel, such as Dr. Adina Schweiger-Baldi, a physician in the Warsaw ghetto, and Mati Rubenova, a Jewish partisan in Bulgaria. One of the students chose to write an entry about Batia Temkin-Berman, a member of Po'alei Zion and a librarian in the Warsaw ghetto. Until then, in the Hebrew Wikipedia, there were only entries about her husband, Dr. Abraham (Adolf) Berman, who was a member of the Knesset, and her son, who is a professor at the Technion. Similarly, a student also wrote an entry about Hansi Brand.

The project drew public attention and appreciation and encountered objections. Anonymous editors and users in the Hebrew Wikipedia community questioned the significance of some entries; sometimes they tried to remove them.[12] According to the Hebrew Wikipedia community rules, senior

11 I entitled the project "Raising Value: Returning Women to History". In Hebrew, the word entry and the word value has the same meaning.

12 Ofer Aderet, Ofer, "Israeli Teacher Blasts Hebrew Wikipedia after Entries on Unsung Women Deleted," *Haaretz*, September 29, 2016. See also: Ofer Aderet,

users may initiate deletion of entries from the database and also remove them by a majority vote. Amongst these entries were entries about Chavka Folman-Raban, Hela Schiffer-Rufeisen, and Batya Temkin-Berman. They questioned their contribution to the underground, by underlining that these women were not commanders, even far from it. This attitude reflected a general perception in Israel, certainly among those who served in the IDF. Even though these women participated in frontline warfare, the term *kashariot* (couriers) can be seen as filling a low profile, supporting role.[13]

My students were annoyed and angry. They had contributed information about women in history to an open access forum. Attempts to delete that information from a popular and open-access database illustrated that women were still on the margins. It also taught them that the topic of women during the Holocaust had not yet received full legitimacy. As for me, it was an effective tool for illustrating the importance of learning and researching women's history, in order to make a change on behalf of women's status here and now. Furthermore, the confrontations within the Hebrew Wikipedia community made the students feel that each one can make a difference – that we are not alone.

Study and research of women in the Holocaust is significant, and not only for the discourse within the framework of academia. We need to learn from it. The first step is raising awareness by sharing it with more and more women, inspiring them to learn about women while they study about the Holocaust, and generating solidarity. This book is also a way to do so. I thank Judy Baumel-Schwartz and Dalia Ofer for inviting me to participating in it, and for the honor of working alongside researchers who paved the way to my own research.

From my experience, among female students, certainly within the framework of women's and gender studies, the legitimacy and importance of research regarding women in the Holocaust, and Holocaust research from a gender perspective, is obvious. When we read the introduction of *Women in the Holocaust* by Dalia Ofer and Lenore Weitzman in class, my students wonder why the editors explain at length the importance of the gender perspective in Holocaust research. Some of them believe that there is even a hint of apology. They do not understand why. This demonstrates the evolution in our field since 1998. Their own responses indicate that it has come a long way. Still, in Israeli academia there are too few classes and seminars about women in the Holocaust.

"Israeli Women Who Made History – Now in Wikipedia Too," *Haaretz*, August 26, 2015.

13 Sharon Geva, "Female Spearheads of the Uprising," *Haaretz*, April 18, 2018.

As for me, following the instructions that I have given to my students for several years, my next research project is to trace in detail the life story of a single woman. Based on new historical sources I recently found and an old ambition of mine, I have begun working on Zivia Lubetkin's life story. I hope that when it is published, there will be no doubt in bookstores that it belongs on the history bookshelf.

Dorota Glowacka

"I Am Polish on My Mother's Side...": A Journey toward Becoming a Feminist Holocaust Scholar

Peregrinations: A Pre-amble

This reflection will *not* begin with the sentence I would prefer to open it with, which would have said that, as a Jewish woman and a Holocaust scholar, I have studied women in the Holocaust for decades. My journey started somewhere else altogether, and it has led me through many cul-de-sacs of this "elsewhere," traversing biography and geography, intellectual passion, and research commitments. It has been a personal and professional *quo vadis*, and I have been reprimanded for allowing the two paths to run into each other. In this essay, I give an account of the journey that led me from my native Poland, where I was a student of American literature in the English Department at the University of Wrocław, via graduate school at the Comparative Literature Department in Buffalo (SUNY), to the University of King's College in Halifax, Canada, where I teach Holocaust and genocide studies, and theories of race and gender. These geographical relocations and professional branding have coalesced with a spiritual exploration of my Jewish roots and of my identity and social position as a woman.

In *The Human Condition*, German-Jewish philosopher Hannah Arendt wrote, "The chief characteristic of this specifically human life [...] is that it is itself full of events which ultimately can be told as a story, establish a biography."[1] If life is a story that must be disclosed to others in order to attain meaning and coherence, then my life can be narrated as a fortuitous account of becoming a feminist Holocaust scholar. It requires that I explore a tangled nexus of identity categories, such as "being" a woman, a Polish Jew, an academic, and a first-generation immigrant. I place "being" in inverted commas to indicate that these are performative rather than essentialist labels, anchored in socially constructed binary categories that I have always hoped to challenge and transcend as I move along. Since all of these designations are unstable, I have never settled into them and occupied them fully, and instead I have travelled across their multiple and occasionally precarious

1 Hannah Arendt, *The Human Condition*, Chicago: The University of Chicago Press, 1998: 97.

intersections. I always remember what a good friend of mine wrote to me in a letter shortly after I left Poland: "Once you cross the Atlantic, you are always on the wrong side." I also wonder whether we are all equally capable of telling our life stories, as Arendt seemed to believe, or if, for some, life circumstances stunt that ability.

Quo vadis? Familial Contexts[2]

My father was a Polish Jew and a Holocaust survivor. He was born, lived, then lived again, worked, and died in Poland. My mother was an ethnic Pole who married a Jewish man at the time when anti-Semitic troubles were resurfacing in Poland, prompting thousands of Jews that remained there after the war to accept a one-way passport out of the country. My father was stubborn and decided to stay. My mother was an embodiment of unbounded generosity idealistically combined with communist indoctrination. An intrepid proto-feminist, she truly believed that all people were equal. My beloved childhood mentor was my paternal grandmother (who had survived in hiding): she taught me how to read, write, and crochet at age four; the skills that have served me well. It would take me forty years to light a *yahrzeit* candle on her grave and say the *Kaddish*. Growing up in Poland, I was unaware of my Jewish background, and my parents sheltered me from that calamitous knowledge for good reasons.

The year 1968 wreaked havoc on our family when my father, a well-known professor of linguistics, became a scapegoat of an anti-Semitic purge at his university. I was appraised of my "Jewishness" by a group of rather unkind high-school classmates: when I confronted my parents about what I thought were malicious rumors, they confirmed the truth about my genealogy but refused to talk to me about it. I was thrown into a precipice of "Jewish shame," which, years later, I intellectualized by studying the writings of Sarah Kofman, Jean Améry, Hannah Arendt, and Viktor Klemperer. It is still very hard for me to say, "I am Jewish" (jestem Żydówką) in my native tongue.

The negative self-conception of Jewishness into which I was pressed in high school began to dissipate when graduate school took me across the Atlantic to the Comparative Literature Department at SUNY, Buffalo (UB), which was sometimes nick-named "Jew-B" on account of a large number of Jewish faculty and students. My relocation allowed me to begin to grow into my Jewish roots: I could finally "be myself," which meant liking the Jewish

2 *Quo vadis* (Latin: Where are you going?) is also a reference to a well-known Polish novel by the 1905 Nobel Prize winner Henryk Sienkiewicz.

part of me, including my dark curly hair that, back in Poland, had made me look unpleasantly different.

Another kind of ignorance, however, befell me in grad school: Martin Heidegger became my major philosophical influence and an exemplar of theoretical prowess to which I aspired. My beloved professor, and later doctoral thesis supervisor, neglected to mention the German philosopher's Nazi sympathies, and I did not inquire into the lives of great philosophers: all that mattered was their luminous ideas. My philosophically inclined doctoral thesis did not include any female thinkers or references to the Holocaust, although one of the authors I theorized about, Polish Jewish artist and writer Bruno Schulz, had been murdered in 1942 during an *Aktion* in his hometown of Drohobycz. It was at that time, however, that I became interested in Polish-Jewish history, literature by Jewish writers, and memoirs by Holocaust survivors.

After I graduated, I was asked, during a job interview for a position in continental philosophy, what elective courses I would like to teach, and I offered to design classes in Holocaust literature and in post-Auschwitz philosophy. I got the job, and, in retrospect, the impromptu decision to teach classes on the Holocaust hardly seems to have been haphazard. Researching and prepping for my Holocaust classes and then presenting a paper at my first Holocaust conference unleashed a new passion and a lifelong commitment, although it also forced me to re-appraise my grad school infatuation with *Sein und Zeit*.

My "about-face" with respect to Heidegger and my radical turn toward Holocaust studies not only brought me into the fold of a very different community of scholars, but also reverberated through my family life. When, during a visit to Poland that summer, I told my father that I had abandoned philosophy for Holocaust studies, he sat me down and, for the first time, opened up about his Holocaust experiences. My father, my Tato, survived on Aryan papers, moving from place to place with the help of my grandfather's acquaintances, some of whom were later recognized as Righteous among the Nations. Dad took pride in his storytelling abilities, and he even put a title on the tales of his improbable survival: "My Great Escapes." He never talked about the fear of having to watch his every word or to hide parts of his anatomy, or about the relatives disappearing into the void one after another. Instead, his narrative focused on the lucky episodes of evading close calls: he duped a German patrol member because he could speak fluent German; on one occasion, he was warned of a search by a German officer who was stationed at one of his hiding places (they played the accordion together: *Jassem und Zelle, die große Kapelle*, he reminisced and laughed); once, he tricked a neighbor who wanted to denounce him.

My father thought it was funny that he, a bookish *schlemiel* with no practical skills, was the one to survive, and I will never know what dark caverns of memory he may have been protecting himself against with that laughter. He would always become taciturn and gloomy, however, when I asked about the year 1968, and he never spoke about his Holocaust experiences with anyone else. During a thaw in Polish-Jewish relations in the early 2000's, he refused to give interviews to Polish journalists who tried to fashion him into a hero. Polish-Jewish sociologist Małgorzata Melchior, whose research focused on the phenomenon of hiding, once observed that, having assumed a false identity during the war, these survivors often continued to "live in hiding," constantly in fear of being "found out" and unwilling to disclose their Jewish identity.[3]

I had always been very close to Tato, so talking to him about the past and discovering family history together allowed both of us to embrace our disavowed Jewish heritage. This part of my peregrinations, gently but persistently encouraged by Tato, culminated in my formal conversion to Judaism, which solidified my Jewishness, halachically speaking. I was also pleased to have officially increased the ranks of Polish Jews, the number of which (3,300 000 before the war) had been so tragically curtailed. As my cousin Piotr, the family genealogist whose road to Jewishness was similar to mine, discovered in his research, the Holocaust had swallowed up dozens of our family members, most of whom had been murdered in Auschwitz-Birkenau and Bełżec.

It was only after I had read Helen Epstein's book that I realized I also belonged to another family – an international network of children of survivors, although it took me a long time to overcome the need to remain "in hiding," a symptom that, as Melchior argued, was often transmitted to the second generation. I hope the buck stopped with me, and my children have grown up comfortable in their skin and unencumbered by these anxious paranoias. Besides, as Efraim Sicher once noted, a parent's history, although a burdensome heirloom, can also become a powerful creative force.[4] Shortly before Tato passed away, I told him that I was grateful to him for having given me "my" Holocaust. In my academic work, I have been beholden to these awkward words of gratitude, now his epitaph.

Although my Holocaust heritage was patrilinear, the new bonds I developed around it were mostly with women. It turned out that I had other Jewish

3 Małgorzata Melchior, *Zagłada a tożsamość. Polscy Żydzi ocaleni na aryjskich papierach*, Warszawa: Wydawnictwo IFiS PAN, 2004.

4 In *Breaking the Crystal: Writing and Memory After Auschwitz*, Chicago: University of Illinois Press, 1998.

cousins in England, France, Israel, and Poland, and I reconnected with all of them. I reached out to my British cousin, writer and journalist Anne Karpf, after I had discovered references to my grandparents on the pages of her book.[5] Another two amazing women with very big hearts who became close friends, kindred spirits, and surrogate grandmothers to my children, were survivors of the ghettoes (Uzhgorod and Warsaw, respectively) and then of Auschwitz; years later, I was honored to write the introduction to a memoir penned by one of them.[6]

Professional Journeys: At the Crossroads of Philosophy, Holocaust Studies, and Feminist Theory

While moving to North America allowed me to assert my Jewishness, becoming a feminist Holocaust scholar was a steep and winding learning curve. In communist Poland, where I spent half of my life, patriarchal attitudes, workplace sexual harassment, and scorn toward women's ambitions were commonplace, despite the official idiom of gender equality. I was often told to tone down my intellectual appetites and to act more feminine. In this respect, moving to Buffalo was liberating since Comp Lit was very progressive in terms of gender politics. Arriving at my job in Canada, however, I found myself to be one of only three female faculty members (behind our backs, we were called the three "muses" or, alternately, the Erinyes). Our famous first-year Great Books program featured one female writer (Simone de Beauvoir), and not a single course on women's literature was being offered in the upper-level program for which I had been hired. In response, I designed a course in feminist theory and literature (which was dubbed PMS), which, over the years, evolved into a much more robust and broad-ranging class in gender theory. I was proud to have become the person who was being asked to speak at International Women's Day rallies or Take-Back-the Night events. Today, if I were to write my "mission statement," empowering female and non-binary students and young scholars would appear in the first sentence.

Already in grad school, I had an inkling that philosophy was a male-dominated discipline and women were not easily admitted to the Parnassus; as one of my (formerly) favorite French thinkers remarked, perhaps philosophy itself is a "male way of thinking."[7] I did not, however, expect to be belittled as a woman in my newly chosen discipline of Holocaust studies, as it happened during one of my first appearances at a Holocaust conference.

5 Ann Karpf, *The War After: Living with the Holocaust*, Mandarin, 1997.

6 Helen Jockel, *We Sang in Hushed Voices*, Toronto: The Azrieli Foundation, 2014.

7 Jean-François Lyotard, "One Thing at Stake in Women's Struggles," *The Lyotard Reader*, ed. Andrew Benjamin, Oxford, UK: Blackwell: 111.

Since, at the last minute, an additional speaker was added to our panel, nine minutes into what was supposed to be my twenty-minute presentation, the chair of the panel put his hand on my shoulder and said, "That's enough, dear." The time of the other female speaker was also cut short, but the male speaker was granted his full slot, as was the additional speaker, a wife of a well-known Holocaust scholar.

This, and another incident at the same conference when a male presenter became rudely defensive in response to a question from a female audience member, possibly marked my re-birth as a feminist Holocaust scholar. After the panel, I and the other female speaker on my panel ran into the woman who had asked the "threatening" gender question, and we held our first witches sabbath in the ladies' room. The formidable woman was Myrna Goldenberg, and this was the first one of many inspiring occasions when Myrna and I would have each other's back. Almost two decades later, I was teary-eyed when I was invited to speak at the launch of Myrna's award-winning volume of women's Holocaust testimonies.[8]

For the next few years after that memorable slight, I deliberately tried to appear on conference panels with mostly female scholars. I became passionately interested in women's Holocaust experiences, while my broader research in gender theory, feminist histories, and literature and art by women allowed me to perceive patterns of exclusion. Not only was Holocaust history dominated by stories of male experiences but also the ways in which it was taught and commemorated was imbued with androcentric norms, regardless of the fact that some of our male colleagues were compassionate, supportive allies. Marginalization of women's narratives in the study of Holocaust history has been contiguous with traditional views of women's supposedly inferior moral agency, their political subordination, and their epistemic vulnerability, since their knowledge has been distrusted on account of their alleged emotionality. These factors have undermined women's status as witnesses to history and dispossessed them of the ownership of their life stories.

Already in my first year on the job, my philosophical allegiances shifted toward Jewish philosophers. I immersed myself in the ethical thought of Emmanuel Levinas, interpreting his work through the lens of his experiences as a Holocaust survivor, although they were deeply buried between the lines of his *magna opera*. I was also looking for a way to re-read Levinas through a feminist lens, finding inspiration in contemporary feminist philosophers such as Catherine Chalier and Tina Chanter, and in feminist theologian Melissa Raphael's *A Female Face of God in Auschwitz*. Soon, I found myself

8 Myrna Goldenberg, *Before All Memory Is Lost: Women's Voices from the Holocaust*, Toronto: The Azrieli Foundation, 2017.

engaging with theory insofar as it allowed me to ask questions about the limits of representation and modalities of witnessing "after Auschwitz." I wrote about female authors and Holocaust survivors, such as Ida Fink, Hannah Krall, and Charlotte Delbo, in relation to Levinas' ethical conception of the subject as primarily a witness to the Other.

My interest in the reverberations of the Holocaust in philosophy led me to an engagement with Hannah Arendt and Sarah Kofman, two female thinkers whose lives were affected by the Shoah, and who both attained a degree of recognition within the traditionally male discipline of philosophy. Although they were indebted to their male mentors and intellectual predecessors and neither had much sympathy for feminism as such, their writings aligned with feminist agendas because of their focus on lived experiences of embodied human agents rather than on universal questions, disrupting traditional philosophical narratives. The work that I found especially insightful was Arendt's biography of Rahel Varnhagen, a 19th century Jewish hostess of a literary salon in Berlin, who, on Arendt's account, struggled both with the "misfortune" of being a woman with intellectual aspirations and the shame of having been born Jewish. Yet, on her deathbed, she proclaimed that this misery "on no account she now wish[ed] to have missed."[9] Kofman's writings projected a similarly complicated intertwining of female and Jewish identity: although she was hostile toward so-called French feminism, she dedicated her work to recovering "the woman," especially the mother, in the works of most influential Western philosophers. She distanced herself from Judaism and Jewish thought (she was known as a Nietzsche scholar), yet toward the end of her life, she wrote a short memoir in which she disclosed that all of her writings had been indebted to the memory of her father, an Orthodox rabbi, who had been murdered in Auschwitz.

In my view, these complex interventions were paradigmatic as a philosophical witness in the feminine, even though neither Arendt nor Kofman embraced the feminist label. Breaking through philosophy's multiple erasures – of women, of Jewishness, and of the Holocaust – they revealed a correlation between philosophy's exclusion of women and its reluctance to grapple with the questions and moral dilemmas posed by the Shoah. In terms of my development as a Holocaust scholar, Arendt and Kofman helped me think about the exclusion of women's experiences in the socially sanctioned narratives of the Holocaust in a broader context, at the intersections of epistemic and sociocultural frameworks.

---

9 Hannah Arendt, *Rahel Varnhagen: The Life of a Jewess*, trans. Richard and Clara Winston, Baltimore, MD: Johns Hopkins University Press, 1997: 85.

En Route: Feminist Engagements with Holocaust Literature and Art

My love of philosophy, at least the kind I imbibed in grad school, was constantly challenged when intersected with questions about gender since Holocaust writings by women questioned some of the basic parameters of these theoretical texts and exposed their hidden assumptions. A pivotal moment in my migratory engagements with continental philosophy and Holocaust studies occurred when I was asked to contribute an essay to a volume on Jean-François Lyotard. I decided to focus on a short, little known catalogue essay Lyotard wrote on French-Israeli artist Bracha Ettinger – in return, Ettinger made stunning photographic portraits of the French philosopher. Ettinger, who is a daughter of Holocaust survivors, developed a technique of photocopying and enlarging documentary and family photos, and then covering their details with inks, charcoal and photocopying dust.

I became particularly intrigued by her paintings from the series *Eurydice*, in which she reproduced a detail from a documentary photograph of undressed Jewish women shortly before their execution in Mizocz, Ukraine, in 1941. As the artist explained in her various texts, her compulsively repeated encounters with that photograph helped her connect with the past across the gulf of her parents' silence (her mother's murdered relatives came from the area where the photo was taken). Finding traditional modes of representing female bodies woefully inadequate to convey the annihilation of matrilineal genealogies, Ettinger searched for a different representational paradigm that would allow her to recover the traces of the murdered women's lives from the grainy photograph. She called her postmemorial art "matrixial" and described it as a space in which the artist and the viewer could affectively connect with the women whose silhouettes she had caressed with her brushes. Pulling away from the Orphic archetype in which the female body was transmuted into beautiful representations while the woman herself was cast into the shadows, the matrixial released corporeal and affective inscriptions of the murdered women's bodies. It was also a sphere in which a multiplicity of wit(h)nessing subjects, together, worked through trauma but also embraced the transformative power of beauty that had been born from those encounters.[10] Ettinger's art moved me deeply, but it also startled me into a realization that conceptions of trauma, at the center of the debates about representations of the Holocaust, were imbued with gendered norms, and

10 Bracha Ettinger, "Wit(h)nessing Trauma and the Matrixial Gaze: From Phantasm to Trauma, from Phallic Structure to Matrixial Sphere." In *Parallax* 7 (4): 89–114.

hence naturalized to align with the criteria that privilege male experience while rendering women's traumatic experiences inarticulable.

Thus, Lyotard led me toward an encounter with Ettinger's art, which became influential in my thinking about Holocaust representations. Yet the experience of writing that paper left me with a conclusion that even he, one of the first male continental thinkers to engage with the question of "sexual difference," remained mired in gendered presuppositions of philosophical aesthetics. On the other hand, Ettinger, a daughter of survivors and a philosopher-artist, empowered me to develop questions about modalities of witnessing in the feminine, the gender of memory, and gendered modes of representing history. Her poet(h)ical art, her theoretical writings, and her autobiographical reflections shone light on prejudices that inhere not only in the structures of knowledge but also in everyday acts of perception, creating epistemic, moral, and even affective blind spots, though perhaps these visual metaphors also belong to the legacy of traditional conceptions of knowledge.

Over the last fifteen years, I often have written about female artists of the second generation, the "daughters of absence"[11] possessed by the history they have never lived, and whose works explore the rituals of memory rooted in the search for identity and belonging. Although I was primarily trained in textual hermeneutics, I have been drawn to these visual testimonies, perhaps driven by a love for visual art that was also gifted to me by my grandmother (who lovingly mistook my copycat daubs à la Van Gogh for a sign of artistic talent). It is striking how many second-generation artists are women: Ettinger's Euridicean bruised-purple paintings; Mindy Weisel's striking-blue canvasses, wounded with the outlines of barbed wire; or Polish artist Ewa Kuryluk's cut-outs from family photographs in soft, yellow silk – all fashion a unique aesthetics of bereavement. I find in their art the traces of what the archive has excluded: the body in its materiality, sensibility, and vulnerability, allowing memory but also historical knowledge about the past to be imbued with sharing, intimacy, and compassion.

The overrepresentation of women in the Holocaust art of the second generation, the category that can be expanded to include postmemorial work by artists that were not necessarily children of survivors (such as Judy Chicago or Nancy Spero), stands in contrast to the marginalisation of female artists in Holocaust art history. In my current project on gendered histories in representations of the Holocaust in visual art, I see a pattern of according the capacity to convey "the truth" about the Holocaust, the courage to defy death and transcend tragic circumstances, as well as artistic merit primarily

11 The term was coined by the second-generation artist Mindy Wiesel, in *Daughters of Absence: Transforming the Legacy of Loss*, Sterling, VA: Capital Books, 2000.

to male artists (Bêdrich Fritta, Felix Nussbaum, Boris Taslitzky, Yehuda Bacon, Christian Boltansky…).

Works by women, however, have been valued as "documents of the time" and, as such, housed in Holocaust museums rather than in national galleries of art. This history of exclusion is consistent with the trajectory of Western art in general, which, however, has reserved for women's bodies the elevated role of the signifier of beauty. It is unsurprising, therefore, that Charlotte Salomon's work is missing from some of the major overviews of Holocaust art (and it took several decades for her work to gain recognition as more than a pictorial equivalent of Ann Frank's *Diary*); gifted artist and printmaker Friedl (Frederica Dicker-Brandeis) is remembered as a selfless art therapist for the children in Terezín; and Halina Olomucki's brilliant expressionist portraits are usually reduced to depictions of scenes from the Warsaw ghetto and from Auschwitz, and condemned to live in the shadow of Karel Fleischmann's and Otto Ungar's drawings. This denigration of aesthetic value in women's art and of female artists' capacity for artistic innovation has perhaps robbed us of important insights both into women's experiences during the Holocaust and into modalities of remembrance. My engagement with visual art of the Holocaust, inflected with feminist conceptions of affective, relational subjectivity and agency, has led me to propose a concept of relational imagination. I understand it as a mode of engaging with the past that acknowledges the interdependencies and vulnerabilities that shape the processes of history and memory.[12]

Veni, Vidi and Beyond: Women in the Holocaust and Interdisciplinary and Comparative Contexts

In all of my classes, conceptions of gender, and especially gender-based violence, are a key issue, coinciding with the reports of high incidence of sexual violence on university campuses and painful struggles to change "the culture of rape." Four years ago, I decided to design a class in comparative genocide with the focus on women's experiences. Being a feminist Holocaust scholar thus began to mean to me engaging with the Holocaust along the axes of multidirectional memory, in the context of other genocides and against the *long durée* background of colonial violence.[13] I thought that, by then, I had developed pedagogical strategies to convey crucial lessons while avoiding causing my students emotional distress. Yet, as we moved from colonial

12 In "Gender and the Shoah: Relational Imagination and the Cul-de-sacs of Remembrance." *Lessons and Legacies* 13 (2018), 310–334.

13 Michael Rothberg, *Mutlidirectional Memory: Remembering the Holocaust in the Age of Decolonization,* Stanford University Press, 2009.

atrocities in North America and Australia to the Herero and Nama genocide and then to Armenia, I realised that I was myself unprepared for how ubiquitous, horrific, and unrelenting had been the sexual violence that we read about day after day. The first time I taught the class, we struck the limit of bearableness by the time we got to Bosnia, and I had to pause the class for a week and regroup before we could discuss Rwanda. It became obvious to us that the apparently neutral concept of genocide, as it emerged in the late 1940's, concealed cultural, political, and gendered biases and, as such, it could not properly address the grievous wrong of genocidal sexual violence. It was not until 1998 that the Rome Statute of the International Criminal Court for the first time recognised sexual violence against women as a crime against persons (under Article 6, "Crimes Against Humanity") rather than as crimes against property and "honor," as in previous legal formulations (such as the 1907 Hague Regulations, the Tokyo War Crimes Tribunal, or the 4th Geneva Convention).

Further research on the subject convinced me that such violence, which stems from dominant, racially structured systems of gender, is not an epiphenomenon, but that it resides at the very core of genocide as its enabling, even necessary, condition. I became convinced that no genocide stands alone, and studying one case of mass atrocities can illuminate, sometimes unexpectedly, previously unexamined aspects of another. We now recognize that knowledge about mass rapes in Rwanda and Bosnia precipitated recognition of genocidal violence on women during the Holocaust.[14] Similarly, I have drawn on recent Holocaust scholarship to think about the role of sexualised subjugation of Indigenous women during colonial conquest and to trace a historical continuum between that past and the contemporary epidemic of Missing and Murdered Indigenous Women in North America.

Hopeful moments always arrive unexpectedly: a year ago, as I was clearing the US customs in Ottawa, a customs officer queried me about the purpose of my visit. When I told him that I was on my way to a conference to give a talk about genocide and sexual violence, he became strangely silent and then told me that, a few days before, he had to interview several women who had arrived in the US as refugees from Syria, and he heard stories he would never have wanted to hear. He said to me, "You have to keep talking about it to everyone because it is better to see people's minds hurt a little than these women totally destroyed." Being a feminist Holocaust scholar,

14 See, for instance, Doris Bergen, "What do Studies of Gender and Sexuality Contribute to Understanding the Holocaust?" in *Different Horrors, Same Hell: Gender and the Holocaust*, edited by Myrna Goldenberg and Amy Shapiro, Seattle: Washington University Press, 2013, 24.

therefore, means to me being able to teach this unbearable material while respecting the victims whose life-shattering stories become our classroom lessons, as well as acknowledging my students' vulnerabilities. I also want to hold myself accountable for what I have failed to teach them, and for the biases and hidden presuppositions that haunt my own discipline. On the other hand, in my gender theory class, looking back to the Holocaust's "same hell, different tortures" often helps me illustrate the mechanisms of binary constructions of gender and the power of social taboos. New scholarship on sexual barter and forced sexual labor during the Holocaust, for instance, has been useful in ferreting out prejudicial stereotypes at the intersections of race and gender in the supposedly progressive debates around Canada's "Prostitution Criminal Law Reform."

During the last decade and a half, I have travelled to Poland for lectures, workshops, and graduate seminars on women's experiences in the Holocaust, which required that I not only translate the subject into my native tongue but also reconceptualize it in the context of a different cultural understanding of gender, female agency, and feminist advocacy. In Poland, teaching feminist Holocaust history became an engaged practice because after class we went to march in a Black Friday protest against Poland's draconian abortion laws or in the Equality Parade in support of LGBTQ+ rights.[15] Polish language itself began to taste feminist on my tongue. In my Canadian classrooms, my cultural difference (the students can hear my accent at "hello!") has been useful: in a seminar room packed with progressive, politically-minded students of all genders, slides with placards from a Black Protest ("Oprócz macic mamy mózgi!" and "PISs-off!")[16] that had just taken place in Warsaw were a powerful reminder of the fragility of our own freedoms, including the ability to express our sexual and gendered identities. Indirectly, they also cautioned us against construing our local contexts as a universal norm.

Travelling the Open Road: Thinking Together and Affective Communities of Knowledge

To some extent, both brightly-colored pieces and painful shards of our autobiographies are imbricated in our professional engagements and scholarly commitments, determining which research subjects we pick up and which we abandon or never choose in the first place, although these connections are

15 At the time of this writing, on August 9, 2019, the news is streaming in with reports of the Pride march in the northwestern Polish city of Białystok being violently targeted by members of the ultranationalist right.

16 "Besides wombs, we have brains." "PIS" stands for "Prawo i Sprawiedliwość, Poland's right-wing party, which has been in power since 2015.

not always easy to claw out.[17] Perhaps, in these auto-theoretical vignettes, I have projected my life story onto my academic interests, although I hope I have been mindful of Marianne Hirsch's and James E. Young's words of caution against the dangers of overidentification. Overall, becoming a feminist Holocaust scholar has helped me overcome my childhood traumas and reconnect with my Polish-Jewish heritage, and settle into my roles as a new immigrant and a female academic and teacher. It has also brought me the joy of meeting extraordinary female scholars and developing meaningful friendships.

If I ever had any doubts about the value of interdisciplinary alliances or about my place in Holocaust studies as a scholar trained in critical and literary theory, they were dispelled when, in 2012, I was asked to co-lead a seminar at the USHMM, entitled "Teaching the Gendered Experience of the Holocaust" with historian Atina Grossmann. Someone's prescient choice of seminar leaders resulted in one of the most rewarding teaching experiences in my career: together behind the teaching desk, Atina and I sparked off each other, exactly because we did not have the same disciplinary background. That wondrous experience of thinking together through gendered histories of the Holocaust allowed me to settle more comfortably into my identity as a feminist Holocaust scholar. It also spurred me to champion interdisciplinary coalitions of knowledge in the study of the subject - and to come up with better rejoinders whenever it was "mansplained" to me (as it happened on several occasions) that true Holocaust scholars were historians, and they did not get emotional during their presentations.

I define my brand of Holocaust feminism as a practice of coming-together to think about the past, take a stance in the present, and exercise our imagination to envisage a less violent future. Women writing about women in the Holocaust is a shared experience that, in Bracha Ettinger's words, "conveys the traces of events that cannot be born and carried alone."[18] I start my day with a glance at a blue-and-purple abstract painting on the wall of my dining room, entitled "The Gift," which Mindy Weisel sent to me in response to an essay I wrote about her work, and I am ready to face another challenge. I would not be able to endure daily experiences of reading, writing, and teaching about rape, mass murder, and other forms of unspeakable violence without these human connections. They involve discussing unbearable subjects, but also chatting about everyday events in our lives and laughing over a glass of wine. And sometimes they also mean that we write a book together.

17 I am drawing here on Sarah Kofman's neologism "autobiogriffure."
18 Ettinger, "Wit(h)nessing Trauma," 112.

Esther Hertzog

A Feminist Serendipity in the Study of the Holocaust and the Power of Suspicion

Introduction

I would like to open this essay with a confession: although I was born to Holocaust survivors I do not perceive myself as 'second generation'. My journey to the Holocaust research emerged from my feminist awareness and involvement and has hardly anything to do with my parents' awful experience and their families' horrific death.

Both of my parents were Holocaust survivors and many of their relatives were exterminated in Auschwitz and in the Ukraine. However, only during the summer of 2000, when by chance I came across an international conference on the Holocaust held in Oxford, did I open up to the subject. This happened mainly due to my unanticipated exposure to studies on the subject, presented in the conference by feminist researchers; among these were Dalia Ofer and Lenore Weitzman, Esther Fuchs and Myrna Goldenberg. I later learned of other prominent gender scholars who had studied the Holocaust, from a feminist perspective, more than a decade earlier. Among these were Joan Ringelheim, Carol Rittner and John Roth, Judith Tydor Baumel and Marion Kaplan. It appears that being a feminist scholar and activist sensitized by gender awareness and being involved in feminist activity since the end of the 80s made the exposure to women's narratives and feminist interpretations in relation to the Holocaust a compelling experience.

The exposure to gender perspectives of the Holocaust research was a revelation for me. It took me by surprise and brought up a trail of fresh insights concerning issues such as motherhood, survivors' testimonies and memories, as well as with regard to personal aspects such as my attitude and identity in relating to the Holocaust. Following that episode in Oxford I became eager to dig deeper into gender aspects of the Holocaust and, consequently, I opened up to absorb my mother's narrative of "her Shoah", documenting it fervently. I was also encouraged by my lifetime mentor and friend Prof. Emanuel Marx, who stubbornly suggested that I "talk with my mother" and later on that I dare write things that are considered as "unsaid". In the years to come I was eager to spread the word and became involved excitedly in organizing international conferences on 'women and the Holocaust', following which I edited two volumes on this subject. Gradually I dared to critically examine widely accepted assumptions; some of them are almost taboos. Thus, for instance, I questioned the widely accepted approach that the Holocaust should not be used in daily life for "irrelevant" matters, suggesting that the instrumental daily use of the Holocaust indirectly serves its commemoration. Based on my conversations with my mother I dared to question the widely perceived totality of Nazi inhumanity. Through these conversations I also revealed the relativity and context-related concepts in survivors' memories, such as the humiliation of walking naked in front of the Nazis. An ongoing issue that bothered me since I started studying the Holocaust was the popular discourse on "second generation". Being frequently affiliated with the title "second generation", I dared to question this taken for granted identification.

Thus, in this essay I intend to examine some bothering concepts and widely accepted assumptions with regard to the Holocaust, with gender lenses and through my intellectual wondering about the Holocaust and hyperactive wandering among activities relating to the Holocaust research since 2000.

From Oxford to Israel: The Spreading Impact of the Exposure to Feminist Scholarship

Coming back from Oxford, I became enthusiastically involved in both academic and public activity that focused on the Holocaust from women's and gender perspectives. I turned to Dr. Batya Brutin, my colleague at Beit Berl College, and to my friend, the late Yonat Klar, who worked at Beit Terezin, and the three of us trurned to Holocaust scholars at Beit Terezin and at the Ghetto Fighters' Museum in Lochamei Hagetaot. We offered to cooperate in organizing a conference on women and family in the Holocaust. The first conference took place in 2002 and was follwed by another five, bi-annual international conferences on this subject. Those conferences brought together prominent Holocaust scholars from Israel, the US, Europe, Asia and Australia. Each event took place in the three sites (one day in each of them), emphasizing the main activity of the specific institution: academic focus at Beit Berl, testimonies at Beit Terezin and the ghetto fighting and fighters in Lochamei Hagetaot. It seems that those conferences served as a catalyzer for expanding and groundbreaking research on women and the family in the Holocaust, as well as a platform for many unknown testimonies. Thus, for instance, according to Judith Inbar, the former director of theYad Vashem museums division, these conferences inspired her initiative of setting up an exhibition on women and the Holocaust at Yad Vashem, in 2007 (followed by a Catalog entitled: "Spots of Light: Women in the Holocaust"). The exhibition travelled to many places outside Israel, thus demonstrating the spreading impact of the conferences that indirectly emerged from the revelation of the Holocaust from a feminist perspective.

Indeed the beginnings were not that encouraging. The de-legitimization of feminist research on the Holocaust was harsh, so I was told by Esther Fuchs in Oxford and by other scholars on other occasions. When I returned to Israel, full of exciting ideas for academic and public initiatives, I also experienced the degrading attitude toward my feminist approach with regard to Holocaust narratives. In April 2001, shortly after my Oxford experience, I published an article entitled "Who is afraid of 'Women and the Holocaust'" in the weekend supplement of *Makor Rishon*. In response Dr. Nadav Shnerb of Bar-Ilan University wrote a long and insulting letter to the editors which they published. In it he claimed that:

> ...Despite the advantages of freedom, not always is there much blessing in it. This is what happens when freedom is the extraction of its opposite to truth, in the freedom of stupidity, in the freedom to choose foolishness and silliness. The academic world is especially vulnerable to this frame of mind and the non-empirical spheres of knowledge in particular. There it is enough that a critical mass of fools is created in order that they will cite, praise and promote each other within the same bubble that they have blown for themselves. All is done under the cover of 'research' and 'science' which they expropriated from the real achievements of the natural sciences.... There is no evil in the things Esther Hertzog brought, but they have more than 10 portions of stupidity and ugly banality which is, in many cases, the mother of evil. The ability of bleary-eyed midgets to take the horrible tragedy of the Holocaust and stare at it through the same distorted lens of the discipline in which they delve, is not a denial of the Holocaust, but is not far from that.

Two comments have to be made in this context. First, when reading the letter to the editors today, it appears to me that the opening of my article revealed a certain sense of apologetics, "inviting" criticism and degradation. The opening sentence of the article wondered: "Is there a place to studying the Holocaust from a feminine outlook or is it, rather, all about trivializing the Holocaust"? Assuming that the title was proposed by me (and not by the editor), I am quite sure that I would not express such a doubt at present, not even for the sake of raising interest or curiosity among the readers.

Second, looking back to 2001 it appears that nowadays no one would dare to say or write such ridiculous and offensive statements. Moreover, already in 2006, when the third international conference on women and the Holocaust took place, an important acknowledgment was published. In an article by Ruti Sinai (*Haaretz*, May 14), she wrote:

> In the beginning of the 80s, when Judy Tydor Baumel started to study the issue of women's place, experience and dealing in the Holocaust, she was politely offered by one of the prominent Shoah scholars in Israel to choose "a more suitable and serious subject" or her promising career may fail before it has taken off. 25 years have passed and Baumel became a professor at Bar-Ilan University and a leading scholar in the sphere of women and the Holocaust, and this sphere became a subject of research and teaching in highly respected universities in the world.

Hence, it seems to me that the studies about women/gender and the Holocaust have become an important and highly esteemed field of Holocaust research. This field is growing rapidly with many young scholars joining this field, forums (such as "Women Recall the Holocaust", headed by Judy Baumel-Schwartz and Dalia Ofer at Bar-Ilan University) are established, the divergence of topics and activities that are developing in academic institutions, in Holocaust institutions, in schools etc., is more than amazing.

Eva – My Mother, Myself and the Holocaust

My exposure and involvement in both research and activity connected to the Holocaust from a feminist perspective, owes much to my mother and my conversations with her, that took place for a whole year after returning from Oxford. It was only then that I realized that I knew almost nothing about her experience in the Holocaust. I am not sure if the reason was sheer ignorance or the need to distance myself from the unbearable horrors. In any case, I prefer to stick to my mother's explanation that she wanted to protect us, her two daughters, from suffering from the exposure to her horrible memories, rather than her claim in some instances that we were not interested in listening to those stories. Nevertheless, my mother has a considerable role in both, identifying my feminine behavior with women's socialization (or with Simone de-Boevoir's claim: a woman is not born as one but rather becomes one). She also has a significant role in my daring to offer a personal-feminine outlook on the Holocaust and in the permission that I granted myself to analyze and publish my insights and even to collect and edit papers written by prominent and exciting scholars from Israel and beyond.

On Motherhood, the Holocaust and Love

My father, Bondy, a Holocaust survivor, was born in Hungary. He met my mother in Italy, where they married and gave birth to me, their first born daughter (Ilana, my sister, was born three years later in Israel). My father was a warm and kind person whom I loved very much. We used to go to football games and war films together. He died from a heart attack when he was 48.

When I used to complain to my father about my mother's toughness and her strict attitude to him and to us, her two daughters, he kept telling me that "this is because she was in the Holocaust". But I did not believe that (as he was also there...). I thought that my father needed an excuse to alleviate the pain caused by my mother's insults directed at him and at us. I suffered from the insults she inflicted on him more than from the ones that were directed at me. I asked him repeatedly why he silently accepted her insults.

Even today, about 50 years after my father passed away I do not think that it was the Holocaust that made my mother a bitter woman, one who used to criticize and reproach us often. Her behavior puzzled me because all the people who knew her in the extended family, at her work place, and in our social surroundings, liked her very much and thought that she was a wonderful woman, kind and gentle. It appeared to me that there was a bothering dissonance between her behavior at home and that outside our home.

My love to my mother developed when I became a mother myself. In fact, through motherhood and daily dealing with childcare, I came to understand my mother's frustrations and difficulties as a woman, a mother, and a housewife. My appreciation of her personal independence and self-esteem grew and deepened gradually. I assume that my feminist awareness, which is profoundly attached to being a mother and to motherhood in general, clarified to me that my mother behaved, in many ways, much like other women-mothers, including myself. Whether we like it or not, we are given the monopoly over caring for babies and children, which is a physically and emotionally demanding and tough task.

My conversations with my mother on her experience in the Holocaust clarified to me the extent of my attraction and interest in the profound connection between 'femininity' and especially 'motherhood' in the Holocaust in general, and to my mother's Holocaust in particular.

Daring to Say Things that "Should Not Be Said"

While telling me about her Holocaust experiences, interwoven in her present-life narrative, daring to say things that 'should not be said', I was overtaken by admiration and compassion for my mother. Her guts and fascinating insights struck me with the understanding that fundamental human ethics lies in free, unbound elaboration on human situations and conduct.

My mother's narrative is embedded in travelling among conflicting and ambiguous perceptions. In our conversations she meandered between descriptions of extreme bad and virtuous good, between dates and periods in the past and various events in the more or less immediate present, between faraway places on the globe and Israel, between collectives and individuals, between seemingly unconnected situations. Listening to my mother, talking with her, and documenting these conversations, made me a companion to her emotional, verbal and intellectual journey between places, periods and ethical positions.

My puzzled reaction, or rather my latent suspicion, regarding my mother's descriptions and views concerning people and events that were part of her past, became an inseparable part of my reactions to her descriptions. Throughout my conversations with my mother some annoying doubts crept into my thoughts, namely her unexpected, inconsistent and inconceivable accounts concerning her experiences during the Holocaust.

In our conversations my mother expressed several provoking statements. One example was a surprising objectionable comparison she made between the Nazis' instrumental use of Jewish collaborators and collaborators with the Americans in Iraq. Another shocking statement was that the time we spent in Cyprus (after the British deported us to the refugees' camps on the island) was harder for her than the time in Auschwitz. Her amazing associations and exclamations inspired my way of thinking and inadvertently encouraged my guts. Thus, I clarified to myself and told others, that more than identifying as "a second generation" I perceive myself as "a refugees' daughter"; I dared to argue that the "use of Holocaust symbols in daily life serves the commemoration of the Holocaust, rather than degrading it"; I took the freedom to doubt prominent scholars' claims about "mothers' heroism in the Holocaust", suggesting that the subjugation of motherhood to social, political and cultural forces better explain women's readiness to sacrifice their lives, accepting the absence of choice when their offspring are endangered or sent to death; Another widely accepted understanding that I dared to question, following my mother's determined reactions, was the one that perceive the enforced nakedness in front of the Nazis as the worst humiliation for women in the extermination camps. I shall soon elaborate on the last two issues, women's nakedness and women's heroism, in detail, by using my mother's testimony and by relating to mainstream research.

The Subjectivity and Relativity of Recalled Humiliation

Elaborating on my recorded reactions to my mother's descriptions and connotations suggests that I, sometimes openly, questioned the sincerity of her accounts and views that she offered while telling me about her past experiences. My questioning and even doubting responses emerged in particular with regard to my mother's descriptions connected to women's experiences. A conspicuous example that can illustrate this problematic attitude is her account of walking naked in front of the Nazis. Indeed being a scholar entails the prerequisite and motivation to doubt taken-for-granted assumptions and interpretations, but my recurring reservations called for self-examination as both a daughter and a researcher.

Following the lead of several feminist scholars, I assumed that the female victims' degrading experiences as women were devastating when they took place, and are intolerable for the survivors when thinking about them in the present. This understanding invoked my skepticism toward my mother's reactions concerning the forced walking naked in front of the Nazis and having their hair shaved. I tried to explain to her that such an experience could clearly have a tremendous impact on the women's basic feminine identity. Yet, my repetitive questions concerning the harsh humiliation I assumed my mother experienced, invoked mostly an adamant denial. Her replies were unanticipated and made me suspect that her descriptions of how she felt in the past could not truly reflect what she felt at that time. She did not express hatred or rage, which I expected. I suspected that while recounting past events she was not really aware of the immense degradation of the experiences she went through and was describing.

When I persisted on raising "difficult" questions about "humiliating experiences" she replied with a vehement negative. "Did you erase it?" I asked, doubting her statement, and she replied: "No, no, they did not humiliate me particularly." "Did they shave your head?" I insisted and she raised her voice slightly and said, "That was humiliating? That was something done to millions, to me too. If you stayed alive, that is the least awful thing they could do." And I don't let up: "You stood there naked, naked in front of the ..." "That was already nothing." I wondered: "Really?" And she continued: "Nothing. Right." And I still kept my distrust reactions: "How could that be? They stripped you naked and you walked around there like some sort of ..."

> Yes, like a what? Like everyone. That's it. You get used to it. So I walked around. So what? It passed. Look, it's one thing when they strip you; a man takes a woman and does it. But when you're in a group, so is it exactly the one standing there who matters? He's looking exactly at you? He doesn't see anyone. He sees women as animals ... no, it shouldn't be taken to heart. I didn't give a damn about him. As far as I'm concerned he humiliated himself.

"Yes? Have you thought about it then?" I wondered whether this was her recollection of the past or whether it was how she perceived the situation at that time. Her reply was: "Yes, Always. This is how I thought then." Obviously, it is impossible to get a valid reply to such question, for my mother certainly spoke from her current thinking. However, she answered confidently that her memory was reliable. It appears to me that this dialogue demonstrates the unstable quintessence of memory, as various scholars suggest. It also reveals my skepticism with regard to my mother's accounts.

My mother's words and resolute reactions to my doubting questions, regarding remembering the humiliating situations, indicated her determination to now perceive her past experiences as bearable rather than exceptional, unconceivable events. She stubbornly interpreted things in a manner that diminished the significance of the humiliation when thinking about events. She did this by denying essentiality and humanness from the situations and the perpetrators, who perceived the naked women before them as non-human. Thus, while the Germans perceived the naked women in front of them as animals lacking human consequence, their conduct in that situation turned them into creatures lacking human consequence, beasts, and so their deeds had no impact on the human value of the women, and their nakedness is like nakedness before non-humans: animals or objects. In other words, humiliation is experienced and perceived subjectively and should be understood in relation to specific contexts and situations.

Similarly, my mother presented the memory of the situation in terms of relativity: Baldness and nakedness lose their de-humanizing, humiliating impact and their relevance to the female identity relative to "what happened", that is: to death. Furthermore, the public humiliation, its collectivized context, is a "trouble shared". The individual has no independent existence and is absorbed in the masses. All are affected and thus the hurt is not individual, and accordingly less severe. The "togetherness" of the humiliation reduces and mitigates its weight and impact. A psycho-social dynamic is manifested here, in retrospect, of processing the experience of nakedness, converting it into something that was "not awful" when there were many others who shared the event, as something that happened to "everyone". The situation in which these things occurred afforded them their reduced impact in my mother's perceptions at present. Nevertheless, it is possible that this cognitive mechanism served the women in the past as a means of adjusting to the devastating situations.

Recollecting the past in alleviating terms, rationalizing the unbearable situations, stand out in my mother's comments also in relating to the cessation of menstruation. She talked about the malicious outcome inflicted by the Nazis on the female physiological functioning as a positive thing, and even as "lucky", in a reality lacking any suitable sanitary conditions and means. Responding to my question, how the women could manage while menstruating without underwear, having only shoes and a striped nightdress, her sharp response was: "One didn't menstruate. They gave us bread with bromide to eat that burned our stomachs. It caused me such heartburn that I couldn't bear. Or they gave us potatoes with their peels to eat. That was the food. It was bitter ..." I cut into her and asked: "So did it immediately stop all women menstruating?" and she replied: "Yes, of course. They thought of that. It's such a satanic thing. And yet, that was luck." And I wondered, "Why was that lucky?" Her response was: "Well, what would we have done there? There was nothing there". The deed was, in fact, satanic, but remembering the results was associated with "luck".

It appears, therefore, that my puzzled reactions, as rising from my reflective curiosity, unrestrained thinking and feminist outlook enabled me the inspiring serendipity that contributed significantly to my understanding of human behavior in the context of the Holocaust and beyond.

Motherhood and the Holocaust: Questioning the Myth of Women's Heroism

Encouraged by my mother's daring to say "things that should not be said" I dared to question the widely accepted view that mothers' going to the gas chambers with their children and endangering their lives, trying to save their offspring is an expression of outmost devotion. In this sense motherhood in the Holocaust is widely perceived as almost sacred heroism.

Many women lost their lives when they walked into the crematoriums with their small children, or died while trying to save them in the concentration camps or hiding places. This behaviour, of walking toward death for the sake of saving their children's lives or accompanying them to their mutual death, is often described as "heroism", "sacrifice", etc. Thus, motherhood in the Holocaust has been idealized as a symbol of the 'sacrificing mother'.

However, this act of "sacrifice" and "heroism" is perceived as taken for granted or even self-evidently expected "natural" performance of women as "mothers". Holocaust research, including feminist studies, implies that women are expected to pay various and tough prices, the most extreme of which is to give up their own lives, as part of their role as mothers. Women's accounts about preferring to stay alive or to increase the chance of being saved, not giving up their lives for the sake of their children's, have been silenced, marginalized or denied. Women's acts of saving themselves are widely considered as taken on account of their children, as deserting or abandoning them. Such instances are often openly or implicitly condemned, by both public discourse and scholars.

My anti-essentialist position aligns (as elaborated in an article in Dapim in 2016) with feminist thinkers, who perceive motherhood as a social construct, rejecting the concept of a woman's body and life as subordinate to those of their offspring and the biologist construction of the mother-child bond as natural and immutable. I challenged the widely accepted perception of mothers willing to walk towards death with children as heroic, and the linked condemnation of women who prioritized their own survival. It was suggested that this fatal behavior demonstrates the feminist interpretation of motherhood as a socially enforced and internalized role, rather than proving heroism.

Thus, for example, in our conversations and in various casual cases, my mother repeatedly encountered the way her mother ended her life in the gas chamber:

> Bobby [my mother's sister] arrived in Auschwitz with Jenny [their aunt], my mother and with their mother's sister [age 43 at the time] and her three small children. And there, mother grabbed her sister, went to help her with the children, straight to the gas chambers. Bobby went with Jenny and remained alive.

My mother's mother (my grandmother) could save her life (at least for some time) if she did not join her sister and her children trying to 'help' her. Yet, this act that is commonly interpreted as self-sacrifice can also be understood as an example of the feminine subjugating socialization that drives women to take care of children, even other women's children, and help care for them, even at the expense of fatal personal price, such as losing their own life.

Consequently, I came to the understanding that the study of the Holocaust, as a most extreme and exceptional experience of violence in human history, offers an opportunity to critically examine a crucial subject in feminist thinking, namely 'motherhood', raising fundamental issues relating to motherhood in the Holocaust and for our times as well.

Reconsidering "Motherhood" and the "Mother-Child" Conflict

As argued above, glorifying mothers for sacrificing their lives for their offspring plays a conspicuous role in studies of the Holocaust. Questioning this approach enabled me to realize the fatal implications of women's socialization in this context, from the perspective of their right to prefer the chance to survive. Prioritizing the child's life over that of the mother's raises a "mother-child" conflict. Challenging the widely accepted implications of this dyad I suggest that even the taken-for-granted preference of the child's life and welfare can be undermined, depending on the circumstances and the situation. The profound social belief in the supremacy of the child's good may even serve to conceal its instrumental use, no less than that of "motherhood", in serving various interests.

Thus, women's socializing mechanisms was used by the Nazis to facilitate the extermination of immeasurable numbers of women, babies and children. Yet, in the context of the ghettos, the concern of the ghetto leadership for the collective's chance to survive pushed them to control women's reproductive nature, prohibiting them, by threatening to sanction them and their families, from giving birth. Such a decision was made, for instance, by the *Judenrat* of the Shavel ghetto, trying to force abortions. Hence, in that context, giving birth and motherhood were perceived as dangerous and negative for the community and therefore penalized. Another example is the social condemnation of Jewish female doctors who carried out abortions in the ghettos and extermination camps, years after the abortions took place and in a 'normal' setting far from their horrendous occurrence. This was powerfully illustrated in the film *Rising from the Ashes*, which tells Dr. Gisella Perl's true story. In the process of applying for American citizenship following the war, a three-member committee interrogated Dr. Perl. All were men, one of them Jewish. The committee members expressed, in various ways, explicit criticism regarding the abortions she had carried out in Auschwitz. Her claim that through these abortions she had saved many young women from definite death did not convince the men that her deeds were morally justified. The moral condemnation of Dr. Perl implies that a woman's right to life independent from her offspring is not self-evident and cannot be tolerated. Moreover, assisting women in getting rid of their unborn fetuses in order to save their lives was considered unforgivable. Although the committee finally approved Dr. Perl's citizenship, they determined that her deeds were "not without guilt."

The post-war context offers another angle to the "mother-child" conflict. Relating to the hidden children in Christian families during the Holocaust, whose mothers came back after the war to take them, brings up the apparent gaps between the rhetoric and the practices relating to this embedded conflict. The surviving mothers were portrayed by some scholars (like Diane Wolf) as "unfit" mothers because they were traumatized, and it was suggested that the children should have been left with their foster families. It appears, therefore, that whereas motherhood in the Holocaust was highly praised, a short time after the Holocaust biological motherhood was denied and rejected and the "good of the child" (to stay with caring foster families) was perceived as superior to the right of motherhood.

A seemingly very different comparison stems from elaborating on the context of the Israeli welfare policy concerning babies and children "at risk". Based on over 27 years of supporting mothers in their struggles against the expropriation of their custody over their offspring I dare to suggest such a comparison, while being aware that it may raise antagonism and opposition. However, I argue that this welfare policy highlights clearly the fragile status of motherhood. Motherhood in the Holocaust was perceived as a highly valued social construct while in practice this value could be adjusted to the relevant needs, conditions and interests. The value of motherhood at present in the Israeli welfare system is also highly praised by social work, the courts and other agencies. However, disadvantaged mothers' custody can be easily terminated by State agencies, through the use of terminology on caring for minors' well being above their mothers' right to motherhood. From a feminist point of view this understanding of the fragile position of motherhood calls for extensive research and activism.

Concluding Remarks

The insights discussed in this paper, are the outcome of both my anthropological training and my critical feminist thinking, adopting the basic requirement of scientific research to doubt taken-for- granted interpretations and perceptions. Suspecting widely accepted beliefs is also crucial in studying society and human behavior. In accompanying "my mother's Holocaust" I went as far as I could in examining critically her descriptions and perceptions, as well as my own, arriving at some unexpected understandings. These elaborations pointed to the veiled gaps between ideological rhetoric, idealization, and practices, hiding away personal, collective and organizational interests. These implications are not novel. Hence, my intellectual trip through documenting and examining my mother's narrative of the Holocaust can merely serve as a reminder of the importance of being suspicious with regard to taken-for-granted perceptions. Suspicion is also crucial in examining the ways in which ideologies serve, whether intentionally or inadvertently, immoral and malicious purposes, especially those of people in power centers and of powerful organizations, such as governments and even of welfare organizations.

The destructive outcomes of the unrestricted power of State agencies and other powerful groups for both children and mothers, in any context, were implied. Hence, I conclude that women's biological and sociological natures are widely, beyond time and place, manipulated and exploited by various agencies. Thus, critical reflection and uncompromising comparative analyses are imperative for women's, children's and society's sake.

Janet Jacobs

Remembering the Holocaust: Gender and the Study of Memorialization

Introduction

My research on woman and the Holocaust resides at the intersection of memory and gender. My entry into the field of Holocaust studies emerged out of a lengthy academic career that, prior to my work on the Holocaust, had been focused on gender, trauma, and memory in diverse social settings. Among these settings was the study of collective memory among descendants of the crypto-Jews, a project that ultimately led to my work on gender, collective memory and the Holocaust. Thus, as a starting point for this essay, I begin with a brief discussion of my research on the descendants of the crypto-Jews and its relationship to the study of gender and Holocaust memory.

At the start of the 1990s, I began a study of Latinx descendants of the crypto-Jews in the Americas, all of whom were raised Catholic, but were seeking to better understand and uncover their Jewish roots and ancestry. In the long history of European Jewry, crypto-Jews refer to Jews of medieval and premodern Spain and Portugal who were forcibly converted to Christianity. In response to the forced conversions, a portion of the forced converts continued to practice Judaism secretly, transferring the knowledge and rituals of Jewish ancestry to succeeding generations. The practice of secret Judaism thus gave rise to a crypto-Jewish culture that spread from the Iberian Peninsula to the colonies of the Americas where many of the crypto-Jews fled to avoid persecution by the Inquisition. Beginning in the twentieth century, scholars discovered that descendants of the crypto-Jews had continued the practices of their forbearers, maintaining Jewish rituals and reciting Jewish prayers in an outsider culture within Catholic Latinx society.[1]

In recording the life histories of the modern descendants of the crypto-Jews, I became aware of the extent to which the memory of Jewish persecution was seared into the collective consciousness of this population, noting

1 Stanley Hordes, *To the End of the Earth: A history of the Crypto-Jews in New Mexico*, New York: Columbia University Press, 2008.

that it was primarily women in the family who had preserved and retained both the memory of Jewish ancestry and a persistent fear of anti-Semitism. Throughout the study, I discovered that memories of violence against the Jews had been passed down from one generation to the next by mothers and grandmothers who carried and transmitted the memory of loss, death, and exile that their Jewish ancestors had experienced centuries before. Especially in the years following World War II, the memory of forced conversion, murder and flight was re-told and re-interpreted through the lens of the more threatening specter of twentieth century Jewish genocide. For the descendants of the crypto-Jews, the Holocaust had become the signifier of the continued threat that being Jewish posed. Secrecy thus continued to be a marker of crypto-Jewish identity.

Through the study of collective memories of fear and Jewish persecution within crypto-Jewish culture, I gained a greater understanding of how the trauma of Jewishness across history and time informs the cultural consciousness of the Jewish people, even among those families who had not self-identified as Jews since the sixteenth and seventeenth centuries. The crypto-Jewish project also led me to consider the role that the Holocaust plays in the construction of collective memories of a terrible past, particularly among Latina women who acted both as memory keepers and as guardians of a secret Jewish heritage. Following this work, I turned to the frameworks of memory that surround the memorialization of the Holocaust to further explore the relationship between gender and memorial culture.

In this next stage of my research, I became more deeply engaged in memory studies and the ways in which societies frame a terrible past for future generations. As a feminist scholar, I approached the study of mass trauma and collective memory from a gendered perspective, seeking to reveal how women's experiences and actions inform the texts of memory that have come to define Holocaust remembrance in contemporary society. In the sections that follow, I discuss the development of my research in the area of gender and collective memory, focusing on my work at sites of Holocaust remembrance in eastern and western Europe. Within this discussion, I draw on my experiences in researching sites of terror, the ethical and political dilemmas that I encountered, and the meaning that an engendered reading of Holocaust memory brings to the discourse on memorialization. I conclude the essay with a discussion of emotion-based research and the importance of doing feminist work on genocide memorialization. Taken together, this essay describes my parallel journeys as a scholar, a feminist researcher and a Jewish woman. Each of these intersecting identities, which are addressed below, has shaped my intellectual and emotional path through the field of memory studies.

Gender and Collective Memory: The Importance of Women as a Category of Remembrance

In my discipline of sociology, the study of collective memory as a social construct originates out of the work of Emile Durkheim and Maurice Hawlbachs. For Durkheim,[2] rituals represented the social acts though which group identity is solidified and through which the memory of a group's past is transferred from one generation to the next. Rituals thus create the social conditions under which collective identity and collective memory are constructed and maintained. Following Durkheim, Hawlbachs[3] argues that, in addition to ritual life, collective memory is produced and preserved in family narratives, oral histories, social symbol systems, and sites of memory that group's create and preserve. Thus, Hawlbach's work provides the foundation for contemporary studies of collective memory across a broad range of disciplines.[4] Beginning in the 1990s, the turn toward memory studies became evident in the large production of scholarship on memory, especially in relation to the Holocaust.[5] As I reviewed the vast literature on Holocaust memorialization, I became aware of the absence of a gendered discourse on Holocaust memory and representation. Recognizing this gender gap in the study of Holocaust remembrance, I began a decade's long ethnographic project that took me to over 100 memorial sites of Nazi terror in eastern and western Europe.

As my fieldwork progressed across the post-Holocaust European landscape, I struggled with the project that I had laid out for myself. When I entered the death camp at Majdanek in Poland, time seemed to stop. Old Zyklon B gas cans sat inside what had once been the gas chambers, the cans neatly piled on top of one another, creating the impression of an aging cement storage closet. Nearby, the barracks of the camp were filled with dust laden shoes and other remnants of the Jews who been murdered there. The sense of death and loss was everywhere—men, women and children's belongings all housed in wire cages, looking much as they had when the camp was liberated in 1945. Here, as later in my fieldwork at Auschwitz, I had to

2 Emile Durkheim, *The Elementary Forms of Religious Life*, New York: Oxford University Press 2001.

3 Maurice Halbwachs, *On Collective Memory*, Chicago: University Press of Chicago 1991.

4 It is important to note that Halbwachs, while not Jewish, was deported to Buchenwald after protesting the arrest of his Jewish father-in law. He died there in 1945.

5 Jeffrey Olick, Vered Vinitzky-Seroussi and Daniel Levy, eds., *The Collective Memory Reader* New York: Oxford University Press 2011.

adjust my scholarly lens – reminding myself to look for the women amidst a gender inclusive horror, to find the women's stories among the visual texts and memorial structures that preserved a history in which women, men and children were terrorized and annihilated.

The first essay I wrote out of this early fieldwork was a reflection on doing feminist work on genocidal trauma. I questioned the meaning of feminist ethics in genocide research both because the policy to exterminate the Jews did not distinguish between women and men, and because, in collecting the data on gender representation and memorialization, I felt as if I was participating in the objectification of the women victims. Their exhibited clothes and their possessions became the objects through which I coded and documented their imprisonment and death. During this period of my research, I worried that in highlighting the memory of women's suffering and embodied death, I would contribute to the objectification of Jewish women's memory through my analysis of a memorial culture that tended to eroticize violence against women and the humiliation to which women were subjected. I feared that my work, while important and necessary, would reproduce and reify the motifs of a collective memory that might further victimize the survivors and the memory of those who had been annihilated. It was only after I wrote the first essay on feminist ethics in research,[6] that I was able to continue the project.

Working through the feelings that I might betray these women in telling their stories, I chose to represent their experiences and their histories through language and description rather than through visual imagery that was clearly available to me at the memorial sites. While I took numerous photographs of the pictures that documented violence against women's bodies and the eroticization of the prisoners' memory, I excluded these images from my analysis, using descriptors that I hoped would capture the meaning of my findings without further exposing the victims through graphic visual representations. I am not sure that this was a successful strategy, but it was my moral compromise. I believed then and I still believe now that women's experiences must not be overlooked in the study of genocide, even while their histories may invoke memories of gendered violence and humiliation. Following the work on Auschwitz and Majdanek, I turned my attention to the memorial spaces in Germany that for the most part had been understudied as gendered memoryscapes. In particular, I turned to sites of synagogue ruins and the women's camp at Ravensbrück to explore how a terrible past is memorialized by a perpetrator nation. Here I consider my experiences as

6 Janet Jacobs, "Women, Genocide and Memory: The Ethics of Feminist Ethnography in Holocaust Research," *Gender and Society* 18 (2004): 223–238.

an ethnographer at German Jewish sites of memory, drawing on my field notes to return to the time and place in which I conducted the research and developed my findings.

Synagogue Ruins as Sites of Gendered Memory

Throughout Germany, the destruction of Kristallnacht is memorialized at sites where the original remains of synagogues are visible alongside restored buildings of the absent Jewish community, many of which now function as museums to a Jewish past. In both small and large cities and towns, these sites are often found in the old Jewish quarter that has been preserved by local and/or the national government. In cities such as Friedberg, Worms and Speyer, the material culture of Jewish religion and practice provides a historical reference point for Jewish life in prewar Germany, with a focus specifically on medieval Jewry. These memorial spaces in Germany are haunted by an eerie sense of silence around the fate of a Jewish community that no longer exists. During my fieldwork in Germany, I learned that the preserved and often abandoned Jewish quarters in these German towns and cities are most often visited by German tour groups on tours of historical and medieval Germany. I thus observed that at these sites of memory, the Holocaust and its relationship to a destroyed Jewish people is obscured and embedded in a national narrative of the past that is signified by a rich German Jewish culture that has been frozen in time. Further, my research revealed the extent to which the *mikveh* (ritual bath) anchors the memorial narrative in these historic archeological landscapes. Among these ruins, the ritual bath stands as a memorial not only to a lost medieval Jewish culture but to the annihilated Jews of the twentieth century. In the following passage from my field notes in Friedberg Germany, I record how the memory of the *mikveh* invokes a memory specifically of the loss of Jewish women:

> Friedberg, Germany
> October 3, 2002
> I arrived at Friedberg and found the *Judengrassse* [Jewish Quarter] right away. I passed a locked gate and memorial park where the synagogue once stood (there is only one wall remaining) and then a man on a bicycle points the way to the *Judenbad* (Jewish bath). Using sign language he shows us where to get the key to enter the centuries old *mikveh*. The *Judenbad* here is an old building in the middle of the street. The proprietor is a woman who lives upstairs. You buy a ticket and she directs you into a small court yard in her house. The court yard walls are covered with plaques of war heroes and also with photographs of Kristallnacht—images of the burning synagogue whose remnants we just passed. Finding the mikveh, I descend into a long and dark stairway. At the bottom of the steep stair case is a dark pool of water. Standing there in the dark, I touched the medieval stones, running my fingers over the moss covered and slippery surface of the *mikveh* walls and

> I suddenly felt dizzy, overwhelmed by the power of all the generations that came before me— women going far down into the darkness to cleanse themselves after child birth, after every menses—how many times did they make this journey below ground alone? I wondered how this cavern of murky water functioned in the minds and emotions of the medieval women and in the lives of their 20th descendants who hundreds of years later were forced from their homes and murdered. In returning to the synagogue court yard, I looked for signage that would describe for the visitor the function of the ritual and its connection to Jewish women. There was none.

In my field notes, I noted the absence of a gendered narrative at this historical site. Here as elsewhere in the many synagogue sites throughout Germany, Jewish religious life is commemorated as a male centered world of ritual and prayer. Through old photographs, contemporary renderings, and medieval drawings of the missing synagogues, men become the symbol of observance and religious faith while the memory of women remains in the shadows. As a Jewish woman and researcher in search of a connection to this medieval past, I considered what it might mean to bring the *mikveh*, as a woman's space, into the memorialization of Kristallnacht. As a text of gendered memory, the *mikveh* might remind future generations that, like other Jewish women, German Jewish women had for centuries descended into these underground structures, following Jewish family law and a religious code that required acts of purification.

As I moved from one Kristallnacht site to another, I felt a sense of loss not only for the synagogue structures and for the people but also for the memory of a Jewish domestic world that women created, preserved and inhabited. In my work in Germany, I found that religious memory was male centered and that the reclamation of a Jewish past was primarily constructed through the lens of Jewish patriarchy. Similarly, in non-religious memorial spaces, such as the labor camps of Dachau and Sachsenhausen, it is men's suffering, death and persecution that are commemorated in the monuments and exhibit halls that frame these commemorative sites. It was only at Ravensbrück, the women's camp in East Germany, that the memory of women became visible and accessible.

Ravensbrück and the Politics of German Memory

At the time at which I began my work on gender at sites of terror, there were two foundational texts on Holocaust memorialization in Europe, the photographic essay by Sybil Milton[7](1991), *In Fitting Memory: The Art and Politics of Holocaust Memorials*; and what has now become the canonical

7 Sybil Miltion, *In Fitting Memory: The Art and Politics of Holocaust Memorials*, Detroit: Wayne State University Press 1983.

work on monuments to this terrible past, James Young's *The Texture of Memory: Holocaust Memorials and Meanings.*[8] Each of these works considers the symbolic and politicized representations at labor camp memorials in Germany, focusing heavily on the memorials that have been constructed at Dachau, Sachsenhausen and Neuengamme. In excluding Ravensbrück, the scholarship on Holocaust memorial culture reproduces the persistence of a gendered memory of the Holocaust that erases women from these frameworks of remembrance.

When I considered what German sites I would include in my study, Ravensbrück thus stood out as a research site that had yet to be fully explored or recognized in the research on Holocaust memorialization. As a woman's camp, Ravensbrück, which officially opened in 1939,[9] was designed to house and imprison criminals; political resistors from Germany and occupied countries; communists; Jehovah Witnesses; Jews; and Sinti and Roma populations. Unlike Auschwitz and Majdanek, where my other fieldwork had taken place, the vast majority of the nearly 140,000 women and children who were imprisoned at Ravensbrück, were not Jewish, although Jews comprised 20 % of the camp inmates. The memory that this camp preserves therefore is a narrative of gendered persecution where women's nationality (seventeen different nations are represented) is the defining trope of remembrance. In addition, the site has been recognized as a German national memorial that invokes Christian themes of martyrdom, especially in the Burdened Woman (*Tragende*) monument that marks the center piece of the camp grounds. The monument, which features one woman carrying another, is comprised of a 25 foot high sculpture that sits at the edge of Lake Schwedt at the lower end of the camp grounds. The lake, which is surrounded by a beautiful wooded forest, holds the remains of the women and children who died there. From the moment I arrived at the camp, it was the lake and the monument (known as the pieta of Ravensbrück) that distinguished this site from other memorials that I had visited. Here is the observation that I recorded in my field notes the night after my first visit to the camp:

> Ravensbrück Women's Camp
> September 29, 2004
> I follow the road into the camp, passing a soviet era sculpture of three muscular women in ragged uniforms bearing the stretcher of a deceased child. Further on down the road, a soviet tank marks the entrance to the camp. The road ends at a large dusty parking lot. I park my car next to three or four school buses and walk to the edge of the parking lot. From where I stand, I can see the vast space where

---

8 James Young, *The Texture of Memory: Holocaust Memorials and Meanings*, New Haven: Yale University Press 1993.

9 A men's satellite camp was opened in 1944.

> the camp was built at the edge of Lake Schwedt. Though I am at some distance from the lake, I can see a large statute at the water's edge and I can barely make out a group of visitors that are congregated around the statute. It is late in the day and storm clouds are overhead. I walk quickly down to the lake, hoping to get there before the rain begins. The closer I get to the lake, the larger the sculpture appears. I look up toward the sky where the figures of two women have been placed on a pedestal and I can see that these are meant to represent prisoners, one emaciated woman holding another dying woman in her arms. At the base of the statute, visitors have placed flowers, stones, and a bible with a cross on the cover, a small crucifix, and candles. School children who appear to be in their early teens stand in front of the monument, singing. The girls hold roses in their arms which they place in the lake as a farewell gesture before returning to the school buses. I look at the lake and the roses floating across the top of the lily strewn water. It all looks so beautiful and bucolic. It is hard to remember that below the water's surface lay the ashes of the dead.

This entry into Ravensbrück was a transformative moment in my study of women and the Holocaust, the point at which I considered the multiple meanings of Nazi genocide with respect to the remembrance of women who were specifically targeted for destruction. The Burdened Woman monument stands as a symbol of gendered suffering and victimization, commemorating the extent to which Nazi terror touched the lives of women and children during World War II. At Lake Schwedt and other spaces throughout the camp, images and renderings of women were everywhere to be seen—in art, sculptures, paintings, and larger than life size portraits of survivors. As I recorded and documented the gendered narratives of camp life and death, however, I became aware of another form of erasure—that of the missing text of Jewish extermination. The texts that describe the history of the camp and the rise of Nazism do not reference Jewish genocide. It was only when I perused the books that were for sale at the memorial that I found the memory of Jewish women's suffering.

Among the few guides to the camp was a booklet entitled, *Through the Eyes of the Survivors*. This small publication, a collection of diary entries from survivors, contained one of the few references to Jewish prisoners at Ravensbrück. In sorrowful and heart rendering accounts, non-Jewish women wrote of the deportation of their Jewish friends to the death camps. Fully aware of the fate that awaited them, the other prisoners collectively and secretly mourned the loss of Jewish women. None of these writings, however, are included in the exhibits within the camp grounds. What makes the absence of these writings particularly poignant is the erasure of women's empathy for one another under the most horrific of circumstances. Reading these journal entries, I was especially moved by the feelings of sadness and loss that the non-Jewish prisoners expressed for the Jewish inmates. In withholding these texts from public view, the memorial not only erases the memory of Jews but also the recollections that reveal the significance of women's relationship to one another during their imprisonment.[10]

Where the trope of relationality is most evident is in the figurative representation of the Burdened Woman statute, one woman carrying another in her arms. Although this monument is the center piece of the memorial, there is no plaque or signage that identifies either the artist or the women on whom this statute is based. After I left Germany, I sought out archival data that might help me to situate the monument within the larger frame of women's remembrance. My research into the background of the Burdened Woman, which is recounted here, deepened my sense that Jewish memory had been forgotten and that the missing signage perhaps was intended to facilitate a Christian reading of the site. Through my research, I discovered that the Burdened Woman sculpture was created by the East German artist, Will Lammert, a Communist who fled Nazi persecution. Lammert's original design, commissioned by the East German government, included the two figures in the Burdened Woman monument and a group of other women prisoners that were intended to be placed at the base of the statute but were left unfinished when Lammert died in 1957. Within two years of his death, the Burdened Woman statute was installed at the newly established camp memorial, the two figures standing alone at the banks of Lake Schwedt. Two of his other sculptures were placed by the camp crematorium and the rest of the women figures were later taken to the Old Jewish cemetery in Berlin where they reside today, a memorial to the Jewish families that were deported from Berlin.[11]

In uncovering the history of Lammert's monument, I came to understand how the politics of memory function through the intersection of gender and genocide. While the group of women at the Berlin cemetery has come to signify Jewish extermination in one memorial landscape in Germany, the Burdened Woman monument occupies a completely different space of memory at Ravensbrück, symbolizing a universal Christian theme of maternal nurturance and sufferance. This bifurcation of Jewish memory is all the more troublesome because the two figures represented in the Burdened Woman sculpture are believed to be the Jewish resistance activist, Olga Benares Prestes, and another Jewish inmate that Benares-Prestes saved when

---

10 Judith Tydor Baumel, "Women's Agency and Survival Strategies during the Holocaust," *Women's International Forum* 22 (1999): 329–47.

11 For a larger discussion of the origins and history of the Burdened Woman, see Insa Eschebach, "Soil, Ashes, Commemoration: Processes of Sacralization at the Former Ravensbruck Concentration Camp," *History and Memory* 23 (2011); 131–156; and Natasha Goldman, "From Ravensbruck to Berlin: Will Lammert's Monument to the Deported Jews 1957/1985," *Images* 9 (2016): 140–163.

she collapsed while being forced to stand for hours during a camp line up. The Burdened Woman thus was intended as a Jewish memory by the artist who sought to capture in his work the suffering particularly of Jewish prisoners. Yet, as a participant observer at Ravensbrück, I was completely unware that the emotionally provocative sculpture of one woman cradling another in her arms, the image that framed my first encounter with the camp, was in fact the most significant site of Jewish memory at the memorial. In discovering this hidden truth of memorialization, I gained a greater understanding of how memory can be obscured and how origin stories can be repressed and forgotten in the politicization of histories of mass trauma and annihilation.

Conclusion: Emotion and the Importance of Engendering Collective Memory

In concluding this essay, I would like to close with some thoughts on the emotional difficulties of doing work at sites of terror and the importance of feminist work in this area. Especially with respect to the Holocaust, scholars have drawn on the psychoanalytic concept of transference whereby the researcher's confrontation with a traumatic past gives rise to deep and sometimes overwhelming feelings that somehow must be managed in the field.[12] This transference may be especially strong if the researcher is connected by kinship, ethnicity or gender to those who were targeted for extermination. Because sites of terror are designed to immerse the researcher/visitor in the histories of a terrible past, the effects of transference may be especially strong. Aware of this emotionally challenging aspect of Holocaust memory studies, I intentionally chose Mauthausen, the men's labor camp in Austria, as my first field site, before making the more arduous transitions to Auschwitz, Majdanek, and Ravensbrück. In choosing to study Mauthausen first, I naively assumed that, as a men's camp that housed thousands of prisoners from diverse countries and ethnic and religious backgrounds, the evidence of genocide would be less visible and thus less emotionally painful.

Once at Mauthausen, however, I realized how unprepared I was for this encounter with Nazi terror. The camp has a brutal history of death, experimentation, forced sexual slavery and homosexual persecution. Below what is now the museum to these atrocities, lies the intact gas chamber that was

---

12 See Saul Friedlander, *Memory, History and the Extermination of the Jews in Europe*, Bloomington: University of Indiana Press 1996, and Dominick LaCapra, "Representing the Holocaust: Reflections on the Historians' Debate," in *Probing the Limits of Representation: Nazism and the "Final Solution,"* edited by Saul Friedlander (1992): 108–127.

used for exterminating the weak, the sick, "racial deviants," and women. When I came to the end of the exhibit hall in what had been the former camp prison, I hesitated before the stairway that led to the rooms below. The signage was concise, "This way to the gas chamber," with arrows pointing downward. It was then that I experienced the immensity of what I had set out to study. Gas chambers are the iconic memory of Jewish genocide and now I was about to enter the space that signified the Holocaust in all of its terror and destruction. Although this was not Auschwitz, the memory of extermination was carried in these structures at Mauthausen that represented the surviving relics of a much larger and vaster use of this technology of genocide.

Slowly and with a sense of dread, I made my way to the basement below. At the bottom of the stairway, I stood a few feet from the entryway to the shower like chamber. I could see that the walls of the chamber were covered with photographs and that memorial candles were burning at the edges of the brick floor. False shower heads were visible among these artifacts of remembrance. I could not bring myself to go inside. Struggling with my own emotions, I could hear people of all faiths offering prayers to the dead and I could see a few elderly men and women taping pictures of their loved ones wherever they could find an open place. Here at Mauthausen, with the passage of time, the Nazi gas chamber had become a touching and moving memorial space, the humanity of the prisoners memorialized in their images and in the notes that their families left behind. As I observed the reclamation of this site of death, my role as researcher gave way to my identification as a Jew, for whom the gas chamber would always signify a terrible death, arousing in me a trembling fear that marked the importance of traumatic transference among scholars of the Holocaust.

My first encounter with the gas chamber at Mauthausen helped me to understand that there are no safe emotional spaces in Holocaust memorial work. In the years of research that followed, and which I have described above, I learned (with lesser and greater success) to balance the fieldwork at sites of terror with the emotions that such work engenders. Although the effort is not without its hardships, the benefits far outweigh the costs. As a feminist scholar, I am committed to creating a new and more inclusive paradigm for the study of genocide and for the study of memorialization, even as such projects present emotional and ethical difficulties. In continuing to do the hard work of trauma and memory studies, I (along with other feminist scholars) seek to provide an intellectual space that makes visible the multiple ways in which genocide across cultures informs the lives of women. The challenge is to stay true to the integrity of women's memory in the representation of atrocity narratives that define commemorative landscapes. Although my current work on gender and genocide has expanded to

Bosnia and Rwanda, my research on the Holocaust remains at the root of my development as a feminist scholar of mass trauma and memorialization. It is through the remembrance of Jewish women that I found my intellectual home as a memory scholar. Holocaust studies is the place where I gained a wider understanding of how gender functions in systems of terror and persecution and thus this area of emotionally arduous but imperative research has been transformative and life changing.

Bożena Karwowska

Women and the Holocaust – Am I an Outsider?

Introduction

Looking at research conducted within Holocaust Studies, it is obvious that academics working in this field, with its interdisciplinary and various national facets, are quite often connected to their research not only on an intellectual level, but on a personal level as well. The same might be said about feminist approaches or women's studies, which are pursued mostly, if not nigh exclusively, by women. I, too, fit squarely within this paradigm. Twisting this around, it also means that who I am is very important for what I do, and this is why I write here both about being a (not-particularly-welcome) feminist in academia, and also about where I come from, not only in terms of the landscapes but also the discourses I grew up with as a child living in the post-war Warsaw. The processes of e/immigration put many things in perspective: being Polish meant growing up in a predominantly Catholic culture, it means having access to the original linguistic version of many accounts of the Holocaust, including first-hand accounts of Auschwitz and those written in the first years after the liberation. This is why, in this article, I write about how feminist categories and concepts helped me to map out and discuss often intimate and sensitive issues that are essential for understanding of women prisoners' experiences of Auschwitz despite how utterly glossed over they have been and continue to be by traditional (patriarchal) approaches.

My Liminal Position as an E/Immigrant and a Feminist in Academia

I was born and raised (both physically and intellectually) in Poland. At the age of 32, with a landed immigrant visa issued on my one-way Polish passport, I moved to Canada. At the time of writing today, I have been affiliated for over 30 years in my new homeland with the University of British Columbia in Vancouver: first, as a graduate student and then as a faculty member. Both Warsaw (Poland) and Vancouver (Western Canada) are very important for my past and current academic life; they both and each have formed and continue to inform who I am, personally and intellectually, and I maintain contacts with both.

Political changes surged in Eastern Europe only a few years after I left, with a landed immigrant visa in my Polish passport, which allowed me only to leave Poland, not to return. Circa 1992, themes and topics related directly to Jewish people returned to public discourse in Poland. It was then that academic circles became much more open to studying the Holocaust, rather than the broader topics of World War Two or the German occupation of Poland. Concurrently, feminisms, which I first began to understand and study in Canada, started to make their way into Polish society. From the point of view of Canadian academics at large, however, my Polish background and education, particularly in the eyes of my colleagues, make my research choice of the Holocaust an incomprehensible one, if not a suspicious one. My being a woman on top of being a Pole does not help. Since I began to teach about the Holocaust and take students to Poland for *Witnessing Auschwitz*, an intensive research abroad seminar, my department suddenly stopped being generous with merit increases for me. A monetary price for my research and teaching choices?

Western Canada, far from any academic centers related to Holocaust Studies, gives me loneliness, solitude and distance - all at the same time. I understand, both as a woman and as an academic, what the meanings of e/immigration are, (a) process(es) many women, among them Holocaust survivors, went through after 1945. As part of my research, I wrote the book *Druga płeć na wygnaniu* (Second Sex in Exile, Kraków 2013), analyzing women's literary accounts of their experiences of displacement, and organizing a new home in their countries of arrival. My closest intellectual friends are in Poland, but the academic texts that feed my thinking and my work are different than theirs. In Poland, various political pressures leave their mark on both research and academic discourses. Living and working between both academic realms has its down sides, but it also provides for a unique sense of freedom.

The Landscapes of My Childhood

Growing up in Poland, a country shattered by the German occupation during the Second World War, in the ruins and rubble of Warsaw, left its mark on me as a person and also impacted me as a scholar. There was not much talk of the war or the German occupation in my childhood home, but, in the late 1950s and early 1960s, the ruins of many buildings still remained around the apartment that we shared with two other families on Marszałkowska Street till I was seven. Like the majority of people in the capital city, my parents moved there after 1945 and did not know (and thus did not miss) prewar Warsaw, the second largest Jewish city in the world. In postwar Poland, each family lived in the shadow of its own tragedies and the official cultural trends of communist Poland additionally framed them in the context of national history. My familial story of WWII was one of loss and absence, but it did not fit the heroic or martyrologic language of Polish suffering and heroism. It was a story that did not exist in national memory, a story impossible to tell in the framework of either official or unofficial postwar Polish discourses. In concrete terms, this absence for me entailed a lack of maternal grandparents; it was an absence that coexisted with the physical marks of the absences of people in the Arian part of Warsaw, where I grew up. There were no stories of Jewish survivors; the survivors I knew did not talk much. Outside the apartment building on Tłomackie, where we got our first flat in 1961, this absence was later also cognitively palpable as empty spaces covered with rubble and overgrown grass. The building stands literally on the border of what used to be the Warsaw Ghetto and the Arian side, providing an interesting metaphor of a liminal space that conditions my perspectives on the Holocaust (or at least some aspects of it).

The ruins I saw made me wonder about the people who once lived there: tall buildings behind "parterowa Marszałkowska" (ground level pavilions on Marszałkowska Street) no longer with front walls, the various colours of walls in rooms, doors leading to nowhere… Mere rubble on the former Warsaw Ghetto's grounds, however, did not invoke much thinking about the people who had lived there. Rubble was physically safer for children to explore, and, unlike partial ruins, one could walk over it without the fear of structures collapsing. The remnants of a bunker on Miła Street were just a hill for sleds for children in the neighbourhood. With the absence of family stories and the lack of Jews and their stories, there was not much that would provide any insight into the life that used to be there, nothing that could call on a child's curiosity and imagination. My family was Polish (within the Catholic tradition); Polish-Jews from my parents' childhoods stayed somewhere in their memories of the small cities they came from, and I knew next to nothing about them. The only glimpse I had into any of this tragedy was offered by literature and memoirs from the camps, which my generation read with deep interest.

From National Narrative to Feminisms

By the late 1950s the "male" heroic war story was already surpassed in Poland by the epic story of rebuilding, which was also told in a symbolically male language. The memory of the Jews faded away together with the disintegrating structures defining their space, but the space itself remained. Growing up in Muranów meant something, even if I did not understand it back then. At school, as a child, I was taught about a nationally united country: Poland being a country of Poles, unlike in the times before the war, when there were also other nationalities. The word "Jew" was not a part of this language; in the mind of a child, Poland and Jews belonged to different spaces and different discourses. Jews were here, but are no longer here, or maybe they are still here. The most important lesson from that time was that Jews were not "us", they were "them".

My formative years did not teach me much in terms of feminisms, but at the same time they taught me everything. I learned that if I wanted to understand the world I lived in, I needed to analyze it with categories from outside of it. Communist Poland controlled the language of its description but it also became very clear that language can create a false reality. Thinking outside the contemporary political discourses and aiming for the traditional, patriarchal society of Poland to be able to see its double victimizing nature, meant that I first had to become familiar with feminist categories that would help me deconstruct its traditional, and thus "natural" structure; from there, I found I also needed to adopt more complex concepts as in, for instance, the feminist ideas of intersections or overlapping. It took me years to learn the ways in which this notion applies to the Holocaust and other human tragedies of WWII as well.

For years, I knew that I was deeply interested in memoirs of Auschwitz, but I was unsure if and how I could express this interest. Only after becoming more conversant with various feminisms did I realize that, regardless of all the fundamental differences between the world views of various groups of prisoners, victims, and perpetrators, their patriarchal understanding of the roles of men and women in families and in societies was almost all the same. In this sense, traditionally (or patriarchally) oriented witnesses and researchers were all in the same blind spot when it came to the question of the victim as a person, who – as a human being - was always clinging to at least some traces of his/her gender identity. This is what my book *Ciało, Seksualność, Obozy Zagłady* (*Body, Sexuality, Concentration Camps;* Universitas, Kraków 2009) is about.

Auschwitz from Feminist Points of View

In my academic work on the Holocaust, I focus primarily on issues related to Auschwitz, with various meanings of it as a place and as a concept. Feminist perspectives allow me to enrich the existing body of research by adding thoughts on deeply personal (and often too personal to share) camp experiences of prisoners, especially those of women who, in general, lack(ed) a language suitable for describing what was happening to them in spheres that they understood as too intimate to discuss. Feminist concepts allow me the possibility of not only adding something important to what has already been stated, but also to touch upon the human identities of victims who were treated by their oppressors as objects rather than as people. The SS selected and then directed "new arrivals" to different camps simply based on how their bodies looked, including whether their bodies looked male or female.

In 1946, Pelagia Lewińska noted in her memoir *Oświęcim* (Paris, 1946) that "People in the concentration camp were all mixed together, as if in a large caldron. All nationalities, all religions, all social classes, all categories of 'crimes'. The entire human mass was divided only according to gender"[1](p. 72). What I realized is that this binary division was not questioned by prisoners or survivors as it overlapped with the traditional designation of space along the sex/gender lines. It seemed quite obvious for everybody that there were "two sexes", and that women and men belonged to different camps and different spaces. This unintended and to a large extent unconscious and unnoticed consensus between patriarchally raised perpetrators, victims and researchers made it impossible to see certain aspects of the victimization of prisoners, and especially of women. This consensus also extended to understanding the world in terms of assigning a higher value to what was symbolically male than to what was symbolically female (see Helen Cixous "Sorties: Out and Out"). It is only quite recently that societal understanding of heroism has evolved from being associated exclusively with what is symbolically male, and has begun to also include, for instance, some people's (symbolically female) decision in the ghetto to accompany their elderly parents in their journey to the extermination camp. This is what I discuss and show is my book *Historia-Kobieta-Literatura* (*Woman–History–Literature*, Warsaw 2016), which also includes chapters about women and the Holocaust (as well as anti-Jewish pogroms).

I am interested in what people, and especially women, seldom talk about openly. Prisoners in the camp did whatever possible to survive; self-reflection, including reflections on (gender) identity, did not help to achieve this task. For years after the liberation, reflections and discussions about the moral and ethical cost of surviving, including survivor guilt, overshadowed all other aspects of the cost of surviving. Moral values and physical and psychological scars have been discussed more openly than the aspects of life deemed by social standards as intimate or private. What is symbolically male has gained more attention than what is symbolically female. It is only thanks to feminisms that researchers now understand that the private/personal is political, and that it should be studied as such.

1 "Ludzie w koncentracyjnym obozie w Oświęcimiu byli zmieszani jak w wielkim kotle. Wszystkie narodowości, wszystkie wyznania, wszystkie klasy społeczne, wszystkie kategorie "przewinień". Całą masę ludzką rozdzielono tylko według płci."

In the late 1940s and the following decades, talking about one's intimate or private life, especially for women, was outside social norms. Thoughts on gender have changed significantly over the years and we now have a much more helpful language for talking about "private" issues; as such, "fresh" readings and reinterpretations of the memoirs of women who survived Nazi-German camps are critical. Reading early writings about the camp in the feminist practice of "reading against the grain" brings forth a humanizing sense of academic purpose: a sense of giving back a voice to the victim as a woman or as a man, with their gender identity formed by and against the culture they grew up in. How do we, as researchers, see women in Auschwitz, and what do the experiences of female prisoners in this camp tell us about womanhood and femininity? Taken out of their domestic roles, placed in the company of women, almost totally deprived of the company of men, women in the camp were deprived of the functions they knew in the "normal" world. But still, they did whatever possible to remain women, whatever this term or identity meant for them at that time and situation. And this was their act of defiance.

Though who I am, or came to be, is crucial for my academic work, what I do is not about me; it is about them – the prisoners of the camp. Let me thus refer here to the first memoirs from Auschwitz, texts women and men survivors wrote shortly after the liberation. Memoirs written mostly in Polish by survivors who went through traumatic experiences in the camp, primarily as "political prisoners", and who also witnessed the mass killings of Jewish people brought to Auschwitz. They do need to be read and analyzed in the original Polish versions, as language, linguistic expressions and word choices are an important part of each memoir. Struggle with the language testifies to other struggles, and among them a struggle to make sense of one's own (gender) identity. It is not only, as many survivors have stated, that they "do not have the words to describe it"; these gaps point researchers to see and analyze where words lack as well as to an insufficiency of language. Many interesting early memoirs and memory-based literary works are written in Polish; not all of them are translated and available translations seldom reflect the linguistic layer of the text, especially when it comes to gender markers.

Authors of the memoirs represent various points of view and come from different backgrounds. It is enough to mention Seweryna Szmaglewska, Zofia Kossak-Szczucka, Krystyna Żywulska and Pelagia Lewińska to see the spectrum: from anti-Semitic and nationalistic to left-oriented or communist, from being a "real Pole" to a Jew whose racial identity was not discovered in Auschwitz. As different as they each were, all of them were, and identified themselves as, women, and thus experienced Auschwitz as prisoners of FKL and as women. Their overseers in the camp, both the SS and kapos, were also women. In my work, I argue that not only did female prisoners see the camp from a woman's perspective; that their camp experiences meant a lot for their gender identity (or femininity), and for our understanding of women as victims of Holocaust. In fact, when writing about Zofia Romanowiczowa's novel *Passage through the Red Sea* (1960) about a girl turning into a woman, or going through puberty and growing into a woman in the camp, I realized that we, as Holocaust researchers, do not really know how to approach this question. Philosophical works about Auschwitz, such as, for instance, the very influential writings of Primo Levi or Georgio Agamben, are gender blind and thus cannot provide help in finding answers. What is the model for performed femininity when the only women you see are your fellow Auschwitz prisoners? On a personal note, I wonder how much my own mother could possibly have known about motherhood when, at the age of ten, during the first few weeks of the Second World War, she was already parentless? It was such sets of research questions that have helped me, as a grown woman, to come to understand my mother and her insecurities.

Recovering the Female Voice of Women Prisoners

While a lot has been done to understand the silences connected with trauma, cultural taboos have proven to be more difficult to overcome. The implementation of feminist categories, however, has allowed me to add to the voices and opinions of victims a critical meta-language and thus to address aspects that the prisoners themselves in various ways signaled in their texts, but were unable to name and analyze. In this sense, feminist work in Holocaust studies is very different from traditional, gender-blind research. It adds a "recovered" voice and thus arguably may be seen as a new way of witnessing. Unlike the task of early feminists in literary studies, feminist Holocaust scholars do not have to concentrate first on bringing to the forefront female voices. There was a significant body of work written by female survivors of Auschwitz right after the liberation and, as Kazimierz Wyka noted in his *Pogranicze powieści*, (*Borderlands of the Novel*, Kraków, 1974) at least in Polish literature, with its important early accounts of Auschwitz, the literary voice belonged to women. Having said this, however, we need to be aware that the authors themselves did not necessarily understand that the same gesture of oppression had a different meaning for men and for women. To understand this myself, I found it fruitful to apply concepts derived from American Black Feminism to Holocaust studies, following Hortense J. Spillers' observation that, while the violence itself might not be gender specific, the same act of violence might have a different meaning for and effect on a man and on a woman.

When, in 1945, Seweryna Szmaglewska, in her book-memoir, *Smoke over Birkenau*, used the third person form "więzień" (male prisoner) to describe her own and other female prisoners' experiences in the camp, readers and critics (but also the translator of her book into English) did not pay attention to this gender transgression. Though all her experiences and knowledge were connected with the camp for women (FKL), Szmaglewska's narrator did not use the feminine "I". In using the male form, in Polish also understood as "generic", the writer created a narrator that shielded her from disclosing traces of her personal identity. A male (or "genderless") voice seemed to do the job of becoming non-personal. (I wonder if I did the same, though honestly not intentionally, when writing here about my childhood, referring to myself as a child and not as a girl.) This private gesture was closely connected with its public meaning, and one can only speculate today as to whether or not Szmaglewska's memoir would be used by the Soviet prosecutor during the Nuremberg trial as evidence, had it been written with the voice of a female narrator. Comparisons of direct and artistic statements in memoirs written almost at the same time by women of similar experiences, jointly capture the dilemmas of womanhood as lived by the prisoners, and also as a category of academic research in the field of Holocaust studies. It also shows that while female prisoners were quite sensitive (though maybe unconsciously) to the issue of gender, even today, several generations later, Holocaust researchers usually overlook it, or gloss over it to move on to "more important things".

Personal Observations on Holocaust Research and Feminism in Poland

I focused on publishing in Polish rather than in English for a reason, though it has been questioned at my university as limiting the impact of my work. While feminisms became an important part of Anglo-American academia, it is still seen in Poland predominantly as a political movement. It was intermittently tolerated in some academic centers in the first years of the new millennium, but has since met fierce reactionary backlash from the Polish Catholic church, as well as a political variant thereof by the governing party, who currently attacks it as an "ideology of gender". There are no feminists among my generation of Holocaust researchers in Poland, so there was a very clear void that I needed to fill. My articles, book chapters and books on the Holocaust have been met with serious interest and, as such, I have been invited numerous times to participate in or jointly organize conferences and to give lectures in Poland. My "foreigner" status was also very helpful as I was not looking for any institutional association and could present my research on various occasions and in various places. While many academics and students, primarily in literary and cultural studies, seem to be interested in this new approach, it is really unfortunate that, in general, Holocaust study centers and their scholars do not welcome feminist approaches or are openly opposed to them. Unfortunately, in both of my academic worlds, Holocaust studies seem to be the domain of men, and of a patriarchal or misogynistic culture. The only conference organized in Poland that was devoted to women and the Holocaust took place in Warsaw in 2011. There were no Holocaust research institutions among the organizers; it was co-organized by the Gender Center Foundation and the Institute of Literary Research at the Polish Academy of Science. Holocaust research centers in Poland (including the Polish Center for Holocaust Research at the same Polish Academy of Science) were quite notably absent from this project.

Similarly, with very positive reviews of my work in literary journals, "Zagłada Żydów" (the major Holocaust Study periodical, which lost state (and other) financial support under the current government) published a review of several feminist books together; its author stressed that though issues of the body, sexuality and women's experiences are important, the role of feminisms is overrated in Holocaust Studies. He argues that there were topics women did not talk about as the result of social taboos, but more so and primarily because of the political realities of the pro-Communist post-war government, and they should thus be studied as such. It is unfortunate, to say the least, that – again – with all the major differences and the binary positions toward the issue of the role of the Poles in the extermination of Jews, the opponents nevertheless seem to agree that understanding women-specific experiences and issues is over-rated, and, therefore reject feminisms as being of a significant value for studying the Holocaust.

The political polarisation and the current major discourse in Poland focusing on Poles helping (the official Polish government position) or denouncing (the officially criminalized position, still taken on by several Polish Holocaust researchers) Jews, has again marginalized feminist thought and research on women and the Holocaust in Poland. It does not mean, however, that it is completely silenced, or that I do not see the results of my efforts. I certainly do, not only in my published work, but in my role as an educator. The up and coming generation of researchers I am in contact with seem to become only more and more interested in this topic.

For six years now I have been bringing groups of Canadian students to Polish institutions (Auschwitz Birkenau State Museum and Memorial and the Jewish Historical Institute in Warsaw) for an intensive research seminar. My students benefit tremendously from working with the best researchers in the field when studying the Warsaw Ghetto and the Auschwitz camp complex, but the exchange of more general knowledge and cultural influence is mutual. It has been a pleasure to see how researchers in both institutions slowly become more open to gendered views and feminist ideas. Again, the seminar has barely been noticed by my Department. The program, standing on its own merits, shows promise to continue regardless of my own Department, thanks to private donors and the institutional support of other parts of my university (and the incredible women working there). In addition to being recently forced to offer a graduate course under my male colleague's name, it is worth noting that historically my department has made my engagement in graduate student supervision extremely difficult. Without getting into too many details, it is worth mentioning the story of one graduate student in particular who insisted on studying the Holocaust under my direction. She had to jump through a number of hoops and faced a myriad of interim problems for her choices regarding her topic and supervisor; she nonetheless succeeded in completing her PhD. Joyfully seeing her triumphs as her own success and one for women in academia and Holocaust Studies in particular, I look forward to the publication of her upcoming book, based on her thesis about the Warsaw Ghetto. There is a lot about women and their experiences in her book; another landmark victory for both the women she writes of and the women she writes among.

A Point of Arrival – and New Beginnings

Recently, a few new books on the topic of women during the Holocaust have been published in Poland. Additionally, a book of my students' research, *The More I Know, the Less I Understand*, (Oświęcim 2017) includes essays related to women's camp experiences; the Auschwitz Museum researchers and educators with whom they undertook their research are more and more open to feminist concepts and topics. There is still a long way to go, but I am very positive that we will continue to move forward and that among the topics Holocaust researchers in Poland will choose to undertake, more will pertain to women and more will take up feminist concepts and views.

I am really glad to be a part of this project connecting feminist Holocaust researchers. For me, this new feeling of belonging to a group sharing common interests and views started when Judy Baumel-Schwartz wrote a meaningful review of my work and examined my article included in the book *Women and Holocaust* (Warsaw, 2015). With so much interesting information about our common interests and similar research topics, Judy's review also helped me to understand that, not despite of but because of our different backgrounds and the different material we work with, we have a heightened chance at finding more authentic and developed answers to the same questions. In at least equal measure, it is very important as well to work with the

Jewish survivors who can still answer our questions and tell their stories, and to re-read memoirs written earlier, especially ones written right after the liberation when the wounds were still fresh, when survivors lacked words, and when their own stories seemed for them insignificant in comparison to what happened to the millions that perished.

Lisa Pine

An Unexpected but Fruitful Academic Journey

Introduction

It is indeed an honour and a privilege to be part of this project, among the pioneering scholars in the field who have influenced my own research and among colleagues whose tireless and important work has forged a significant place in the development of Holocaust historiography. It is an excellent opportunity for me to reflect upon both my personal and my professional identities, to look back on the path that led me to where I am today, to recollect from childhood and family experiences, and to consider where my future research and writing may take me.

Family History and Education

To begin with my family history, I was born in London in 1966 and grew up in a suburb of London within a strong Jewish community. However, among Anglo Jews my interest in the Holocaust and the development of my writing in this and related areas, is perhaps not the most likely or expected, as I come from the community of Bukharian Jews. My father was born in Tashkent in the USSR, now Uzbekistan, and my mother, though born in the UK, was of the same ethnic and religious background. Not only was our community much, much smaller than the Ashkenazi community in Britain, but also my family - on both my parents' sides - had no direct experience of the Holocaust. Fortunately, Hitler made it neither to Central Asia nor to Great Britain. Hence my personal and professional journey to Holocaust studies was not a direct result of my family's history.

In terms of education, I went to a Jewish (and orthodox) primary school, which of course played a very important role in instilling Jewish religious traditions and values in me. In my home and family life too, I was imbued with this ethos and especially the concept of *Tikkun Olam* (repairing the world). I have no doubt that these early socialisation influences had a bearing on my eventual profession as a university lecturer and author, but I shall return to that later. My secondary education was at a leading private girls' school, where the pupils came from a variety of different religious backgrounds. My university education consisted of three degrees, all at the London School of Economics and Political Science. My first degree was a BSc (Econ) Government and History. After this, I completed my MSc International History and my PhD, awarded in 1996, was on the subject of 'The Family in Nazi Germany'. In all regards, together with my older brother David, I had a privileged and fortunate education throughout and a happy childhood in which I knew my identity and had a strong sense of how I fitted into both the Bukharian Jewish community and British society.

My first introduction to the subject of the Holocaust growing up was a visit to Anne Frank's house in Amsterdam in 1977. However, I was quite young and do not have much recollection of this. A key moment of exposure to the subject was the four-part television mini-series *Holocaust*, which was made in 1978. I think that my parents had made a conscious decision at that point to sit us down in front of the television to watch that series together. Of course, it was shocking and made me cry, but I suppose what it really did was to make me wonder, as I still do today, what made people behave in that way. It was difficult to conceive and to understand. It still is. Whilst I do not recall all the details of the series, I do remember my shock and disbelief that the Jewish people of Europe were transported in cattle cars to camps where they were slaughtered en masse.

My Academic Path to this Subject Area

In tracing my academic path to this subject, I make a jump from my early teenage years to the second year of my undergraduate degree to a course on 'Fascism and National Socialism in Interwar Europe'. This was without doubt the course that most interested and inspired me as a student, so that when I did my Master's degree, I wrote a dissertation comparing Italian Fascist and Nazi Germany film propaganda, which I thought was a fascinating subject. When it came to trying to find an original topic for my PhD, I started with the idea of wanting to research on the subject of women and film in Nazi Germany.

My initial explorations of the historiography in the early 1990s led me to discover that a new field was emerging in women's studies and women's history, with some pioneering studies of women in Nazi Germany, especially by Jill Stephenson.[1] In addition, very influential to me at that time was the book *When Biology Became Destiny* (that I am now contributing to a book with some of its co-editors and writers is very pleasing to me).[2] It became clear to me that whilst perhaps my initial idea was not as viable as I had hoped, there was certainly a gap in the historical literature on the subject of the family in

1 Jill Stephenson, *Women in Nazi Society*, London: Croom Helm, 1975, and J. Stephenson, *The Nazi Organisation of Women*, London: Croom Helm, 1981.

2 Renate Bridenthal, Atina Grossmann and Marion Kaplan (eds.), *When Biology Became Destiny: Women in Weimar and Nazi Germany*, New York: Monthly Review Press, 1984.

Nazi Germany and that became the focus of my PhD research. I had a lot of support from my former MSc supervisor, the great Donald Cameron Watt (who passed away a few years ago and whose memorial service I attended in London in 2015) and benefitted from the intellectual eminence of Michael Burleigh, who supervised my PhD.

The course of my PhD research led me to examine not only what the Nazis considered to be 'valuable' families, but also the extremes of German family policy, between the promotion of "Aryan" German families on the one hand, and the destruction of those who did not fit in to the Nazis' "national community" on the other. I looked at "asocial" families in one chapter, as an example of people who did not conform, but I also had a chapter on Jewish families, to further explore this seed in my mind from my early teenage years and my finding out about the Holocaust, to discover what happened to "racially inferior" families in German society. My doctoral research took me on many visits to a variety of German archives, including the Bundesarchiv (Federal Archive), which was then at Koblenz, but subsequently moved to Berlin. As I researched the chapter on Jewish families, however, I also visited Jerusalem, where I spent valuable time at the Yad Vashem archive, reading testimonies, as well as to New York, where I did the same at the Leo Baeck Institute. Once again, I was very fortunate to have been awarded research funding both in the form of a grant for my doctoral research as a whole, as well as additional funding for some of these archival research trips. My PhD research provided me with the material for my first book, which was published in 1997.[3]

Writing in the Area of Holocaust Studies

My first foray into writing anything at all directly in the area of Holocaust studies was the outcome of a request from Dan Stone to write a chapter for his edited book *The Historiography of the Holocaust* on the subject of 'Gender and the Family'.[4] Of course, this was a very new and emerging area of study at the time, with just a few scholars having written on this topic previously. The chapter was a discussion of the state of the academic literature in the field of Holocaust Studies. The main points to be made were that the perspectives of gender, children and the family were becoming established within the broader field of Holocaust studies, which added an entirely new dimension to the historiography and to our understanding of the subject as

3 Lisa Pine, *Nazi Family Policy, 1933–1945*, Oxford: Berg, 1997.

4 Dan Stone (ed.), *The Historiography of the Holocaust*, Basingstoke: Palgrave Macmillan, 2004.

a whole. I was subsequently invited by the editor of the *Journal of Jewish Identities* to write an article on 'Gender and Holocaust Victims'.[5]

Over the years, my main research and writing has centred on my abiding interest in the social history of the Third Reich, in particular, women and the family, education and youth groups, the "national community" and the themes of inclusion and exclusion in Nazi society. I am primarily a social historian and have always been interested in how the Nazi dictatorship functioned and in the complexities of the relationship between the regime and the German people. In the burgeoning historiography of the Third Reich, this too was an area that needed to be developed beyond the earlier historical interest in the politics of the Nazi regime and the mechanisms of the dictatorship. But, of course, these studies of the Third Reich could not preclude analysis of aspects of Nazi anti-Semitism and the Holocaust, because these formed an intrinsic part of what Nazism was about and the consequences of its government.

Researching and Writing on Gender and the Holocaust

And so, at the same time, I continued to give some attention to looking more at gender and the Holocaust and came to consider a need to explore female Holocaust narratives, which I did over the course of a number of years. My work in this field has focused on the importance of the social construction of female identities and roles in the history of the Holocaust. It has analysed the structural sources of gender difference in relation to Nazi persecution before the war and then the distinctions between the ways in which Jewish men and women experienced the Holocaust, using significant examples from both male and female survivors' accounts to underline and illustrate the key points. In particular, it has discussed gender-related experiences at Auschwitz. It has examined female behaviour that conformed to traditional gender norms, such as adaptation and coping mechanisms and social bonding among female victims.

My work additionally considered female behaviour that differed from the expected female type. While this is an uncomfortable topic, it is nevertheless an important one. The literature had tended to overlook the desperate actions taken by Holocaust victims in order to survive under the appalling conditions in which they found themselves. But this does not mean that they did not occur. The purpose of such discussion is not to judge, but to offer

5 Lisa Pine, 'Gender and Holocaust Victims: A Reappraisal', *Journal of Jewish Identities* 1 (2008): 121–141.

a more complete picture of Holocaust experiences and to try to establish a greater historical understanding of the subject.

The lens of gender provides a useful tool for interpreting the behaviour and experiences of Holocaust victims. Gender is a characteristic of all human experience. Both masculinity and femininity have been socially constructed and shaped by historical circumstances and expectations. Moving away from universal interpretations, both women's experiences as specifically female and men's experiences as specifically male, are significant to our understanding of the Holocaust. The field of Holocaust studies that was gender neutral until the 1980s now includes a substantial literature on gender. Furthermore, a comparatively recent, yet substantial output of memoirs and testimonies by female Holocaust survivors has ensured that women's voices are no longer unheard. These developments in the historiography have meant that scholars are now in a much better position to understand the diversity and complexity of the experiences of Holocaust victims.

My work has contributed to this field by analyzing survivor narratives from the perspective of gender. In many ways, women were placed in a position of "double jeopardy". They were in a position of blame not only for behaving in a particular manner or for carrying out an act or deed, but also because by doing so, they contravened the social construction of femininity that they should not prostitute themselves or kill their babies in order to survive.[6] During their imprisonment at Auschwitz, women had to opt for agency and make choices in a variety of ways that were distinctive from those made by men. Survivor Viktor Frankl notes that for men too, the "choice of action" existed even in the face of the terrible privations they faced at Auschwitz.[7] In the end, all Jews were equally destined for death, but there were differences on the road to that destination for men and women. Women's and men's experiences of the Holocaust were not identical, but as Myrna Goldenberg has suggested, they were "different horrors" within the "same hell".[8] Hence, an analysis of gender-based distinctions in Holocaust experiences and the ways in which they have been narrated by female (and male) survivors, adds an important angle to our knowledge and understanding of this dark chapter in modern history.

6 This concept of 'double jeopardy' features in the title of Judith Tydor Baumel, *Double Jeopardy: Gender and the Holocaust*, London: Vallentine Mitchell, 1998.

7 Viktor Frankl, *Man's Search for Meaning*, London: Simon & Schuster, 2004: 74–75.

8 Myrna Goldenberg, "Different Horrors, Same Hell: Women Remembering the Holocaust." in R. Gottlieb (ed.), *Thinking the Unthinkable: Meanings of the Holocaust*, New York: Paulist Press, 1991: 150–66.

The Impact of the Subject on me as the Researcher

It has not been an easy subject area to work on, but it is one I regard as significant and compelling. In seeking to understand the enormity of the Holocaust, an examination of survivor memoirs and testimonies is essential. Nevertheless, we must acknowledge the fact that survivors, male or female, are unable to bear witness to the suffering of the six million Jewish victims of Nazi policy who did not survive. As Primo Levi has written: 'we, the survivors, are not the true witnesses'.[9] This point is underlined in the memoir of Henry Wermuth, who wrote: 'How could I even attempt to describe all the wretched misery, the death cries of millions of innocent people? ... Being in these camps does not, contrary to the assumptions of many, imply that I knew all and everything there was to know about them'.[10] Each and every aspect was either experienced or remembered differently. In the end, the examples that historians and other scholars use from memoirs and testimonies are illustrative, not comprehensive.

Not only the narrative, but also the concept of the survivor and what the survivor represents to us, is very significant. Survivors have a special, although unenviable, status characterised by what Robert Lifton has called "the death imprint", an imprint formed by having survived death or having witnessed the deaths of others and still remained alive. Lifton suggests that we should not glorify survivors though, as doing so, "diminishes the survivor and interferes with our understanding of both what is particular to his or her ordeal and what insight it might reveal about our own psychological and historical condition".[11] Yet, we do feel distinct from them. They have lived through an experience we can only try to imagine. We feel overwhelmed by their recollections and we tend to see them as 'different' precisely because of what they have experienced and survived.

What was the impact of researching this "hell" upon me as a researcher? I think that the most important thing to be said is that is that it is harrowing work to read survivor memoirs and testimonies, especially when I was going about the business of reading many of them over a sustained amount of time and became immersed in the world of the concentration camps and the death camps, in particular, Auschwitz. Researching a subject like this certainly put my routine concerns and problems into context, making them

9 Primo Levi, *The Drowned and the Saved*, New York: Summit Books, 1988: 83–4.

10 Henry Wermuth, *Breathe Deeply My Son*, London: Vallentine Mitchell, 1993: 1; 139.

11 Robert J. Lifton, 'The Concept of the Survivor', in J. Dimsdale (ed.), *Survivors, Victims and Perpetrators: Essays on the Nazi Holocaust*, Washington: Taylor and Francis, 1980: 115–30.

seem very trivial by comparison. It is very difficult to read the details of victims' experiences. Accounts of the barbarity and the brutality can be very graphic and disturbing. Furthermore, accounts of betrayal and unkindness on the part of fellow victims towards each other, even former friends or family members, make unpleasant reading. What are the lessons to be learnt about human nature? The human capacity for cruelty, violence and betrayal is still shocking to me, however many accounts I read. There has been comparatively little written about emotions and stress on researchers of traumatic subjects. Yet, exposure to the traumatic experiences of victims can have a profound impact upon us. We internalize their words. They change us. We almost inevitably take in some of the emotional pain through reading traumatic survivor accounts. A recognition that is usual to feel an array of emotions, such as outrage, sadness, horror or vulnerability is a significant part of the mechanism for coping with the impact of such work.

The accounts of Holocaust survivors also have made me feel sad, have made me cry, have made me angry, and have made me feel vulnerable and anxious. They are made up of very painful and difficult material. Whilst survivor accounts are a testament to the endurance of the human body and spirit, they are also a testament to the worst type of evil that human beings are capable of inflicting. Hatred, discrimination, prejudice and violence are a part of humanity, the darker side, which must also be acknowledged. It is unpleasant to keep returning to this fact. I am forced to re-examine my cognitive schema. It has been important to acknowledge all of this and to have in place some support system for myself at times when I am immersed in working on such painful and emotive material. This has usually taken the form of personal support from close family members and friends, as well as the practice of yoga and meditation. However, I supplement this whenever possible, with a "work" support system, in the form of discussions with colleagues working on the same or similar types of subjects. This particular project has been very beneficial in this regard, giving me a sense that I am not alone in my endeavours and of camaraderie with other scholars in this field. It has been important to me to tell the stories of survivors whenever I have an opportunity – to my students, at talks at secondary schools and at academic conferences. I have been fortunate to present aspects of this work at conferences in the UK, Denmark, Poland and the USA, and not only at history conferences, but also at multi-disciplinary ones.

Auschwitz

During the course of undertaking my research on gender and Holocaust victims, I was invited to present my findings at an international conference on "The Legacy of the Holocaust" at the Jagellonian University in Krakow in

2009. Whilst in Poland, I took the opportunity to visit the site of Auschwitz-Birkenau. The site of Auschwitz is one whose public perception has largely been shaped by second-hand accounts and images from films and documentary programmes. A personal visit to Auschwitz, and hence a first-hand opportunity to see the site, was a very unsettling, odd and emotional experience. Images that had been constructed from films, memoirs and testimonies suddenly became concrete and real. They were not constructs any longer. I had read many accounts and memoirs of survivors bearing witness to the horrific events that took place here, but my physical presence on the site itself added a different dimension to my perception and understanding of the place and its part in modern history.

Auschwitz represents the epitome of an event in history that has shaped and impacted not only Jewish, Polish and German history, but also that of Europe as a whole and indeed has had global ramifications. It has disturbing and chilling associations. It symbolises evil. Here, the worst type of atrocities that human beings are capable of perpetrating upon others took place. As a museum and a memorial site, Auschwitz-Birkenau stands as a highly significant point in European society, culture and history. It generates controversy, elicits strong emotions and evokes horrific images. It is a bleak and grim representation and reminder of some of the most heinous acts and events in our history. It makes us question humanity and consider issues of morality.

At Auschwitz, extermination and the Nazi conquest of *Lebensraum* ("living space") came together, conceptually, temporally and spatially. The site of Auschwitz comprises the original forced labour camp (Auschwitz I), Birkenau, the death camp (Auschwitz II) and the sub-camp, Monowitz (Auschwitz III). The remnants of barracks and other buildings, barbed wire fences, chimneys and railway lines stand as a stark reminder of the history of this place. The scope and barbarity of the events that occurred here have left their mark on the site. It is nowadays visited by large numbers of tourist groups, scholars, students and school groups. In fact, it feels very much like a tourist site, even "attraction", on the Polish map, with trips to Auschwitz amply advertised around the main square in Krakow, which seemed rather strange. It also felt odd to see so many tour buses arriving at the site itself, with large groups of tourists, equipped with their cameras and guidebooks. Nevertheless, on further reflection, it is better that the place is visited and remembered, rather than forgotten, even though it felt somehow rather incongruous to see tourist buses rolling up and coffee shops and bookshops trading in an everyday way at a place with such a horrific historical record.[12]

---

12 On this, see Daniel P. Reynolds, *Postcards from Auschwitz: Holocaust Tourism and the Meaning of Remembrance*, New York: New York University Press, 2018.

As Duane Mezga has noted: "The overwhelming nature of the Auschwitz experience seems to require an opportunity to reflect on what has been seen in an attempt to comprehend its scope and meaning. The memorial provides such an opportunity".[13] It also stands as a lasting monument to the victims of National Socialism who perished here. Auschwitz-Birkenau creates a profound impact on the visitor. A trip here is a highly emotional experience, as visitors try to comprehend the enormity and scale of what happened here and to grapple with its meaning. For me, the visit underlined and concretised, in a sense, all I had read in survivor accounts, but even so, it was and still remains very hard to accept man's inhumanity to man. This is an aspect of working in this subject area with which I am unable to come to terms and which I still find hard to understand, however many accounts I read or however many times I teach the subject. The horror, terror, brutality and barbarity narrated by survivors of the Holocaust are incomprehensible.

The Holocaust and Genocide from the Perspective of Gender

The study of this particular subject has had a bearing on the direction of my wider research and writing interests too. It has led me to reflect not only on the debate in terms of Holocaust studies, but also in genocide studies. I have been teaching an undergraduate course on genocide for more than a decade, and recently wrote a book on this subject for students.[14] Here, too, I included a section on gender, because it is so crucial in this field of study as well. This is exemplified by many publications on this subject, in particular, Amy Randall's edited volume on *Genocide and Gender in the Twentieth Century*.[15] Indeed, the subject is growing with such speed that Randall is currently preparing a new edition of the book to encompass the most recent developments in the field.

My work has led me more recently to think that the time was ripe to reconsider men's Holocaust narratives previously regarded as universal, but which we now know are not so from work we have seen on women's testimonies from the perspective of male gender. I became interested in masculinity and, in particular, in what male Holocaust survivors chose to relate in their narratives, and what made these distinctive from women's narratives. My work in this area sheds light on the experiences that pertained to the gendered particularities of male victimisation. It interrogates men's words,

---

13 Duane Mezga, 'The Imagery of Auschwitz', *Landscape Research* Vol. 15 (1990): 28.

14 Lisa Pine, *Debating Genocide*, London: Bloomsbury, 2019.

15 Amy Randall (ed.), *Genocide and Gender in the Twentieth Century*, London: Bloomsbury, 2015.

deeds and behaviour under extreme conditions, as well as the choices they made in relation to these circumstances.[16] It also considers both male behaviour that reflected expected gender norms, such as egotism, strength, and identity through work, and male behaviour that deviated from these expectations, such as social bonding to enhance chances of survival. A revisiting of men's testimonies, previously regarded as "universal", through the lens of gender allows us to understand them as the testimonies of men specifically.

Additionally, the memoirs of the *Sonderkommando* (special detachments) allow us to begin to comprehend the ambivalent position of these male victims at Auschwitz, who served the machinery of death. A fresh reading of these accounts enables us to understand aspects that have not been previously analysed in relation to the gendered experiences of male Holocaust victims. The accounts of *Sonderkommando* survivors are particularly revealing as expressions of male behaviour and choices. The *Sonderkommando* were engaged in the extremely gruesome task of working in the crematoria where the victims' bodies were burned. Much discussion on the *Sonderkommando* has been concerned with the moral ambivalence of their positions, as they were living in more privileged circumstances in the camp and had a chance to survive longer, whilst carrying out this unenviable and grisly job for their captors. Revisiting their testimonies from the perspective of gender sheds light on the particularities of their experiences, as only male prisoners, selected for their strength, were *Sonderkommando*. A number of salient themes emerge from their testimonies, including their experiences upon arrival at Auschwitz; separation from their families; their attitudes to their work; their association with other workers; their relationship to their overseers; and their use of cigarettes and alcohol. These themes suggest important responses and reactions to their circumstances that were male-gendered.

My recent research has examined the experiences and conduct of male Holocaust victims at Auschwitz specifically in relation to their gender. It has shown the significance men placed on work as a means of dealing with their situation, trying to gain control of it (in a similar way to which women used home making skills to do the same) and surviving. As long as they could perform their work tasks, the chance of survival remained. Inability to work almost inevitably signalled selection and death. Men also chose to portray in their narratives the qualities of strength, courage, autonomy and independence as expected gender norms. Once separated from their wives and

16 Lisa Pine, 'The Experiences and Behaviour of Male Holocaust Victims at Auschwitz', in B. Krondorfer and O. Creanga (eds,), *The Holocaust and Masculinities: Critical Inquiries into the Presence and Absence of Men*, Albany: SUNY Press, 2020.

children, an obvious aspect of their familiar pattern of behaviour (responsibility for their family members) was taken away. This left them bereft and bewildered, along with the rest of the extreme circumstances in which they found themselves placed at Auschwitz. An analysis of gender-based distinctions in Holocaust experiences, and the ways they have been narrated by men (and women), adds an important angle to our knowledge and understanding of life and death at Auschwitz.

Concluding Thoughts

Working in this field has given me an appreciation of the courage and resilience of Holocaust survivors. The will to survive and to bear witness is an enduring part of the spirit of humanity and survivors are a testament to this. Despite their trauma and the horror that they experienced, they went on to start new lives and to make their narratives known in order to try to encourage toleration and a better world for the future through their presentation of their past experiences. In addition, my empathy, compassion and sensitivity towards others have been increased as a result of this work. I have a more heightened awareness of prejudice and discrimination. Reading survivor accounts and reading about the atrocities of the Nazi death camps, in particular, has made me appreciate my family and all the other good things in my own life. Furthermore, it has put into perspective difficulties that I face from time to time, and the mundane problems of everyday life. It has made me think harder about my life, my relationships and my priorities. Overall, this has been an illuminating journey for me. Analysing agency and choices made by both female and male victims and how these either conformed to or deviated from accepted gender norms has taken my research and knowledge in directions I had not expected when I started my academic career. It has been personally satisfying and intellectually rewarding and fruitful to engage in research that is meaningful to me. In terms of future research and writing, I still intend to do more work on the Holocaust, as well as on other aspects of the history of Nazi Germany, the Second World War and its impact on civilian populations.

*I would like to express my thanks to David Brauner, Corinne Linskell and Julien Morton for reading and commenting on the draft chapter.

Na'ama Shik

Can You Gaze upon Medusa's Face without a Mirror?

For my mother, Hava Shik, who is unparalleled

For the truly wonderful Ruth Bondy z"l, who meant so much to me
With love

> "For a poem is not timeless. Certainly it lays claim to infinity, it seeks to reach through time—through it, not above and beyond it. A poem as a manifestation of language and thus essentially dialogue, can be a message in a bottle, sent out in the—not always hopeful—belief that somewhere and sometime it could wash up on land, on heartland perhaps. Poems in this sense too are underway: they are making toward something. Toward what? Toward something standing open, occupiable, perhaps toward an addressable Thou, toward an addressable reality. Such realities, I think, are at stake in a poem [...] These are the efforts of someone who, overarced by stars that are human handiwork, and who, shelterless in this till now undreamt-of sense and thus most uncannily in the open, goes with his very being to language, stricken by and seeking reality."
>
> Paul Celan

Academia

The rules suddenly change a bit when writing a professional autobiographical article. Where do you start and with what? In which direction will the article take you? What will be its tone? Something that may also please the cognitive process, but first and foremost will allow the flow of those silently read words, observing their rhythm and what they create. Then we turn to meaning, the search for meaning in places where it cannot be found. There is no meaning. This causes you to object - how can there be no meaning? It is this objection that stands at the base of it all.

I once lectured to a group of teachers. I began with our inability to understand, which to me seems basic, almost primordial, I'm even tempted to write atavistic. A reversion to something primal and ancient, a retreat to the source of all things human. It is difficult for us to understand, as we were not there. Neither our bodies, nor that which they contain, our souls, were scarred. One teacher became terribly angry with me. In truth, she got up and left during the break. She was livid at me for saying that we, who were not there, could not fully understand the Holocaust body and soul. I remember the incident upset me somewhat. I truly could not understand how this was not obvious to her.

Yesterday, during a phone call with my mother, we talked about someone who was a member of my Kibbutz many years ago, had left, and today, in his retirement, is writing poems. I asked my mom what his poems were about. And she replied - about the Holocaust. I responded that that's quite interesting, as I didn't even know he was a survivor. And my mom said - yes, of course, that's why he married Esther. I then asked what that has to do with the matter, and she stared at me through the phone, with a kind of surprise that I can identify and see clearly, even though she's sitting miles away, and said - Esther's father arrived at Auschwitz from Salonika, with a wife and four sons. He was the only one who returned. In Israel he married Esther's mother, who had not lost a thing during the Holocaust, and they had four daughters. Esther came to the Kibbutz with her youth movement. And I still didn't understand what the relevance was to the poet. Well, my mother tells me, he, the poet, came to the Kibbutz after the Holocaust, alone, and here he met Esther, and she had three sisters, a large family, and they got married. Now that they are older, the four siblings from Saloniki who were murdered in Auschwitz are finally returning.

Well, can you understand it? Constantly searching for a way to write about the Holocaust, examining how best to teach it, how to describe it - is it even possible? Until now, I have dealt with these issues mainly through the academic prism. It's a cold one. Judgmental. It has stylistic limitations, defining how things should be written, read, and published. It is in this context that I wrote my doctoral dissertation as well as articles relating to the topics it examined, such as sexual abuse in Auschwitz-Birkenau, mother-daughter relationships, early primary sources compared to later ones, and more. But as strange and puzzling, even dissociative, as it may sound, to this day I have not dealt with the subject on the closest, most personal sense, possibly because too much sadness comes into play.

Why did I choose to research the topic of women in the Holocaust? Why Auschwitz? When I let myself examine these questions, or rather when I allow myself to do so, or if I am truly honest - when my defenses are weak, I think the answers lie with my father having been in Auschwitz, though he died when I was two years old, and my mother having survived as a convent child. This is how I dealt with my dead father's story, writing about his "place" from her female perspective, but my living mother's personal history remained untouched.

Women and the Holocaust, women in the Holocaust, that topic. As others who came before me have, as my current-day peers do, and maybe as those who follow us will, I too have encountered difficulties arising directly from the subject matter itself - from within the academic world and at times also from outside of it. A kind of opposition to the essence of the topic itself. Not only was it said that Jewish women were murdered just as Jewish men were, but research of the female experience was perceived as less important, irrelevant, and at times even as unnecessary. It was viewed as a "female sub-field" within Holocaust studies, less academic and less serious.

One of the clearest examples of this in my own case, took place in Israel in 2006 during an international conference on the history of the camps. At the time, I had already completed my Master's thesis, which I had written at Tel Aviv University under the supervision of Prof. Billie Melman and Dr. Raya Cohen, entitled: "'This Poor Body': The Female Experience as Seen Through Autobiographies Written Between 1946–2000 by Female Auschwitz-Birkenau Survivors". I was in the midst of writing my doctoral dissertation, supervised by Prof. Shulamit Volkov, on Jewish women in Auschwitz-Birkenau. During the conference I presented a lecture which dealt with the uniqueness of the Jewish female experience in Auschwitz-Birkenau in which I examined sexual abuse in Auschwitz, focusing mainly on the rape of Jewish women in the camp. I still hold a copy of the lecture. The following section would later spark the debate:

> ***A. Sexual Abuse***
>
> Cases of harsh sexual abuse, especially of female inmates, in the camps in general and in Auschwitz-Birkenau, were a prevalent practice, and they were committed by both SS men and inmates, generally by non-Jewish inmates with privileges. Although, as I note, we can find a variety of sexual abuse practices in the camp, the exceptional one is rape. The Nazis, because of their ideology, were not allowed to do it. It does not mean they didn't, but it was not genocidal rape. Most of the cases where Germans raped Jewish women were in the eastern front. Unlike in other genocides, the rape of Jewish women in the Holocaust was not an end in itself, nor one of its defining characteristics. This does not mean that Jewish women and girls were not raped during the Holocaust, by Germans and others. And it certainly does not matter to the victims of genocide in what ideological framework the crimes were committed against them — it does not diminish their pain, nor the importance of acknowledging the effects of rape on their lives later on.
>
> [***]

Following my lecture, as often happens at conferences, there was a lively discussion among the researchers. That was when a senior historian intervened and addressed me in an extraordinarily harsh fashion, practically hurling the following criticism at me which I remember word for word, even after all of these years. Absurdly he also completely inverted the meaning of what I was saying. I was discussing how there were many cases of sexual abuse in Auschwitz-Birkenau, but relatively few incidents of Jewish women being raped by Germans in the camp. I also showed how Jewish female prisoners were not "allowed" or forced to serve as prostitutes in the two brothels established in the Auschwitz complex in 1943. The historian responded harshly by saying - "what did you think you would find? There were obviously many cases of rape of Jewish women by Germans in all the camps, all the ghettos, everywhere. It was war and there were male soldiers and female victims."

He was not only mistaken by asserting this, he was also stressing some deeply rooted misconceptions. These have to do mainly with the rape of Jewish women by Germans and with the issue of forced prostitution of Jewish women during the Holocaust. He was actually "contributing" to this image of Jewish women being raped and serving as forced prostitutes during the Holocaust, which emerged in the consciousness of Israeli society immediately at the end of World War II.

It was a difficult experience, kind of double negation - personally of course it was humiliating - of the research, the historical truth and in a way which reinforce misconceptions. I think that this reaction is deeply connected with the field of women and the Holocaust and arguments and opposition it raised.

Research proves that my findings were correct. These stereotypes and misconceptions need to be clarified, refined, and uprooted.

The Right Amount of Distance or How to Write About the Holocaust

Israeli poet and author Nurit Zarchi, responding to Israeli translator and editor Helit Yeshurun, wrote the following: "You wrote: 'the dead that we cannot converse with are actually directing our lives.' [My] answer: they become our destiny."[1]

Sometimes I think that dealing with the Holocaust, particularly for the "Second Generation", brings with it uncontrollable moments and places where suddenly, the ability to distance yourself collapses. This is a negative form of collapse. It's harmful for both research and soul. I think you're taught how to evade it, but it's like a scent - you cannot avoid it, unless you're anosmic, but even then you have other senses that keep reminding you. When that happens I think of Rachel Bluwstein and her beautiful love poem, which always seems to me like a poem about post-trauma. The love discussed in the poem is obviously post-traumatic, but it's also a beautiful representation of the "collapse of distance": "The dam of oblivion - I had built in my defense - is as if it had never been." However this love has a redeeming value, as it allows hope, the hope to find a cure in the living

1 Helit Yeshuron, *How Did You Do It? Interviews with Poets*, (Hebrew), Menachem Peri Ed., Tel Aviv: Hakibbutz Hameuhad, 2016: 491.

water, to quench thirst by drinking from its unrest, "I kneel on the shore of the roaring sea and drink my fill."[2] The Holocaust doesn't have that. The collapse is total, you remain unshielded.

In her brilliant essay "I carry it in my blood" Esther Peled wrote that "it" in her blood. Since it in her blood she doesn't need any outside reminders such as names, or memory days or movies or interviews with Holocaust survivors. In this way it can also stay tangible, not symbolic, which is harsher: "This even has theoretical support; it's tangible, and when it's tangible, it's not symbolic. The symbolic is somehow supposed to control the tangible so that the tangible won't drive the person who carries it in his blood mad, but I didn't go mad because of what I carry in my blood, I've been living with it ever since I can remember myself and even before that, and I manage it."[3]

How do people select their professions? Their paths? To what extent do the circumstances of our lives dictate the roads we travel? Are we aware of this? Is it a choice? Does the choice also entail an attempt to understand? To make peace with something (our parents' pain, the humiliation - one of the hardest things to confront is the thought of your parents being humiliated, helpless)? To repair? Do we choose history, literature, other disciplines, to avoid writing in the first person? How painful is it to write in the first person? Once, someone addressed me as a "Second Generation". For a second I didn't understand. Then I quickly understood. Then suddenly, as if struck by a sharp object, I truly understood. For twenty-five years, half of my lifetime, I've been dealing with Holocaust study and research, yet I never gave account to the fact of my belonging to the "Second Generation". Not truly, not internally.

Maintaining the right amount of distance. Is that even possible? What happens when this distance collapses? For instance - the unthinkable thought that our parents died in the Holocaust. Do they exist or did they remain there? What remained there? What's in the here and now? If I were observing this from "the outside", I would have written that it's enigmatic - because it's a pretty word, and even more ambiguous when we think about it in Hebrew, but also because it allows a detachment, and in an elegant form. But it's wrong. The correct word would be, yes, detachment, I would say, real detachment. I didn't fully understand until today, and I did not perceive myself until recently, as a "Second Generation".

2 . *The Poems and Letters of Rachel, in Manuscript*, (Hebrew) Kineret Publishers, 1969

3 Ester Peled, "Its in My Blood", *The Daughters of Those Who Were There. The Second Generation: Life Stories*, (Hebrew), Ester Peled ed., Bavel, 2018: 216.

Yolanda Gampel wrote about relinquishing the need for certainty when truly listening to survivors of the Holocaust, of trauma. "Testifying is difficult for Holocaust survivors, as it is for any survivor of state violence. At the same time, the opportunity to testify, and even more so the opportunity to be heard, is these survivors' only demand. Yet hearing about laws that were trampled on, about human beings who had been broken, listening to the chaos, to the cruelty and the crimes, this demands relinquishing the need for certainty."[4] This is a difficult, complex concession for every person. Since you have to listen to something awful and scary, which does not have the basic trust in men and in the world. I think it's harder when it comes to your parents. I mean, when it's about your parents, which due to psychoanalysis actually lives within you.

To me this is a true form of "the Uncanny" (*Das Unheimliche*) - experiencing something as strangely familiar, yet foreign at the same time. It is therefore a distressing and extremely threatening foreignness. It creates a cognitive dissonance, and the subject, let's say you yourself, chooses avoidance rather than acceptance. Yet it's there, it's in the ever knowing and ever remembering body. Yona Wallach wrote: "I remember many things. Much more than I remember."[5] The *Unheimliche* worsens, it becomes an unbearable sense of anxiety. I think it's an existential fear - what would happen if that thing you've been holding on to for so long would collapse, that thing that's "in your blood", as Esther Peled wrote. This is the deepest, yet most tenuous, form of knowing, yet its place within the individual is almost physiological - a thin membrane held by just a few tendons and muscles and blood, and it can erupt at any time. The fear is that it will collapse inwards.

I still don't truly understand that I am a descendant of a rabbinical dynasty that was nearly extinct, of families that were destroyed, had disappeared. That is the right amount of distance. It doesn't collapse because of, or thanks to, my academic and scholarly work. For instance I have yet to view my mother's testimony.

I once attempted to write a novella on women in the Holocaust. This might have been an attempt to acknowledge something, to mark it, to understand, or rather to distance myself. I wrote it and there was an interest in publishing it. I suddenly became nervous, it seemed like sacrilege to me. I reread it now, before writing this article, and I understood that the parts dealing with Auschwitz (actually the text in its entirety deals with Auschwitz), are

4 Yolnda Gampel, *The Parents Who Live Through Me*, (Hebrew), Keter: Tel Aviv, 2010: no page.

5 Helit Yeshurun, *How Did You Do It? Interviews with Poets*, (Hebrew), Menachem Peri Ed., Tel Aviv: Hakibbutz Hameuhad, 2016: 70.

historically accurate. This is of course my "area of expertise". I realized how it was actually my parents' biographies, I just switched the genders, keeping a "right amount of distance." The following is a short passage from it. You constantly feel as if there's an attempt to attack, to reach, to describe, to name, to find the right words, to understand.

"Esther gazes outside. Morning zephyrs. Morning zephyrs - what a beautiful expression, she thinks to herself. She remembers how, when returning from visiting Leah in New York, she had gone through a difficult time. Suddenly it all resurfaced. Not that it ever disappeared, but following her return it seems as if things became magnified. The memories, like a menacing worm, crawled out of abandoned corners of the mind and penetrated everything. Those things that she thought were dead suddenly became a glowing monster. Yosef was still alive. At night time he would try to calm her down, to stroke her, to send the worm back into the hole it crawled out of. It didn't help. She was awoken every time by a different cry of pain. Why does this only happen during the night, and almost always during cold nights? As if from a fire, but made of cold. When she arrived at the camp the night would burn as well, but the cold was petrifying."

[***]

"The noise, the horrifying noise, she could not find release from it. Yosef strokes and strokes, and she only hears the noise, blinded by the white light, by the screams, by the smell. The smell. How many children were there? It seems as if whole battalions of children would wander around terrified over there. The largest playground in history, and God dividing them into groups from the heavens. All children to the left, all the elderly, all the mothers. Unequal groups, she remembers thinking to herself. Unequal. Her sister Miriam. 29 years old, so beautiful. A doctor. One of the first female doctors in their town. Tall, redheaded, they used to call her "angry Miriam". Not anger in the irritating sense of the word, but an anger of passion, a passion to live, of one who does not submit to authority and does not accept norms, who has such an independent way of thinking. And courage."

"She stood there with her only daughter, Shulamith. Years later when Esther would read Celan's poem, and Shulamith's ashen hair, she would recall that moment. And with it, almost instantaneously, Isaac and his binding. Except that in Isaac's case God intervened, directing the slaughtering knife to a different victim. And in Shulamith's case God was busy with other things and didn't even see her beautiful sister Miriam and her singular daughter, radiant and tiny, standing there. She sometimes thinks to herself that it would have been better if God had not have stopped Abraham, maybe then there would be no "people" and no "holy" and there would be nothing. And then simply nothing would have happened. But God was there for Isaac, halting the swaying of the knife. But he did not give Miriam and

Shulamith a second glance. Maybe he too was blinded by the white light and was deafened by the noise - their view blocked by everything."

[***]

"Every day Miriam would return with something else: once with a baby porcupine who had to be fed with a dropper, once with a basket filled with blueberries, her mouth blackened by the fruit, once with a snake's egg that had to be raised, and once with a deep gash adorning her forehead - she had climbed to the top of a tree to pick chestnuts, where she found a birds nest from which a fledgling had fallen. She of course had to return the fledgling, climbing down and losing her footing on a rock that was lying at the foot of the tree, but she didn't give up. Miriam never gave up and was never silent in the face of perceived injustice. Maybe that's why she didn't survive and why her death was so horrible. A *Sheigetz* child."

"When she reached the age of 18, miraculously, our father Mendel would say, she announced to the family on the eve of the Sabbath, at the Sabbath table, that she's travelling to the neighboring city to study medicine. Study what? Suddenly there was silence, and it was obvious to everyone, to Miriam, Esther, Yaakov and Ruschka that this silence would not remain for long. And before the silence was interrupted, each family member had time to ask him or herself how it was possible that this *Sheigetz* child, who never lasted more than two days straight in school, would go and study medicine at the university. And then Mendel rose, his anger so extreme that everyone was afraid that he would collapse and die right then and there, and he banged on the Sabbath tale so strongly that one of the candles went out and the *Challah* slipped from the table."

[***]

"A week and a half later, Miriam and one suitcase left for the city on their neighbor Eliezer's carriage. Miriam studied there for seven years, returning aged 25 with a diploma in family medicine, husbandless and with Shulamith, a two year old red-headed girl. Mendel once again thought that he was going to die, but Ruschka kissed Miriam and embraced the red-headed Shulamith tightly, then turned to find them both a room where they could be comfortable. And Miriam became the town doctor."

"She returned from the city the same wild being that she always had been, but now there was an added wrinkle on her forehead caused by deep pondering and a sense of newly found peace - the peace of those who know that they can provide true relief."

"But her anger, her holy anger, did not vanish. She would treat everyone. Those who had enough to pay, and those who didn't. Jews and gentiles, it didn't matter. She would work day and night, once it was with porcupines, now it was with people. Why weren't there sufficient medications, why weren't there appropriate hygiene conditions, and why do you give your children home remedies. Rushing, raging, endlessly occupied with healing and mending. And the townspeople would observe her, this *Sheigetz* child, and they adored and admired her. They would flock to the family home, bringing with them, when they had no money to pay, anything they could find: farm eggs, vegetables, rustic sourdough bread, woolen shawls, and many gifts for Shulamith, because if there was a child who brought light to the world, it was Shulamith. No one knew who her father was and no one dared ask. As opposed to her mother, she wasn't a *Sheigetz* child at all, she was a child of light. The same red hair, the same freckles and the same patrician build, but all expressed through a calm and luminescent demeanor. She had green glittering eyes, and she wore dresses that Ruschka would make her, playing and softly singing to herself. She would wander around our town, picking wildflowers, laying them in different corners to "make things pretty." She would accompany her mother during her home visits, sitting outside and stroking with her tiny fingers those waiting for Miriam to finish taking care of their loved ones. And smiling. She was always smiling. And when Miriam would finish, she would exit the room and would search for Shulamith, and when she saw her stroking someone, singing softly to him, or giving him flowers, a soft glow would spread across her face. And she would tell Shulamith - come my love, let's go home to grandmother, come, she already prepared soup for us, or baked potatoes in the oven, or a steaming slice of bread with a pinch of salt. And she would pick her up with her strong and soft arms and they would return to their home, our home. And we used to eat there, and laugh, and relax, and Miriam, the *Sheigetz* child, and her enlightened daughter Shulamith would fall asleep together, bodies entwined, until the next morning. Even when they were sent to Auschwitz, when we were sent, Miriam continued to take care of everyone on the cattle car and Shulamith continued to smile. It was hot and stifling, there was no air, and the old and young were dying, but Miriam continued to tend to everyone and Shulamith continued to smile. When we reached the ramp, Miriam embraced the seven year old Shulamith and they stood across the doctor who was carrying out the selection."

But "only an ongoing wail or complete silence can express the horror itself, all the rest are the pursuits of life for the sake of living," Ruth Bondy wrote about how to write about the Holocaust.[6] "I have returned/ from a world beyond knowledge/ and now must unlearn/ for otherwise clearly see/ I can no longer live."[7] Charlotte Delbo writes about the blur that separates

6 Ruth Bondi, Whole Fragments, [Hebrew], Gvanim: Tel Aviv, 1997: 51–52.

7 Charlotte Delbo, *Auschwitz and After*, "Useless Knowledge", New York and London, 1995: 230.

between the reality of "that world", of Auschwitz, and the reality of the world she returned to. But, "As far as I'm concerned/ I'm still there/ dying there/ a little more each day/ dying over again/ the death of those who died/."[8]

One of the foundations of the human experience is the ability to transmit knowledge - of the body, of the soul. A knowledge that can be shared and passed on. A knowledge that can be imparted through words, descriptions, that can be absorbed and spread further. But when we talk about tacit knowledge, one that was acquired through extreme suffering and that has no purpose as it cannot be transmitted, it becomes, in Delbo's words, useless knowledge. And thus it turns into an eternal Sisyphean pain, as its solitude is acute, sentenced to everlasting silence and nothingness. How do you write about the Holocaust.

The ever present and constantly unsettling question - is it even possible to testify about the Holocaust? Based on the perspective that says that those who experienced the true essence of the Holocaust were those who were murdered, who did not return to testify, and those who did return, the survivors, are sharing an "incomplete" and "unfinalized" experience - is it possible? And furthermore those survivors who did share, are recounting events that cannot truly be transferred - there are no morals, no lessons, no solace. Survivors agonized over the question whether the true, authentic testimony, can only be expressed by those who experienced it to the fullest - remaining painful ghosts, existing only in the horror of the constant discontent they create. Whereas they, the survivors, the carriers of knowledge and the storytellers, remain powerless in their inability to provide the words, language, meaning and names. "What's burning is me," Dahlia Ravikovitch wrote in her horrifying poem, which is a form of personal testimony turned aflame - the body sizzling, annihilating the soul until nothing remains, besides the remnants of the body. And maybe it is the act of testifying itself that is the "dress of fire" that burns itself and the body with it. Did they not alert the poet, Jason's wife, Medea's revenge? They warned, they cautioned: "they made you a dress glowing like an ember/ burning like coals/ [...] What will become of you, she said, they made you a burning dress." But the poet, the witness, still cannot understand nor trust ancient and modern Greek tragedies, and only when reaching the end, the complete downfall, the end of all ends, is the blaze revealed, the pillar of fire, the final light which accompanies those who walk and those who will remain alive: "But the dress, she said, the dress is on fire./ What are you saying, I shouted, what are you

---

8 Delbo, *Auschwitz and After*, "Useless Knowledge", New York and London, 1995: 224.

saying?/ I'm not wearing a dress at all, what's burning is me."[9] Does the testimony not burn also the bodies of those who returned, their souls trembling?

In her book "A Certain Kind of Orphanhood" Eleanora Lev writes: "Isak Dinesen wrote - 'one can bear anything, withstand anything, if only you turn it into a story'. No one has been able to turn Auschwitz into a story, that is to paraphrase it, to illuminate the nightmare in a way that will enable catharsis; to name it by its true name (usually, the method to overcoming the horror is by getting to know it closely, by coming to terms with it in some form. With Auschwitz that's impossible: the more you attempt to look at it directly the more the horror worsens)."[10] But can you gaze upon Medusa's face without a mirror?

---

9 Dalia Ravikoivitch, *A Dress Of Fire*, (Hebrew) Trans. Chana Bloch, The Menard Press, 1978.

10 Eleonora Lev, *A Certain Kind of Orphanhood. Report of a Journey* (Hebrew), Tel Aviv: N.B. Books, 1999: 254.

Louise O. Vasvári

Towards a Portrait of a Transcultural Academic Life

The Cultural Imprint of My Hungarian Origins

The 1880s building where I live in Budapest was part of the original Parliament complex, built when Hungary was still part of the Austro-Hungarian Empire. In the interwar period, with a country reduced to one third its former size and racked by political turmoil and economic instability, the building was turned into gradually-decaying apartments. In the summer of 1944 it came under the protection of the International Red Cross and provided temporary refuge to some Jews, among them Jewish children and orphans, some reportedly hidden in the bowels of the cellars that connect the former government buildings. Because it faced the offices of the dictator Mátyás Rákosi, from the early fifties the same building only housed families of reliable Communist functionaries, and there are still a few surviving family members of the tenants of that time among my neighbors.

Today that building across the street, which had been kept empty since the fall of the Communist regime, has suddenly been sold to a crony of the current government and is in the process of being restyled into a boutique hotel. My building and my street are like locations described by János Terey in his *Passage Through Budapest* (2014), where citizens walk on buried scenes and when they move into a building do not necessarily know which revolutions or wars those four walls have seen or which terror organization was lodged there. Those who, as we say in Hungary, were "affected," who had relatives "who didn't come back," are well aware that today's flourishing tourist "ruin pubs" are in the area of the blood-stained former ghetto. We follow the recent project (funded by George Soros) to construct a city-wide memory bank of the darkest period in Budapest's history through the interactive mapping of the yellow-star buildings in the city, some 2,000 apartment buildings which from June 1944 were designated to forcibly house over 20 % of the city's inhabitants. About three-quarters of those buildings are still standing today, so this knowledge changes the milieu of those homes and of our daily relationship to the past of our city.

Budapest is the site of my own family history, of a place and a time that has determined much of the structuring force of my later life, and also of my (rather belated) work in Holocaust scholarship. If I feel compelled to preface my own story with the socio-political history of Hungary into which I place my family, it is because when family histories are intimately bound up with momentous historical events, they become communal and generational. But also I think that such a brief excursus is necessary to help clarify the complicated story of the Hungarian Jews from the 1867 *Ausgleich*, the historical compromise in the Hapsburg Empire that created the Dual Monarchy of Austria-Hungary of 1867–1919.

In 1867 the Hungarian National Assembly enacted a law making Jews equal to Christians in practicing all civil and political rights, a declaration unique in Central Europe. Hungary's ruling elite welcomed the assimilation of its Jewish minority during the Dual Monarchy, and Jews came to identify nationally, culturally and linguistically with the Kingdom of Hungary, participating in the economic development and modernization of the country. However, among themselves they were split along social, political, geographical, and religious lines. The educated middle class, much like their coreligionists in Vienna and Berlin discussed by George Mosse in *German Jews beyond Judaism* (1985), were particularly intent on adopting national customs and loyalties. The particular route of Jewish self-fashioning that was open to them when other avenues in society were still closed was social attainment through the gymnasium system and the liberal professions.

By the early 1920s there were just under half a million Jews in Hungary, roughly 6 % of the population. They were the most educated segment of society, extraordinarily represented in most of the educated liberal professions, and were the core of Hungarian middle and upper middle classes, including some 60 % of doctors and 40 % of privately employed engineers. In the same decade there was an exodus of an unprecedented number of assimilated Jewish students and young graduates, with over 40 % of those who emigrated in the interwar period being Jewish. Some left because of 1920 *numerus clausus* law, which strictly limited Jewish (and female) attendance at universities, others because of their inability to find professional employment in the shrunken and anti-Semitic postwar Hungary, and due to the rivalry between the Jewish bourgeoisie and gentile middle class in the free professions. Because U.S. quota laws of 1921 and 1924 enabled very few Hungarians to enter the country, chain- or step-migration was not uncommon, with the first step often Latin America (a route that was to be repeated later by many pre- and post-Holocaust refugees).

As Tim Cole discusses in "Constructing the Jew, Writing the Holocaust: Hungary 1920–1945" (1999), to be a "Jew" in interwar Hungary, was a complicated and shifting political category through anti-Semitic legislation. Both the 1920 *numerus clausus* and the definition of "Jew" in First Anti-Jewish Law of 1938 focused on Christian underrepresentation, so that it failed to define the "Jew" but did define those who were exempt, those who served the nation, and those who converted prior to

August 1919 (because when the short-lived Communist government of Béla Kun toppled there were large numbers of conversions). It was the Second Anti-Jewish Law of 1939 that finally defined the "Jew" in pseudo-racial terms, as a member of "Israelite faith" or a person with at least one parent or two grandparents who were members of the Israelite faith when the law came into force. The Third Anti-Jewish law of 1941 prohibited marriage of "Jews" and non-Jews; the former now defined as with two or more grandparents who had been born as members of the Israelite faith. However, a person was deemed Christian if born a "Christian" to parents who were "Christian" at the time of their marriage, regardless of the status of their grandparents. In other words, in Hungary there was no *Mischling* category in the 1941 Law. Under the terms of these laws, while in Germany I would have been categorized as a *Mischling* in Hungary in 1944 I was legally a Christian, the offspring of a pure Christian mother (who could prove her ancestry to the seventeen hundreds) and a father who, although born a Jew, had been a Christian since the age of eight.

During the war in Hungary the very heterodox branches of the Jewish community, as well as the large number of converts out of Judaism, lacked solidarity with each other. Most, however, tended to have blind faith that Hungary would prove the exception to what was happening around them and that they would be spared. (Imre Kertész in the first chapter of his *Fatelessness* provides a magisterial satire of futile Jewish popular discourse on this issue as late as in 1944.) Ultimately, while the Jewish population of provincial Hungary was decimated within a few months through brief ghettoization and subsequent deportation to Auschwitz (where at one point Hungarians formed the single largest population), roughly half of the Budapest Jews survived. As Peter Tammes (2007) has documented, survival correlated mostly strongly with the level of education and assimilation, including having close social ties with non-Jews and those having non-Jewish family members showing the highest level of survival.

Even today, Hungary continues to be unique in regard to its Jewish population. Already before the war, an extensive self-imposed silence about one's Jewish origins had existed, which became much more prevalent among survivors, many of whom kept the secret from their own children This pervasive familial secrecy was augmented by the discussion of Jewish identity and history being a taboo topic in the Socialist regime, which was broken open by the seminal article, "How Did I Find Out I Was a Jew" (Erös, Kovács, Lévai 1987), about some Second Generation survivors who eventually found out about their origins. It seems many never did find out, or did not want to know, because while today those who self-identify as Jewish in surveys is about 47,500, on the basis of recent DNA tests taken by sample populations it now appears that at least 130,000 actually have from 25 % to 100 %

Jewish ancestry, the highest in the world relative to the total population, outside of Israel. This means that the majority are not aware of, or intentionally repressed their origins, and that cultural intergenerational transmission of Holocaust awareness is sorely lacking.

My Hungarian Family

It is into this history, hidden today in plain sight both in its buildings and on the bodies and the faces of many of its inhabitants, that I was born in 1943. I belong to what Susan Suleiman (2002) has aptly dubbed the 1.5 Generation. I have no independent memories of the war (except for the sirens), but certainly many fragmented traumatic childhood memories of the immediate postwar years. My family background on both sides, gentile and Jewish, has instead instilled in me the feeling that I am somehow one of the last survivors of the Austro-Hungarian Empire, in part because I am an only child and the very youngest member of my generation in my family, much attached in my childhood to loving older relatives on both sides, who were all born in the multi-ethnic Austro-Hungarian Empire, and who experienced its forceful transformation in the course of the First World War and the Second.

Perhaps a brief microhistory of the paternal side of my family can serve to illustrate in personal terms the history of the achievements and failures of Jewish assimilation in Hungary that I have previously described. My paternal grandfather was born in 1862, that is, before Jewish emancipation, in the Western and most developed part of Hungary, where many Jews spoke German rather than Yiddish. His native knowledge of German and some university education helped him obtain a reasonably prestigious and very secure job in the Hungarian State Railway system, which by 1910 had become one of the largest European railway companies. Family lore has it that already at the age of six he rebelled against religious instruction. By the early 1880s he and his brothers Hungarianized their last name, which was the earliest date that Jews could do so without also converting. In 1896 he married a Jewish schoolteacher from a more traditional background in Eastern Hungary, where he was posted as a stationmaster.

My father, the youngest of their three sons, born in 1904, was already born with a Hungarian name into a non-observant family. When he was eight, his father took the next step to radical assimilation by converting to Calvinism with his three sons, but my grandmother, claiming respect for her forbearers, would refuse to convert until 1938. Their family life was typical of the assimilation most prevalent among educated Jews: adaptation to the national outlook, culture and social customs of surrounding society, combined with preservation of elements of Jewish identity. Yet, as Zygmunt

Bauman has discussed in his *Modernity and Ambivalence* (1990), while secularization meant the rejection of religious forms, it often entailed the retention of social and cultural traditions or habits associated with Judaism. As evidenced by interwar family letters, my grandfather's family socialized exclusively with other secularized Jews, in part perhaps because converted Jews faced the scorn of both their former co-religionists and their new ones. Like many of his peers, my father's middle brother, born with the century, emigrated as soon as he received his medical degree in 1926. It was too late to gain entry into America, so he and a classmate ended up practicing in the outback in Argentina. After a few years his classmate managed to emigrate to New York, but my uncle lived out his long life in Argentina, forever hiding his origins.

When my father's brother left for Argentina, the plan was for the other two brothers to follow him, but neither showed the slightest inclination to leave. Even as late as 1938, when relatives in Slovakia were already in trouble, my father was writing to his brother that he feared emigration and that anyway he was doing well in Hungary (although I don't know how much his reluctance to leave was actually due to his involvement in a complicated relationship with my mother, who was married to someone else). Meanwhile my father's older brother who was even less interested in leaving, married a Jewish woman, who, much to my grandfather's satisfaction, also converted when they married. My parents married at the last minute in 1940, before the Third Jewish Law outlawed such marriages. Because my mother could prove that she was pure gentile, my father was protected until 1944. When many were taken to Ukraine for forced labor service he was not drafted. Only in 1944, when doctors and engineers were called in, some even from the ghettos, did my father, who was an engineer, get drafted, although eventually he did have to go into hiding with my mother's help.

In this story, I must also mention the gentile side of my family, all from German-speaking stock, who also became important participants in the events of 1944. My maternal grandparents lived in Győr, in Western Hungary, from where my grandfather, a lifelong Social Democrat activist, was deported to Dachau in a convoy in late November 1944, where, as I have traced in the camp records, he was registered as Prisoner 129367. He survived and walked back to Hungary, weighing some eighty pounds. In that same month, my father's brother, who was on a Death March through Győr on the way to the Reich, was pulled out of the line by my gentile uncle and then hidden by my grandmother, thus saving his life. While all my immediate family survived, it was only half a century later that I realized that among the many family stories, there was never mention of what happened to all of those provincial relatives, the families of those numerous siblings of my grandparents. A more touching coda to my family stories of the Holocaust is that I also had a beloved aunt and uncle on my mother's side, who had no children, and who were like parents to me after the war. Only by chance did I find out recently through the Yad Vashem site that in 2002, decades after their death, they were declared Righteous among the Nations for hiding an eight-year old little girl, the daughter of a Jewish lawyer colleague of my uncle. Today that child, now an eighty-six-year old lady, and I are in joyful contact.

After the war, my father still had no intention of leaving. Immediately after liberation he became involved in a national reconstruction engineering project for a system of tractor repair so that spring planting could begin. However, by March 1948 he had a sense that the communists would take over power and that he would be imprisoned. Luckily, having obtained a six-month business visa to go to the US to buy used ball bearings, he left Hungary a week earlier than planned. He was already crossing the Atlantic on the Queen Elizabeth when he heard the news that the power grab he had feared had indeed taken place. He was granted political asylum in the US by President Truman, although not without difficulty, the problem being that since he had left Hungary at the last minute he was suspected of being a planted spy.

Meanwhile, by 1951, trapped in Hungary, my mother and I were in danger of being deported to the countryside as class a aliens, as indeed some relatives were. Because engineers were in short supply in the US at the time, after getting his first papers (equivalent to today's temporary green card) my father was able to get a job and with political help from his then-congressman, Gerald Ford (who was to become President much later) he was able to get us out of Hungary, but could not yet legally sponsor us for a visa. He did get us visas for Argentina, but his brother refused to take us in, as he was afraid that his Jewish origins might be revealed. My mother and I ended up alone in a most terrible first immigration in Bogotá. Perhaps because we had been able to leave Hungary in a year that no civilians had done so, my mother was smeared as a Communist agent by a right-wing newspaper, where a headline appeared with her photo, calling her the "red Mata Hari." While my mother and I had absolutely no knowledge of the McCarthyism rampant in the U.S. at the time, we still lived in fear that the Americans would never admit us. Because my mother spoke only Hungarian it was my job as a nine-year old Spanish speaker, to try to salvage our situation at the American Embassy in Bogotá, speaking in Spanish.

My father did succeed in getting us to America, but there was no happy end. I, by then a trilingual child, was not to find a new forever home, in part because my parents were never able to assimilate either to each other or socially to American culture, or allow me to do so. To complicate life further, we also we moved coast-to-coast several times due to my father's work. Even before we had arrived in the U.S, he had gotten into the space program as an aerospace engineer, and eventually culminated his career working on the Apollo Program. I was fortunately an excellent student, aided by my multilingual background, which helped me master additional languages. And in 1964 I was accepted with full support for doctoral studies in Romance Philology at the University of California, Berkeley, where I received my Ph.D. in 1969.

Berkeley in the Sixties, Graduate School, and Emerging Feminism

In the fifties and into the early sixties I can only say that I remained a refugee in the US. True, only months after my arrival my first teacher praised me to the other students because although I could not yet speak English, I could do the daily spelling tests perfectly. The secret was that I could read phonetically in three languages while my poor classmates were mired in the "look-see" method. In my second year my luck changed: one day my teacher sent me home early and told all the other students that they should give me the silent treatment because my father had taken jobs from Americans. My parents were too cowed to dare to go and complain. The first years we lived in a big complex in New Jersey, where we found a few other Hungarian refugees, women who gave me amazing affection, and who were the first people I gradually began to recognize as survivors, although I could then have no idea that some of them had likely lost their own children. In retrospect I realize that my deep thankfulness to them is an additional source of my obsession with the past.

It was only in early adulthood that I can say I discovered America. At twenty I was able to graduate from college prematurely, and was able to escape my home life by getting married (of course to another refugee). For a year I taught German and Spanish in a high school, which was to become the beginning of my lifelong teaching career. By twenty-one I arrived in Berkeley and the five years I spent there from 1964 to 1969 formed the beginning of my Americanization –inasmuch as I have achieved that – at a time and in a place which was then at the epicenter of cultural change in the U.S., bursting forth in October 1964, one month after my arrival in this new American land of California.

No decade produced more protests and more frenzied change than the 1960s, and no community in America had a richer involvement in protest than Berkeley. That was the city which stood at the center of the political, social, and cultural upheaval that made the 1960s unique in American history, changing the landscape of American life in a dramatic rupture of the 1950s middle class ethos. The 1960's that put Berkeley on the map as a center of militant political awakening in the US included a wide range of countercultural and political movements, first centered in the Free Speech Movement. By 1968 the Free Speech and Civil Rights movements had shifted into the antiwar phase, and with an evolution of student protest from liberalism to radicalism (with its split between the Old Left and the New Left). These multiple entangled issues through this contentious decade also led to the gradual emergence of feminist consciousness and the early Women's Liberation Movement.

Berkeley radicalism in the sixties was male-dominated by the latent and not so latent sexism of both "liberated" hippies and self-righteous radical men. Many male activists considered women's issues to be irrelevant. In the documentary on some of the founders of the Second Wave Women's Movement, *She's Beautiful When She's Angry* (2016), Ellen Willis expresses succinctly what sexual liberation really meant for women: "In the 1960's we were all subjected to a double message: that first of all sex was okay now, but if we were pregnant it was our problem." Women attended rallies and sit-ins, passed out thousands of leaflets and did most of the grunge work, but very few were in the leadership. Writing this piece I again watched the 1990 documentary *Berkeley in the Sixties* and was struck by how literally *all* the student leaders were male, as were *all* the administrators. In a scene showing faculty emerging from a Senate meeting, exactly one female head appeared among scores of men. I was there *in vivo* every day in Berkeley's Sproul Plaza but I simply didn't notice it then.

Two books specifically on the situation of female graduate students in the sixties in Berkeley cover many more points than I can deal with here: Jo Freeman's *At Berkeley in the Sixties* (2004) and Marsha Hudson's edited volume (2005), which details the experiences of eighteen women. Several testify how painful it is to realize how narrow our vision as young women and students was, how although sexual discrimination was all around us, we didn't perceive it as such but as personal, rather than political, difficulties. Freeman adds that she not only never had a woman professor, she never even saw one. Nor did we notice that even in graduate disciplines such as the foreign languages, which by that time were full of female students, virtually all the faculty were male. Hudson's book recounts the story of the founding in Fall 1969 of the first "female caucus," of female graduate students in the Comparative Literature Graduate program, who began to challenge the male-centered curriculum and created and taught new courses about women authors. It must be noted that very few of these women actually ended up in an academic career, but their work was part of the very beginning of a larger political context in which women at all levels at the university were reconsidering their status, and making demands on the institution.

As far as my own situation during those years I can only claim to have been involved in the periphery of these movements. My first priority was always that of scholarship in the famously demanding program of Romance Philology, where we were examined in four living languages plus Latin and had to know literatures and historical linguistics in three languages, a program in which many fell by the wayside and many others took a decade to finish. Also, as a refugee from Communism I found it hard to sympathize with the radical wing of the protesters, which included old-line communists. Ironically, Bettina Aptheker, the daughter of Herbert Aptheker, a US Communist Party leader, was one of the few female leaders. Later, she was to turn her activism to lesbian feminist liberation and her brutally honest memoir, *Intimate Politics: How I Grew Up Red, Fought for Free Speech, and Became a Feminist Rebel* (2006), offers invaluable testimony of a paradigmatic female activist of the period.

In my own home department of Spanish there actually *was* one woman professor, who recalled in later years how when she was a Teaching Assistant in the early 1930s, male classmates informed her she should leave since she was taking a job from a man. In the department she was ostracized by her male colleagues, who freely shared their view that they didn't "need" any more women. After I had already left Berkeley, an Academic Senate Committee concluded in May 1970 that women faced a large number of obstacles due to discriminatory practices, including anti-nepotism rules, reluctance to tenure, and giving priority to men in graduate admissions and intellectual support. However, it was only in 1972, when the Berkeley's League of Academic Women filed a class action with Federal Office of Civil Rights, that some change slowly began (although in my own former department not until 1977). Unfortunately, just as change was mandated, the hiring market in most humanities and social science fields dried up.

In 1969, I did get a job offer in UC Davis, but my husband and I wanted to return to Europe, so we chose his less favorable but better-located postdoctoral position in Geneva. Had I been able to get permanent employment there I would likely have never returned to the US, but I could only work illegally, and three years later I reluctantly returned to start my university career in a tenure-track position at Stony Brook University.

My Transcultural Academic Career

My original field, Romance Philology, is a discipline located at the intersections of the literary, linguistic, and cultural study of medieval culture, and my teaching and scholarly work, as well, have always been interdisciplinary, before word was common currency. For the first decades of my career I worked primarily in the more traditional area of medieval studies but increasingly theorized by concerns for gender and sexuality, including queer sexuality. Women's themes were already of interest to me in my medieval work and I published on topics such as women's voices in the *Frauenlied*, and on the motif of taming of the shrew as wife battering. I was fortunate to have my primary line in a department of Comparative Literature, which already in the eighties took the turn to Cultural Studies. At the same time I also regularly taught in two other graduate departments, the Department of Hispanic Studies, and the Linguistics Department, where in 1982 I co-taught one of the first courses in the country in Language and Gender. Since 2000 I have also taught sociolinguistics and gender in the Linguistics Department at New York University.

My publications in this area have been primarily in studying the evolving queer terminology as well as coming-out stories in Hungarian, and in examining how Hungarian, a language with no grammatical gender (including having no gendered pronouns) is not in any way less sexist than, say, the highly gendered Romance languages. What I have not been able to discuss in this essay is the impact on me both in a personal sense and later in my scholarly work, of the writing of some of the feminist theoretical writings of the eighties, as well as of the academic memoirs and immigrant memoirs of the nineties. I was particularly hooked on what Suleiman (1993) dubbed "autobiographical reading," reading in order to understand one's own life experiences, and on what Edwige Danticat (2010), called the "immigrant reading," on the immigrant writer's obligation to bear witness to the crisis in her country of origin.

During my career in Stony Brook I also served as Associate Provost, which was a tremendous experience in learning how a university functioned, including gaining access to knowledge about gender inequality in the salary structure. I subsequently interviewed for several deanships and provostships but was not able to move into a career in academic administration.

Since 1970 I have returned to Hungary yearly and for the last twenty years I have reestablished a life there about half of each year, perhaps seeking that idealized but in any case lost childhood that I have also read about in so many of the Holocaust women's memoirs I came to study. I was lucky enough to be able gradually to become involved in the intellectual life of the country, in part because I have proudly and even arrogantly maintained native competence in the language, and because I have taught linguists there in the Central European University and also in Hungarian universities under two Fulbright grants. When Imre Kertész won the Nobel Prize, with Steven Tötösy de Zepetnek, another refugee Hungarian scholar, I published the first in English book on him, *Imre Kertész and Holocaust Literature* (2005), which we followed with two other related volumes on Hungarian Cultural Studies. While working on these projects I realized that women's Holocaust memoirs had not received sustained attention, and I also realized that my insights derived from feminist theory and my earlier theoretical projects of feminist and queer criticism as an "analysis of difference", could also be relevant to my reading of Holocaust memoirs. I began to study and collect memoirs by survivors, my first aim being a bibliography. But soon I realized it was important to know who they were, who survived camps, who in hiding, who wrote early, who late, and what was the effect of religious and class differences, and the effects of their gendered oppression. I was also keenly interested not only in the women's Holocaust experiences but also on their differing diasporic experiences. I also began to collect and write about female Hungarian survivors who remained in postwar Hungary and who, with very few exceptions, could begin to be published only post-1989, but whose work due to it being in Hungarian, remains essentially unknown.

Out of this large and ever-growing corpus of memoirs, augmented by many others in a total of five languages, I wrote a number of studies, including on alimentary life writing, on women prisoner doctors, on wartime rape, on women's Hungarian-language wartime diaries (most of which had lain dormant until recently in archives or in private hands), and most recently on the interwar Jewish *Miss Hungaria/Miss Europa* 1929 and her wartime fate. Because I began to publish on the Holocaust so late in my career, I did not face any opposition. Most of my work has been published both in English and in Hungarian, so that I have been able to accomplish part of my additional motivation for this research, which was to provide information on the Hungarian Holocaust in English and at the same time, more theoretical work on the Holocaust to Hungarian readers. A new project brings me back to my family origins, since the archive I am working with consists of some two hundred family letters written between 1926 and 1938 that recently came into my possession. The letters uncover family dramas, some of which have become falsified in later family memory, and at the same time even in some of their seemingly mundane details, capture the complexities of assimilated Jewish life and of forced emigration in the interwar period that I outlined in the first section of this essay.

Conclusions

As I discussed at the beginning, the principal factors affecting the course of my professional life have been my family history and my subsequent childhood refugee life in two new cultures and two new languages in quick succession. Nevertheless, this personal essay has also sought to invoke the intellectual and cultural forces that shaped my generation of American feminist scholars. In this sketch towards an intellectual self-portrait, I feel like an ethnographer who at times writes from within her society but remains emotionally detached. Due in part to emigration early in life, migration through different cultural spaces, and subsequent multiple socializations, I have lived a transcultural life, or, perhaps better, a diasporic life. I am lost to Judaism but yet feel like the last survivor of a polyglot Central European culture that vanished before I was born, and I am obsessed with the responsibility of remembering and passing on that collective memory through the retrieval of as many women's voices as possible. I would conclude with the words of George L. Mosse who in his memoir, *Confronting History* (1999), confessed he would remain an emigrant, but that this did not suggest a simple continuity with his early life; rather that many factors had shaped his life, particularly his pleasures in living and communicating in different cultures and languages, all of these informed by scholarly interests and choices.

Zoë Waxman

A Journey without End: Reflections on Holocaust Research

Beginnings

A few months ago, I had the great honour of meeting the German-born author and illustrator Judith Kerr shortly before she died at the age of ninety five. Probably best known for her children's book, *The Tiger Who Came For Tea,* and a series of beautifully illustrated picture books about Mog the cat, Kerr also wrote a trilogy based on her own experiences of escaping Nazi Germany and life as a refugee in Switzerland, Paris, and finally England. Introduced to Kerr rather grandly as 'an historian of the Holocaust', I was able to tell her quite truthfully about the profound impact her writing has had on my career – and, indeed, on my life.

Without doubt it was the first volume of Judith Kerr's trilogy, *When Hitler Stole Pink Rabbit*, which started my interest in the Holocaust. This told the story of her family's narrow escape from Germany, and the awful dilemma with which she was presented, aged only nine. Travelling light, the family insisted she chose only one toy to bring with her. She chose her newest, leaving behind her oldest, most beloved pink rabbit. As a child myself, the image of a faithful toy left to fend for themselves in Nazi Germany without family or friends was almost too much to bear. Yet I had to know just what had happened to Pink Rabbit, why it was that Anna and her brother Max needed to leave Germany so urgently, and what it meant for their father – the German-Jewish theatre critic and essayist Alfred Kerr – to be wanted, dead or alive, by the Nazis.

I was six when I first read the book. I have read it countless times since, and come to realise that in many ways, this formative encounter with the subject has continued to shape my interest in the Holocaust. I wasn't particularly interested in the Nazis then, and I'm still not desperately interested in them now. What I wanted to know about was a nine-year-old girl called Anna and her family; about what they felt as they were forced to face the increasing inevitability that the Nazis would come to power and life for them and other Jewish families would no longer be tenable in the country that was their home. I was horrified by the idea that one day you could be buying crayons after school, and the next you could be escaping for your life. Although I have now read countless stories of both those who managed to escape the Nazis and those who did not, I am still awed by the enormity of what it meant to be forcibly robbed of the life mapped out for you in childhood. To be cut off from your history and your native tongue. Not only did Anna and her brother have to flee for their lives leaving behind the objects and comfort they had grown up with, but they were not allowed to let anyone know that they were leaving least they were betrayed. They never even got to say goodbye.

With the vantage point of time and now having children of my own, I sometimes wonder about the wisdom of giving such a book at such an early age. While we are certainly more cautious today about what is and what is not suitable reading material for young children, I think my introduction to the Holocaust was by any standard precocious. Growing up in suburban England in a secular Jewish family, my father was very keen to remind his children that they were Jewish, and that this identity should never be lost or forgotten. We might not have been religious, but this did not mean that we could celebrate Christmas or eat ham when it was offered at school.

My father had grown up in the East End of London in a community which included many Jewish refugees and survivors. The Holocaust was a constant, unspoken but ubiquitous and somewhat menacing presence. From a young age he understood, without explanation, why the woman in the flat above sometimes screamed out during her nightmares. He knew how to respect people's privacy, how not to ask them about where they had come from. As he grew up, and grew away from his East End roots, he was also increasingly confronted with the precarious place of Jews in British society, an ambiguous situation well documented by Anglo-Jewish historians such as Tony Kushner and David Cesarani. The sense of never quite belonging, of never quite being accepted however seemingly successful and assimilated you might be. He was also very alert to the nuances of anti-semitism, of decoding "but you don't look Jewish", or detecting anti-semitic undertones in the British press. He also well understood the violent potential of anti-semitism and the need to be constantly vigilant. Perhaps he appreciated what I until very recently have not – the peculiar resilience of anti-semitism and anti-Jewish prejudice both in Europe and the wider world. To be forewarned is to be prepared might have been his motto.

This background undoubtedly shaped his desire that I should be told about the Holocaust: that nameless thing which had haunted his childhood. Yet the effect of this early disclosure was surely not quite what he expected. Telling me a little bit about the terrible tragedy that had befallen the Jews, left me, an inquisitive six year-old, desperately wanting to know more. And so he told me more – and more. I was warned, however, that the Holocaust was not a suitable subject to share with my friends at school: an injunction which inadvertently left me with the belief that it was a terrible secret only I knew about. It was, I now recognize, a terrible burden for a small child to bear.

Reading stories and first hand witness testimonies about the Holocaust became something of an obsession, and my father was reluctant to shut down his daughter's burgeoning interest in such an important subject. As time went by, I read whatever I could get my hands on about ghettos, concentration and death camps, cattle trucks, and gas chambers, trying to work out how these things fitted together like some nightmarish jigsaw puzzle. Too young really to comprehend what I was reading, I amassed material without really processing it. The puzzle remained incomplete, and apparently incompletable.

Yad Vashem

I had more or less resigned myself to this state of frustrated ignorance when I was taken to Israel as a young teenager, and most importantly to Yad Vashem, Israel's official memorial to the victims of the Holocaust. Not only was I confronted with a chronological framework for the Holocaust for the first time: from pre-war Jewish life, to the rise of Nazism, to ghettoization and deportation; I also began to see the bigger picture, not least the sheer enormity of the Holocaust and the magnitude of the catastrophe. The somewhat random selection of testimonies I had read, I now realized, represented just a handful of the estimated 6 million Jews murdered during the Holocaust.

For the first time I viewed some of the photographs of the victims: the iconic picture of the little boy with his hands up in the Warsaw ghetto, the naked woman holding her small child as she is shot from behind. The museum I visited was the one built in 1957 and not the extraordinary new museum designed in 2005 by the Israeli Canadian architect Moshe Safdie, which I have now been to many times. I can see now that the old museum needed replacing, that there were too many photographs, and not enough focus on individual stories; yet I can still vividly remember the impact of that first visit. I now had not only words and Judith Kerr's charming sketches, but visual images of real people and of real suffering as well. I did not know what to do with many of the images I saw, so I filed them somewhere in my mind to be considered later. One in particular I returned to again and again – the terrible sight of a group of naked women lining up to be shot by the Einsatzgruppen. Where were their menfolk I wondered? Was there anything specific about their fate?

Writing the Holocaust

I would like to think it was then, standing in the halls of Yad Vashem, that I realized I would one day study the Holocaust. Yet, in truth, I think that

I still saw it as a huge, unmentionable secret: a private, personal tragedy, rather than the subject of serious, scholarly research. In some ways, I still think that to some extent.

Rather than studying history, I read sociology at university and then undertook a master's in social and political thought. Slowly, but surely, I found I was returning to my childhood obsession. My master's supervisor was Gillian Rose: a brilliant interpreter of Hegel, and also one of the most creative and exciting philosophers of Jewish thought. Through working with her, I found a way of integrating my personal experience with my intellectual life: something that I had rather imagined was impossible.

As a doctoral project, therefore, I began to think about how I could interrogate the testimonies I had grown up with and think about the silences that had surrounded my father's upbringing in England. Almost inadvertently, I began a historical project and with the untimely death of Gillian Rose, I transferred from philosophy to history and from Warwick University to the University of Oxford.

Attempting to build something of a history of testimony, I traced the genre from the ghettos to the camps to testimonies written after the war, trying to take the story up to the present day, as new testimonies continued to appear. What fascinated me then, and continues to fascinate me now, is that the need to write down one's memories remained so strong, even in the terrible conditions of the concentration and death camps. Even as the events were unfolding, Jewish men, women, and children were using their words in an effort to understand the unprecedented tragedy that was befalling them and the terrible suffering they were experiencing.

The decision to attempt a history of Holocaust testimony from the Nazi enforced ghettos to survivors writing as part of a collective memory was, in hindsight, fraught with problems. I became increasingly aware that the archival projects of the ghettos, the scraps of testimony written in the concentration camps, the oral interviews conducted in the Displaced Persons camps, or the memoirs written after the war, could each have been the subject of a doctoral thesis in their own right.

What this approach did allow me to do, however, was to appreciate more fully that the Holocaust was not just one event, but a plethora of different events experienced by a wide diversity of individuals from numerous different countries and communities. This in turn enabled me to consider more deeply the identities of the victims. Men and women, children and the elderly, the religious and the secular, the affluent and the impoverished, were all singled out for persecution and murder, yet experienced and narrated that same fate differently.

Women in the Holocaust

Perhaps in part because the very first Holocaust stories and testimonies I read were by women or about women, I have always been drawn to women's testimonies. As a graduate student finally researching the Holocaust, I started specifically thinking out the particularities of women's Holocaust experiences and how they might be different to those of men. What could that terrible image of naked women huddled together about to be shot that I had first seen at Yad Vashem tell us? However, although becoming increasingly interested in gender, I was at this time only confident enough to devote one chapter of my thesis to the role of women. I did decide, however, that if I ever managed to complete and publish my doctoral thesis, the next book I would write would be about women's Holocaust experiences.

I was further motivated by attending a lecture given by a distinguished historian who had recently published a very important book on women's Holocaust experiences. It was both an extremely informative and a remarkably moving presentation, particularly when hearing about the women who bravely accompanied their children to the gas chambers knowing they would, as a result, share their fate. However, when I asked the speaker about the female Holocaust victims who didn't sacrifice themselves for their children I was simply told 'Well, most women did' and any discussion was quickly shut down. I found this immensely frustrating. Suffering is rarely an ennobling experience and doesn't make all people behave in a heroic way. Surely – I thought - there must have been some women who, for whatever reason, didn't sacrifice themselves for their children but sought to separate themselves in a desperate attempt to live? This also made me recall a talk I listened to at Yad Vashem several years earlier when I had the privilege of hearing a Jewish survivor named Ruth Elias recount her terrible story of survival. As is often the case we don't always realize the importance of what is being said to us until sometime later.

Elias became pregnant while in the ghetto-camp of Theresienstadt but as her pregnancy was not yet noticeable she was able to survive selection on arrival at Auschwitz-Birkenau. Later, however, her pregnancy attracted the attention of the sadistic Dr. Mengele. He allowed her to give birth but bound her breasts in an 'experiment' to see how long it took for her baby to die without nourishment. When Mengele's curiosity was satiated Elias was told that she and her dying six-day-old daughter were to be sent to the gas chamber. She saved herself, and killed her baby by injecting her with morphine obtained from a fellow inmate. She was only 22 years old and not yet ready to die herself. Remarkably she did survive and went on to make a new life for herself in Israel married to a fellow survivor. However, it took her many years before she felt able to talk about her experiences. She said that she lied to her children, that when they asked why she had a number on her arm she told them 'So I won't get lost'. It was eventually for her children and also her grandchildren that she decided to speak about her traumatic past.

As I thought further, I came to realise that if Elias and others like her are willing to revisit the past and speak about these terrible times, then it is only right for us to listen to them – to listen to them and to recapture the experiences of all those millions who didn't survive. Truly to understand the enormity of the Holocaust, we need to encounter real people when we read and write its history. They are not helped and we are certainly not helped when they are turned into paragons of virtue, exemplars of cheap hope, or one-dimensional women who unthinkingly conform to rigid notions of femininity or maternity. Instead, I resolved to try and give an account that captured the real experiences of real women faced with the terribly enormity of the Holocaust.

The research for my book, *Women in the Holocaust: A Feminist History* began with less exalted aims. Initially based on the simple premise that I wanted to find out more about women's lives during the Holocaust, I set out to try to capture something of the diverse nature of women's responses to the Holocaust, and to show that in a world of unimaginable brutality both men and women were forced to make desperate decisions. Whether it be the young girl starving to death in the Warsaw ghetto who finds herself stealing her families miserable food rations, or the woman forced to smother her baby while hiding in one of the city's filthy sewers so its hungry cries wouldn't alert the Germans to the group of Jews hiding there, these were desperate people acting in desperate times.

When I started my research about the specificity of women's lives during the Holocaust I found the existing literature surprisingly sparse. Perhaps unsurprisingly, but no less depressingly, men's experiences were taken as normative. The situation has changed less than some might think. Although in recent years there has been some very important work done by feminist scholars, most historians of the Holocaust still seem reluctant to engage with gender as a serious category of analysis. While it is now an accepted part of historical research in most other areas, for some reason it remains a blind spot in Holocaust studies, as if looking at gender somehow diminishes the atrocity. It's wrongly regarded as a softer topic.

That the Holocaust was an appalling event of almost unimaginable suffering for all involved in its wake, male or female, old or young, religious or secular, should be self-evident. A focus on women does not deny the experiences of the male victims of Nazism, but rather allows us to look more closely at what happened to women as women, as well as to men as men.

Moreover, as I have sought to show, far from being an undifferentiated or somehow gender-neutral attack on the Jewish people, the Holocaust was in its very nature gendered. It affected men and women differently, and male and female experiences were different. While Jewish men as the leaders of their communities and potential political opponents were the first to be targeted for persecution and murder, Jewish women were specifically targeted because of their biological role as child-bearers – as mothers or potential mothers of a future Jewish race.

Pregnant Jewish women had forced abortions, and any visibly pregnant woman arriving at the death camps was immediately sent to death, as were women accompanying children. There is also the little-discussed history of the rape and sexual abuse of Jewish women during the Holocaust. Although both men and women were degraded, dehumanized and desexualized by the Nazis, for example in the shaving of heads and body hair in concentration camps, and the destruction of families, the Nazis acting with 'violent, murderous sexism' especially targeted female prisoners for brutal sexual violence.

Increasingly I came to feel that *Women in the Holocaust* had to be a quite transparently feminist account, even if it meant that I lost any potential readers I might have started with. Sitting down, after years of research to write the book, I not only wanted to explore the experiences of women during the Holocaust, but also hoped to challenge contemporary assumptions about gender, including our very understandings of what it means to be a woman. I wanted to make it clear beyond any reasonable doubt that my writing is predicated in the belief that gender operates as a system of oppression intended to subordinate women. At the heart of my book, therefore, was the understanding that, as Sara Horowitz has argued, under Nazism gender needs to be understood as 'a central political category.'[1]

For a feminist historian, the experience of women in the Holocaust is especially important and particularly revealing. Women's lives in the Holocaust were different *because* they were women. This insight, I believe, is not only important for women's history; it can radically transform what we mean by the Holocaust, demonstrating that it was not a totalizing event, but rather a series of different, and differently experienced, events. Furthermore, writing a feminist history exposes the Holocaust as an especially revealing example of genocide in action. Developing a feminist approach to women's lives during the Holocaust involves not just exploring, but re-examining and re-conceptualizing, experiences such as pregnancy, abortion, menstruation, consensual sex, sexual molestation, and familial relationships. By reducing women to their biological functions – rape, pregnancy, childbirth, motherhood, and

1 Sara R. Horowitz, "Gender, Genocide and Jewish Memory", *Prooftexts*, 2./1 &2 (Winter/Spring 2000), 181.

so on – the institutional and genocidal patriarchy of the Nazis specifically targeted Jewish women as a distinct biological and racial group. National Socialism, while premised on a monolithic hatred of the Jews, nevertheless saw Jewish women as being separate from Jewish men and persecuted them accordingly.

When discussing the writing of my book with friends and colleagues the response was far from encouraging. Warned that I would be "pigeonholed as a women's historian", or "wouldn't find enough material" or might even be accused of hijacking the memory of the Holocaust for my own political agenda, the reactions I received were certainly less than positive. Despite, or in fact, because of this, I decided to press on with the project. Historians are rightly wary of politicizing their history, fearing the distorting effects of an explicit agenda. But there comes a time when a pretence at disinterest simply will not do.

Any potential doubts were finally laid to rest when attending a conference on the Holocaust in Oslo in 2004. As usual, I was the only woman on my panel – I was one of only a handful of women at the conference – and I presented a paper on the subject of rape and sexual abuse during the Holocaust. My research, like my career, was at a very preliminary stage, and I was therefore eager for feedback from my more established colleagues. The first question I was asked after citing testimonies from women who had experienced sexual molestation in the ghettos and concentration camps was 'So what? Is this really worth discussing?' At the very least I was warned my research could never have more than a very minimal impact on the field. As if in some warped time machine I found myself transported back to the 1970s alongside such feminist luminaries as Joan Ringelheim, Judith Baumel-Schwartz, Lenore Weitzman and Dalia Ofer, furiously defending the study of women and the Holocaust.

Dalia Ofer and Lenore Weitzman's edited collection *Women in the Holocaust*, published in 1998, marked a significant landmark in the field of women and the Holocaust. Containing essays by scholars such as Marion Kaplan, Myrna Goldenberg, Sarah Horowitz, Joan Ringelheim, and Paula Hyman, as well as survivor writers such as Felicja Karay and Ruth Bondy, it opened up important areas of women's experiences such as life in pre-war western and eastern Europe, in the ghettos, as partisans, passing as Aryans, and in forced labour camps. Their book was premised on the simple belief that 'questions of gender lead us to a richer and more finely nuanced understanding of the Holocaust.'[2] The book influenced a generation of scholars, myself among them.

2 Lenore J. Weitzman and Dalia Ofer, 'The Role of Gender in the Holocaust', in Dalia Ofer and Lenore J. Weitzman (eds.), *Women in the Holocaust*, New Havven, CT: Yale University Press, 1998: 1.

The challenge, as I saw it, was to write gender into the Holocaust, without homogenizing or valorizing women's experiences. Most major works on the Holocaust seem to assume that the Holocaust was somehow gender neutral, or, worse still, that women' experiences are somehow a side-line, a distraction from the main events. For example, an important work by a distinguished former colleague includes a separate index entry on 'women', but no entry headed 'men'.[3] This assumption that men's experiences were normative and that women were wither an addendum or that their specific experiences can shed no broader light onto the Holocaust, has proved surprisingly long-lasting.

My book was intended to contribute to a deeper understanding of the distinctive experiences of men and women both in and after the Holocaust, by exploring different layers of gender. It was also – in part I must admit in angry frustration at the climate I was writing in – specifically intended to challenge the status quo of an overwhelmingly male narrative. Drawing on the work of a new generation of scholars such as Atina Grossmann, Kirsty Chatwood, Monika Flaschka, Rochelle Saidel, and Helen Sinnreich, I wanted to focus on areas of research that I regarded as hitherto ignored or marginalized. In 2010 Sonja Hedgepeth and Rochelle Saidel published an interdisciplinary anthology by a group of international scholars on subjects such as sexual abuse, forced prostitution, pregnancy, and forced sterilization. My book and a series of articles attempted to develop some of these discussions.[4]

Conclusions

The field of Holocaust studies has come a long way since I started my research on women's Holocaust experiences. Women's history and the history of sexuality are now firmly established academic fields. It is relevant too, that history departments are no longer overwhelmingly, even though they are predominantly, male. However, sexual violence remains a difficult topic. When writing my book I encountered a survivor who acknowledged the existence of rape and sexual abuse during the Holocaust, but didn't think such things should be written about. She believed that they were private

3 See David Cesarani, *Final Solution: The Fate of the Jews 1939–1949*, London: Macmillan, 2016.

4 See Sonja M. Hedgepeth and Rochelle G. Saidel (eds.), *Sexual Violence against Jewish Women during the Holocaust*, Waltham, MA: Brandeis University Press, 2010.

matters and not for public consumption. The woman who had survived the war with her mother further argued against the use of nude photographs of women in Holocaust exhibits. It desecrated, she argued, the memory of the dead. I thought back to my experience viewing such photographs in Yad Vashem. Yes, they shocked. But to what purpose? I have thought about this often, and indeed, often changed my mind. Ultimately, I think that those of us born after those terrible events have a duty to try to find out as much as possible about the sufferings women were forced to endure, even those parts which disquiet us.

As a result, my recent work has continued to interrogate testimony, but to very different ends and with very different results. I have been reading ever more against the grain, looking for silences, ellipses, elisions and other signs of something more. I have written a small clutch of articles about rape and sexual abuse in the Holocaust and in other genocides. I have been thinking hard about what the problems are with this and I am not quite sure where this will quite take me. But I have grown more confident that it is right to pursue your intellectual obsessions even if – especially if – you don't know quite what the results will be, and even if – again, especially if – it takes you far from where you are comfortable and where others would want to put you.

This has taken us a long way away from where we started and where I started, as a confused, slightly frightened but nonetheless fascinated young girl. There is, I believe, no greater fan of *When Hitler Stole Pink Rabbit* than myself. I'm not ashamed to admit that I felt a real sense of loss when Judith Kerr died. I look forward to reading the book with my own children when the time seems right. However, as Kerr herself acknowledged, it was a book written as a way to begin to speak to her children about her experiences, and not a book about what she had escaped from. Kerr's books are as much about the adventure of starting a new life in a new country as they are about the loss of what she left behind.

Kerr found a great deal to enjoy despite the challenges of being a refugee, not least because she had her parents and her brother with her. Nevertheless, for many years she refused to return to Germany. When she finally did so, she found that the railway station where she and her brother used to take the train to the local swimming pool was the station from which Berlin Jews were transported to Auschwitz. She never wrote about the fate of those she left behind.

As a historian, I am now as interested in that unwillingness to speak as I was intrigued by her story as a small girl. I remain committed to the serious business of trying to understand what was said and what has never been said – what could not be said, or was not recorded. Despite the mountains of testimony that exist today, it needs to be remembered that the vast majority of the victims of the Nazi genocide perished without ever writing down their experiences. I now realise that it is impossible to capture all of this, but I have made it my life's work to capture some of it and to seek to communicate this as best I can.

List of Contributors

Natalia Aleksiun is a Professor of Modern Jewish History at Touro College, Graduate School of Jewish Studies, New York. She specializes in the social, political, and cultural history of East European Jewry in the twentieth century.

Judith Tydor Baumel-Schwartz is the Director of the Arnold and Leona Finkler Institute of Holocaust Research and a Professor at the Israel and Golda Koschitzky Department of Jewish History and Contemporary Jewry at Bar-Ilan University, Ramat Gan, Israel.

Pascale Rachel Bos is an Associate Professor of German and Netherlandic Studies, Comparative Literature, Jewish Studies, and Women and Gender Studies at the University of Texas at Austin. She works on cultural memory and gender in relation to traumatic events, and is a member of the international working group on Sexual Violence in Armed Conflict (SVAC).

Batya Brutin, Bar-Ilan University, Beit Berl Academic College, Emerita, is an art historian researcher and a curator of art during and after the Holocaust and of Holocaust monuments in Israel and worldwide.

Sarah M. Cushman is the Director of the Holocaust Educational Foundation of Northwestern University and a lecturer in the Department of History at Northwestern. Her research centers on women's experiences during the Holocaust.

Insa Eschebach is the director of the Ravensbrück Memorial Museum, Fürstenberg, Germany. Her main areas of research are the history and post-history of the concentration camps, women's and gender studies, and the history of commemoration.

Esther Fuchs is Professor Emerita at the University of Arizona and the author of numerous publications on feminist theory and Holocaust Studies, as well as other areas including Hebrew Literature, Biblical Literature, Zionism and Jewish Studies. She edited *Women and the Holocaust: Narrative and Representation* (University Press of America, 1999). Her most recent books are *Feminist Theory and the Bible* (2016) and *Jewish Feminism: Framed and Reframed*, (2018).

Sharon Geva is a lecturer at the Kibbutzim College and a teaching fellow at Tel Aviv University. Her book, *To the Unknown Sister: Holocaust Heroines in Israeli Society* (in Hebrew) (Hakibbutz Hameuchad Publishing Group, Israel) was awarded the 2011 Mordechai-Ish Shalom Prize by the Yad Itzhak Ben-Zvi Institute in Jerusalem.

Dorota Glowacka is Professor of Humanities at the University of King's College in Halifax, Canada. Her teaching and research interests include Holocaust and genocide studies, gender studies, philosophy of race, and critical theory.

Myrna Goldenberg (Montgomery College, Emerita) uses memoirs and testimonies, as well as a wide variety of histories, to write about Jewish women's culture and how it affected their survival in ghettos and camps during the Holocaust. *Before All Memory Is Lost: Women's Voices From the Holocaust* is her award-winning groundbreaking examination of Jewish women survivors who emigrated to Canada.

Atina Grossmann is a Professor of History in the Faculty of Humanities and Social Sciences, Cooper Union, New York. Publications include *Jews, Germans, and Allies: Close Encounters in Occupied Germany* (2007) and (co-editor), *Shelter from the Holocaust: Rethinking Jewish Survival in the Soviet Union* (2107).

Esther Hertzog (Beit Berl Academic College, emerita) is a social anthropologist and Professor who teaches and studies "gender" and "bureaucracy", at Zefat Aacademic College, and is a social and feminist activist.

Sara R. Horowitz is a Professor of Comparative Literature and Humanities and former Director of the Israel and Golda Koschitzky Centre for Jewish Studies at York University in Toronto. She is the author of *Voicing the Void: Muteness and Memory in Holocaust Fiction*, which received the *Choice* Award for Outstanding Academic Book.

Janet L. Jacobs is a Professor of Distinction at the University of Colorado and Director of the Honors Program for the College of Arts and Sciences.

Marion Kaplan is the Skirball Professor of Modern Jewish History at New York University. She is a three-time National Jewish Book Award winner for books about the making of the German-Jewish middle class; Jewish life in Nazi Germany; and gender and Jewish history.

Bożena Karwowska is an Associate Professor at the Department of Central, Eastern and Northern Studies and a Chair of Modern European Studies Program at the University of British Columbia (Vancouver, Canada).

Phyllis Lassner is Professor Emerita in the Crown Center for Jewish and Israeli Studies at Northwestern University and the author of *Anglo-Jewish Women Writing the Holocaust, British Women Writers of World War II,* and *Espionage and Exile*, as well as many articles on Holocaust literature and film.

R. Ruth Linden is the founder and president of Tree of Life Health Advocates in San Francisco, where she works with clients with serious illnesses to navigate the healthcare system and access the best possible care.

Dalia Ofer is the Max and Rita Haber Professor of Holocaust and East European Studies at the Hebrew University of Jerusalem (emerita). Her main research areas are the Holocaust in Eastern Europe, Women in the Holocaust, memory of the Holocaust, and Immigration to Palestine and to the State of Israel.

Lisa Pine is an Associate Professor of History at London South Bank University, UK, where she teaches modern history courses, especially on Nazi Germany and Genocide. She is author or editor of six books, most recently *The Family in Modern Germany* (Bloomsbury Academic, 2020).

Melissa Raphael is Professor of Jewish Theology at the University of Gloucestershire and teaches at Leo Baeck College, London. She is the author of numerous books and articles including *The Female Face of God in Auschwitz* (Routledge, 2003). Her most recent book is *Religion, Feminism and Idoloclasm: Being and Becoming in the Women's Liberation Movement* (Routledge, 2019).

Joan Ringelheim was Assistant Professor of Philosophy at DePauw, Northeastern, Connecticut College, Univ. of Bridgeport, and SUNY/ Stonybrook. She was Project Director for the first conference on Women and the Holocaust (1983) and received an ACLS and a Kent Fellowship for that subject (1982–83). She spoke widely on women and the Holocaust and published a number of articles. Among them: "The Unethical and the Unspeakable," "Women and the Holocaust—A Reconsideration of Research," and the "Split Between Gender and Genocide." She worked at the United States Holocaust as Research Director for the Permanent Exhibition (1991–93), Director of Education (1997–99) and director of Oral History (until she retired in 2007).

Rochelle G. Saidel, the founder and director of Remember the Women Institute, is an author, researcher, and curator on the subject of women and the Holocaust. Details of her related activities are at www.rememberwomen.org.

F. K. Schoeman is director of the Jewish Studies Program at the University of South Carolina. She is an Associate Professor of English and Jewish Studies, and Peter and Bonnie McCausland Fellow of English Language and Literature. She is the author of *Holocaust Mothers and Daughters: Family, History and Trauma*.

Na'ama Shik is a Holocaust historian who deals with subjects concerning women in the Holocaust, Jewish women in Auschwitz-Birkenu camp, sexual abuse, early Holocaust testimonies, female Auschwitz survivors lives after the Holocaust, and trauma. Since 1999 she lectures, teaches and works at The International School for Holocaust Studies at Yad Vashem.

Louise O. Vasvári is Professor Emerita at Stony Brook University and currently she teaches at NYU. She works in medieval studies, diachronic and sociolinguistics, Holocaust Studies, and Hungarian Studies, all informed by gender theory within a broader framework of comparative cultural studies.

Lenore J. Weitzman is the author of 5 books including the awarding winning *The Divorce Revolution* and the pioneering volume with Dalia Ofer on *Women in the Holocaust*. She was a professor at Stanford University, Harvard University, the University of California, and George Mason, and is currently the Vice President of the Jewish Book Council.

Zoë Waxman is Lecturer in Modern Jewish History at the University of Oxford. Publications include *Writing the Holocaust: Memory, Testimony, Representation* (2006) and *Women in the Holocaust: A Feminist History of the Holocaust* (2017).